The Story of the Coins and Tokens of the British World

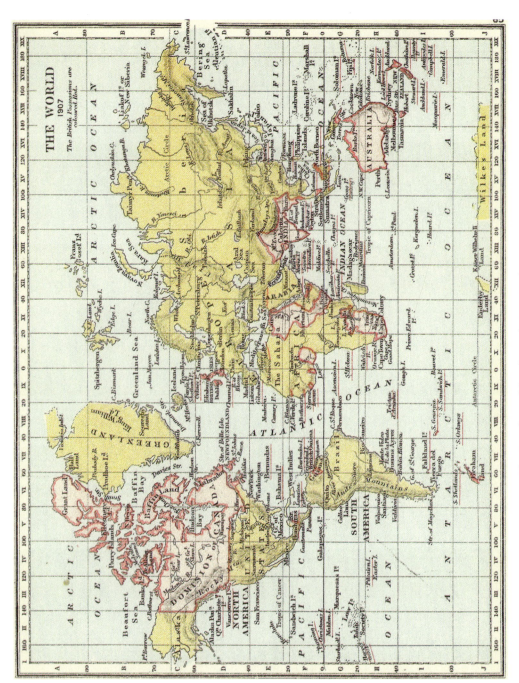

The British World in the early twentieth century.

The Story of the Coins and Tokens of the British World

by
Peter R. Thompson

2020

First published in Great Britain in 2020 by
Token Publishing Limited, 410 Southernhay East, Exeter EX1 1PE
Telephone: 01404 46972
e-mail: info@tokenpublishing.com   Website: http://www.tokenpublishing.com

© 2020 Peter R. Thompson

The right of Peter Thompson to be identified as the author of this work has been asserted in accordance with Section 77 and 78 of the Copyright, Designs and Patents Act 1988

British Library cataloguing in Publication data:
a catalogue for this publication is available from the British Library

ISBN 978 1 908828 46 0

No part of this publication may be reproduced, stored in a retrieval system or transmitted in any form or by any means, electronic, mechanical, photocopying, recording or otherwise, without the prior permission of the publishers. Whilst every care has been taken in compiling this work, the publishers do not accept any responsibility for errors or omissions or for any consequences caused thereby.

Printed in Great Britain by
Short Run Press, Exeter

Contents

Introduction   vii

CHAPTER 1

The Beginnings   1

    The need for European expansion • Portuguese and Spanish monopolies • Challenges to the monopolies • Defeat of the Spanish Armada • Settlement in Virginia and Bermuda • Settlement in the Caribbean • Settlement in New England and Maryland

CHAPTER 2

The Seventeenth Century   11

    Acquisition of lands • Founding of the East India Company • Portcullis coins • Earlier coins for overseas use • Somers Islands hog pieces • Coinages for Massachusetts and Maryland • Development of the East India Company • Madras mint • Problems in the Far East and the founding of Bencoolen • Bombay mint • Settlement of St Helena

CHAPTER 3

Consolidation and Control   27

    Proprietary grants • The Old Colonial System • Systems of government in the colonies and at home • Proclamation and Act of Queen Anne concerning colonial currency • The Act proves inadequate Effects of the Act • Consignment merchants and colonial development.

CHAPTER 4

Settlement, Slavery and War   41

Indentured servants • Early transportation • Slavery • The Navigation Acts and the Dutch wars • Scotland's Darien Company • The Union of Great Britain • The French wars • American independence • Coin use in the American colonies • Colonial small change

CHAPTER 5

The End of the Old Colonial System   59

    Alien colonies (Senegal, Canada and Caribbean islands) • Loyalists in Canada and Nova Scotia Losses and gains in the Caribbean • Cut and countermarked dollars • Plugged and marked gold coins • The abolition movement and Sierra Leone • The Company of Merchants Trading to Africa • The penal colony of New South Wales

CHAPTER 6
Pax Britannica   77
Abolition and anti slavery • Expansion of Sierra Leone • Development of New South Wales • Introduction of sterling to the colonies from 1825 • New sterling denominations for the colonies • A uniform coinage for the East India Company • Free Trade

CHAPTER 7
Britain and Europe   97
Britain's foreign policy • Balance of power in Europe • Isle of Man and Channel Islands • Britain and Hanover • Mediterranean interests • The Colonial Office • Crimean War • Germany's rise to power

CHAPTER 8
The Americas   117
Hudson's Bay Company • The American war of 1812 • The Monroe doctrine • Building the Dominion of Canada • Currency of the Canadian provinces and the Dominion • Currency of Newfoundland • Economic problems in the Caribbean • Currency of the Caribbean colonies • Currency of the Bahamas and Bermuda

CHAPTER 9
Africa and the Atlantic   149
The Atlantic Islands • West Africa • Southern Africa

CHAPTER 10
Egypt and East Africa   173
British interests in Egypt • Aden and British Somaliland • The Maria Theresia dollar • Zanzibar • Uganda • Imperial British East Africa Company • East Africa Protectorate (Kenya) • Tanganyika • East African Currency Board

CHAPTER 11
The Indian Ocean   189
The Persian Gulf • British India • Coinage of British India to 1947 • Native States of India coinage • Afghanistan • Burma • Ceylon • Mauritius and the Seychelles • The smaller islands

CHAPTER 12
East of India   225
The Malay Peninsula • Raffles in Java, Sumatra and Singapore • Straits Settlements • Hare in Maluka • The White Rajahs of Sarawak • North Borneo • Dr Jardine, Mr Matheson and Hong Kong

CHAPTER 13

Australasia and the Pacific — 267
Australia • New Zealand • Fiji • New Guinea • The Pacific Islands

CHAPTER 14

Climax and Decolonization — 305
The First World War • Demise of the German and Ottoman Empires and the mandate system • Palestine, Transjordan and Mesopotamia • The Dominions • Ireland • The Second World War • Indian independence • Decolonization • The Commonwealth • Withdrawal east of Suez • Britain and Europe • British Overseas Territories

Gazetteer — 336

Glossary — 349

Note on Sterling Denominations — 358

Select Bibliography and References — 360

Index — 369

Abbreviations

BCCB   British Caribbean Currency Board.

BNJ   *British Numismatic Journal.* The journal of the British Numismatic Society.

EACB   East African Currency Board.

ECCA   East Caribbean Currency Authority.

HMS   Her Majesty's Ship.

IBEAC   Imperial British East Africa Company.

SCBI   *Sylloge of Coins of the British Isles.*

SCMB   Seaby's Coin and Medal Bulletin.

SNC   Spink *The Numismatic Circular.*

VOC   Verenigde Oostindische Compagnie (the Dutch East India Company).

Z.A.R.   Zuid-Afrikaanche Republiek.

Introduction

THE coins and tokens which form the subject of this book are those that are associated with British activity overseas. These are sometimes referred to as "British colonial coins" or "Commonwealth coins" but in fact neither of these terms will correctly suit our purpose. Some of the coins described in this book are the issues of private companies like the East India Company, some even of private individuals like the Brookes of Sarawak and none of these can be defined as "colonial" or "Commonwealth" coins. Tokens were often an important part of the circulating medium so must take their place alongside the coins as an essential part of our story. Foreign coins were frequently a legal tender in the colonies and these too must be taken into account. Some of the territories involved were protectorates, dominions or mandates rather than colonies. Some later joined the Commonwealth (which did not exist until the twentieth century) and some did not. Some pre-date the Union so were initially "English", in one case "Scots", rather than "British". India is an important part of our story but was never a colony at all and the British Indian coinage ceased before India and Pakistan joined the Commonwealth.

We must therefore accept that, in order to be comprehensive, our subject matter defies a collective definition of any sort and even the title of the book must be a compromise. This conveniently allows us to spread the net wide in selecting the material described and to include everything of interest in the various overseas territories that became the complex organization known as the "British Empire".

The story of the coins and tokens cannot be told in a vacuum. The history of the Empire and of the world in which it existed is therefore covered in some detail with the intent of better understanding the coins and tokens, of explaining the reasons for the various issues and of providing a foundation on which the story can be built. This book is not a new classification of the series; for detailed listings the various standard catalogues noted in the Select Bibliography must be consulted. This is simply the story of the coins and tokens, of the period in which they were used and of the people who used them.

The first two chapters look at the reasons for European maritime expansion, the challenges to the Portuguese and Spanish monopolies, the early settlements, the movement of bullion from the New World, and at the early coins. Chapters three to five describe the Old Colonial System (the Navigation Acts, competition with other European powers and the wars with France culminating in 1815). They look at the ways in which the colonies were administered, the coins they used and the first attempts to legislate for colonial currency.

The East India Company had little to do with the colonial empire but did play a major part in overseas expansion. The Company and its coins are therefore brought into the story where appropriate. Apart from the activities of the East India Company and until the later 18th century, British overseas adventure was limited to West Africa and the Plantations. Although on opposite sides of the Atlantic these two regions were strongly linked in that one provided the labour for the other and made the whole system work. Up to this time the Empire can therefore be dealt with in a single chronological narrative and this is what the first five chapters have done.

Chapter six looks at the situation immediately after the Napoleonic War which resulted in Britain becoming the world's foremost maritime power. This coincided with and complemented her industrial might. It is during this perod that Britain attempted to introduce sterling to all her colonial posessions and this chapter goes into this in some detail. The last French wars resulted in the acquisition of colonies worldwide and the penal colony in New South Wales had also been established.

The extension of Empire continued during the 19th century, including the informal empire encouraged by free trade, and it is now easier to treat our subject geographically. The next seven chapters therefore deal with "Britain and Europe", "The Americas", "Africa and the Atlantic", "Egypt and East Africa", "The Indian Ocean", "East of India" and "Australasia and the Pacific". The history of each region for the period 1815 to 1914 is covered in detail but for the sake of continuity each chapter usually takes the story of the coins and tokens to its conclusion.

The final chapter draws the whole story back together and looks at the Colonial Empire, the Indian Empire and the Commonwealth from the First World War to decolonization. It is therefore devoted mainly to the historical events that brought the old Empire to an end and established the Commonwealth. The coins and tokens of this period have mostly been covered in the previous seven chapters but some still remain to be examined here.

Numismatically I have attempted to include everything of relevance but with such a broad subject it is difficult to know exactly where to start, what should be included and what should be left out. Paper money, bills of exchange, commodity money and barter items are outside the scope of this book. They were an important part of the currency and are mentioned in passing where appropriate but our primary purpose is to examine the coins and tokens.

A sensible place to begin is the first voyage of the East India Company which left Woolwich on 13th February 1601 with coins specially struck for use in the east (the "portcullis" coins of Elizabeth I). As we set sail though we must remember that these are purely trade coins and not a specific colonial issue. We might also recall, as noted in Chapter two, that they were by no means the first coins struck in the name of English monarchs for overseas use. Nevertheless, it is a useful beginning and the story is then told chronologically and geographically as noted above until the twentieth century. The Empire though did not have a specific end date so we must then decide where to bring the story to a close. Britain's military withdrawal east of Suez in 1971 and her entry into the European Economic Community in 1973 are landmarks of change but not all the colonies had achieved independence by that time. Some of them still remain as "British Overseas Territories" today. Many members of the Commonwealth still recognize the British monarch as their head of state and still use her portrait on their coins. It is therefore difficult to decide exactly when and where our story should close and unlikely that everyone will agree with the parameters I have chosen.

For each individual colony an obvious end date is independence but in some cases coinages had already been changed in anticipation and it is sensible to leave our story at that point. The independence of India and Pakistan in 1947 gives a specific end date to the British Indian coinage. For Hong Kong, which did not become independent, our story must continue until the territory was handed back to China in 1997.

The Dominions effectively became independent Commonwealth countries under the Statute of Westminster in 1931 but this is too early to bring our story of their coinage to a close. For Australia and New Zealand I have therefore continued the story to decimalization and the adoption of the dollar in the 1960s. From a British perspective this is a convenient line to draw but we cannot use the same criteria for Canada. Here, decimalization and a dollar currency were adopted in the nineteenth century and the story had by no means run its course at that time. I have therefore continued the Canadian story also to the 1960s selecting the change from silver to nickel as a convenient though arbitrary time to bring it to a close. South Africa left the Commonwealth in 1961 bringing her own connection with our story to an end. Ireland was unique among the Dominions in several ways, not least with her coinage. Like other Dominions she introduced her own sterling denominations but although this coinage began in 1928 its design is more akin to the coins of newly independent colonies in the 1970s. Ireland left the Commonwealth in 1949 making no change to her coinage at that time. Although these coins look decidedly out of place among their contemporary Commonwealth cousins, those struck until 1949 have been included.

The ending of our story is therefore a rather ragged affair as indeed was the end of the Empire itself. For the sake of completeness the sterling denomination coins still issued by some of the remaining British overseas territories are noted in the final chapter; perhaps a reminder that the story is not quite finished yet.

Some explanation of the spelling of place names and foreign words used in this book is called for. By and large the spellings used are those that I have most frequently met with in the records and published works consulted. In older works the actual spellings in English are hardly worth argument as they are transliterations from one script to another, many of them in an era when English spelling itself had still not been formalized. "Kabul" for example can appear as "Cabul", "Cabool" and in other ways as well. Nevertheless, new systems of romanization like that adopted by China have led to specific spelling changes which can cause confusion when using older works. "Peking" for example becomes "Beijing" under the new system. Confusion can also arise where the names of towns or states have reverted to original names or been changed in later years and in many cases it would be unhelpful to stick rigidly to the modern form. Students today for example could miss many references to "Lesotho" in older works if they did not also search for "Basutoland" and to "Chennai" if they did not also look for "Madras".

The spellings and nomenclature used in this book are therefore those that seem least likely to cause confusion and it is hoped that none of them will cause offence. Alternatives are usually noted in the text, in the footnotes or in the Gazetteer.

In writing this book I have attempted to look at the coins and tokens of the British world in a new perspective. Although some new information is brought to light I have drawn heavily on the research of others and have tried to acknowledge most of this in the Select Bibliography.

Acknowledgements are due to Eric Hodge who read the first draft of the text and to Bob Lyall who read relevant sections. Both have offered useful suggestions but any errors that remain are my own.

Most of the images are by Alan Dawson but some have been supplied by Bob Lyall and Dr. Paul Stevens. I am also indebted to the auction houses of Baldwins of St James's, Dix Noonan Webb, Heritage, Noble, Spink and Stacks for generous permission to use images from their archives.

The Story of the Coins and Tokens of the British World

The "Boyhood of Raleigh" by Millais.

The Beginnings

OVERSEAS settlement evolved from a desire to seek profit in ways that were not possible at home in Europe. While the earliest voyages sought precious metals, trade or plunder it was soon realized that settlement and the plantation of exotic crops could also give a return on investment. With plantation came a need for labour, at first attracted by future prospects. This soon had to be supplemented by the transportation of convicts and then by the purchase of slaves. Those seeking greater freedoms, political or religious, also began to see emigration to a new land as an attractive alternative. Once settlements had been made, they had to be administered and defended. In this chapter we will look at how and why European expansion began and particularly at early English colonization.

By the late 15th century the population of Europe was beginning to recover from the losses of the worst plague years and rising standards of living demanded more trade and new resources. To secure these, direct access was sought to the eastern spices which had always come overland through the Middle East and to the gold which had trickled across the Sahara. Gaining direct access to these resources would increase supply but it would also circumvent Islamic influence in northern Africa and the eastern Mediterranean, an important consideration for the countries of Christendom at that time. Islam, less complex and less prone to violent schism than Christianity, had spread swiftly after its inception using a combination of coercion and toleration. The decline of the Roman and Sassanian Empires made this rapid advance possible and in the 8th century Islam moved into the Iberian Peninsula and crossed the Pyrenees. In the west its spread was halted by the Franks at Poitiers in AD 732 but it was not until 1492, when European expansion was in its infancy, that the expulsion of Islam from Grenada returned the whole of the Iberian Peninsula to Christian rule. In the East, however, Constantinople had fallen to the Ottoman Empire in 1453 after which all the overland routes from the East to Christian Europe were in the hands of potential enemies.

The merchants of Amalfi, then Genoa and Venice were those who had benefited most from the overland spice trade to Europe from the East. It would be Portugal and Spain (primarily Castile) who initially gained most from direct imports of spices and precious metals to Europe.

Portugal explored the African coast, first bringing back gold dust from the Rio de Oro region in 1443 and reaching the area later known as the Gold Coast in 1471. Seventeen years later they rounded their Cabo das Tormentas which was soon more optimistically renamed

Cabo da Boa Esperança ("Cape of Good Hope") and in 1498 they reached India. Portugal would soon control a growing trade in eastern spices and pepper to the European markets.

Spain also pushed south, claiming the Canary Islands in the process, but voyages for them by Cristoforo Columbo were soon seeking a direct route to the Indies by sailing west[1]. Columbus knew very well that the world was round but had little idea of exactly how far he would have to sail. The exact circumference of the globe was still open to debate and the Indies themselves were thought to extend much further east than was the case. When he reached the Bahamas and then Cuba in 1492 he was convinced he had found the Indies. He would make a further three voyages to his "Indies" before his death in 1506 mapping much of the Caribbean and remained convinced that he had discovered the direct route to the East. Although others were sceptical it was left to Amerigo Vespuchi, appointed *Piloto-Mayor* of Spain in 1508, to formally recognize that a new continent and another ocean lay between Spain and her goal. The Indies had not been reached by sailing west although Magellan would do that for Spain in 1521. They had though discovered the Pacific Ocean across the Isthmus of Panama, a route to the East that they would exploit. Perhaps more significantly, they would discover undreamed of quantities of gold and silver in Central and South America.

The Pope, as the leader of Christendom, assumed ascendancy over the discoveries being made by Portugal and Spain and divided the vast regions now available for exploration between them.

Papal bulls in the 15th century granted to the kings of Portugal whatever should be discovered between Cape Bojador (on the West African coast, just south of the Canary Islands) and the easternmost lands of the Indian Ocean. When Columbus returned from his 1492 voyage claiming to have reached the Indies by sailing west there had to be some recognition of Spanish claims. The bulls of Pope Alexander VI drew a line 100 leagues west of the Azores and Cape Verde Islands and assigned everything westward of that as far as the east of India to Spain. The Pope's division of interests seemed to the Portuguese to be heavily in favour of Spain and some negotiation was necessary before Portugal was granted exclusive interests in the east, Spain in the west

The Treaty of Tordesillas between these two countries finalized this arrangement in 1494 and was eventually accepted by the Pope. It was though imprecise on several points. The Portuguese were now granted everything to the east of a meridian 370 leagues west of the Cape Verde Islands. This meridian was deemed to be halfway between the Portuguese Cape Verde's and Spanish Cuba and would ultimately give Portugal control of Brazil. In the East the exact division between Portuguese and Spanish interests was not settled until later. Nevertheless, as a result of the treaty, Portugal would claim Brazil, most of Africa, the Indian Ocean and the Spice Islands while Spain would claim the Americas and the Philippines. There were differences from time to time but by and large these two countries were in agreement with each other, were backed by the Pope and hoped to exclude all others from the riches of empire and world trade.

These monopolies and the readiness of Portugal and Spain to defend them was the situation that faced the countries of northern Europe in the 16th century. Papal support for the monopolies came in the form of excommunication for unlicensed discoverers, fishers, traders and travellers and this was a powerful tool in the Europe of the day. Those who still chose to venture on the seas allotted to Portugal and Spain would be guilty of piracy, a capital offence.

---

1 *The Spanish claim to the Canaries from 1404 was the first European colonization to take place as the world began to emerge from the medieval period.*

When they came, the principal challenges to Portugal and Spain would be from the Dutch, from England and from France.

One way of gaining access to the riches of eastern trade without risking excommunication and execution would be to find an alternative route. As Portugal and Spain between them claimed rights almost everywhere south of the Azores the only remaining option was to find a more northerly passage. For years English, French and Dutch navigators would seek such passages without success but their efforts to find them would lead to the establishment of unforeseen trades and settlements.

The first English attempt to find a northern route to the East was undertaken by the Venetian navigator Giovanni Caboto with the support of King Henry VII[2]. Caboto had experience of the Mediterranean and Red Sea trade in India goods and had settled in Bristol some time before 1490. Known in England as John Cabot, he sailed from Bristol in the "Matthew" on 2nd May 1497. Some 52 days later he sighted a "new-found-land" which, as Columbus had done on finding Cuba, he assumed to be the north east extremity of Asia. Cabot claimed this land in the name of Henry VII and among other things noted an abundance of great cod. He sailed from Bristol again in 1498 believing that he only had to coast southwards from Newfoundland to reach the Spice Islands but on this voyage he suffered the fate of so many early navigators. His expedition was lost without trace.

European fishermen may already have been exploiting the Grand Banks and may even have known of Cabot's new found land. It would soon be used on a seasonal basis by fishermen of various nationalities (Portuguese, Spanish, French and English) for salting fish but the English claim to Newfoundland would not be forgotten.

Cabot's claims to have found Asia, like those of Columbus before him, were treated with some doubt. To most it was now apparent that a whole new continent lay between Europe and Asia and if a northern route was to be found it would be a narrow strait or a way through the northern ice.

In search of a north west passage the Frenchman, Jacques Cartier, set sail in 1534 with a commission from his King, Francis I. On this voyage he discovered the promising Gulf of St Lawrence but a second voyage in 1535 came to a stop at what became known as the Lachine Rapids. It was clear that this was not a deep water route to China. On this voyage he over-wintered in the St Lawrence returning to France in 1536. His sojourn in the ice and snow did not unduly discourage him and his next voyage, in 1541, was intended to found a settlement. Although this first attempt would end in failure, it would lead eventually to French colonization and settlement in this part of North America – *Nouvelle France* (New France).

French explorers and adventurers would push on through the lakes and river systems beyond the St Lawrence still hoping to find a route to "La Chine" (China) until the Mississippi, reached in 1672, was found to run into the Gulf of Mexico rather than into the Pacific. Although the Mississippi was not the route to the East the vision of a New France extending from the St Lawrence to the Gulf of Mexico was born.

In September 1609 the English navigator Henry Hudson entered the river that now bears his name also seeking a route to the East. At that time he was in the employ of the Dutch and although his river did not lead to the riches of Cathay it became the only effective overland route to the fur trades of the St Lawrence basin[3]. Dutch trade and the New Netherlands were the result.

---

2 *Caboto was actually born in Genoa in 1450 but became a Venetian subject as a young man.*
3 *In English employ Hudson would soon be seeking the North West Passage.*

In May 1553 three ships set sail from London to find a north east route to Cathay by sailing north of Russia. The voyage was planned by Sebastian Cabot (one of John's sons) and was under the command of Sir Hugh Willoughby with Richard Chancellor as Pilot-Major. These were dangerous waters and the ships were separated by a storm after rounding the North Cape. Willoughby decided to over-winter in Lapland where he and his men were frozen to death[4] but Chancellor went on to the White Sea and reached the Dvina River where Archangel now stands. This and subsequent voyages by English and Dutch navigators did little to find a route to the East except to show that it was not feasible. From his anchorage however, Chancellor travelled to Moscow at the invitation of the Tsar. He had with him a letter of accreditation from King Edward VI addressed to "*all kings, princes, rulers, judges, and governors of the earth, and...*" (perhaps as an afterthought) "*...all other having any excellent dignity on the same, in all places under the universall heaven.*" This was the sort of comprehensive address that was deemed suitable when no one knew to whom it may need to be presented. It was just as appropriate for the Tsar of Russia as it would have been for the Emperor of China or the head man of a tiny island.

Ivan (soon to be "the Terrible") seems to have been suitably impressed and as a result the Muscovy Company, often referred to as the "Russia Company", received its Royal Charter from the new Queen of England and her Spanish husband in 1555. This was the first of the great shareholder (or joint stock) companies that would play an important part in the development of English overseas trade and settlement.[5] It had exclusive rights to English trade with Russia and other northern lands and was also granted major concessions within Russia from the Tsar. Several permanent agency houses were soon established in Russia to service annual fleets sailing to the White Sea and, when circumstances allowed, trade extended as far as Persia.[6]

If a northern route to the Indies could be found, the right of first discovery would establish a lucrative monopoly. If the north east looked unlikely and a river passage across North America could not be found the only remaining route was to the north west. It is for this reason that England, later Britain, made strenuous and sustained efforts to find the legendary North West Passage before anyone else. The geographical names in this region are a tribute to those who tried, failed and sometimes died in the attempt. Davis Strait, Frobisher Bay, Hudson Strait, Hudson Bay, Baffin Island, Foxe Channel: these are enduring memorials to the intrepid mariners who pitted wooden, wind powered ships against heavy arctic ice in the pursuit of fortune for themselves and for their nation.

The lasting result of these efforts to find the North West Passage was the founding, much later, of the Hudson's Bay Company which not only developed a fur trade but played a major part in the exploration of what would become Canada.[7]

As time progressed it became apparent that if anyone else was to share the wealth created by overseas adventure the monopolies of Portugal and Spain would have to be challenged directly. There were several ways in which this could be done.

Privateering was a legal method of practicing what may have seemed very much like piracy. When nations were at war letters of marque (privateering commissions) could be issued which allowed individuals to attack enemy ships and property. The system would

---

4 *Willoughby's two ships were eventually discovered and found to be structurally sound but were both lost on the voyage home.*
5 *The most important would be the East India Company.*
6 *The Company carried finished cloths, tin, lead and re-exports such as wine and salt to Russia and brought back tallow, wax, train oil, furs, skins, cordage, etc. From Persia, occasionally, came some silks and spices.*
7 *The Hudson's Bay Company was incorporated on 2nd May 1670. The role it played in the development of Canada will be discussed in Chapter eight.*

become strictly regulated. Although equipping a private naval expedition was very expensive the profits could be large and there was never a shortage of entrepreneurs willing to take the risk. Once a privateer was at sea of course attention to the rules depended very much on the individual commander but there was legal redress if the rules were shown to have been broken. Also there was sometimes a fine line between an official state of war and a warlike threat which, in the early years at least, meant that the difference between a privateer and a pirate was frequently a matter of opinion. A share of the prize money went to the Crown, the remainder being split between the owners and the crew. There was no pay for the crew of a privateer other than their share of the prize money creating an obvious incentive on board for the success of the venture.

Prime targets for privateers were Spanish treasure ships on their return voyages. French privateers seized Spanish treasure off the Azores as early as 1523 but apart from stragglers the Atlantic fleet sailed in company and was well defended. A bigger prize, and one which sailed independently, was the rich Manila galleon which each year plied the long and lonely route from Acapulco to Manila. Carrying bullion westwards and rich Asian goods on the return voyage (much of which went overland to the Caribbean for onward shipment to Spain) the "Santa Ana" plied this route in 1587. This ship was captured while closing the American coast on her way back to Acapulco by Sir Thomas Cavendish, carrying the Queen's commission as a privateer. Loading what he could into his smaller ships Cavendish burnt the rest in the "Santa Ana" where she lay beached. This was an enormous financial loss to the Spanish Empire.

Some 235 English voyages with privateering commissions are estimated to have been made to the Caribbean between 1586 and 1603 – a big enough presence to seriously challenge the Spanish monopoly of that region.[8]

While privateering was necessarily restricted to times of war, trading voyages could be made in defiance of the monopolies at any time. In blatant defiance of the monopolies John Hawkins made three slaving and trading voyages to West Africa and the Caribbean in the 1560s, perhaps getting away with it because the Spaniards needed his cargo.

Prior to these slaving voyages English trade to West Africa had existed for many years almost certainly inspired by the Portuguese discoveries there. As early as 1481/2 the Portuguese, claiming a monopoly of the region's trade, complained of a planned English voyage to Guinea. English merchants would point out that there were large areas of the coast where the Portuguese were not established and which should be open to English trade. Nevertheless, from the late 1480s to about 1530 there seems to have been little English trade to West Africa. There was certainly strong Portuguese opposition but English navigators of the period may perhaps have been more interested in the possibilities opened up by Cabot's attempt to find the Indies. The next recorded English voyage to West Africa is that of William Hawkins, father of the more famous John, in 1530. He visited the Guinea Coast buying ivory and other commodities before sailing on to Brazil to buy valuable dye wood. The elder Hawkins would make three such voyages but none of these were slaving voyages like those of his son. The Guinea trade, conducted on areas of the coast not firmly held by the Portuguese, can now be seen almost as an extension of English trade to the Barbary Coast. By 1560 that trade was well established and there were English Factors resident in Morocco.

Voyages to "Africa" often made little distinction between Barbary and Guinea. Although the first permanent English trading establishments in West Africa would not be made until the early 1630s (at Kormantin and elsewhere) English trade to West Africa predates her first settlements in the Americas by many years.

---

8 A.N.Porter (Editor), "Atlas of British Overseas Expansion", 1991, P.24.

Francis Drake's round the world voyage of 1577–1580 was an example of how privateering could be combined with a disregard for the monopolies. He struck at the Spaniards by plundering Valparaiso and Callao and capturing a treasure ship on the South American coast. He searched for the Pacific entrance to the North West Passage and claimed Nova Albion (somewhere in what is known as California today) for his Queen. He then struck at the Portuguese monopoly by buying cloves from the Sultan of Ternate in the Moluccas and obtaining a promise from him for future English trade.

Although privateering could be used as a legitimate tool to attack the monopolies in time of war and brave souls like the Hawkins's and Drake may challenge them directly, these were not permanent solutions. However, Francis I of France openly questioned the monopolies and in England the Papal bulls on which they were based were little heeded. Many assumed that areas not actively occupied by the Iberian powers should be available for others and in practice it was often difficult for Portugal and Spain to enforce their monopolies. They were vulnerable to any European state that had sea power and the will to use it and events would soon combine to make enforcement even more difficult.

In 1580 Philip II of Spain annexed Portugal and this altered the status quo. Until Portugal again became independent of Spain in 1640 both east and west were in Spanish hands and both would be liable to attack by Spain's enemies. Also in 1580 Spain actively assisted rebellion in Ireland and soon had plans for the English succession if Elizabeth could be deposed. The Spanish king was at war too with his rebellious Netherlands. This exposed all Spain's overseas interests, east and west, to attack by English and Dutch privateers.

In 1588 Spain launched her attack on England to depose Elizabeth I and to bring England back into the Catholic fold with a huge armada of ships assembled in Lisbon. It was presented to the Pope as a crusade although, shrewdly, Sixtus V's promised financial support would only materialize on a successful conclusion of the enterprise. The Spanish Armada which sailed from Lisbon in May 1588 was a combined fleet of the two most powerful maritime nations of the world (united under the Spanish king since 1580). It comprised about 130 ships and 30,000 men. The plan of action was for the Armada to force its way up the Channel, rendezvous with the Duke of Parma's army in Flanders, ferry them to the Thames and march on London.

The expedition had taken a long time to prepare so the English knew it was coming and prepared to meet it as best they could. By the summer of 1588 the navy had been reinforced with armed merchant ships and had perhaps a hundred vessels in the western Channel under the command of Lord Howard of Effingham. His Vice Admiral was Sir Francis Drake. Ashore, the county militias were mobilized and reorganized but with no standing army England would have been hard pressed to resist an invasion. The people knew all this and were fearful of what may happen. When word reached Plymouth that the Armada had been sighted Drake finished his legendary game of bowls on the Hoe and his ships put to sea. The English ships were smaller than their Spanish counterparts, more maneuverable and had developed the art of long range naval gunnery but were nevertheless unable to inflict any serious damage on the Armada before it anchored in tight formation off Calais some eight days later. Here things began to go badly wrong for the Duke of Medina Sidonia who commanded this great fleet. The Duke of Parma's army was not ready to embark and was unlikely to be so for some time. The next night, 28th July, the English sent fire ships in on the tide and in the ensuing confusion the Spanish fleet slipped anchors and was carried into the southern North Sea. The Battle of Gravelines the next day marked the end of any chance of success for the Armada. Its ships were viciously attacked among the unfamiliar sandbanks off Dunkirk and the prevailing wind made it impossible for them to make back for the Channel. The weather in the northern seas accounted for more ships as the remnants of the once proud fleet found their way back to Spain round the north of Scotland. Armada wrecks are strewn around the coast of the British Isles from Fair Isle to the west coast of Ireland. Perhaps seventy ships, many of them severely damaged and their crews depleted, arrived home by the end of September.

The Armada losses, in both men and ships, seriously damaged Spain's ability to police her commerce and added considerably to the growing confidence of English seafarers. The long rebellion in the Netherlands also weakened Spain at a time when Dutch shipping was expanding rapidly. Dutch trading voyages to the East began in earnest in 1594 and the six individual companies who were trading there from Dutch ports were formed into a United Company in 1602.[9] In England, the "*Governor and Company of Merchants of London trading into the East Indies*" was incorporated by Royal Charter in December, 1600. The founding of these great East India Companies was the result not only of increased confidence. The closing of Portuguese ports to the Dutch and English after 1580 had disrupted the flow of eastern goods from Lisbon to northern Europe.

Portuguese and Spanish overseas enterprise had combined trade with missionary zeal. A major concern for both these nations was the spread of Christianity. For the Dutch and the English the quest was purely for profitable trade, initially avoiding existing Portuguese settlements. The Dutch though were soon attacking Portuguese (Spanish) interests wherever they could, viewing this as an extension of their struggle for freedom in Europe.[10] By about 1640 the old Portuguese Empire in the East had been all but destroyed.

English overseas adventure was thus first concerned with trade and commerce and in securing the spoils by force when chance offered. Apart from the Crown's share in the (declared) profits of privateering there was little official involvement in this other than to give privateering commissions, to encourage exploration and to charter the companies involved. It had not though escaped notice that some of the lands discovered enjoyed a reasonable climate, fertile soils or other attractions which may make settlement worthwhile.

Cabot had claimed his new found land for Henry VII in 1497 and Drake, on his round the world voyage had made a similar claim for Elizabeth I in California in 1579 but the first deliberate attempt to found a colony was that undertaken by Sir Humphrey Gilbert in 1583. The intention was to found a settlement somewhere north of Spanish claims in Florida from which it would be possible to attack Spanish shipping and where, hopefully, gold would be discovered. The main attraction of New World settlement was, and would remain for some time, the possibility of finding serious mineral wealth as the Spaniards had done. Plunder and riches, not peaceful settlement, were the aim. Gilbert optimistically made huge grants of land to his financial backers but was lost on the voyage without having made any permanent settlement. All he had done was to lay formal claim to Newfoundland. His rights, granted by Elizabeth I, were taken over by his half brother, Walter Ralegh, who made careful preparations for another voyage.[11] His settlement would be called Virginia in honour of the unmarried Queen who donated one of the ships and the gunpowder for the voyage. Other finance was attracted by promises of shares in captured Spanish booty and the first settlers arrived off the North American coast in June 1585. Roanoke Island was the selected spot. Buildings and a fort were erected but much of their food and most of the seed grains which would have provided the first harvest had been damaged by sea water when the main store ship grounded.

---

9   *The Verenigde Oostindische Compagnie (VOC).*
10 *Spain did not formally recognise the independence of the Dutch Republic until the Treaty of Münster in 1648.*
11 *A reconnaissance voyage in 1584 brought two Indians to London where their language was studied and much useful information obtained. Ralegh issued strict rules for his projected colony concerning relations with the Indians.*

Although Ralegh had worked very hard at developing relations with the Indians he was not himself present in the colony. The settlers' constant need of food from the Indians soon soured relations and fighting took place in which the Chief of the Indians was deliberately killed by the settlers. When Drake arrived off Roanoke in June 1586 on his way home from a marauding voyage to the Caribbean the settlers took the chance of leaving with him. A re-supply voyage which arrived shortly afterwards found the place deserted and left only a small garrison of soldiers to maintain Ralegh's claim to the place.

When the failure of the settlement and the hardships endured became known in England it was extremely difficult to attract new settlers. Nevertheless Ralegh organized one further voyage with the intention of settling further north in Chesapeake Bay where he was assured silver mines would be found. This time the expedition included women and children but, having called first at Roanoke, the ships which had brought them refused to take them on any further. Their fate is uncertain as when the next ship arrived in 1590 Roanoke was deserted, the would-be colonists dispersed or dead.

The first attempt at English colonization in the New World was thus a failure. James I, who succeeded Elizabeth in 1603, had little interest in the land named after her. Ralegh fell out of favour at court and his claim to Virginia reverted to the Crown.

Those who had returned to England in 1586 however, like earlier visitors to North America, had brought with them an aromatic herb that was rumoured to cure almost anything and examples of the pipes through which it was smoked by the Indians. Tobacco was soon very popular at court and was destined to be an important factor in the development of the English settlements in North America.

It would not be until 1606 that interest in settlement was again sufficient for the formation of a Virginia Company. Their first settlement was established at Jamestown in Chesapeake Bay where they arrived in April 1607. Once again there were problems with food supplies and with the Indians. Once again there were those among the colonists who were more interested in seeking gold and silver than in growing their food but England now had her first permanent settlement in the New World. By 1612 tobacco was planted and was soon being sent to England. Labour for the plantations was provided first with indentured servants from England but by 1619 slaves were being imported. The growth of the settlement alarmed the Indians to the extent that in 1622 a major attack on Jamestown and the plantations nearly destroyed the colony. The Virginia Company was abolished in 1624 following these attacks and Virginia became England's first Royal Colony. From then on Governors of Virginia were appointed by the Crown.

Other settlements in North America would follow and those islands of the Caribbean which were not actively held by Spain would also attract English adventurers.

In 1609 one of the ships of a Virginia Company supply fleet was wrecked in the Bermuda Islands. On board the "Sea Venture" were some 150 colonists and the Governor elect bound for Virginia all of whom eventually reached Jamestown.[12] Also on board was the Admiral of the supply fleet, Sir George Somers. Somers seems to have been very much impressed with the islands which he claimed for England and the Virginia Company. In 1612 Bermuda was granted to London investors as a subordinate part of Virginia but, making no profit from it, they relinquished their claim back to the Crown in 1614. The next year exclusive rights to the Bermudas were granted to "The Company for the Plantation of the Somers Islands". England had her first island colony. Although tobacco was grown for some time in the Bermudas it

---

12 They and the ship's crew built two pinnaces from the remains of the "Sea Venture" and also saved most of the cargo.

could not compete with Virginia. Bermudians turned increasingly to maritime activities from shipbuilding, whaling and salt production to trading and privateering. The Somers Island Company would run the Bermudas until 1684 when they passed to the Crown.

Barbados may first have been claimed by English seamen in 1605 but was not settled until the 1620s. St Kitts (St Christopher) was settled at about the same time and Nevis in 1628. This was followed by settlement in Antigua and Montserrat in 1632.

Because Columbus had assumed this region to be the Indies it would eventually be termed the "West Indies" to differentiate it from the real Indies in the East. The indigenous population of all these islands and of North and South America too would be referred to as "Indians" for the same reason.

The Caribbean islands produced a variety of crops but from about 1640 sugar would become the most important. The sugar plantations, manned by slaves from West Africa, would become an important part of England's (later Britain's) overseas empire and of her economy.

Jamaica was the first English colony to be taken by force by the state. It was captured from Spain in 1655 by a Cromwellian expedition which had tried (and failed) to capture Santo Domingo. Although Jamaica was not heavily defended by Spain its capture was the first major loss suffered by the Spanish Empire in the west.

On the North American mainland the next notable arrival was that of the "Mayflower" in 1620 with a group of religious separatists from England many of whom had been living in the Netherlands for some years. This group, often known as the "Pilgrim Fathers", were dissenting Puritans looking for religious freedom. They had permission to settle in Virginia but actually landed west of Cape Cod and named their settlement Plymouth. This was the first settlement in what became known as New England which sat between New France to the north and New Netherlands to the south. The area soon attracted more Puritan settlers. By 1640 settlements had been established in Massachusetts, Rhode Island, Connecticut, New Haven and New Hampshire which became stable agricultural communities. Although most of these settlers had crossed the Atlantic to find religious freedom the intolerance practiced by some of them was probably worse than anything they had suffered themselves in England. The first settlement in Rhode Island was founded by a group of settlers from Massachusetts seeking their own freedoms.

Further south Lord Cecil Baltimore was granted a patent in 1632 to establish a colony on Chesapeake Bay which would be named Maryland after the wife of Charles I. This was just north of Virginia. Settlement began here in 1634, many of the early settlers being indentured labourers to grow tobacco.

By the mid 17th century there were thus thriving agricultural colonies in New England and plantations producing tobacco around Chesapeake Bay and sugar in the Caribbean islands. The East India Company, which we will look at in the next chapter, had trading settlements in the East and English merchants had been trading to West Africa for many years.

As colonies of Englishmen far from home, settlements would naturally have been run on English lines. Just like English ships at sea they would have been governed by English law and the colonists were subjects of the reigning monarch. For money they would have used what they could but their accounts were in pounds, shillings and pence.[13] In time there would be variations in both government and currency but for the moment these colonies were simply English settlements abroad.

---

13 For a full explanation of the English (later British) monetary system see Note, page 358.

Deptford, River Thames, where many East India Company ships were built.

The Seventeenth Century

WHEREVER settlers arrived in the New World they assumed some sort of right to the lands on which they settled. Indeed many of them had obtained grants of land before they left home and often assumed that the indigenous people would become their tenants. Certainly agreements were reached with native peoples from time to time but the basic assumption was that those who tilled the soil had a right to the land while those who simply hunted and gathered across it did not. Exactly the same assumptions would be made many years later in Australia and in parts of Africa. For those who thought about it the belief that these primitive people would benefit culturally, spiritually and materially from the colonial experience was not questioned.

In the East, however, the European explorers and traders would meet civilizations older and perhaps more sophisticated than their own. Here, trade rather than settlement was the prime concern and for England this eastern trade would be developed by the East India Company.

Chartered companies of the day were given monopolies for their respective trades as recompense for the large investment required. The East India Company was granted all English trade beyond the Cape of Good Hope and the Strait of Magellan and on the basis of that wide ranging monopoly raised the necessary funds for its first voyage to the East.

The money raised was invested in ships, goods and bullion and the first voyage also carried with it some specially struck coins. These are usually called "portcullis" coins because of the prominent use of that device in their design and are often considered to be the first British Colonial coins. At this time of course these coins are "English" rather than "British" and they are certainly not colonial. They were struck for the use of a private Company for general trade in the East, but why did they need to be struck at all?

Spanish American pieces of eight (eight reales) were the international trade coin of the day. These were the often crude coins struck in vast quantities by the Spaniards from newly mined silver in the mints of Central and South America. The Company knew that these were the coins required for its trade but knew also that it would be difficult to raise the numbers required so they requested that some be struck at the Tower Mint. It was probably not expected that the Mint would strike direct copies of foreign coins. What was required was an English version of the Spanish piece of eight at the same weight and fineness and with similar design features. The four, two and one real denominations were also struck. These portcullis coins together with Spanish coins comprised the specie taken to the East by the first voyage.

The Company's Charter allowed them to export up to £30,000 worth of bullion on each voyage provided that £6,000 was first struck at the Mint. Whether or not there was a shortage of Spanish pieces of eight, the striking of the portcullis coins fulfilled that obligation. In fact, just over £6,000 worth of these special coins was struck. In the East they were not popular perhaps because of their rather different appearance. Although the design features were similar the products of the London mint at this time were generally better than those of the Spanish mints and far superior to the "cob" coins produced at the Spanish American mints. Although the requirement to strike coin for each voyage remained in the Charter, subsequent voyages were exempted from it and were able to ship Spanish coin as required. A new Charter of 1609 made no mention of such a requirement so the portcullis coins were struck for the first voyage only.

It is interesting to note that not all of them accompanied the first voyage to the East. The Company opted to strike an extra £20 worth for presentation to the Lords of the Council and to other worthies and it is probably mostly these coins which are available to collectors today. Most of those that went to the East are likely to have been melted.

Portcullis eight and four reals struck for the Company's first voyage.

Spanish American "cob" eight reals of Mexico, typical of those exported by the Company as bullion.
Note the similar design features: crowned arms on obverse and symbol on reverse although the Tower Mint products are of better style.

2 The Seventeenth Century

Although they are not colonial coins the portcullis pieces nevertheless have a prominent position at the head of any study such as this. They are a tangible link to the beginnings of English oceanic expansion and to a company that would play a major role in that story.

When Elizabeth's Privy Council agreed that these special coins should be struck for overseas use, however, they were perhaps not the innovation that we imagine them to have been. Her father, Henry VIII, had struck coins for the city of Tournai which he captured in 1513 and held for five years. He struck groats there, most of which were similar to those struck for English use at that time but with reverse legend **CIVITAS TORNACEN**. For many years before that English kings and princes had struck coins for the lands they held in fief from the French kings. These of course were part of the French coinage but are known today as the Anglo Gallic series. They were struck from the time of Henry II (1154 – 1189) to the mid 15th century. Associated with them are the coins struck by Henry V and Henry VI as claimants to the throne of France towards the end of the Hundred Years' War. Calais, an English town and seat of the wool staple, struck English coins from Edward III to Henry VI and from the 12th century English rulers had struck coins for Ireland.

Groat struck at Tournai under Henry VIII from about 1513.

Anglo Gallic coins of the 12th to 14th centuries.
Richard Duke of Aquitaine, son of Henry II (denier), Edward III (gros tournois) and the Black Prince (leopard d'or).

13

Grand blanc of Henry VI (1422-1461) claiming to be king of France.
Saint Lô Mint.

Groats of the Calais mint.
Edward III (1327-1377) (left), Henry VI (1422-1461) (right).

English kings as Lords of Ireland.
Penny of John (1199-1216) (left), groat of Henry VIII (1509-1547) (right).

Shilling of Elizabeth I (1558-1603) as Queen of Ireland.

So for hundreds of years English monarchs had produced overseas coinages when needed. At a time when the concept of nationality hardly existed, these overseas territories were the personal interests of the monarch rather than "English" so none of these can be considered to be colonial coins. Nevertheless the portcullis coins do not need to be seen as the beginning of a new era. In fact in some ways they can be seen as the end of an old one. Like all the coins noted above the portcullis coins were official issues in the name of the monarch which some of the later East India Company coins and some of the colonial coins were not.

Before looking at developments in the East we must return briefly to the New World to see how the North American and Caribbean colonies, by that time often referred to collectively as "the Plantations", were providing currency.

The early colonies were proprietary colonies and were run by the Proprietor who had been granted the original charter by the monarch. When the Proprietor was present in the colony it tended to be governed in a very independent manner and if he remained in England it would be governed by his appointed governor. It would be some years before there was direct royal involvement. Provision of a coinage would therefore have been the responsibility of the Proprietor and was not always a major priority. The chronic problem in all developing colonies was that specie was continually exported in return for supplies and stores arriving from England so there was always a shortage of circulating coin. Settlers would presumably have brought some money with them, some perhaps in the form of English coin. The export of English coin though was discouraged and at a time when all coins had an intrinsic value anything that came to hand would have been used. In the New World this was usually Spanish American silver. Colonial products like tobacco and sugar were also frequently given a circulating value and, alongside foreign coins at locally declared values, formed an important part of the currency. The accounts of the Plantations were kept in sterling but the coins most frequently used were the piece of eight reales and its fractions.

At this time there was no difference in standard between the eight reales of Spain and those of her colonial mints. Those of Spanish America though were produced in much larger quantities and were the basic method of transferring the wealth of the New World to Europe. The products of the Spanish American mints were generally quite crude although those of the Spanish mints were often little better.

Large silver coins had appeared in Europe from the late 15th century following the introduction of new mining methods at the silver mines of Tyrol and Bohemia. One of the largest of these mines was at Joachimsthal, the coins produced there being known as Joachimsthalers. This word was soon shortened to "thalers" and eventually corrupted into English as "dollars". As the Spanish and Spanish American pieces of eight became established as international trade coins the terms "dollar" and "Spanish dollar" would be applied to all of them too. For convenience, in this book and elsewhere, the term "Spanish dollar" is often used indiscriminately to refer to both Spanish and Spanish American dollars. Although other coins would be used it was mostly these that were familiar to the early English colonists and that were exported by them in return for the supplies and stores coming from England.

Typical English coins in use during the early period of colonization.
Shilling and half pound of Elizabeth I (1558-1603).

Spanish American coins of the same period.
Eight reals and two reals of Philip II (1556-1598). Mints of Potosi (left) and Mexico (right).

In fact in the early period of settlement there was little need for a circulating currency within the colonies. The northern colonies were mainly rural communities where barter and private credit provided a sufficient exchange between individuals. Official dues were often paid in commodities at agreed rates. In the southern plantation colonies wages were not required for the indentured and slave labour employed. In all colonies military service was usually an unpaid requirement and most towns also required men to work on roads and public buildings for a few days each year. As the colonies developed, the need for a currency would obviously increase.

Perhaps the first attempt by a proprietor to provide a circulating coinage which would remain in a colony was that made by the Somers Island Company for Bermuda. When the first governor was appointed by the Virginia Company in 1612 he was advised that a supply of base metal coins would be sent out in the next supply ship for use in the colony. It is not known if any were sent before the proprietorship of the islands changed but the new Somers Island Company was allowed similar rights in 1615. They were able to manufacture a local coinage which could be used by the governor for paying weekly wages to colonists working on public projects. The coins could not be exported. They were for island commerce only and could be used to buy goods from the store.

The coins that resulted from this are very rare today and were probably not produced in great quantity. They show a hog on one side with the value in pence (XII, VI, III or II) and a ship on the other.[1] They have a brassy appearance but some at least originally had a coating of tin which would have given them a silvery appearance when new. At the time they were introduced barter and foreign coin were establishing themselves as a means of exchange and an unofficial report of 1624 speaks of these "hogge pieces" in the past tense[2]. They should not

Somers Island "hogge" piece shilling, about 1615.

---

1 *The hog commemorates the abundance of these creatures on the islands when first settled (a good source of food). The ship may be Sir George Somers' "Sea Venture".*
2 *By Captain John Smith, an early leader of the Jamestown settlement in Virginia.*

however be dismissed as unimportant. They were years ahead of any other attempt to provide a circulating currency that would remain within a colony and were also the first English overseas coins not struck in the name of the monarch or his deputy.

Accounts in all the colonies continued to be kept in sterling but it would not be until 1652 that anything other than barter, commodities, and foreign coin would again form part of the circulating medium in a New World colony. In that year the General Court of Massachusetts ordered the setting up of a mint to produce silver coins. The New England colonies had been founded by dissenters and right from the start were reluctant to accept government authority from England. Massachusetts in particular refused to permit Anglican worship and all the New England colonies openly flouted the Navigation Acts[3]. The introduction of a coinage was a right which they had voted to themselves and was perhaps typical of the independent way in which matters were settled. All this would lead eventually to an annulment of the Massachusetts charter (in 1684) and to the subsequent appointment of a royal governor but in the mean time a substantial coinage had been produced.

The first coins put into circulation by the Massachusetts Bay Company were simple silver discs impressed with New England's initials, NE, on one side and the value in pence (XII, VI or III) on the other. Because these were easily clipped a fuller design with legend, date and the representation of a tree where a royal portrait could have sat soon replaced them. Over the years the design of the tree was changed (from willow to oak and then to pine). Apart from the two pence, which was presumably introduced in 1662 and bears that date, all the Massachusetts tree coins are dated 1652 but continued to be struck until the early 1680s. Although struck in sterling silver these coins were lighter than their English counterparts, the intention being to keep them in the colony. Nevertheless they were soon being exported and legislation had to be introduced to limit this.

The only other New World colony to introduce a coinage of its own in the 17th Century was Maryland under the second Lord Baltimore. In about 1659 a small issue of silver coins in three denominations (XII, VI and IV pence) was produced in England. Unlike the hammered coins of Somers Islands and Massachusetts the Maryland coins are machine struck and perhaps did not circulate to a great extent. The coins were of good silver but the XII pence (the "shilling") was lighter than its English equivalent. The shillings of both Maryland and Massachusetts were intrinsically worth nine pence sterling, the lower denominations in the same proportion.

It has often been remarked that the Massachusetts coins avoided the use of a royal portrait but in fact so did those of Maryland where Lord Baltimore's portrait was used. Both these coinages were introduced during the Interregnum when there was no king in England[4]. Even a staunchly royalist colony would have been unlikely to use a royal portrait at that time. The Massachusetts coinage of course continued long after the Restoration even though the colonists were reminded in 1665 that coining was a royal prerogative. Only when the Boston mint was threatened with closure in 1678 was the colony's agent in London instructed to stress its importance and suggest a change of coin design acceptable to the king.

Nevertheless, with increasing royal control after the Restoration of the monarchy in England, this coinage had to come to an end. There was little inclination on the part of the

---

3 *The Navigation Acts were the laws governing English overseas trade and introduced in 1651.*
4 *Charles I was executed for treason after a trial by Parliament in 1649. After a period of rule by Parliament a Protectorate was established under Oliver Cromwell followed by his son, Richard. Parliamentary rule was briefly re-established in 1659 and the monarchy was restored in 1660 under Charles II. The period 1649-1660 is termed the "Interregnum".*

Coins from the Boston mint in Massachusetts.
The New England shilling struck about 1652 (left) and the later pine tree shilling (right).

Maryland shilling of Lord Baltimore, about 1659.

new Massachusetts administration to reopen the mint after 1684. Foreign coin, commodities and credit again had to serve.

While these few New World issues attempted to supply the need for a circulating currency none of them addressed the problem of the higher value coins in silver and gold that were required for larger transactions. The need here was still supplied by locally rated foreign coins and the few English coins available. Neither did they address the problem of small change which must have been required from time to time for lesser transactions and to give change. Presumably sufficient copper coins and tokens from England and Ireland filled any gap which could not be satisfied with barter items or credit. We will return to this matter in a later chapter.

Although this book is primarily concerned with the coins and tokens that were used in the colonies, we will look in the next chapter at how commodities and paper money also played an important part in their currency. All of these though are only the visible money supply. As our story unfolds we must never forget that the book credit arranged through consignment merchants and merchant houses was a major part, perhaps the largest, of the money supply Consignment merchants in effect acted as bankers and often risked their own financial security by honouring planters' bills payable in London before their produce was received. This allowed trade to develop with a minimum of actual specie passing either way and played an important part in facilitating the development of the colonies.

We must now return to the East where the establishments developed by the East India Company, some of which would eventually become colonies, are beginning to become an important part of our story. The first voyages of the East India Company had been very successful. A main factory[5] had been established at Bantam in Java with minor settlements around the East. In building up this business the London Company met fierce opposition from the Dutch who were determined to monopolize the spice trades to Europe. There was also opposition in England which came from those who were excluded from these riches by the Company's monopoly and from those who accused it of exporting the nation's wealth in return for expensive trivia. Unlike earlier joint stock companies it was set up primarily to import expensive foreign luxuries, not to export English goods.

---

5 *A factory was a secure establishment in which the Company's factors could carry out their business.*

The excluded English merchants would eventually force a merger with the old London Company to form the United East India Company in 1708. Dutch opposition in the East forced the Company to concentrate its trading activities more on the Indian sub continent and less on the East Indies. Those who complained of harmful bullion exports led the Company to seek additional trades between ports in the East which would raise funds for the home investment. Together, these various circumstances combined to build the Company into a rich and powerful organization although not altogether in the manner originally intended.

To carry on their trade the East India Company needed bullion and plenty of it. English goods were also exported but silver was the main requirement. The obvious answer to their critics when exporting this bullion was that India goods would find a market in England whoever brought them to Europe and it would be dangerous to allow anyone else to gain a monopoly of those trades. Soon they could also argue that much of the bullion exported was obtained through the re-export of India goods. London, as well as Amsterdam, soon surpassed Lisbon and Seville as the commercial centres and entrepôts of Europe.

The bullion carried to the East, mainly in Spanish American silver, was used to purchase the investment for the homeward voyage but in India itself where there was already a sophisticated economy it had usually to be changed into local currency. In the north of India, mainly under Moghul rule, the silver rupee was the current coin. Here were the main commercial centres like Surat in the west and Bengal in the east. In the south, where the Company was soon purchasing large quantities of calicoes for eastern trade, gold coins were in use.

To obtain the necessary coins in India the Company could either take their bullion to a banker (or "shroff" as they were usually known) who would exchange it for an agreed percentage or they could take it to a local mint and pay to have it re-coined. The Company used both of these methods as circumstances dictated but both of them tended to be expensive and were subject to negotiation. Most local rulers of substance operated a mint. In the Moghul areas the products of all the mints were similar in appearance, were in the name of the Moghul and were of remarkably consistent standard. In the areas outside Moghul control there were many different coin standards but wherever it traded the East India Company would always need an acceptable form of currency.

When the Company first began buying calicoes in India for resale in the East their main port on the Coromandel (south east) coast of India was Masulipatam. There had though been problems between the Company and the local authorities and in 1639 Francis Day, a member of the Company's Council at Masulipatam, was entrusted with an important mission. He was sent south to examine the coast in the region of the Portuguese settlement at St Thomé to find somewhere more congenial to settle and trade. He reached agreement with the Raja of Chandragiri that the Company could erect a fort on a point of land just south of the fishing village of Madraspatam. This new settlement was named Chennappa Patam (often "Chinapatan") in honour of Chennapa, the father of the local Naik who had brokered the deal. The English referred to their new settlement as Fort St George and later simply as "Madras".

Madras was held by a grant which included the right to strike coins, a standard right for any local ruler. This gave the Company the opportunity to reduce its currency exchange costs by using its own mint to strike local coins and they seem to have begun minting operations about 1643. Like any local ruler, the coins which the Company would be allowed to produce would be part of the local coinage and it was no doubt required to operate under the same rules and restrictions as any other local mint. A start was made (in this gold using region) by striking gold pagodas and fanams of local type. As time went on and their establishment at Madras grew in importance they would begin to strike silver and copper coins for their own use within the "garrison and city."[6] These subsidiary coins bore English devices, the silver fanam coinage bearing the two interlinked "C"s used on the English silver coins of Charles II while the copper coins bore the Company's balemark as its main design.[7] In this way the Company first began to influence coinage in India.

By this time trade with Bengal, for which the silver rupee was required, was increasing rapidly but nowhere in Bengal did the Company have the status which would have allowed it to run a mint. For some years, as Moghul influence spread southwards, the Company had sought to gain permission to strike rupees at their Madras mint in order to service the Bengal factories. By 1692 the Company had sufficient influence to obtain a Moghul grant for its activities at Madras which included permission to strike coins in the name of the then Moghul Emperor, Aurangzib Alamgir I.

The rupees produced at Madras under this grant were the same as rupees produced elsewhere in the Moghul Empire except for the mint name *Chinapatan*. The initial dies were provided by the Moghul authorities to ensure that the correct design of coin was struck. The real benefit of the grant was that it left the Company able to produce a Moghul rupee at its own mint. These were not for circulation at Madras where the rupee would not become the unit of account for many years. The Madras (Chinapatan) rupees were used to finance the Company's Bengal trade as were rupees subsequently struck at Madras bearing the mint name Arcot. For many years, until the Company was able to open its own mint at Calcutta (in 1757) both these types of rupees were exported in large numbers to Bengal. The gold pagoda continued to be struck for the Madras investments as too did the subsidiary silver and copper coins for local use.

Early Madras mint coins.
Gold pagoda, silver fanam and copper dudu.

Madras struck rupees for the Bengal trade.
Madras (Chinapatan) rupee (left) and Madras (Arcot) rupee (right).

---

6 *The relative security of a fortified settlement attracted weavers and spinners to Madras in some numbers.*
7 *A balemark was the mark stencilled on a company's bales of goods to identify ownership. Its use on the coinage was also a guarantee of quality.*

Although the East India Company was well established in India by the mid 17th century its influence further east was on the wane mainly because of Dutch opposition. The first voyages of the Company had been to Java and other East Indian islands seeking freedom to buy pepper and spices. The Dutch however were there before them and felt that as they, not the English, were actively displacing the Portuguese they were entitled to exclusive access to those trades. This led to hostility between the Dutch and English companies in the East. Because the Dutch were better financed and better organized the East India Company found it necessary to close some of its smaller settlements and concentrated its far eastern trade at Bantam.

The Dutch continued to make life difficult for the Company in the East and in 1682 matters came to a head. The Dutch and English supported different sides in a local Javanese power struggle. The English had supported the wrong (losing) side and were expelled from Bantam by its new ruler. The Company's remaining goods were moved to the Dutch settlement at Batavia from which the English were expelled the following year, leaving Java altogether. By this time the price of pepper had fallen considerably in Europe and Bantam's main importance was as an entrepôt for eastern trade in general. This trade could well have been carried on through Madras but the East India Company still considered it important to have a base further east. Accordingly, in 1685, they reached agreement with the ruler of Bencoolen in Sumatra to build a fortified settlement which they named York Fort and agreements were soon reached with other local rulers as well.[8]

The Company built up a plantation system for the production of pepper around its various outstations in Sumatra, a system that was never popular with the producers and which never generated a great profit. The pepper could be purchased with Spanish American pieces of eight (dollars) but within the settlements (as at Madras) the need for a subsidiary coinage soon arose. To supply this need a coinage of copper cash was produced at Madras in 1687 and in 1693 this was supplemented by one and three fanam silver coins. A double fanam was added to the series some time later and these various denominations would remain in issue, intermittently as required, until at least 1768. The obverse design of all these denominations was similar to the Madras copper coins and showed the Company's balemark while the reverse was a usually crude attempt at "English Company" in Malay Arabic.

Bencoolen (Sumatra) coins in use from 1680s.
Copper cash and silver one, two and three fanam coins.

---

8 *An eastern settlement was useful as a rendezvous point for ships bound for China but would also deny the Dutch a monopoly of eastern pepper. The original site of York Fort was found to be unsuitable and in 1714 it was rebuilt some 2 miles to the south and renamed Fort Marlborough. The East India Company would maintain a presence at Bencoolen until 1824.*

By this time Madras was not the only Company mint in India. On the west coast the Company's trade was centred on Surat which was the main commercial port for the whole region. Bombay had been in Portuguese hands for some time and in 1661 the treaty of marriage between Charles II of England and Catherine of Braganza granted it to the English king.[9] For the better running of the place the king transferred it to the East India Company in 1668. It was to be held by the Company in free and common soccage as of the manor of East Greenwich on payment of an annual rent of £10 in gold. This form of neo–feudal grant was a common way of granting proprietary rights in overseas settlements at that time. It was a formula which left the proprietors in permanent leasehold subject only to a requirement to develop the land and pay the annual quit rent.

Although Bombay would eventually eclipse Surat as the main commercial centre for the region the Company had no particular desire in 1668 to develop it or to move from their existing quarters at the centre of things in Surat. However, possession of Bombay gave them one very big advantage. As undisputed rulers of the place the Company was entitled to run a mint. At Bombay it was subject to the king of England, not to the Moghul, and the first coinage struck at Bombay clearly illustrates this unusual status.

Silver rupees and copper pice were struck from 1672 with the Company's shield of arms on the obverse and an English legend on the reverse. Small tin coins bearing the Company's balemark began to be issued at about the same time. These were primarily for the internal use of the settlement although the rupee (usually referred to as the "anglina") was very close in weight and standard to the Surat rupee. It was no doubt hoped that the English rupee would become acceptable in trade alongside that of Surat but its very "foreign" appearance almost certainly ensured that it did not. Although local coins were useful the main advantage to the Company of having a mint at Bombay was to be able to strike their own coins for trade.

The Company therefore set about producing a rupee that looked more like the local product. Holding Bombay from the King of England, it did not occur to them to seek permission from the Moghul to do such a thing. The coin was a local style rupee in that the legends were in Persian but it bore the names of English monarchs on the obverse and proclaimed the authority of the English Company on the reverse[10]. They simply went ahead and produced these coins at Surat weight and fineness. Coining, after all, was a right and even a proof of sovereignty.

These rupees are known in the names of James II and of William and Mary. The Moghul had tolerated the anglina as a purely local phenomenon but with these coins with a Persian legend he was furious. The Company had to stop producing them and humbly apply for permission to strike Moghul style rupees in the Emperor's name. The Company did not get that permission for many years so initially their mint at Bombay was of limited use.[11]

Early Bombay coins.
Rupee (anglina), 1670s and pice (copeeroon), 1694.

---

9 Tangier in North Africa was granted at the same time.
10 Persian was the language used on Moghul coins.
11 Permission to strike Moghul style coins at Bombay was finally obtained in 1717.

Bombay rupee 1694 in the name of William and Mary.

It can be argued that none of the coins struck by the East India Company are colonial coins and that their settlements were trading posts rather than colonies. Bombay though had been granted to the Company by the king and its early coins are little different in function and status from the coins struck by the Somers Island Company for Bermuda or the coins struck by Lord Baltimore for Maryland. In fact many of the subsidiary coins of Bombay continue to bear a crown and the king's initials until the 1770s clearly indicating the difference between them and the coins struck by the Company for local use at Madras.

As we shall see in future chapters, the Company would eventually become involved in large scale administration as well as trade. In the end its territories in India would pass to the Crown and territories elsewhere would become colonies. Although a story in its own right the East India Company therefore cannot be ignored in this study.[12]

One of the early East India Company settlements however did become a colony of Englishmen living abroad. Unlike the other Company settlements of the period St Helena owed its importance to its geographical position rather than to any potential for trade. From its earliest days the Company's ships had called there for fresh provisions and water. The Dutch laid formal claim to the island in 1633 but seemed to have lost interest in it when they settled at the Cape in 1652. In that same year the Company's homeward bound ships, finding it deserted, took possession and, with the Dutch at the Cape the East India Company could see the wisdom of fortifying St. Helena to secure it for their own use.

It was not though until 1659 that the island was permanently settled and even then it was not officially intended. Many years before, in 1616, the inhabitants of Pulo Run, one of the Banda Islands, had sworn allegiance to the English Crown. They had done this through visiting Factors of the East India Company who had accepted it in the name of James I. The Dutch, although recognizing the claim, had remained in occupation closely guarding their spice trade. After the first Anglo Dutch War of 1652-1654 Cromwell became interested in reasserting English rights there and in December 1658 a group of prospective settlers was assembled to colonize the place. The Company was not too keen on the idea of further confrontation with the Dutch in the East where English trade was becoming difficult so, at the last minute, the scheme was aborted. The Court of Committees diverted the fleet to St Helena where it arrived on 5th May 1659. It went no further, St Helena was fortified and the East India Company had what was in effect a colony.

The royal rights to Pulo Run itself would be surrendered to the Dutch at the Treaty of Breda in 1667. As part of the same treaty England gained what many considered at the time to be a far less important territory. The Dutch rid themselves of the tiresome English claim in the East while the English claim to the New Netherlands in North America, which she had

---

12 For details of both the Company and its coins see Peter R Thompson, "The East India Company and its Coins", 2010.

taken from the Dutch in 1664 was recognized. What had been New Amsterdam was confirmed in its new name of New York.

By the end of the 17th century the East India Company had settlements in the East but had lost much ground to the Dutch in the Spice Islands. These settlements were for trade and existed only by agreement with local rulers. The firmans agreed though were often very generous usually allowing freedom to govern themselves without interference and sometimes granting land revenues for their support[13]. These agreements were sometimes reached on the promise of military support from the Company or for protection against piracy and other European powers. As the trade grew in importance the Company was granted wider ranging privileges through their successive charters concerning defence and settlement but charters from England alone did not guarantee settlement. The only exception to this in the East was Bombay which had been granted to the Company by the King of England and was theirs by right. Royal claims to Pulo Run in the Spice Islands had finally been exchanged with the Dutch for territory in North America. St Helena in the South Atlantic supported a colony of settlers in the Company's employ. It was of no use as a trading settlement, was not a source of rare or exotic crops and was the first territory occupied by the Company for a purely strategic purpose.

On the North American mainland the New England colonies were successful agricultural settlements and the plantation colonies further south were producing exotic crops in increasing quantities. The West India Islands were producing sugar and the Bermudas were in English hands. There was an English claim to Newfoundland where settlements had been established and St John's fortified. In the colonies royal government was replacing proprietary rule.

On the west coast of Africa English interests had been consolidated under the Royal African Company which we will look at in Chapter four.

England could consider herself to be a world power. There was a new concept of what we can begin to call "Empire" and in the next chapter we will look at how some sort of central control began to be attempted.

---

13 A firman was an order, mandate or imperial decree allowing for settlement, trade, etc.

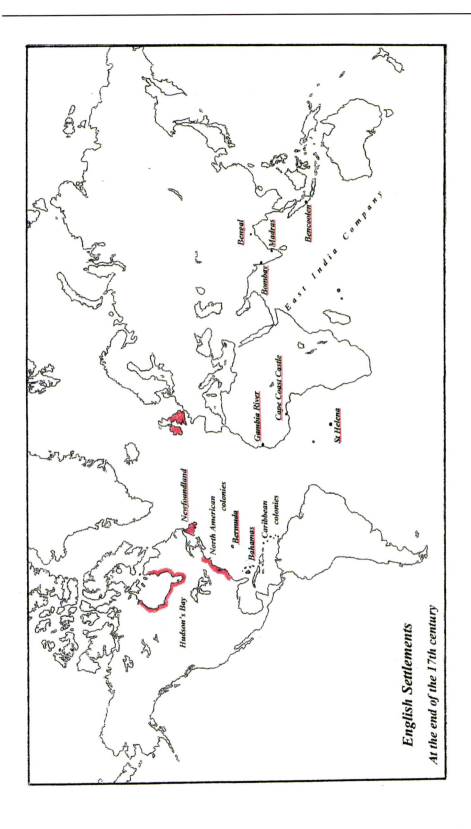

English Settlements
At the end of the 17th century

Title page of the 1651 Navigation Act.

3

Consolidation and Control

THE general assumption of all European nations was that their overseas settlements should benefit the mother country which, in the final analysis, was the reason for their existence and the guarantor of their security. France and England in particular strove, through the produce of their colonies, to be as self sufficient as possible, aiming never to rely on a potential enemy for their essential supplies. In England it was assumed that global commerce, properly protected, would provide national security and economic advancement. The produce of the colonies should go only *to* England from where any surplus could be re-exported. Manufactured goods required in the colonies should come only *from* England. The nation would benefit from the customs dues and only English merchants and manufacturers would benefit from the trade. This mercantilist ideal was one of the prime motives for English colonization.

In the early period of settlement these general assumptions were the natural scheme of things but they were first codified in the Navigation Act of 1651. This Act required all colonial produce to be carried in English or colonial ships and was passed by Parliament not long after it seized power from Charles I. Among other things it was designed to secure a large proportion of the seaborne carrying trade for English ships. Most of this had fallen into Dutch hands and this was the cause of some concern. After the Restoration of the monarchy in 1660 a re-enactment of the Navigation Act was necessary[1]. This clarified the earlier Act by decreeing that English or colonial ships should be built in England or the Plantations, that they should have a Master and Owner in England or the Plantations and that three quarters of their crews should likewise be from England or the Plantations. Colonial imports and exports were all to be in English or Plantation ships. The 1660 Act also "enumerated" certain colonial products which could only be exported to England, Ireland or another colony. "Non-enumerated" goods could be exported anywhere but only in English or colonial ships.[2] The Staple Act of 1663 made England the staple for all European goods destined for the colonies thus ensuring that these too had to pass through England, pay duties and be carried by English or colonial ships. There was now no reason, other than stress of weather, for a foreign vessel to visit an English colonial port.

The colonies at that time were not seen as developing nations but as outposts of the mother country and it was natural that controls such as these should be put in place. The system of control through the Navigation and Staple Acts is referred to as "The Old Colonial System". It

---

[1] Acts passed during the Interregnum were considered to be Acts of a usurping government and were therefore invalid.
[2] The initial list of enumerated goods included sugar, tobacco, cotton wool, indigo, ginger and dye woods. The list would be amended from time to time but some items, like grain and timber, were never enumerated.

benefited the mother country by expanding the customs revenues and increasing imports, exports and re-exports. It benefited the colonies because import duties on colonial goods were relatively low and colonial producers were reasonably sure of a market for their enumerated goods. It encouraged English and colonial shipping and the development of plantations. The East India Company, backed by its Charter, policed its own monopoly of English trade with the East, as yet without any interference from Parliament. The Royal African Company supervised the trade and forts of the African coast.

By and large the Old Colonial System worked reasonably well, not least because the laws preventing smuggling in and out of the colonies were not rigidly enforced. Only when colonial trades had considerably increased and when the rules began to be more strictly applied would the cracks begin to appear.

New England was always of particular concern, politically as well as commercially. The Massachusetts Bay Company received its royal charter in 1629 and it very soon decided to move its governing body and administration to New England. Unlike other colonial companies there was now no governor in England to whom it was responsible and on whom the Government could bring pressure if the need arose. The colony became a refuge for dissenting Puritans and there was soon grave concern in England about where this may lead. In 1634 a Commission was set up to examine the activities of the new colony and the conditions of its charter but that important document was in Boston along with the patentees. A writ of *quo warranto* failed to produce it and no action could immediately be taken against absent patentees. It seemed inevitable that Massachusetts would become a Crown colony as was already the case with Virginia but such were the problems in England at the time, between King and Parliament, that the matter was quietly forgotten for some years.

Commercially, New England lacked a staple crop to export to England in return for manufactures. She therefore tended to develop trades and manufactures of her own that were not in England's interest. Having mainly the same agricultural produce as the mother country, New England would soon be exporting those products to the West India islands and elsewhere in return for sugar and other staples that should usually have been going to England. Politically too New England, colonized mainly by dissenters of independent view, was reluctant to accept the laws of an English Parliament where it was not represented when they were not perceived to be in its best interests. Like the laws of trade and navigation which by the 1660s made much of her trade illegal.

New England was thus out of accord with the spirit of English (later British) imperialism. It did not fit the scheme of a self sufficient empire where trading and fishing settlements and plantation colonies complemented the mother country for the common wealth of all. She was a reluctant member of the Old Colonial System and the laws of trade and navigation were of little use to her. Nevertheless, New England's various trades did provide her with the bullion required to pay for imports from England. Although various attempts would be made to restrict colonial trade to that allowed by the Acts these made little difference to the trading patterns of New England perhaps because, until the mid 18th century, it was in nobody's real interest to change them.

Although the activities of the East India Company and of the Royal African Company were strictly controlled by their charters and by agreements with local rulers, the colonies themselves originally operated under little restraint. It was understood from their charters that these settlements were attached to England, were subject to the laws and freedoms of England and that representative institutions should be based on the English model. Beyond that though there was little direction from government as to how the colonies should be run.

The original grants to proprietors were in effect grants of land from the monarch and were based on old established English practice. That practice, the old feudal tradition, was based on a strong link of loyalty between the king and his tenants in chief. It implied a similar link between the king and his colonial proprietors.

It was therefore not surprising that during England's Civil War the colonies sided with the king or remained neutral. Even puritan New England was unwilling to commit fully to what may have been the losing side. When Charles I was executed for treason in 1649, Virginia and Barbados immediately recognized his son as king and Barbados went as far as to pass a resolution giving commercial preference to the Dutch. The central authorities in London had to take action against what it saw as traitorous colonies and in 1651 a fleet was dispatched to the West Indies under Sir George Ayscue. Its purpose was to remind the colonies of their allegiance to and dependence on England rather than, specifically, the Crown. Ayescue's arrival persuaded the Barbadians to expel their royalist leader who surrendered under generous terms in 1652. Similarly the royal governor of Virginia was disavowed. In spite of Admiral Ayscue's successes Parliament realized that more specific control was needed to ensure the continued ties between England, the colonies and their trade.

Because the original colonial settlements had been made by royal grant to proprietors or chartered companies any regulation of the colonies had been the business of the Privy Council, not of Parliament[3]. After Charles I's execution in 1649 the House of Commons became the supreme power and the House of Lords was abolished. The three estates of the realm had been reduced to one; the Commons, and membership of that was restricted to those (the "Rump") who had agreed to the proceedings against the king. The Speaker of the Commons was now the highest dignitary in the land and the only check on its activities was a watchful army under the command of Cromwell. It was Cromwell, appointed Protector in 1653, who limited the power of the Commons by bringing back an appointed Council. Less than two years after Cromwell's death, which took place in September 1658, the monarchy itself was restored.

From 1649 to 1660 the Colonies were therefore the responsibility of Parliament and the Protector. During this period events had occurred which brought changes to colonial administration, changes which would continue after responsibility reverted to the Crown. Unlike his father and grandfather Charles II had little choice but to accept the competence of Parliament to legislate for the colonies.

The Navigation Act had formalized trade and Ayscue's expedition had brought the West India islands under direct government control. Jamaica was England's by right of conquest and had never been subject to a proprietary grant. At the Restoration it had to be decided whether Jamaica should continue to be held (it was), whether the Navigation Act should be retained (it was) and whether proprietary grants lost by Royalist sympathizers under Parliament should be restored. In order to return to normality as swiftly as possible the proprietary grant for the Islands was restored but eventually replaced with a financial arrangement which lasted many years.

New England's reluctant membership of the colonial system continued to cause concern. Complete independence was hardly an option at this time. Colonies and their trade (legal or otherwise) still needed the ultimate protection of a mother country. If New England was not to be part of the English colonial system it was likely to fall prey to France so no one was keen to force the issue. Eventually, in 1684, the Massachusetts charter was annulled and in 1686 the Dominion of New England was formed under one Governor in an attempt to ensure tighter royal control of the region.

---

[3] *In practice this was carried out by subcommittees and boards of the Privy Council.*

In the meantime, in 1664, the area which included the New Netherlands was granted by Charles II to his brother, the Duke of York. The time was thought ripe to enforce England's claim which was based on the right of first discovery (Cabot's voyages) and a fleet was dispatched for that purpose. Lacking the means to resist, the Dutch surrendered but managed to do so on reasonable terms. Most of them retained their property and remained in the colony which was named New York after its new proprietor. The western part of this region was almost immediately granted to other proprietors by the Duke of York and would become New Jersey.

England was not at war with the Netherlands at that time but the region was becoming a centre of colonial trade where her laws of trade and navigation could be circumvented. The Second Dutch War though soon erupted and ended with the Dutch in a position of strength. The Treaty of Breda which concluded the conflict in 1667 left England with what was considered the relatively unimportant trading post of New York but confirmed to the Dutch the plantations of Suriname and the nutmeg island of Run.

The Dutch would briefly reoccupy their New Netherlands in 1673 during the Third Dutch War but the region was again confirmed to England at the Treaty of Westminster in the following year.

New York and New Jersey would eventually become part of the short-lived Dominion of New England mentioned above.

England's Glorious Revolution of 1688 replaced the Catholic absolutism of the Stuarts with the Protestant parliamentary government of William of Orange. This was a fundamental change in the governance of England but it had consequences for the colonies too.[4] After the Glorious Revolution colonial Assemblies, like Parliament in England, felt better able to influence their own affairs. An immediate result though was the ending of the short lived Dominion of New England which fell apart in 1689. A major objection to its existence was that it had never had an elected Assembly and after the changes in England this could not be allowed to continue. Although there was some consolidation the New England colonies went their separate ways and it was some time before the legal status of their various charters was sorted out or new ones granted.

The changes at home (the Civil War, Parliamentary rule, the Restoration of the monarchy and the Glorious Revolution) thus brought about changes in the way England's colonies were governed. Proprietary rule would continue to play its part but by the early years of the 18th century many of the colonies were run directly by royal governors, a move intended to tighten central control. Royal governors, with mandates from the monarch, governed with the help of an appointed Council and were increasingly subject to laws passed by Parliament. Those settlers and planters who had a right to vote elected an Assembly to look after their own interests. In very general terms the Governor, Council and Assembly of a Crown colony had similar functions to the King, the Lords and the Commons at home.

At the same time the administration of the colonies from England began to develop and mature although a specific uniform method of governing them, either individually or as a whole was never achieved. In post Restoration England colonial matters continued to be handled by standing committees of the Privy Council or by separate councils specially commissioned. The specially commissioned councils may have had planters, merchants or

---

4 The Bill of Rights of 1689 when accepted by William of Orange legalised the bloodless revolution that had deposed James II. William was to rule jointly with James II's daughter, Mary, and provisions were made for a Protestant succession and a constitutional monarchy. The revolution was soon termed the "Glorious Revolution".

others with expert knowledge appointed to them in addition to members of the Privy Council. The Committee for Plantations was appointed in July 1660 to deal initially with matters concerning proprietary rights in the West Indies but their work was soon overshadowed by the Council for Foreign Plantations which was nominated in December 1660. From 1675 matters were again dealt with solely by a standing committee of the Privy Council usually referred to as the Lords of Trade. In 1696 this committee was superseded by the newly formed Council of Trade and Foreign Plantations. This became known as the Board of Trade and existed until 1782.

These committees and councils within and without the Privy Council could not issue their own orders direct to colonial governors. They had to be authorized by a Secretary of State of which there were two at this time. The Secretary of State for the north dealt mainly with home affairs and important foreign matters. The Committee for Plantations and its successors were responsible to the Secretary of State for the south. Only in 1768, with disaffection mounting in the American colonies, would a third Secretary (the Secretary of State for the American Colonies) be appointed to deal specifically with colonial affairs.

In addition to Privy Council responsibility for the colonies, Parliament also involved itself in colonial affairs as necessary. Until the early 18th century Parliament generally did little more than reinforce royal authority but it soon began to assert its own power passing Acts dealing with matters such as trade, customs and piracy. There was now an unquestioned assumption, in England at least, that the authority of Parliament extended to the colonies.

Royal control and a developing interest from the home Government did not automatically result in stricter superintendence of colonial affairs. The increasing power of the representative Assemblies often made the Governor's job a difficult one. It was the Assembly who authorized the expenses of the colony including often the Governor's salary. If the Governor and his Council were not in agreement with the Assembly the funds to carry on the business of the colony were not readily forthcoming. It is partly for this reason that royal revenues like quit rents became important to the Crown and were often resisted by the colonial Assemblies. They provided an independent income from which the salaries of royal officials could be paid and over which the Assemblies had little control[5].

Laws passed by the Assembly of a Crown colony had to be agreed by the Privy Council in London but even this did not give the level of control over colonial affairs that may be imagined. A law passed by a local Assembly and signed by the Governor would come into force temporarily until examined by the Board of Trade and ratified by the Privy Council. Allowing for voyage times and press of business in London it would be some time before a reply could be expected. Although most colonial laws were either ratified or laid by for future consideration, those that were disallowed could be replaced with similar legislation by a colonial Assembly and the process started again.

As important decisions concerning the future of the colonies and their financial wellbeing were made in London, many of them appointed London based agents to look after their interests. Representations from these and from other interested parties sometimes also delayed decision making.

Even under royal governors the colonies therefore enjoyed considerable freedom and whatever sort of machinery was put in place at home, strict control over the internal affairs of

---

5 *Only in some of the colonies did the Crown have sufficient quit rents, etc to fund its government at this time. There was no general funding from England to cover these expenses although specific items such as governors' salaries were sometimes allowed for.*

the colonies was difficult. It was thus the case that legislation from London concerning the colonies tended to be of a general nature only. The Navigation Acts to control colonial trade are examples but the regulation of colonial coinage was also seen as a general responsibility of central government. By the early years of the 18th century it was a matter that required urgent attention.

By that time the East India Company was producing coins at two mints in the East but this was of no concern to Parliament or the Privy Council. As long as the Company acted within the terms of its charter the administrative details were solely its own responsibility. This included provision of coinage for use in its settlements and for trade. The only colonial coinages had been those for the Somers Islands, Massachusetts and Maryland. Of those only that of Massachusetts had met with any success but even this was now suppressed. Other than these the various colonies had to make their own decisions regarding the currency value of foreign coins in use.

In 17th century England the Spanish piece of eight was generally rated at 4/6d sterling (four shillings and sixpence). In the colonies it often passed at five shillings, perhaps because of its similarity in size to the crown piece[6]. In Jamaica however the real was originally rated at sixpence giving the piece of eight a currency value of only 4/- (four shillings). This resulted in the clipping of the Spanish coins in Jamaica to bring them into some sort of relationship with ratings elsewhere. Unlike the other West India islands, Jamaica was well supplied with specie because it was at the centre of Spanish activity in the region and a major base for English buccaneers. Jamaica was the main source of specie for the other English colonies where attempts to keep Spanish (usually Spanish American) coins in circulation tempted many of them to raise its value above 5/-. As we have seen, the trading patterns of the New England colonies attracted part of this bullion to the north. The main currency in most of the New World colonies by the later 17th century was therefore clipped pieces of eight with currency values of 6/- or more but an intrinsic value of less than 4/- sterling.

As economies developed there was an increasing need for a circulating currency within the colonies. The best way to provide for this was to have an adequate supply of coin but because much of this disappeared in external payments, other methods had to be devised. Simple credit and promissory notes continued to be of use together with bills of exchange and eventually paper money of various descriptions. Commodities though were also used as a method of payment and it is important to make the distinction between "barter" (the straightforward exchange of one item for another) and "commodity money".

Commodity money was a legal form of payment at rates agreed by a colonial government in the same sort of way that they fixed the rate for foreign silver coins. Once a rate was fixed the commodity had a legal standing as current money within the colony for both taxes and public debts. For private payments the rates were not usually guaranteed. In general though, a person receiving the commodity as a money payment could do so with confidence knowing that ultimately the colonial government would accept it for taxes at the stated rate. The commodities used most consistently as money were tobacco, sugar and corn but, particularly in the northern colonies, many other products would serve. Over the years these comprised most of the main agricultural products including grains, wood, beef, pork and fish, often a whole range of items at the same time.

The system worked but had several faults. Colonial Assemblies, consisting mainly of planters, tended to overvalue commodities when fixing the rates. Governors and their

---

6 *In Massachusetts the General Court of 27th September 1642 ordered that the piece of eight should be current at 5/- although a previous Court (14th June 1642) had voted that it should pass at 4/8d.*

Councils were often in contention with their Assemblies when salaries were paid in commodity money and it was not usually accepted for royal payments such as quit rents. When exported, these commodities (like overvalued silver coins) obviously reverted to their market value. Storage, transport and deterioration were also problems when commodities were used as money as was the fact that those producing the commodities were effectively running their own mints. There was an obvious tendency for the poorer quality product to be packaged as money and the best retained for export with obvious implications for the final owner of the commodity.

In 1713 Virginia would introduce a scheme to protect against such frauds and make the system more workable. Public storehouses were erected where tobacco could be inspected and stored and notes issued in return for that of good quality. The notes, backed entirely by tobacco in the storehouses, then passed as an approved currency. The owner of a note for the time being was the owner of the tobacco.

Long before that time though, paper money had come into general use in many of the colonies. Private credit, often in the form of promissory notes, had existed from the earliest days and the laws of the colonies usually recognized the endorsement of such notes. They thus passed from hand to hand as currency until repaid to the final holder. A promissory note was simply a promise to pay a certain sum on a stated date. Bills of exchange were similar in function but involved a third party. The drawer of the bill instructed his agent (the drawee) to make payment of a certain sum to the payee on a certain date. The easiest analogy is the modern cheque where the drawer is the person who writes the cheque, the drawee is his or her bank and the payee is the person to whom the cheque is made out. In fact most bills of exchange in use in the colonies in the early days were basically cheques drawn on deposits lodged with English agents. These, endorsed from person to person, passed freely in public and private payments.

Bills of exchange were also the common method of transferring Government funds to the colonies and could then be used to make payment in London. Bills on Government departments were drawn to maintain troops, refit warships, etc[7]. The total paid in this way was not large until the War of the Spanish Succession (1702-1713) but was the favourite method of sending funds as it represented the least risk to the Government. The colonial merchants to whom they were paid (for stores, services or colonial currency) would endorse them to English merchants in payment for goods sent to the colonies. The system was not perfect as many bills drawn by colonial governors and officials were contested when presented and there were delays (sometimes years) in payment. The merchants involved would have preferred payment to be made in Spanish dollars or even in trade goods but Government bills were a method of making returns to England other than in specie or commodities. This was particularly important to the colonies north of Maryland who had no staple crop with which to make returns. Because the bills were subject to discount and delay specie would though remain the cheapest way of making payment to England.

Promissory notes and bills of exchange accustomed the colonists to the practice of securing ready cash on account of future resources or by drawing on existing credit. It was then a small step for the treasurers of the various colonies to issue promissory notes in order to pay public debts and these too could pass from person to person on endorsement and serve as currency.

Public bills of credit were similar and were first issued in anticipation of specific taxes. They

---

7 The Government departments on which bill were usually drawn included the Treasury, the Navy Board, the Victualling Office, the Ordinance Board, the Commissioners for Sick and Wounded Seamen, the Transport Board and the Paymaster of Guards and Garrisons.

were redeemed and destroyed when the specific tax was paid. Massachusetts issued public bills of credit in 1690 and in the early 18th century other colonies followed suit. It is these bills of credit that are considered to be the first real issues of colonial paper money. The usual reasons given by the Assemblies for the issue of such bills were a shortage of coin and a need to encourage trade and commerce. The initial issues were made mainly to pay military expenses but they were soon being issued for all manner of public debts. They became the commonest form of paper money in the colonies. As long as there was adequate security in the form of taxes due, etc these public bills of credit circulated at par with the current lawful money of the colony but as time went on the period set for their redemption was moved further into the future. Occasionally bills were reissued without adequate security. Although they were payable to bearer and could be used to pay tax, they were not payable on demand as would be the case with bank notes in future years. For all these reasons colonial paper money would soon depreciate against coin, particularly after 1712 when their issue increased significantly.

The colonial governments who produced these bills of exchange did not have the legal power to create money. It is perhaps for this reason that the term "bill of exchange" was adopted and then retained for them. It implied a borrowing rather than an issue of money. London always objected to the legal tender status given to some of them and consistently treated bills as they would have treated private promissory notes rather than as official money.

The various methods described were used as necessary in order to provide an adequate circulating medium and to pay public debts. Commodities would continue in use well into the 19th century and paper money would eventually become a normal part of the currency in most colonies, particularly when banks were established which could issue notes payable on demand. In the early 18th century though there was still no doubt about the superior advantage of an adequate supply of coin to facilitate small dealings and increase trade. Commodities and the types of paper money available were cumbersome. It was therefore advantageous for the colonies to retain coin. Export of coins could be banned but laws of this nature would not be ratified by the Privy Council and were unlikely even to be signed by the Governor. Alternatively coin in circulation could continue to be given enhanced currency values and this was the method invariably used by a colonial Assembly to attract coin to their colony and keep it there.

The currency values arrived at were based on what the various administrations thought was proper at any one time. While these local values were perfectly comprehensible in each particular colony they were extremely confusing for commerce and there were often problems with remittances home and the movement of coin between colonies. The Board of Trade therefore felt that something had to be done to bring the various rates into line and this led to the first central legislation concerning colonial currency. The aim was to establish a uniform rate for foreign coins throughout the Plantations.

In deciding what that rate should be the Board of Trade had to take into consideration the rates currently in use and any existing legislation. In 1697 the Massachusetts Assembly had legalized the current rate for the piece of eight at 6/-[8]. After submission to the Privy Council in London, their Act had received Royal assent in 1698. Having been confirmed by the Crown this Massachusetts Act had the same force as an Act of Parliament made in England. A proclamation altering that value would contradict the law.

Other colonies had passed Acts giving different rates to the piece of eight but it was the Massachusetts Act which came to the particular attention of the Board of Trade and the Massachusetts rating that was adopted.

---

8 A considerable advance on the 1642 rate of 5/- (see footnote 6).

The Board of Trade therefore suggested to the Queen in Council that a uniform rate for foreign coins should be established throughout the Plantations based on a maximum rate of 6/- for a piece of eight reales with other foreign silver coins in proportion. After consultation with the Royal Mint, where the sterling values of foreign coins were ascertained by assay from time to time, a Royal Proclamation was signed by the Queen on 18th June 1704. It was to be transmitted to the colonies by the first conveyance.

The Proclamation proved impossible to enforce *"owing to no slackness in the Government, butt to the liberty that Trading men will always take in their own bargains"*[9] Coins continued to circulate at their old values or even higher. The Board of Trade consulted the Attorney General on what action it could take and, in October 1705, was advised that only an Act of Parliament would make it definitely illegal to receive coins at more than their declared value.

The resulting Act (of 1707) provided that after 1st May 1709 anyone paying or receiving coins at above the Proclamation rates was liable to imprisonment and forfeit.[10]

TABLE 1
The coins listed in the Proclamation of 1704

Coin	Stated weight (equivalents)	Value according to Weight and Assay
Seville Pieces of Eight, Old Plate	17 pennyweight 12 grains (420 grains = 27·20g)	Four Shillings and Sixpence
Seville Pieces of Eight, New Plate	14dwt (336grains = 21·77g)	Three Shillings Seven Pence One Farthing
Mexico Pieces of Eight	17dwt 12gr (420 grains = 27·20g)	Four Shillings and Sixpence
Pillar Pieces of Eight	17dwt 12gr (420 grains = 27·20g)	Four Shillings and Sixpence Three Farthings
Peru Pieces of Eight, Old Plate	17dwt 12gr (420 grains = 27·20g	Four Shillings and Five Pence, or thereabouts
Cross Dollars	18dwt (432 grains = 27·99g)	Four Shillings and Four Pence Three Farthings
Ducatoons of Flanders	20dwt 21gr (501 grains = 32·46g)	Five Shillings and Six Pence
Ecu's of France, or Silver Lewises	17dwt 12gr (420 grains = 27·20g)	Four Shillings and Six Pence
Crusadoes of Portugal	11dwt 4gr (268 grains = 17·37g)	Two Shillings and Ten Pence One Farthing
Three Guilder Pieces of Holland	20dwt 7gr (487 grains = 31·56g)	Five Shillings and Two Pence One Farthing
Old Rix Dollars of the Empire	18dwt 10gr (442 grains = 28·64g)	Four Shillings and Sixpence

---

9 Letter from John Evans, Deputy Governor of Pennsylvania, to the Board of Trade dated 13th February, 1704/5 as quoted in R. Chalmers, "A History of Currency in the British Colonies".
10 Act 6 Anne, c. 57. 1707.

It may be useful to explain some of the terms used in the list of Proclamation coins. Seville pieces of eight are listed for both old and new plate. This is because there had been changes to the Spanish monetary system during the 17th century that resulted in the mainland real being 20% lighter than that of the Spanish American mints. The Spanish new plate coins were for circulation in metropolitan Spain only while the Spanish American mints continued to strike at the internationally accepted standard. It is unlikely that the new Spanish coins found their way to the colonies in any quantity until the pistareen (the two reals of new plate which we will look at in a moment) began to be imported in large numbers some years after the Act.

Old plate Peru pieces are the only coins in the list not to be given an exact value. At this time the Viceroyalty of Peru still extended to the whole of Spanish South America thus including the Potosi mint as well as that of Lima. All pieces of eight that were not of Mexico were therefore often termed "Peruvians". Malpractice at the Potosi mint had come to light in the 1640s so there was some doubt in the minds of the Royal Mint officials as to the standards maintained there. Hence their insistence on "old plate" Peru coins and the slight and uncertain discount placed even upon them. The pillar and waves design was introduced on the coins of the Peruvian Viceroyalty from 1651 in order to restore confidence. It was a design that had been used occasionally before but now came into general use at the South American mints. The Mexico coins, whose standards had never been questioned, were unchanged and continued to use the long cross reverse. The Proclamation list therefore assigns the 4/6d value to pieces of eight of the Seville (old plate) and Mexico types only.

The cross dollar was the patagon of Flanders and the old rix dollars of the Empire were those of some of the German cities of the Holy Roman Empire. These were simply the coins that had been assayed at the Royal Mint. In practice the colonies would have made no distinction between these and the patagons and rix dollars of other mints. Again the list indicates that ducatoons of Flanders were assayed while the ducatoon most often seen in the colonies at the time of the Proclamation was probably that of the Dutch mints which showed a horse and rider on the obverse (usually termed a "rider ducatoon" today).

Pieces of eight and their fractions were the commonest foreign coins in use. The other proclamation coins would not all have figured prominently in day to day usage but would have been familiar to colonial merchants and traders.

The Seville (old plate), Mexico and Pillar pieces of eight of full weight were not to pass at above 6/- in colonial currency, disregarding the marginally higher assay of the Pillar type. Halves, quarters and lesser fractions were to pass in proportion, the other coins in the list according to their assay relative to the piece if eight. Light pieces would pass in proportion to their weight.

The Act failed to achieve what was intended. The individual colonies still faced the problem of retaining specie. In finding ways to do this most of them managed to avoid complying with the main provision of the Act which was to fix a maximum value for the piece of eight. The Act made no mention of gold coins which had previously been treated as multiples of the silver. In the West India islands advantage was taken of this by giving independent ratings to gold coins, primarily those of Spain and later Portugal. Instead of silver having a fixed value it became simply a fraction of the gold pieces and it was perfectly legal to adjust the circulating value of the gold coins in each colony as required. The West Indies thus moved onto a gold standard.

The mainland colonies generally retained silver for their metallic currencies but increasingly issued paper money which drove coin out of use. In these ways the Act of Queen Anne was largely ignored and the currency problems resulting from the variety of rates continued.

A further complication was that the Act provided for full weight coins while most of those in circulation were light. In fact even the Massachusetts valuation of 1697 was for a coin of 17 pennyweights rather than the full weight of 17½ provided for in the Act. Light weight coins would have to be weighed and pass in proportion to the rates noted in the Proclamation.

Looking at the Act and its effects in some detail clearly shows the problems that existed and how people grappled with them. Opinion in the colonies themselves was that the problems could only be solved by the establishment of colonial mints which could re-coin all the foreign silver into English coins of full sterling standard to be used for home payments. The Board of Trade, remembering the independence of the Massachusetts mint, would not agree to that. For the modern numismatist this is a disappointment as it would certainly have resulted in some interesting coins.

Coins noted in the 1704 Proclamation and their sterling values.

Seville piece of eight, old plate.
Four Shillings and Sixpence

Mexico piece of eight.
Four Shillings and Sixpence

Pillar piece of eight (Potosi mint 1679).
Four Shillings and Sixpence Three Farthings

Peru piece of eight, old plate (Potosi mint, Philip II).
Four Shillings and Five Pence, or thereabouts

Cross dollar (Patagon of Flanders, Brugge mint 1653).

Four Shillings and Four Pence Three Farthings

Ducatoon (this one of the Antwerp mint 1638).

Five Shillings and Six Pence

"Rider" ducatoon of Holland, Dordrecht mint 1673).

Five Shillings and Six Pence

Ecu of France (Rouen mint 1652).

Four Shillings and Six Pence

Cruzado of Portugal (Lisbon mint 1687).

Two Shillings and Ten Pence One Farthing

Three guilder piece of Holland (Utrecht 1682).

Five Shillings and Two Pence One Farthing

Rix dollar (this one of West Frisia 1620).
Four Shillings and Sixpence

What the Proclamation and Act tell us is that the main coin in circulation was the Spanish American piece of eight reales most of which were assessed at 4/6d sterling and given a maximum circulating value in the colonies of 6/-. They also tell us that a variety of other coins were known and used although not all of them would necessarily have been in use in every colony. It can be imagined how difficult it must have been to agree a total value for a payment tendered in different coins often clipped to a greater or lesser degree between colonies where different rates were in force for each coin. Had the Act succeeded it would have gone some way to sorting things out. No further attempt to reform colonial currency in general would be attempted until 1825.

In the years following the Act the term "dollar" tends to replace "piece of eight". In the West Indies it is rated in terms of gold and is used for overseas payment while in the North American colonies it is largely replaced by paper. For day to day transactions in most of the colonies a baser coin came into general use. This was the *Spanish* two reales of new plate, soon known as the pistareen. It was equivalent to one fifth of a Spanish American dollar but its similarity to the quarter dollar and the fact that both were denominated as two reales led to its ready acceptance in the British colonies. It was soon being imported from Spain in large quantities and, being overvalued, remained in circulation.

Pistareens were soon being cut for small change as was the whole range of Spanish American silver coins. As those who cut these coins usually erred on the side of economy cut silver segments were also overvalued and remained in circulation as small change.

The people who evaded the Act of Queen Anne and the Navigation Acts before it were seeking workable systems and were not deliberately defying the law. They came predominantly from England and the British Isles and, in spite of the way things stood in New England, would have had little real problem accepting the authority of Parliament or the laws of England if they were workable. In the next chapter we will look at how and why this began to change during the 18th century.

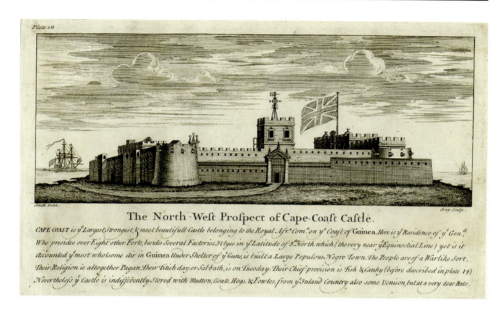

One of the West African forts at which slaves were gathered for export.

Slaves cutting sugar cane in Antigua.

4

Settlement, Slavery and War

INITIAL settlement in the colonies was primarily from England with the original proprietors. The first settlers came to seek their fortunes and in the early years most were male. This, and a high mortality rate, meant that populations were difficult to maintain without further immigration. Only in the New England colonies, where the settlers were mainly family groups and where subsistence rather than plantation farming was the norm, was there natural increase from the start.

New free settlers were recruited in a number of ways, most being attracted by expectations of wealth and land ownership which would not have been in prospect had they stayed at home. However, an increasing requirement for labour as the colonies flourished meant that other systems of recruitment had to be developed. Those who were unable or unwilling to pay their own way often went as indentured labourers. In return for their passage and their keep they contracted for a set period, usually four to seven years, during which time the settlers who employed them could sell or hire them out as if they owned them. Indentured servitude of this type continued until the 1780s.

Settler groups seeking greater religious freedom were soon also arriving in the New England colonies and by the later 17th century many new settlers were arriving in the Plantations from other parts of the British Isles, some of them exiled after the upheavals of the Civil War.

As the plantations developed it soon became obvious that free settlement would not be enough. There was no great surplus of labour in 17th century England and if colonies were required for commercial reasons some of the labour required would have to be forced.

Under English law any offence more serious than a misdemeanour was classed as a felony and usually led to the death penalty. The list of felonies was a long one and would increase as time went on. It was early recognized that in many cases transportation of convicted felons would be a merciful alternative to hanging and an ideal solution to the shortages of labour in the colonies. A new start in a new land where there was plenty of honest work away from the corrupting influences of large cities would give offenders an opportunity to reform. At the same time the mother country could rid itself of undesirables and provide a work force for the plantations, all of which was to the common good. Transportation of criminals and vagabonds began soon after the colonies were founded but increased from the mid 17th century. The Transportation Act of 1718 made it a specific penalty in England except for the most serious offences. It has been estimated that until 1776, when the North American colonies declared their independence, about 50,000 convicts were sent to the Americas[1].

---

1 See for example Peter Wilson Coldham, "Emigrants in Chains".

These of course were not the only forced labour that would come to the Plantations and nor were they the largest number. Up to 1807, when Britain banned her slave trade, perhaps 3 million slaves were imported to British colonies from West Africa in British and colonial ships[2]. The total number of slaves brought to the colonies over that period could have been three times the total number of white immigrants. The slave populations, like the settlers themselves, eventually began to increase naturally. This was not so marked in the West Indian Plantations but by the 1750s it has been estimated that only about 10% of the slaves in the mainland Plantations were African born[3].

The preference in the early colonies was for European indentured labour, occasionally referred to as "white slaves", and up to about 1660 Barbados was the only colony using large numbers of African slaves. Indentured labourers though were hired only for a specific period and, like transportees, were well aware of the opportunities available to them when their time expired. Complaints in England about shortages of labour made it difficult to attract sufficient numbers of indentured servants and a fall in the price of slaves made the African economically viable. The preference gradually changed and the huge increase in the numbers of imported slaves in the 18th century made them the main source of labour in all the colonies from Maryland southwards.

For many years (long before the Plantations were founded) English merchants had traded to West Africa. They went in the wake of the Portuguese seeking the gold that was known to be found there but filling their ships with other cargoes too. The various parts of the coast came to be named after the commodities most readily available. The Grain Coast, Ivory Coast and Gold Coast were the main sources of melegueta pepper[4], ivory and gold. The area to the east of the Gold Coast (the Bight of Benin) would also come to be named after a rich export commodity. Although slaves were available all along the West African coast this region to the east would come to be known specifically as the Slave Coast.

When they first came though, the English were not seeking slaves. They came intermittently looking for gold and traded mostly to the west in the areas around the Gambia River. For many years this river was assumed to be the gateway to Africa's gold mines. The Portuguese though were already well established in West Africa and English trade could not flourish without a fortified base to protect it. Perhaps with this in mind the Company of Adventurers of London trading to the parts of Africa known as "Gynney and Bynney" (Guinea and Benin) was chartered by James I in 1618. Although known as "the Guinea Company" and in spite of the geographical areas assigned to it, trade was still largely carried on further to the west. In 1631 a new charter was granted to what was essentially the same Guinea Company. Now termed the Company of Merchants Trading to Guinea its purpose was to extend English trade further east and England's first permanent factory on the Gold Coast, soon fortified, was established at Kormantin.

By now the Dutch had replaced the Portuguese as the main traders on the West African coast and were determined to protect their interests. This made life very difficult for the Guinea Company who also had to contend with English interlopers. At home, during the Interregnum, the Company was accused by Puritans of having exercised undue influence in gaining its royal charter and a review was carried out. In 1651, as a result of this review, the

---

2   *The figures are difficult to calculate with accuracy. An attempt is made in the "Oxford History of the British Empire" volume II, pp. 441 et seq. to determine the numbers shipped in British and colonial ships. For the period 1662 to 1807 this probably accounts for about half the total slaves shipped from West Africa by all nations to their various plantations. The slave trade was continued after 1807 by nations other than Britain. The total number of slaves shipped across the Atlantic from the 16th century until 1867 was probably more than 11 million.*

3   *See for example M. Craton, "Empire, Enslavement and Freedom in the Caribbean".*

4   *The seeds of melegueta pepper were termed "grains of paradise" because of their flavour. They were much sought after by 16th century merchants.*

Council of State reduced the geographical extent of its monopoly and much of the coast was thrown open to free English trade. The Guinea Company lost most of its business and in 1657 leased its rights and factories to the East India Company.

These arrangements were made during the period of Parliament and the Protectorate and it will be remembered that the Navigation Act and the First Dutch War date to the same period. At the Restoration the time was therefore ripe for another royal charter for the West African trade and the Company of Royal Adventurers Trading into Africa came into being in 1660. The rights of the old Guinea Company (which legally lasted until 1662) had to be sorted out but a new charter of 1663 confirmed the English forts of the Gold Coast to the Royal Adventurers and appointed the Duke of York as the Company's Governor. The 1663 charter changes the Company's name slightly to "The Company of Royal Adventurers *of England* Trading into Africa" (my italics) and for the first time mentions slaves among its interests.

There was still though strong opposition from the Dutch and several warlike acts occurred in West Africa before the outbreak of the Second Dutch War in 1665. This crippled the Royal Adventurers who, after bankruptcy in 1672, were superseded by the Royal African Company of England.

Before the formation of the first royal company most slaves bound for the English colonies had been carried in Dutch ships but one of the purposes of the Navigation Act was to secure some of the Dutch carrying trade for English ships. While the earlier English companies had traded between London and Africa for the produce of the land the Royal Company's 1663 charter specifically mentions the buying and selling of slaves. From now on many of the ships of the African Company would ply the infamous triangular route carrying trade goods to West Africa, slaves to the Plantations and colonial products home to England.

The Royal African Company carried on its business from forts scattered along the West African coast of which Cape Coast Castle became the most important. Goods and slaves could be kept securely in these forts awaiting shipment but the company did not own these establishments. The forts were rented from local rulers. Not all of them remained open all the time and some changed hands now and then between the various European nations buying slaves on the coast.

Because of its importance we will return to the slave trades and slavery in general in later chapters but before we leave West Africa it is interesting to note that the direct trade brought home quantities of gold. Much of this was coined at the Tower Mint into English gold coins. To indicate the provenance of the metal used these coins bore the African Company's badge (an elephant, later an elephant and castle) below the obverse portrait. Such was the quantity of gold coming from the Guinea coast that the denomination itself became known as the "guinea".[5] Of course these are not colonial coins but they are an interesting insight into overseas adventure.

English guinea of Charles II (1660-1685).
Struck from gold supplied by the African Company.

---

5 *Gold is recorded as arriving at the Mint from Guinea as early as 1649 (SCBI 57, P. 18). The first guineas to bear the mark of the African Company are dated 1663.*

While England was busily pursuing her mercantile policy by developing the plantations and protecting their trade it was inevitable that she would come into conflict with other European nations who were attempting to secure their own positions. Competition for the riches of the world inevitably led to wars between nations aimed at protecting their own interests and damaging those of others.

The Navigation Act of 1651 was a direct attack on the Dutch carrying trade and triggered a series of wars with the Dutch whose strength lay in their domination of the seas. By the end of the 17th century these matters had largely been settled in England's favour even though William of Orange now sat on the English throne.

Scotland had had the same kings as England since James VI of Scotland succeeded Elizabeth I in 1603. In addition to his Scottish title he became James I of England but his two kingdoms remained separate. They were still separate kingdoms in the 1690s by which time William of Orange had become William III of England and William II of Scotland. Perhaps to avoid confusion, William omits the regnal numeral on his Scottish coins.

For many years Scotland had wanted her own overseas trading company and, with the promise of financial backing from merchants in England, the Company of Scotland Trading to Africa and the Indies was founded by an Act of the Scottish Parliament in 1695. The Act was given royal assent by the King's Commissioner at Edinburgh but in a hurry and without the king's specific permission. There were soon complaints from the East India Company in London that a Scottish Company would breach their monopoly and the result was that all English investment (about half the total required) was stopped. The Scottish directors decided to go ahead but now had to raise all the necessary capital in Scotland. This was achieved but only by raising funds from some 1,400 investors, many of them towns or boroughs, across the land. The Scottish company had become a patriotic cause and it has been estimated that perhaps half the available capital in Scotland was raised to fund it.[6]

Although the Scottish company commissioned voyages to West Africa and the Indian Ocean it is usually known as the "Darien Company" because its main venture was the setting up, in 1698, of a merchant colony at Darien in central America. The purpose of this was to tap overland into the trans Pacific trade as the Spaniards had already done. The English were concerned that a Scottish colony in that region would cause problems between Spain and England (William III was after all the king of Scotland too). Colonial governors throughout the Plantations were therefore told that the king had been unaware of the true intention of the Scots to set up a colony instead of limiting their activities to trade. They were instructed not to trade with the new colony or to assist it in any way. By and large these instructions were obeyed. For a number of reasons, including the lack of support from the English colonies, the Darien colony failed and was finally abandoned in 1700.

Apart from the loss of many lives the failure of the colony was a very serious blow to Scotland threatening huge financial loss for a large number of people. Inevitably England was blamed for the disaster and this could well have brought about a Jacobite rising in Scotland against the king. The necessity to ease tension over the Darien failure was one of the factors which led the two kingdoms towards Union. Among other things the Act of Union of 1707 dissolved the Scottish company and granted a substantial sum of money to Scotland for the company's shareholders.

The Union of the two nations gave all citizens of the new Great Britain the right to trade to the colonies. The formation of the United East India Company at about the same time similarly extended participation in the eastern trades.

---

6 *For the full story of the Darien Company see John Prebble, "The Darien Disaster", 1968.*

An interesting numismatic relic of this period is the gold brought back to Leith by the "African Merchant", a ship on charter to the Darien Company. The gold arrived in Scotland from West Africa in 1700 and a Scottish Act of August that year allowed it to be struck into coin. In the same way that English guineas of the period bore the badge of the African Company, it was agreed that the Scottish coins would bear the crest of the Darien Company below the king's bust[7]. Although obviously not colonial coins this small issue of Scottish gold is a further reminder of overseas adventure.

Scottish pistole.
Struck from Darien Company gold.

With Dutch sea power curbed and matters in the north largely settled Britain could now face challenges from other European nations with growing confidence. Although Spain continued to oppose British expansion the main threat to Britain's old colonial system was now seen to be that of France.

By the late 17th century France had become the most powerful Catholic country of Europe. Louis XIV envisaged universal monarchy for himself and a great colonial empire for France. The main object in his way was England in both the Old World and the New. This and England's determination to secure her own interests resulted in the great struggle that developed between the two countries for world supremacy which we must now examine.

The wars that were fought in the period 1689 to 1815 between England (later Britain) and France involved many other countries and were fought for a variety of reasons. Underlying the particular occasion for each of the wars though was the perceived need for both of them to secure their assets. The whole period can thus be seen as a lengthy duel for domination of the world's trade, almost a second Hundred Years' War with France[8].

In 1689 all of England's colonies were still in North America and the Caribbean. The regions east of the Cape of Good Hope and west of The Strait of Magellan were the preserve of the East India Company as was St Helena in the South Atlantic. The forts on the West African coast were in the hands of the African Company. France also had colonies in the Americas and an East India Company (the Compagnie des Indes Orientales). Like England she also had interests in West Africa. At this time though France's prime concern was the domination of Europe.

The Nine Years' War (1689-1697) forced France to accept the Protestant William III as king of England and thus drop her support for the deposed James II. Like all the wars of this period this was not simply a war between England and France but a war that involved other European states. Nor was the result all in England's favour or to the detriment of France. The treaty of Ryswick which ended it confirmed some French territorial gains in Europe which the war had been designed to reverse.

---

7 At about the same standard as the French Louis d'Or these coins were soon termed "pistoles". They were tariffed at £12 Scots which was the approximate equivalent of £1 English at this time. Half pistoles were also struck.
8 See for example J.R.Seeley, "The Expansion of England", 1884. The original Hundred Years' War resulted from the 14th century claim by Edward III of England to the crown of France.

The War of the Spanish Succession (1702-1713) confirmed Bourbon control of the Spanish Empire. It was during this war (in 1704) that Gibraltar was captured and when a British naval base was established in Minorca (1708). By this time Britain had grown powerful enough to gain considerable advantage at the peace of Utrecht which concluded the war. France accepted the legality of the Protestant succession in Britain and recognized Nova Scotia and Newfoundland as British colonies. She ceded to Britain her claims to the Hudson's Bay Company territories and there were commercial benefits too. Britain was granted the *asiento* (the contract to supply slaves to the Spanish dominions in America) and gained rights to trade to Spanish America[9].

Britain's next major war began in 1739 as a result of various disputes, some of which had involved military action, with Bourbon Spain. There was British logging on the Yucatan Peninsula which Spain considered illegal and a territorial dispute between Spanish Florida and the British colony of Georgia. Spain resented the rights that Britain had gained at Utrecht and argued that British traders were abusing the privileges granted. The British complained of the "piratical" actions of the Spanish *Garda Costas* whose job was to police Spain's trade. Matters came to a head in 1738 when Captain Robert Jenkins is reputed to have exhibited his severed and preserved ear to a furious House of Commons committee. It had been torn off, he alleged, when his ship was boarded for search in 1731 and was typical of the barbaric treatment British seamen could expect while engaged in their lawful trade. His Spanish adversary, Jenkins asserted, had threatened the English king with the same treatment should he also dare to meddle in Spanish waters. In the atmosphere of the day this was enough to plunge Britain into the "War of Jenkins's Ear". This colonial war with Spain was not settled before it became part of the more general European war: that of the Austrian Succession, and Britain was again at war with France.

Although many European states were involved in the war of 1739-1748 the Treaty of Aix la Chapelle which concluded matters was dictated by Britain and France who were now indisputably the two most important nations of Europe. It did not though settle very much between them and has been considered to be more of a truce than a peace settlement. The Seven Years' War of 1756-1762 was inevitable.

The struggle for influence in Europe and domination in the Atlantic was now extended to India where conflict between British and French interests had already occurred. In North America the British coastal colonies were seen as hemmed in and possibly under military threat from forts along the Ohio and Mississippi rivers as the French extended their influence south from the St Lawrence and north from the Gulf of Mexico. Some of the West Indian islands were vulnerable to attack and in India the Compagnie des Indes was actively working to extend French influence at Britain's expense.

War was declared by Britain when news came of the French landing in Minorca in 1756. Britain's naval base there was temporarily lost after a seventy day siege and the war had begun badly for Britain. By its end though the French had been effectively expelled from North America, the Caribbean was largely under British control and French ambitions in India had been halted. The old colonial system had been preserved. Britain, her colonies and her trade were secure.

The Seven Years' War had been a decisive victory for British arms but it had been an expensive one. At its end the National debt stood at more than £130 million, a debt which had to be serviced through taxation of one sort or another. Much of this debt had been incurred

---

9   *The South Sea Company rather than the Royal African Company was granted the asiento and also the right to send an annual ship to Vera Cruz in Mexico and Cartagena on the Spanish Main for trade.*

removing the French threat to the colonies so it seemed reasonable to the British Government that the colonies should pay a fair share of it. Parliament set about passing the necessary Acts. Until this time Parliament's right to pass Acts governing colonial affairs had not been seriously questioned but soon the cry would be heard that there should be "no taxation without representation". The colonies were not represented in the British Parliament and, in the days of sail, it would have been difficult for such to have been the case. Most of them exercised a considerable amount of freedom through their Assemblies and exerted influence, sometimes large, through their agents and other personal contacts. This had always worked sufficiently well in the past but when direct taxation began to be applied the legality of the necessary Acts began to be questioned.

The Thirteen Colonies south of Nova Scotia that rebelled on 4th July 1776

Ministers and Parliament stuck firmly to the view that they had an unalienable right to pass legislation for the colonies. When the duties imposed by the Stamp Act of 1765 were stubbornly resisted in North America they were forced to try other measures (Townsend duties, Tea Act, etc) but they would never accept the American view that Parliament had no right to legislate for the colonies. In doing so and in insisting on colonial taxation Parliament reflected the mood in Britain but steadily alienated the colonies. At the same time the provisions of the Navigation Act were tightened up to increase revenue and this caused further friction. The Seven Years' War, the root cause of the revenues disputes, had of course removed the French threat to the North American colonists making many of them less inclined to contribute to the costs incurred. The West Indian colonies, where the threat of French attack still existed and where there were large slave majorities, paid their duties with little complaint.

With Parliament's insistence that it had the right to legislate and the colonial view that it did not there could be only one end result. When thirteen of the North American colonies declared their independence it was a mutiny that had to be met with force. The bitter War of Independence lasted from the date of that declaration, 4th July 1776, till 1782. In the end the colonists had their way and the United States of America was born but although a preliminary peace was agreed between Britain and the United States in November 1782 the war did not come to a negotiated end for some time. When it had become obvious that Britain could not control her colonies France, Spain and eventually the Dutch all entered the war against her. It is ironic that the old enemy should now assist British colonies in a contest brought on by the costs of a war which had secured those colonies against her. The involvement of other nations delayed the final settlement of the war until agreements had been completed at Versailles in September 1783.

The loss of most of the North American colonies was an enormous blow to the principles of the mercantile system. It came though at a time when Adam Smith was formulating his economic theories based on free trade and in fact British trade to North America increased considerably in the years following American Independence. Also there were soon large acquisitions of territory by the East India Company which would be considered a compensation for the American losses.

A further consequence of American Independence was the founding of a new, purely penal, colony on the other side of the world as an alternative destination for transported convicts (New South Wales).

Importantly, France had not been able to reestablish herself in North America by taking the side of the colonists and by 1790 was no longer considered to be a large scale threat to Britain or to her commerce. It seemed as if the great contest was over but in 1793 the two countries were yet again at war. Revolutionary France had to be curbed in Europe and this war continued until a peace was agreed in 1802. It was not long though before war resumed and this time Napoleon's grand ideas of conquest had to be countered. The Battle of Waterloo which finally ended his dream in 1815 not only marked the end of a war. It was the end of the great duel between Britain and France for world domination: a duel that Britain had won.

In India the events of the 18th century led to fundamental changes in the function of the East India Company. It changed from a commercial to an administrative organization which would eventually bring most of India under British rule and lay the foundation of British Empire in the east. Through the Regulating Act of 1773 and the India Act of 1784 the Company lost its independence and became little more than a department of the British Government. (see Chapter eleven).

It is now time to look at what was happening to the coins used in the colonies while the great contest between Britain and France was shaping these fundamental changes to the Empire. In fact the practices that emerged after the Act of Queen Anne had failed in its intent continued with little change. Gold remained the basis of denominational values in the island colonies with the dollar rated to it. In the mainland colonies paper money was much used and everywhere the silver pistareen provided a circulatory medium. Cut fractions of the dollar also provided small change; particularly in the Caribbean colonies as did imported French billon coins.

Two escudos of Philip V. Bogota (Colombia) mint c.1730.
A popular denomination in the West Indian colonies after 1707.

Spanish two reals (pistareen).
Circulated extensively in the colonies in the 18th century.

The Spanish American dollars and fractions in use up to now had been the very basic cob type coins. These coins may have been referred to as cobs because of their rather lumpy appearance or perhaps because they were *"cabo de barra"* – the end of the bar from which they were cut. It was not until 1732 that the process of introducing a milled coinage at the Spanish American mints was begun. Mexico was the first mint to produce the new coins and adopted a pillar reverse for them which it had not used on its cobs. It was some years before the other Spanish American mints followed suite with their own milled coins but when the process was complete there was a standard uniform coinage of milled pillar dollars throughout Spanish America. The new coins were at a slightly reduced weight and fineness. It was not long before another change was made introducing a portrait obverse in 1772 when the fineness was again slightly reduced. The justification for these changes in standard was that the Spanish American dollar was now a much improved milled coin. Nevertheless its standard was now changed a little from that laid down in the British Proclamation of 1704.

The Proclamation coins listed in 1704 were not the only foreign coins familiar to the colonists. Perhaps a surprising omission from the list was the lion dollar. This was a Dutch coin somewhat lighter and baser than the rix dollar but more or less the same weight as the eight reales. It was much favoured by Dutch merchants as an export coin wherever they traded

Milled "pillar" dollar (Mexico 1755).   "Portrait" dollar (Lima mint 1774).

and as such had come into use in the New Netherlands (which later became New York and New Jersey). It found its way in trade to most of the English colonies of North America. It is interesting to note that no fewer than 22 lion dollars were recovered from the wreck of H.M.S. "Feversham" which was lost on an expedition to Canada in 1711. The ship is known to have drawn cash from the Victualling Office of the British Treasury in New York before sailing and the coins recovered are assumed to be indicative of the coins in use in New York at the time[10].

The lion dollars and other European silver coins were popular in the colonies partly because of their superior fabric. The Spanish American cobs could be clipped without substantially changing their appearance so were often of uncertain value. With the introduction of milled Spanish American dollars (from 1732) other foreign silver lost that aspect of its appeal.

Netherlands "Lion" dollar (Gelderland 1611).
Popular in the North American colonies.

Another coin which was familiar in some of the colonies was referred to variously as the "Arabian chequine", the "zequeen" or the "Barbary ducat". This was the gold *ashrafi altin* struck at the Ottoman mints to the same weight as European ducats (3.49g) and usually

---

10 The 22 lion dollars recovered compare with 504 Spanish American coins of all denominations, 126 silver coins of Massachusetts (a surprise at this late date) and just 13 English and Spanish coins.

"Barbary ducat". (Mehmed III, 1595-1603, Misr mint).
Used extensively in the North American and West Indian colonies.

known today as the sultani. It circulated quite extensively in some English colonies where it was usually taken as the equivalent of two dollars. In the later 17th and early 18th centuries it is noted in the records of several colonies including Antigua, Nevis, Bermuda, Virginia and Maryland and was presumably brought in mainly by privateers and pirates.

The Barbary ducat perhaps remained in circulation until about 1740 but after the Act of 1707, when the Caribbean colonies moved towards a gold standard, the weight and fineness of gold coins became more important. Although all manner of coin was familiar to the colonists the preferred gold was initially that of Spain and Spanish America.

The Spanish gold in use in the early 18th century, like the silver, was of the old cob type and easily clipped. The basic unit of gold currency was the escudo. There were multiples of the escudo up to eight but it is only two of these denominations that regularly appear in British colonial records. These were the eight escudos, termed the "doubloon," and the two escudos, often termed the "pistole". The fineness of Spanish gold was reduced from 22 carats in 1772 with a further reduction in 1786.

Spanish American doubloon (eight escudos). Popayan mint (Columbia) 1796

The Portuguese gold retained its standard throughout the period and was already a milled coinage. The main gold coin of Portugal at the start of the century was the Moidore. This had originally been 4,000 reis but by 1688 had been raised to 4,800. In spite of this the figure 4000 continued to appear on the coin. The moidore had achieved considerable circulation in Ireland and in the west of England by the early 18th century where it usually passed at 28/- but had less influence in the colonies. By the time gold became an important part of colonial currency the moidore had been superseded by the larger "Johannes" series of gold, so named because they were introduced during the reign of John V (1706-1750). The largest unit of the series was the *dobra* of 12,800 reis but the most popular denomination was the *peça* of 6,400 reis. Officially the "half joe," it was the *peça* rather than the *dobra* that came to be called the johannes in common usage and which is referred to as the johannes in this book. It was this coin together with the Spanish doubloon that would dominate the currency of the New World.

Portuguese gold coins.
Left, Moidore of 1704, Lisbon mint. Right, Johannes (6,400 reis) of 1771, Rio de Janeiro mint. Portuguese gold became more popular than Spanish gold in the West Indies in the later 18th century.

The maintenance of the fineness of Portuguese gold while that of Spain declined led not only to a preference for Portuguese gold in many of the colonies but also to the clipping and imitation of the johannes.

By the later 18th century light weight imitation and clipped johannes had become a major problem in the colonies and in some of them steps were taken to restore weights by adding plugs of gold. We will look at this in the next chapter but for now it should be noted that this was not an entirely new practice. Silver cobs of various denominations are known which have been plugged to bring weights up to standard and another interesting feature of the "Feversham" finds is that several of the Spanish American coins recovered have had plugs applied to them. It will be remembered that many of the coins on board this ship came from an official source in New York.

Plugged Spanish American eight reals (Mexico).
This coin has had two plugs added to bring it to a required standard and is one of the "Feversham" coins.

In the late 17th and early 18th centuries there were some specific attempts at providing small change for colonial use. There is little doubt that most of these were profit motivated rather than altruistic and it is to Ireland as well as Britain that we must look for much of the small change arriving in the North American colonies during this period.

In 1681 an emigrant named Mark Newby left Dublin bound for New Jersey with a large supply of copper coins. These were the Saint Patrick coins struck for use in Ireland, perhaps about 1670, because of a shortage of small change in that country. There is evidence that these were still in circulation in Ireland as late as 1724 but Newby, no doubt aware that there was a great dearth of small change in New Jersey, was able to obtain large numbers of them before he sailed from Dublin. In May 1682 the New Jersey General Assembly authorized the St Patrick halfpenny as legal tender up to five shillings. The coins are of two sizes, assumed to be halfpenny and farthing. The smaller coin though is usually more than half the weight of the larger and has a slightly different obverse so it is possible that it could be a subsequent, lighter, issue of the halfpenny. Only the halfpenny is specifically mentioned in the colonial records but both sized coins circulated in New Jersey.[11] Presumably Mark Newby derived some profit from the venture although he was required to change them on demand.

Another early attempt to provide small change for the colonies is a tin coinage in the name of James II denominated as one twenty fourth of a real. There is evidence to show that these were produced by one Richard Holt in 1688 under a similar patent to those granted for the English tin coins of the period. The intention was that they would be current in the plantations in general and supply the need for small change wherever Spanish coin was in use. The number of die varieties known indicates a moderately large production but there is no evidence to show that they were actually sent to any of the plantations.[12]

An unusual copper token of the late 17th century may have been struck specifically for overseas use. The obverse type of this piece is an African elephant. Its reverse type is a shield bearing the arms of London with legend **GOD PRESERVE LONDON.** It is undated and approximately halfpenny size but somewhat heavier than the official halfpenny of the day. Some early writers have suggested that this piece could have been struck for use in Tangier which was in English hands from 1662 to 1684.[13] Two further tokens, both extremely rare, use the same obverse die. Both have a legend only on the reverse: **GOD PRESERVE NEW ENGLAND** or **GOD PRESERVE CAROLINA AND THE LORDS PROPRIETORS** and both are dated 1694. These may have been intended for currency in North American colonies but are more likely to have been presentation pieces or medalets designed to encourage interest in the Plantations.

Another Irish issue which found its way to North America was the copper coinage struck under patent by William Wood in 1722-1724.[14] Wood's "Hibernia" coins were not popular in Ireland partly because the Irish Parliament had not been informed of the scheme but also because they felt that a large issue of base metal coins would drive gold and silver from circulation. In addition to his patent for Irish coins Wood obtained a patent to strike copper coins for the Plantations – the "Rosa Americana" coins, so named because of their reverse legend. With coinage patents for both Ireland and the Plantations it would have been easy for Wood to ship unwanted "Hibernia" coins to North America where they could circulate at double their original value. Wood's Irish coins were struck in two denominations (halfpenny and farthing), the "Rosa Americana" coins in three (two pence, penny and halfpenny) the

---

11 William Nicholson (Bishop of Derry) "The Irish Historical Library" 1724, p.170 states "These are still common in Copper and Brass..." and further states that (in Ireland at that time) "...being of different dimentions are current for halfpence and farthings."
12 See Eric P. Newman, "The James II 1/24th Real For the American Plantations" in American Numismatic Society Museum Notes, 11, 1964.
13 For the Tangier suggestion see particularly Ralph Thorsby writing in 1713 as noted in Peck p.138.
14 A patent coinage was one struck under contract by a private individual rather than at the Royal Mint. Wood paid a fixed sum for his patent and made what profit he could from producing the coinage.

penny being approximately the same size and weight as the "Hibernia" halfpenny. The "Rosa Americana" coins were no more popular in North America than were the "Hibernia" coins in Ireland and currency examples are dated 1722 and 1723 only.

Copper coins though, like silver, nearly always passed at a premium in the colonies so it was advantageous for individuals to import copper coins when they could. Halfpennies often passed at a penny. Other copper coins and tokens from Britain and Ireland that found their way to North America during the 18th century and entered the currency system include the "Voce Populi" tokens of Dublin and regal copper coins from William III to George III. By the middle of the 18th century though many of the coppers being imported were light and counterfeit and eventually contemporary copies, particularly halfpennies of George III, were produced in North America. Some tokens like the Higley coppers of Connecticut, the Barbados tokens of Sir Phillip Gibbs and tokens of Kingston, Jamaica were also produced in or for the plantation colonies from time to time.

Colonial small change, 17th and 18th centuries

St Patrick halfpenny used in New Jersey.

Tin Plantation token in the name of James II.   The "God Preserve London" elephant token.

"Rosa Americana" coins.
Left, penny of 1722. Right, twopence of 1723.

4 Settlement, Slavery and War

Wood's Hibernia halfpenny 1723.

"Voce Populi" halfpenny 1760.

Imitation George III halfpenny.

Barbados penny token 1788.

Jamaica. Kingston token, late 18th century.

Although the preferred method of making government payments to the colonies was by bills of exchange official payments were sometimes made in coin. As the export of British gold and silver coins was prohibited these payments were made in Spanish silver and/or British regal copper coins. Perhaps the largest payment to be made in this way was that to Massachusetts in 1749 as reimbursement for the expenses incurred by the colony for an expedition against Cape Breton some years earlier. The shipment is recorded as 650,000 ounces of Spanish silver in 217 chests and 10 tons of copper halfpence and farthings in 100 casks. The purpose of this particular payment was not to provide small change but to allow the withdrawal of much of the colony's paper money.[15]

---

[15] Sylvester S. Crosby, "The Early Coins of America and the Laws Governing their Use", 1875, pp. 226-229.

There were thus several individual attempts to provide a circulating small change for some of the colonies during this period and official shipments from time to time. As with the precious metals though there was no real attempt by central government to solve the problem.

The only official copper coinage struck for a mainland colony in the 18th century was that of copper halfpennies for Virginia struck at the Royal Mint in 1773 after requests from the Virginia House of Burgesses. They arrived early in 1774 but were not put into circulation until February or March of 1775 as the governor insisted on waiting for the necessary proclamation.[16]

Pennies were struck at the mint of Matthew Boulton in Birmingham in 1793 to supplement the small change of the Bermuda Islands but their relative value against the dollar was too high and most were exported. Birmingham also struck an issue of pennies for the Bahamas in 1806.

Virginia halfpenny 1773.

Bermuda penny 1793.

Bahamas penny 1806.

In general the northern colonies sought to solve their small change problems with copper coins and tokens of various kinds. The southern colonies (mainland and island) preferred cut Spanish silver and pistareens and French billon coins for their small change requirements.

Colonial paper money continued to be a problem because of its persistent depreciation. By 1740, for example, the exchange in North Carolina was £1,000 in paper currency to £100

---

16 *The coins arrived in the ship "Virginia" owned by John Norton and Sons, Merchants of London and Virginia. John Norton handled the arrangements for the Virginia coinage.*

sterling[17]. There were similar rates in other colonies and, where notes were legal tender, debts were being paid in depreciating currency. The Home Government continued its opposition to the legal tender status of colonial paper with an Act, effective September 1751, which applied to Rhode Island and Providence, Connecticut, Massachusetts and New Hampshire and a further Act of 1764 applying to all colonies.[18] The 1764 Act effectively banned the legal tender status of all new paper issues and insisted that existing legal tender bills were redeemed by their due date. Nevertheless, because of the continued shortage of gold and silver, an amending Act in 1773 allowed for secured issues if voluntarily accepted.[19] This is the way things stood as the North American colonies moved towards independence.

****

At the beginning of the 18th century Britain's maritime empire consisted of settlement and plantation colonies of Englishmen united with the home country through family ties, shared beliefs and traditions. It was a maritime and commercial empire held together by British shipping and policed by the laws of trade and navigation. Conquest and the rule of alien people had no place in this system.

By the end of that century it had fundamentally changed. Thirteen of the English speaking colonies of North America had left. A penal colony had been established in New South Wales. Alien peoples, from French Canadians to the Hindus and Muslims of India, had come under British or East India Company rule. The ways in which these were governed would have to be different from those adopted for the old English colonies. Also, the slave trade and the whole concept of slavery which were the bases of plantation labour were being seriously questioned in Britain.

---

17 R. Chalmers, "A History of Currency in the British Colonies", p.18.
18 24 Geo II c. 53 (1751), 4 Geo III c. 34 (1764).
19 13 Geo III c. 57.

Typical of the ships that seized victory in the French wars, HMS "Victory" was Nelson's flag ship at Trafalgar in 1805. She is still in commission in the Royal Navy today. (Image courtesy of the National Museum of the Royal Navy.)

5

The End of the Old Colonial System

THE events described in the last chapter spelt the beginning of the end of the old colonial system. The acquisition of alien colonies, the loss of the American colonies, the notion of free trade, the humanist approach to the slave trade, the development of a new dominion in India and the founding of a penal colony on the other side of the world amounted in total to a fundamental change to Britain's Empire but they did not all occur at the same time. Changes had begun several years before the American colonies declared their independence and elements of the old colonial system lingered on well into the 19th century. The Empire changed a great deal between the 1760s and the 1860s but there was no specific end to the old order. It was a process of evolution and reform rather than of violent change. Attempts to classify the British Empire into periods labelled "first" or "second" Empire can never wholly succeed.

Alien colonies began to come to Britain mainly as a result of the Seven Years' War (1756-1762) and can be defined as colonies that were not peopled primarily from the British Isles. The term "British Isles" is a geographic term which it may be useful to explain at this point. They comprise England, Wales, Scotland, Ireland, the Channel Islands and the Isle of Man, but these have never formed one political entity.

Although from time to time there had been fiercely independent Welsh princes most of them had paid homage to the kings of England and to the Anglo Saxon kings before that. The country did not develop a permanent national unity and in 1536 all of Wales was incorporated into England by the creation of shires which sent knights to Parliament[1]. From an early date the term "England" was thus generally understood to mean "England and Wales". The union of England and Scotland in 1707 therefore automatically included Wales in the new "United Kingdom of Great Britain". When Ireland joined the Union on 1st January 1801 it became the "United Kingdom of Great Britain and Ireland". In 1922 the Irish Free State was formed but the six counties which made up the district of Northern Ireland immediately opted out in order to remain within the United Kingdom. The correct title of the nation then became, and is still, the "United Kingdom of Great Britain and Northern Ireland". The Isle of Man, Jersey and Guernsey have never been part of Great Britain or of the United Kingdom but are self governing British Crown dependencies.

---

1 *This could perhaps only have been done by a Tudor king (Henry VIII), the Tudors being of Welsh extraction.*

The Union Flag, often misnamed the Union "Jack", was a combination of the English and Scots national flags from 1707 and from 1801 included an additional element from the flag of Ireland. There is no Welsh element in the Union Flag.

We have noted that the early colonies were peopled mainly from the British Isles. They were subject to the laws of England.[2] The colonists jealously guarded their rights as free Englishmen through their proprietors and their colonial assemblies but, as in Britain itself, these liberties were limited to free men. Those, like indentured servants, who were not free had little say and the increasing slave populations had no say at all in the running of the colonies in which they toiled. Slaves did though have some effect upon colonial legislation which was often used to ensure their continued subjection; legislation that was soon a little out of step with English law. The democratic rights of free Englishmen on which the colonial assemblies were based had, of necessity, to be used to pass draconian laws protecting the planters against the possibility of slave revolt. By the 18th century slaves formed the majority in many of the colonies. They laboured under harsh controls which would not have been allowed in England and which did not sit well with the concept of English liberty. Nevertheless these colonies were still considered to be very English.

While the opinions of slaves did not have to be taken into account when governing a colony this was not the case when dealing with the European populations of colonies taken from other powers. Nova Scotia had been ceded to Britain at the Treaty of Utrecht in 1713 and over the years there had been serious problems concerning the loyalty of the existing French settlers. The solution to this was the eventual deportation of many of them in 1755 to other British colonies and the encouragement of Protestant settlers. As a result of the Seven Years' War Canada[3] and several Caribbean islands were taken by Britain and so too was Senegal on the west coast of Africa. With all these new colonies expulsion was now clearly not an option. It was clear too that the traditional method of running British colonies with a powerful colonial Assembly was not suitable where there had been no such tradition and could have been difficult where those who would be elected were of an alien disposition and practiced Catholicism. These colonies therefore had to be run initially by autocratic governors and appointed councils. The integration of "alien" colonists into those councils and the acceptance of Catholicism was a lengthy and gradual process often fiercely opposed by British settlers, by neighbouring colonies, by the Church of England and in Parliament.

Senegal, which was taken from the French in 1758, was the centre of the gum trade. It was little more than a couple of trading forts servicing an inland river trade. Nevertheless these were added to similar forts in Gambia run by the Company of Merchants Trading to Africa and constituted a colony (Senegambia) in 1765. Its constitution was modelled on that of the New World colonies with a Governor and Council for the legislative and administrative responsibilities and a Chief Justice in charge of an elaborate judicial system. There were though few people to govern and, fort for fort, Senegambia proved much more expensive to run as a colony than the areas further east still administered by the Company. The Chief Justice was hampered in the working of his judicial system in that when he opened his courts he could find only twenty two Europeans from whom to choose his jury of twelve.

The French retook some of Senegal during the American War and in 1783 all of it reverted to them. The Gambia forts were returned to the Company's administration and the first British colony in West Africa had proved to be a temporary one.

---

2 *Even after the Union of 1707 this continued to be the case. Scotland retained, and still retains, her own separate legal system.*

3 *A Royal Proclamation of October 1763 named the new colony "Quebec". It continued to be the Province of Quebec until divided into the Provinces of Upper and Lower Canada by the Constitutional Act 1791.*

Canada was very different. The vast majority of the European population, about 60,000, was French and Catholic when Canada was confirmed to Britain by the Treaty of Paris in 1763. Their faith would normally have barred them from holding any office in Britain or in a British colony and it was assumed that their natural inclination would be towards insurrection. They had no experience of representative government and could not be granted an Assembly. It would have been out of the question to grant an Assembly to the few hundred British Protestants resident in Canada. A military Governor was therefore appointed to administer the new colony until something could be worked out.

As the colonies to the south began to question Parliamentary authority a solution for Canada became more urgent and the result was the Quebec Act of 1774. This Act recognized Catholicism and guaranteed freedom of worship. French civil law and laws of tenure were recognized but English criminal law adopted. The colony was to be ruled by a Governor and appointed Council, some of whose members would be French Canadians. The bounds of the colony were also defined. It extended west to the Mississippi, south to the Ohio River and east to Labrador thus including the whole of the Great Lakes and St. Lawrence basin.

The American colonies to the south did not like the extent of this autocratic colony which may have threatened their own expansion westward. Neither did they like the idea of Catholic tolerance in a British colony. They saw Canada with its appointed Council as a model of British plans to curb English liberties in the New World. But they had other more important wrangles with Britain at this time which would soon lead to their independence.

One of the results of the American War of Independence was a movement of settlers and loyalists to Canada and Nova Scotia from the thirteen colonies to the south. In Canada they were not encouraged to settle among the Quebecoise but were given grants of land in the area around the Great Lakes. Many of them were of British stock, well used to representative government and they would be unhappy with anything less. A number of those who settled in Nova Scotia were freed slaves who had joined the British forces but many were also of British stock. It was considered unwise to admit these newcomers to the existing Nova Scotia Assembly so here a new province was formed where most of them had settled. It was called New Brunswick and was granted a representative Assembly in 1784. Canada itself was divided into two parts by the Constitutional Act of 1791. Upper Canada and Lower Canada roughly corresponded to the British and French settled areas. Both now had Lieutenant Governors and appointed Councils but both also had elected Assemblies – their first representative institutions. The division of Canada allowed movement towards full representative government to move at a different pace in each province.

The main British Caribbean islands at the start of the Seven Years' War were Jamaica, Barbados and the Leeward Islands of Antigua, St. Kitts, Nevis and Montserrat. There were also settlements in the Bahamas, the Virgin Islands and on the Spanish mainland (in Honduras and on the Mosquito Coast). During the war Britain captured Dominica, St. Vincent, Grenada, Tobago, Guadeloupe, St. Lucia, Martinique and the Cuban port of Havana but at its end Guadeloupe, St. Lucia and Martinique were returned to France and Cuba was confirmed to Spain. As in Canada Britain inherited French settlers and Catholicism in the retained islands. There was though an influx of British planters and attempts were made to set up representative governments. Attempts were also made to include Catholics who had sworn allegiance to the king but there would be problems with this, particularly when war again broke out between Britain and France.

In the American War St Lucia was once more taken by Britain while St Kitts, Nevis, Montserrat, Grenada, Tobago, St Vincent and Dominica were all taken by France. The war was going badly for Britain in the Caribbean as well as in North America but the Battle of the Saintes in April 1782, which took place near Dominica, put paid to French and Spanish designs on Jamaica and other British islands[4]. In a four day battle Admiral George Rodney defeated a large French fleet under the Compte De Grasse. At the conclusion of peace in 1783 all the islands except Tobago were returned to their previous owners. Islands would again change hands during the Revolutionary and Napoleonic wars but by 1816 possession of the Caribbean colonies was settled.

The Dutch colonies of Essequibo, Demerara and Berbice were confirmed as British possessions in 1814 and would be combined to become British Guiana in 1831. The British logwood cutters of Honduras remained in Spanish territory although their right to be there was reluctantly recognized by Spain. This region would become the colony of British Honduras in 1862. The main islands in British hands were Tortola in the Virgin Islands; Dominica; St Kitts, Nevis, Antigua and Montserrat in the Leeward Islands; St Lucia, St Vincent and Grenada in the Windward Islands; Barbados; Jamaica; Tobago and Trinidad. The Bahamas and Bermuda were also in British hands as were several smaller islands.

As the 18th century drew to a close there was still little change to the actual coinage in use in the colonies. The pistareen continued in circulation everywhere supplemented in many colonies with cut fractions of the Spanish dollar and whatever British and foreign coin came to hand. The preference for Portuguese gold was greater in the West Indies (particularly Barbados and the Windward Islands) than elsewhere and the remaining northern colonies used copper for small change. Spanish American silver and Portuguese gold figure prominently in lists of coins current everywhere but in Canada the continued presence of French coins is evident too.

"Portrait" type pistareen (Madrid, 1793).

"Portrait" dollar (Mexico 1799).   Cut half dollar ("pillar" type, Mexico).

In the West India islands in particular there was continuing competition between neighbouring colonies to retain specie for circulation. We saw in Chapter three that in order to retain coin in the islands many of them were tempted from an early date to raise the

---

4   *The Saintes were a group of small islands between Dominica and Guadeloupe.*

currency value of the dollar. This practice had tended to continue but became particularly prevalent again in the later 18th and early 19th centuries. Some colonial administrations now opted to guarantee a finite number of coins at an enhanced value. In putting Spanish dollars into circulation at an increased value backed by a colonial Act these administrations were not seeking profit. Once issued at an enhanced value these coins would have to be accepted by the treasuries at the same value. In order for this to work the coins issued under the various Acts had to be marked in some way and this resulted in a whole series of cut and countermarked coins being produced, gold as well as silver.

The first British colony to mark coins in this way was Jamaica in 1758. The new Spanish American milled "pillar" dollars which replaced the old cobs had been introduced long after the assays on which the 1707 Act was based. Their value was therefore not defined by any British statute and they were in fact at a slightly reduced standard[5]. Milled gold coins had also appeared and, like all gold, were not covered by British statute. The Jamaica Assembly therefore decided to put its own circulating value on these coins. The doubloon was given a circulating value of £5 and the new milled dollar was rated at 6/8d. A finite number of these and their fractions was authorized to be countermarked on both sides with an ornate GR assigning them these values. This first attempt at controlling the increased value of the dollar was not successful. The countermarking was not able to prevent all coins, countermarked or not, passing at the new rates (or close to them). The practice was abandoned in 1759 and in any case the colonial Act was disallowed by the home Government.

Jamaica. Mexico pillar dollar countermarked "GR" in 1758/9. Rated at 6/8d.

The minutes of a meeting of the Dominica Council in 1798 allowing for an issue of holed coins at enhanced value (the dollar to be valued at 8/3d) mentioned earlier coins with a heart shaped hole[6]. The earlier coins (both dollars and fractions with a heart shaped hole cut in them) are of several different types, the dates of the host coins indicating that they may have been cut about the 1760s. Interestingly the same mutilation is recorded for Gibraltar from the 1740s onwards[7] and the practice may have been imported into Dominica with troop movements during or after the Seven Years' War. The 1798 cut coins were dollars only, the centre plug circulating at 1/1½d. Other cuts and countermarks in Dominica would further increase the currency value of the dollar in the early 19th century.

---

5   Neither this reduction nor the further reduction in 1772 appears to have affected the rate used for the dollar in any of the colonies or in Britain at the time. This is probably because the market price of silver had risen above the official London mint price (see also Chapter six). A further covert reduction in the fineness of Spanish American silver in 1786 is noted by C. Faulkner, "The Holey Dollars and Dumps of Prince Edward Island", P.73. This also went unnoticed in Britain and her colonies.
6   F.Pridmore "Coins of the British Commonwealth Part III West Indies", P.308.
7   Bob Lyall, "Gibraltar Hearts" in SNC December 2007, Pp 306/8.

Cut and countermarked coins were soon common throughout the region; everyone was competing for the available specie. For the British colonies the main period of countermarking was c.1795 to c.1818 with currency values soon at nine or ten shillings to the dollar, sometimes more.

While British and colonial legislation often rated the dollar it is important to remember that the coin referred to was still a piece of eight reales. In Spanish America it was the real itself that was the unit of currency and the dollar was eight of them. The rate assigned to the real thus governed the rate for the dollar. When the real was 6d, as was originally the case in Jamaica, the dollar was 4/- currency. As the value of the real increased from 6d to 7½d the rate for the dollar increased from 4/- to 5/-. In many of the colonies the real was rated at 9d and the dollar at 6/-.

The pistareen which became so popular in the colonies during the 18th century rather complicated matters. It was two reales of Spanish "new plate" and was equivalent to a fifth, not a quarter of the Spanish dollar. Because of the popularity of the pistareen the fractions of the Spanish American dollar fell out of use in the colonies and here too the dollar began to be rated at ten reales instead of eight.

As well as increasing the rate for the real (and thus the dollar) to compete for specie against neighbouring colonies it soon became the practice also to further increase the number of reales (or "bitts") to the dollar. If the number of ninepenny reales in the dollar was increased from 8 to 10 (which occurred about 1740) and then to 11 (in the 1780s) the rate for the dollar automatically rose from 6/- to 7/6d and then to 8/3d.

The competition between the islands for the available specie led to ever increasing currency rates for the dollar which in Dominica in 1813 reached 16 bitts (12/-). Even this did not allow for the segment being cut from the centre which was also countermarked for circulation. A newly cut Dominica dollar and plug between them circulated for 18 bitts in 1813.

The cut and countermarked coins of this period form a very interesting series. Although made from foreign specie, the British issues are colonial coins by any definition. They were produced under British colonial authority for use in British colonies.

The countermarks used on these coins were usually quite simple devices and could therefore be easily copied[8]. Most colonies attempted to police this as best they could but in Tortola the countermarking proved so useful that when the official issues lost their legal tender status in 1805 they remained current. Private issues with similar countermarks appeared and were probably in issue for a number of years. The Tortola cut and countermarked coins, official and unofficial, continued to circulate in the Virgin Islands for many years after such pieces had been demonetized in other colonies and were not withdrawn until 1892.

Although the cut and countermarked coins draw our attention because of the marks upon them it is important to remember that in all the colonies at this time the practice of cutting the dollar and its divisions for small change was common practice. Unmarked cut coins circulated at whatever was their accepted value. In Barbados full weight cut money was authorized as a legal tender in 1791 at the rate laid down in the Act of 1707. By that time cut money had formed the main circulating medium of the island for many years and the reason for the 1791 proclamation was that most of it was very much underweight.

---

8 *Collectors today should also be aware that modern copies and concoctions exist.*

5 The End of the Old Colonial System

Some cut and countermarked coins of various West Indian colonies

Heart cut. Mexico two reals 1750.
Similar cuts are known for both Gibraltar and Dominica.

Dominica.
The 1798 cut dollar (11 bitts) and the plug, or "moco", cut from it (1½ bitts). The bitt was rated at 9d making the holed dollar current at 8/3d.

Dominica.
The 16 bitt dollar of 1813 (12/- currency).

Tortola.
Quarter dollar with official "Tortola" countermark. Half dollar with later "Tirtila" countermark.

Montserrat.
Left. Countermarked quarter dollar (Mexico, 1780).
Right. Mexico quarter dollar cut and countermarked to circulate at one bitt.

St Lucia.
Centre and side cut of Spanish American dollars. The rating for these in 1813 gave the full dollar (centre and two side cuts) a currency rating of 11/3d.

St Vincent.
Mexico quarter dollar countermarked to circulate at IV½bitts.

Granada.
Cut and countermarked third of a pistareen.

Trinidad.
Holed dollar current at 9/- in 1811.

Guadeloupe (British occupation).
Mexico dollar cut in 1811 to circulate at 9/- currency. The centre plug was 1/- currency

While the countermarking of silver coins generally guaranteed their legal tender at an enhanced value gold coins were usually marked for a different reason. In many of the West India islands gold, particularly the johannes (6,400 reis), passed by tale and for many transactions it was convenient that it should continue to do so. Only in Barbados and Jamaica was the full weight standard maintained for gold coins with a penalty per grain of deficient weight. Because Portuguese gold was overvalued against that of Spain it tended to be clipped to bring it into line. As the johannes became more heavily clipped (beyond the level that brought it into line with Spanish gold) it became profitable to import light weight copies of them into those islands where they could still pass by tale. The clipping of genuine johannes probably began in the 1760s or 1770s. Forgeries began about 1790 and by 1794 large numbers manufactured in Europe and North America had flooded the islands. Something had to be done and the plugging and marking of clipped and forged johannes was the solution adopted. In none of the remedial actions taken was there any suggestion that the forgeries should be banned. It was recognized that they were of good gold (it was probably sourced from genuine johannes) so all that was necessary for them to be able to pass by tale was to add plugs of gold to bring them up to the required standard.

The first colony to take such action was Martinique when under British rule in 1798 and this was quickly followed by other islands. To guarantee that the coins had been brought up to the required standard the plug was usually marked with the responsible goldsmith's initials and other marks were often applied to the coin.

The countermarking of gold coins was therefore not to enhance their value but to guarantee them at a recognized standard. The standards adopted included 7½ pennyweights (180 grains) in the Windward Islands, 7 pennyweights (168 grains) in the Leeward Islands and probably 8 pennyweights (192 grains) in Tortola. None of these approached the full weight of an unclipped johannes which was 221·3 grains.

Plugged and marked johannes.
This one, for Grenada, on a genuine but heavily clipped coin. Countermarked G three times to limit further clipping and the plug marked by goldsmith's initials JR in script. At 180.1 grains this piece is remarkably close to the Windward Islands standard.

Martinique.
A lightweight forgery of a johannes (6,400 reis) countermarked under the French administration but still current under British control after 1809. The coin on the right is a full weight genuine johannes for comparison.

For smaller transactions, in addition to cut Spanish coins and pistareens, the British colonies also used billon coins imported from the French colonies. These included the sol marqué which had been introduced into the French colonies in 1640, the metropolitan two sous introduced in 1738 and the later Cayenne two sous introduced in 1782. In the British colonies these were all termed "black dogs" on account of their dark colour and usually circulated at ⅙ of a bitt. In 1763 the French introduced the billon sol tampé at an enhanced value for her colonies. These also found their way to some of the British colonies where they were termed "stampees" and usually circulated at ¼ of a bitt.

The overvaluation of the black dog and stampee throughout the Americas soon made them prime targets for forgers and by the late 18th century large numbers of these, produced in Birmingham and elsewhere, were being sent to the West Indies. Such was the problem that in 1797 St Vincent passed an Act prohibiting their import and requiring genuine black dogs and stampees already in the colony to be countermarked. A British Act of 1798[9] sought to prevent their export from the United Kingdom and this was followed by local legislation in several of the West Indian colonies requiring genuine coins to be countermarked.

Nevis
Black dog (1½d currency) countermarked c.1801 on a Cayenne two sous.

The countermarking of cut dollars was not confined to the West India colonies. In 1813 one thousand dollars were officially cut and countermarked in Prince Edward Island. A circular piece was punched from the centre of these dollars, the outer ring circulating at five shillings and the piece punched from the centre (the "dump") at one shilling. The official rate for the Spanish American dollar in most of British North America at this time was the "Halifax" rate of 5/- but, as the price of silver rose above that, the dollar was hoarded rather than circulated in Prince Edward Island. The punching and countermarking was designed to attract dollars back into circulation at a rate that would keep them in the Island. The countermark was a simple one, sometimes described as a "sunburst" but usually made up of a ring of small triangles and it was not long before counterfeit marks, generally assumed to have been made by the merchants of Charlottetown, began to appear. Because of this the Executive Council decided to withdraw the official issue after less than a year. There is no way today of distinguishing the official countermark from the copies and nor is there a record of how many were redeemed. The "merchant counterfeits", which were probably more numerous than the official issues, remained in use until the 1820s but were not officially accepted after 1814.[10]

Later in our narrative we will see cut and countermarked coins of New South Wales and of Sierra Leone as well as some coins countermarked for use in the Ionian Islands.

---

9   38 George III, c. 67. See also Chapter six.
10 See C. Faulkner, "The Holey Dollars and Dumps of Prince Edward Island", 2012, for details of this coinage.

5 *The End of the Old Colonial System*

Prince Edward Island.
Holed dollar made current at 5/- in 1813.

Until the early 19th century Britain was a major participant in the slave trade and for most of the 18th century was the main participant. There is no doubt that slavery played a major part in the development of colonial plantations and it is difficult to see how sufficient labour could have been secured in any other way at that time. However, it is not the purpose of this book to make moral judgments on bygone eras; simply to record what happened. Slavery had existed for many years in Africa before the European nations came on the scene. The merchants who came to Africa purchased what commodities they could which included slaves. They bought them from local rulers who had enslaved others through war or because they had broken the law or failed to repay debts. The rapidly increasing demand for slaves from the European traders inevitably led to more people being enslaved in Africa than would otherwise have been the case, sometimes to the extent of "panyaring" (kidnapping) innocent persons. Nevertheless the European traders were buying persons who were already enslaved and the forts on the coast were not European colonies. They were rented to the slave traders by local rulers to facilitate that trade. It is a fact that the traders of Europe bought and used large numbers of slaves for many years. It is also a fact that they bought them from African traders who were very pleased to sell and who objected strongly when the trade was ended.

The humanitarian movement with which such names as William Wilberforce, Granville Sharp, etc are associated gathered pace in the later 18th century. It led first, in 1807, to the abolition of Britain's slave trade and eventually to the abolition of slavery itself throughout the British Empire in 1834.

Some years before abolition humanitarian endeavours led to the founding of a settlement at Sierra Leone on the west coast of Africa. In the 1780s there were increasing numbers of free Africans in London many of whom were living in straitened circumstances. The Committee for the Relief of the Black Poor felt that a settlement in West Africa for freed slaves was not only a solution to the problem of destitute Africans in London but also an opportunity to produce tropical plantation crops without slavery. This would demonstrate to the world that the slave economies of the Americas were not just morally indefensible: they were not a commercial necessity either.

At a time when the first fleet of convict ships was fitting out to sail for New South Wales there was some suspicion among those encouraged to embark for Sierra Leone that a similar fate awaited them. Nevertheless more than 400 settlers were persuaded to embark and their fleet arrived in the "Province of Freedom" in May 1787. Their number is generally stated as including some sixty whites, mainly women of the lowest order. A more recent study finds no specific evidence that the women were of ill repute and implies that many of them were married to the departing Africans just prior to embarkation. Nevertheless, it also notes that *"during the voyage scarcely any white lady had more than one white eye, the other being usually black from blows. Battles have been carried on even under the oratory of the chaplain."* [11]

The commander of the small fleet of naval ships and transports which carried this first expedition to Sierra Leone purchased a tract of land for £59-1-5d in trade goods from the local Chief who was himself subject to the king of the surrounding country. The Province of Freedom though was a free and self governing settlement, not a British colony, and once the settlers and their supplies had been properly landed the authorities left them to themselves. They struggled to survive, there were some desertions and in 1789 the settlement was ruined by the local Chief in revenge for action taken against him by a British naval vessel.

The philanthropist Granville Sharp had been keenly involved in the settlement scheme. He felt that sufficient settlers remained for it to be viable and urged British Government support. A British settlement there, he argued, would discourage French ambitions and encourage trade. As a result the Sierra Leone Company was founded in 1791 and a new settlement expedition planned. This time the settlers would come from a different source. During the American War many loyalists had made their way north. A number of these had been slaves promised emancipation if they joined British units and many of these had settled in Nova Scotia. In 1790 there were still complaints that many had not received proper grants of land and to these the promise of generous grants in a warmer land where they could govern themselves would prove very attractive.

The newly formed Sierra Leone Company was delighted at the prospect of attracting English speaking manpower with plantation and farming experience to their settlement and the British Government offered free passage to all those who wished to go. The response was much larger than expected. More than eleven hundred embarked at Halifax and all the ships arrived safely at the place that would become Freetown in February and March of 1792.

Under the Sierra Leone Company the settlement was not quite as free as the new settlers had been led to believe. The Company owned the place and was increasingly aware of the need to satisfy their investors through trade, quit rents, etc. With little capital available to them the settlers found it difficult to develop their farms beyond the subsistence level and soil and climate did not encourage plantation agriculture. There was general dissatisfaction in the settlement at the way the Company ran Sierra Leone and an eventual acceptance in London that it could never make a profit while pursuing a philanthropic goal. The hope that trade and plantation, requiring hard physical work, would naturally replace the lucrative and easy slave trade of the region was a forlorn one. Nevertheless the settlement was an unique experiment and although the Company would fail the settlement did not[12]. It became a Crown colony on 1st January 1808 and Freetown would later become the centre of the Royal Navy's anti-slaving activities.

It will be remembered that the Royal African Company, a joint stock company, originally held the monopoly of English trade to West Africa. The trade though had been thrown open in 1698 and in 1752 that Company had been dissolved. It was superseded by a regulated company, the Company of Merchants Trading to Africa[13]. It may seem strange that a Royal Charter should be granted to the Sierra Leone Company, part of whose function was to develop trade,

---
11 Ellen Gibson Wilson, "The Loyal Blacks", 1976, quoting a contemporary journal.
12 Sierra Leone also inspired the founding of Liberia in the 1820's for freed American slaves.
13 A regulated company controlled individual merchants in a particular trade. A joint stock company raised funds from investors and traded as a single organization.

when a chartered company already existed for the same region[14]. In fact the trade was still open but the founding of the Sierra Leone Company reflects the changing political scene in Britain as the abolitionist movement gained ground. For several years, until the abolition of the slave trade, these two chartered British companies worked in close proximity to each other, one involved heavily in the slave trade, the other inexorably opposed to it.

Both the Sierra Leone Company and the Company of Merchants of Africa had coins struck for them from the 1790s. As private company issues they are not of course colonial coins but they are nevertheless of considerable interest.

The coins struck for the Sierra Leone Company all came from Matthew Boulton's Soho Mint in Birmingham. The first of them bear the date 1791, the founding date of the Company, although they were actually produced in 1792. Two denominations only were struck for this first coinage: a silver dollar (bearing the numeral 1 and with a local currency value of five shillings) and a penny in copper. Some British halfpennies were also sent out for small change. The dollar was the first precious metal coin produced by Boulton and it is interesting to note that although penny tokens had appeared in Britain a regal copper penny was not struck for use there until 1797.

After only a few months it was decided that sterling denominations were not suitable and a second coinage was produced in decimal values. This time the silver dollar (bearing numerals 100) was slightly lighter and of token value. Also struck for this coinage were fifty, twenty and ten cent pieces in silver and a copper cent. These were struck at the Soho mint in 1793 but still bore the Company's founding date of 1791. The coins were stored on board the Company's ship "York" in Freetown Harbour when, in November 1793, she caught fire. Although the silver was saved most of the copper cents were destroyed. Because of this the sterling system had to continue in use until a further supply of cents arrived in 1796, the silver pieces being assigned sterling values in the mean time. The salvaged copper from the "York" was presumably sent back to Britain because some of the less badly damaged 1791 cents were later returned for use in Sierra Leone. Further supplies of the ten cent piece were sent out in 1796, 1802, 1803 and 1805, all except the last being dated 1796.

The Company of Merchants of Africa had no specific responsibility to supply a currency for use in its forts or for its trade. The main medium of exchange for the region was gold dust, a troy ounce of gold being divided into sixteen ackeys, each ackey being divided into eight takus. It was very inconvenient for the Company's servants to buy small value items in the market place with gold dust which had to be weighed and was often of uncertain fineness. In 1796 the Company received a letter from their Governor in Chief at Cape Coast Castle requesting a silver coinage to resolve the problem. Realizing that profit could be made the Company was happy to oblige and sent out coins of sterling silver in four denominations. The largest coin is designated the trade ackey and is similar in weight to the British half-crown but on the coast, where it could be used to pay the Company's servants, it had a currency value of five shillings. The other denominations were in proportion: the half and quarter trade ackey and the trade taku. A further supply of these coins was struck in 1801 but was still dated 1796. All of these were struck by Boulton.[15]

There is evidence that by 1807 all the coins sent out by the Company of Merchants had disappeared probably because silver was rated more highly on the coast than its currency value. In that year the Company lost its main item of trade with the abolition of the slave

---

14 The Sierra Leone Company was incorporated on 1st July 1791. It did not receive its Charter until 1800.
15 For details of the Africa Company and Sierra Leone coinages see D. Vice, "The Coinages of British West Africa and St Helena 1684-1958", 1983.

trade. Its members would now have to limit their trade to more conventional commodities and, if it was going to survive in the new humanitarian climate, the Company would have to show some commitment to the civilizing of Africa. Its final coinage reflects the Company's new image. Two denominations only were struck this time: the trade ackey and the half trade ackey both dated 1818. Unusually for a private Company issue these coins show the bust of George III on the obverse but the Company was now little more than an agent of the Crown. Its main function was to maintain the forts with a Government subsidy while the actual trade was the business of individual merchants. The coins were struck at the Birmingham mint of Edward Thomason and evidence implies that their purpose was to make payments to encourage local children to attend school. The slavers had become philanthropists.

Coins of the Sierra Leone and Merchants of Africa companies.

Sierra Leone penny 1791.

Sierra Leone dollar and half dollar 1791.

Sierra Leone cents.
The 1791 fire damaged issue and the replacement of 1796.

Gold Coast.
Ackey, 1796 issue.

Gold Coast.
Half ackey and takoe dated 1796.

Gold Coast.
Ackey and half ackey 1818.

As the founding fleet for Sierra Leone was preparing to sail from the River Thames another, more famous, fleet began taking on prisoners from the hulks down stream. The loss of the American colonies deprived Britain of the usual destination for transportees and there was soon a build up of prisoners awaiting transportation. There was no adequate prison system in Britain at the time so, as a temporary measure, these were housed on prison hulks in the Thames.[16] When it became obvious that the ex colonies would never again accept convicted felons another destination had urgently to be sought. Various places were examined including the remaining parts of British North America, southern and western Africa and the Falkland Islands but in August 1786 it was finally decided that New South Wales should be the location of a new purely penal colony. Botany Bay had been examined by James Cook some years earlier and it was felt that such a distant colony would eventually prove advantageous for navigation and trade.

The First Fleet left England in May 1787. It consisted of eleven ships carrying some 786 convicts, a detachment of marines with some wives and children, officials and a few passengers together with a large quantity of stores and equipment. There were some deaths on the voyage and a few births as well but all the ships arrived safely in Botany Bay in January 1788 after an eight months voyage. It was realized at once that Botany Bay was unsuitable and the fleet was moved north to Port Jackson. Here, on 26th January 1788, Captain Arthur Phillip raised the Union Flag at Sydney Cove and took formal possession of the land.[17]

As a convict settlement New South Wales had a military government and was run autocratically by the Governor who was always an officer of high military rank. It was policed initially by the First Fleet marines who were not relieved until the New South Wales Corps, raised in England in 1789 for that purpose, had arrived. The system of military government would not substantially change until the provisions of the New South Wales Act of 1823 came into force.

---

16 Prison hulks were soon established in other ports as well and did not finally go out of use until 1857.
17 Captain Phillip was the overall commander of the expedition and the first Governor of New South Wales. Sydney was named after Lord Sydney, the British Home Secretary.

Initially there would have been very little need of a circulating medium in this military settlement other than Commissariat store receipts, paymasters' bills and private promissory notes. Barter and commodities played their part. The ships and personnel arriving in the First and subsequent fleets no doubt brought some specie with them and a Proclamation of 1791 gives the Spanish dollar an enhanced currency value of five shillings. An official consignment of some 4,500 dollars to Governor Phillip is known to have arrived in the "Kitty" in 1792. As in other colonies the dollar is known to have been cut for small change but, also as happened in the plantation colonies, specie tended to be quickly exported in return for imported goods[18]. As the population began to increase and diversify with businesses and farms being set up there was an increasing need for a satisfactory circulating medium and we shall see how this was attempted in the next chapter.

****

In 1783, after the loss of the thirteen colonies in North America, it had been assumed by some that the other colonies would soon follow suit and that Britain would become an unimportant European nation with little influence on the world stage. The French however had been denied any ascendancy over the American ex colonies and we have seen that the Caribbean colonies (often isolated and with large slave majorities) had good reason to remain within the Empire. Canada too was reluctant to go the way of the thirteen as her Catholic faith and French institutions were more likely to be preserved within the Empire than as part of the United States. The East India Company was expanding its influence in India and new settlements like Sierra Leone and New South Wales were being established.

In fact the ending of the great duel with France in 1815 left Britain as undisputed master of the oceans and of world trade, a position from which she would effectively rule the world for most of the 19th century.

---

18 For details of early currency provision in New South Wales see Dr. W.J.D.Mira, "Coinage and Currency in New South Wales 1788-1829", 1981.

5 The End of the Old Colonial System

Sydney Cove 26th January 1788.

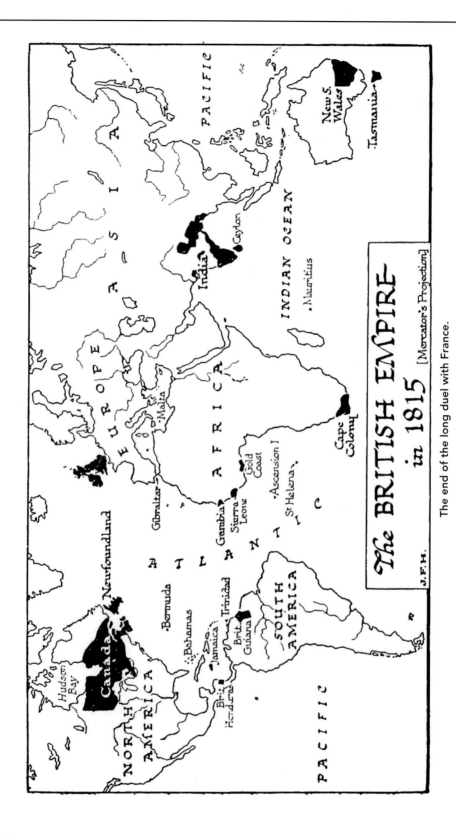

The end of the long duel with France.

6

Pax Britannica

ON 18th June 1815 at Waterloo Napoleon's dreams were finally shattered. Britain did not seek to become the preeminent power in Europe but the long series of wars culminating in 1815 had made her the supreme maritime power. This, coupled with her great commercial strength as a supplier of manufactured goods to the world, created a situation in which Britannia could truly be said to rule the waves. She set about doing this in a variety of ways, imposing peace as she saw fit and developing commercial and maritime practices which in many cases still form the bases of international business today.

Other European nations retained great strengths but on the world stage Britain assumed the role of policeman. This was a period when Adam Smith's "Wealth of Nations", first published in 1776, and Thomas Paine's "Rights of Man" (1791) were still hotly debated, a period also of reasoning and enlightenment, of abolition and emancipation and of electoral reform. A heady mix when mingled with unfettered power. The peace imposed on the world by Britain for most of the 19th century was of course evolved in Britain's interest but as she increasingly saw her interest to be free trade it was not an unduly onerous system as far as other developed nations were concerned. Enforcing the "Pax Britannica" though led to many colonial wars in the less developed parts of the World, indirectly to the Crimean War of 1854-1856 and to the unseemly scramble by the European nations to secure whatever territories were still available for colonization in the later 19th century. All of this will be discussed in subsequent chapters. One matter however that did affect several western nations and the colonial empires of most was the abolition of the slave trade.

In 1807 Britain abolished her own slave trade and was soon sending naval patrols to the West African coast to enforce that. Britain could of course impose what rules she liked on her own nationals but from her position of strength and from her newly acquired moral high ground she now attempted to impose her views on others. It proved difficult to do. Firstly, many African rulers depended on the slave trade for their economic wellbeing and felt that in banning it and encouraging others to do the same Britain was interfering in their affairs and traditions. In 1810 for example the king of Dahomey sent an ambassador to Brazil to reassure his customers that, for his part, the traffic would be maintained and in 1817 the king of Ashanti wrote to George III asking him to allow resumption of the slave trade.[1] Secondly, there was resentment from other nations still engaged in the trade, particularly from France, Spain, Portugal and the United States. Although the United States also banned her international

---

1 See for example H. Thomas, "The Slave Trade", p.563 and W. St Clair, "The Grand Slave Emporium", p.249.

slave trade in 1807 the ban did not apply to her coastal or inland trade. Many slaves continued to enter the southern states from Texas, Mexico and Florida and many of the ships that challenged Britain's blockade of the West African coast were American owned. The Americans in particular but the European nations as well would always object to stop and search at sea during peace time. International agreement that would have allowed searches of vessels suspected of slaving always proved impossible to achieve (Britain even attempted to have it classed as piracy). Undaunted, Britain set about securing bilateral agreements with all the nations involved. Most of these whether in Africa, Europe or the Americas found Britain's new moral crusade puzzling and viewed Britain's anti slaving stance with cynicism. They felt that she wished only to damage their own colonial economies, flex her muscles at sea and gain influence in Africa but, over the years, Britain achieved agreement with most of them including more than forty African rulers. Because of her maritime strength, this determination to destroy the slave trade wherever it existed had to be taken seriously and her persistence in doggedly attacking it undoubtedly had a major effect. Eventually other nations began to take part in the anti slavery patrols although Britain always played the major role. Over a period of nearly sixty years the Royal Navy freed some 160,000 slaves and by 1865 the Atlantic slave trade was over. As in the British Empire, the abolition of slavery itself would follow (in 1865 in the United States, in 1886 in Cuba and in 1888 in Brazil).

Ascension Island was first occupied by British forces in 1815 as a precaution when Napoleon was exiled to St Helena and soon became a useful base for the ships of the West Africa (or Preventative) Squadron which was suppressing the slave trade. In 1823 a ship arriving with fever on board resulted in many deaths not only on the ship (HMS "Bann") but among the small garrison ashore. A separate quarantine anchorage was then designated to the north of the settlement where infected ships could be better controlled. Close to it there was a pleasant little sandy beach where it was possible for boats to land and where in 1899 the Atlantic cable would come ashore. There was nothing else remotely pleasant about Comfort Cove. Here, in a volcanic landscape under a merciless sun and short of water, sick British seamen spent their last days under makeshift shelters. Their shipmates buried them as best they could, scraping together enough rocks to cover them before leaving what was soon called "Comfortless Cove" and returning to their task at sea. Although the men involved had no choice in the matter, no one who visits this place today can come away unmoved by the sacrifice made by them in suppressing the slave trade. The numbers who will remain forever in Comfortless Cove are not large but they are a cogent reminder of the men of the Squadron and the conditions they endured. In total more than one thousand five hundred British seafarers died fighting the slave trade, due mainly to the effects of the climate and poor conditions.

Most of the slaves freed by the Royal Navy were taken to Sierra Leone where they were registered as British citizens. Sierra Leone had become a Crown colony when it was taken over from the Sierra Leone Company at the beginning of 1808 and it was here, at Freetown, that the various courts of mixed commission allowed for in the bilateral arrangements with other nations were set up. The courts made legal decisions concerning the ships which had been intercepted. The new British citizens were given the choice of an apprenticeship in the British West Indies, of signing up with one of Britain's West India Regiments or of establishing themselves in Sierra Leone where they would be safe from re-enslavement. Those who chose to remain in Sierra Leone would be allotted a quarter of an acre of land and given a small cloth to wear, a pot for cooking and a spade. It is perhaps no surprise that most opted to stay so there was soon a requirement for more land. Various agreements were made with local rulers to secure it, the peak period for resettlement being the 1830s and 1840s.

While Britain was busily taking steps against the Atlantic slave trade (in which African prisoners were exported to the Americas) she was still exporting her own prisoners to New South Wales where they would build towns and roads, clear land and develop farms. Much of their work would have been familiar to the slaves of the Americas and, like the slaves, they would have no choice of to whom they were assigned or what they would be required to do. Also, like the slaves taken across the Atlantic, there was no intention that the convicts should ever return home. Here though the similarities ended. After serving their time convicts were free. In theory they could have paid their way home but in New South Wales they could expect generous grants of land. Some of their crimes had been petty but not all of them. The low level of re-offending in Australia shows that most convicts became useful members of this new society so the system worked far better than anything tried before or since. It was though an expensive system. As had been said by critics of the scheme in the early years, it would have been cheaper to feed the convicts on turtle and venison at the London Tavern than to send them half way round the world and feed them in New South Wales.[2]

When the settlement was first made at Sydney it had been hoped that the colony could be self sufficient after two years. This proved wildly optimistic, food and stores still being imported twenty years later. The penal colony was within the area of the East India Company's monopoly and early governors were always reminded of this. Any opportunities there may have been to develop trade were therefore limited. However, as the East India Company became more and more involved in the administration of India its trading monopoly was attacked by free trade interests at home and steadily dismantled by Parliament. In Bengal the Company had received the grant of Diwani (financial jurisdiction) in 1765 involving it heavily in administration.[3] In other parts of India too the Company was assuming the right and duty of revenue collection and it was not considered proper for a commercial company to be involved in government. However, as there was little alternative to the Company's government in India its involvement in commerce was steadily reduced. In 1813 it lost its monopoly of the India trade entirely. It retained its monopoly of trade to China until its next Charter renewal in 1833 when it lost all its trading rights and became an administrative organization only.[4] The loss of the Company's trading monopolies established free trade to the East but also, incidentally, allowed New South Wales more commercial freedom.

Initially the term "New South Wales" referred to the whole of eastern Australia (or "New Holland" as it was still called). Additional convict settlements were soon being established. Some convicts were taken to Norfolk Island in 1788 immediately after the arrival of the first fleet in Sydney. Discovered by Captain Cook in 1774 Norfolk Island was noted as having flax and giant spruce, both useful items of naval stores. Captain Arthur Phillip, the expedition's first governor, had been told to secure the island for that reason but in the end the settlement would mostly be known for its harsh regime – a place where only the worst convicts were sent.

Convicts were first sent to Van Diemen's Land (later known as Tasmania) in 1803. The prime reason for this and for an attempted settlement at Port Phillip on the mainland at the same time was to forestall any French claims to the region.

Free settlers began to arrive in New South Wales in the early 1790s, spreading inland and finding the Aborigines more numerous than they expected. As with the earlier settlements in North America the assumption of the settlers and of the British authorities was that as the

---

2 See A.G.L. Shaw, "Convicts and the Colonies", 1998, p.55.
3 Chapter eleven gives more details of the Diwani grant.
4 For details of the East India Company's changing role see Peter R. Thompson, "The East India Company and its Coins", 2010.

Aborigines did not cultivate the land they had no right to ownership. Merino sheep, the foundation of a major Australian industry, were first imported in the 1790s and by 1820 sheep and cattle were beginning to attract settlers with capital. The first move away from the direct rule of a military governor was the New South Wales Act 1823 which legislated to provide for the colony's government and judicial system. The Act allowed for the appointment of a Legislative Council to advise the Governor and for greater independence for the judiciary through the creation of a Supreme Court for New South Wales. This was a first step on the long and difficult road that would eventually bring a penal colony to full representative government. At the time of the Act the population of New South Wales was about 30,000 of whom perhaps 20,000 were free.

A growing settlement needed to have a circulating medium and it was desirable that the various paper receipts, promissory notes, barter items and commodities should be replaced by something more regular. The currency of account was of course sterling but like earlier colonies the problems were finding specie in the first place and then keeping it in circulation. We have seen that the Spanish dollar was given an enhanced rating of five shillings in 1791 and of course any coin, British or foreign, would have an intrinsic value.

Just as Queen Anne had placed maximum sterling values on foreign coin in her Proclamation of 1704 and her Act of 1707 the Governor of New South Wales did the same in 1800. His Proclamation of 19th November assigns sterling currency values for various gold and silver coins, British, Portuguese, Dutch, Indian and Spanish. Interestingly it also gives a circulating value of 2d to the one ounce British copper coin which circulated at 1d in Britain. Large numbers of these had recently been received in the colony and this was a simple method of keeping them there and of increasing the total value of copper coin in circulation. Unlike the 1707 Act the New South Wales Proclamation of 1800 simply assigned conventional or convenient rates to the various coins, not all of which bore a strict relationship to each other or to sterling. The Spanish Dollar retained its five shillings rating and the rates assigned to the other coins were all designed to keep them in the colony.

Although various coins are noted in the proclamation not all of them were in common use and private notes and other forms of paper continued to be the main form of currency together with copper coins. In November 1812 some 40,000 Spanish dollars arrived in the colony from India on HMS "Samarang" and before these were put into circulation the method used in many of the West India islands was adopted to keep them in the colony. Each dollar had a

The New South Wales Holey dollar and dump of 1813.

circular piece cut from the centre and both parts were countermarked with their value, the date and the name of the colony – **NEW SOUTH WALES**. In this way Australia's first colonial coins came into existence. The holey dollar was put into circulation at five shillings (5/-) giving it the same currency value as the uncut dollar. The "dump" cut from the centre weighed about 83 grains which was one fifth of the dollar. Nevertheless it was given a value of fifteen pence (1/3d) and thus circulated as a quarter dollar. There were severe penalties for exporting the cut coins but between them the holey dollar and dump circulated at 6/3d and the overvaluation seems sufficient to have kept them in the colony.

Commissariat notes and other forms of paper continued in use but no further dollars were cut. As long as the dollar, holey or whole, was accepted throughout the colony at the nominal rate of five shillings sterling there was little problem but the intrinsic value of the Spanish dollar at this time was only about 4/2d. By 1822 the enhanced value of the Spanish dollar in New South Wales compared with its price in England was attracting large numbers of them to the colony and their increased availability allowed the Commissariat to purchase supplies with coins instead of Commissary notes. As colonial duties and quit rents could also be paid in dollars at the five shillings rate, a metallic circulation had been achieved. Although the Government rate for the dollar remained at five shillings increased quantities tended to reduce the rate in general circulation, sometimes as low as its intrinsic value. The Bank of New South Wales[5] and other interested parties pointed out that a dollar that varied in rate day by day like merchandise was little use as current coin and urged that something be done in terms of fixing an equitable rate for the dollar.

It was at this point that the Governor attempted to introduce the dollar as the legal currency of the colony in place of sterling. Having achieved a general circulation of Spanish dollars a Proclamation of July 1822 ordered that the holey dollars could be exchanged at their original rate of issue (5/-) within a period of six weeks. A further Proclamation in November allowed a period in which the dumps could be presented in exchange for bills at the rate of 1/3d sterling after which they would circulate as one fourth of the Spanish dollar only. The holey dollars were reissued in 1823 at three quarters of a dollar.[6] These two coins were now rated in terms of the dollar instead of sterling. From 5th February 1823 the accounts of the Naval Officer and Colonial Treasurer were to be kept in dollars and cents, the British halfpenny to be the equivalent of a cent and government salaries were to be paid at the rate of five dollars per pound sterling. Colonial dues would be taken in Spanish dollars but only at the variable market rate. The dollar that was paid out by the Government at five shillings for goods (the Commissariat was still the major purchaser of agricultural produce) was being received back at a variable rate while salaries were being paid at four shillings.

All this caused confusion and outcry and in September of 1824 a committee finally fixed the value of the dollar at 4/4d that being the average rate for the dollar in buying government bills over the last few years. The holey dollar was to pass at 75 cents, the dump at 25 cents, the British shilling at 20 cents and the halfpenny at a cent.

With the dollar now in general circulation promissory notes and bills of exchange payable in Spanish dollars were given the same status, by the Currency Act of 1824, as if they "had been drawn payable in Sterling Money of the Realm". Hardly had these last provisions been made for a dollar currency when instructions were received from London concerning the currency of all British colonies. We shall see how this affected New South Wales in Chapter thirteen.

---

5   *The Bank of New South Wales was founded in 1817.*
6   *General Order of 31st December 1822 published in the Sydney Gazette 2nd January 1823.*

At home, the British Government had currency problems of its own. The mint price of silver had been fixed for many years at 5/2d an ounce but since the mid 18th century its price had generally been higher than that. As a result very little silver had been brought to the mint for coining. Copper also had increased in price during the Napoleonic War and no copper coins had been struck since 1807. With the exception of gold and what remained of the regal coppers the metallic currency of the United Kingdom by 1815 consisted largely of bank and private tokens. Even gold had been largely displaced by paper and it was time to sort this out. The problems stemmed from bimetallism. If both gold and silver were to circulate at intrinsic value a price change of one relative to the other would always cause problems. The solution was to place the United Kingdom on a gold standard after which the silver coinage (although still of sterling fineness) was lighter, token in nature and fixed at 20 shillings to the gold sovereign.[7] The gold standard was introduced in 1816 after which gold was the only legal tender in Britain for sums of more than two pounds.[8]

Having resolved matters at home attention was turned to the colonies. Some attempts had been made to control paper currency and some copper coins had been supplied to the colonies as noted in Chapter four. In 1798 the Act mentioned in Chapter five was passed to prevent the exportation of base coin to the colonies.[9] This Act specifically targeted the light and false johannes and false foreign minor coins being manufactured in Britain and sent to the colonies but it covered silver coins too. No attempt though had been made to reform colonial coinage in general since the 1707 Act and, as Britain now saw herself as the commercial ruler of the world, it was high time something was done.

Enquiries were made of the colonies as to what this should be and they were all in favour, like New South Wales, of a currency based on the Spanish dollar. That there was no basic objection to the dollar as the colonial currency is apparent from the issues of "anchor money" (so named because of the prominent use of that devise in the design) in the early 1820s. In Mauritius, which had been taken from the French in 1810, a need for small value silver coins led to a request to Britain (in 1817) that such should be supplied. In 1820 the Home Government finally ordered that 50,000 Spanish dollars should be bought and struck into quarter, eighth and sixteenth dollars (the "anchor" coins) for the use of the island. A further issue of 1822 included the half dollar and this time anchor money was also sent to the West Indies. The anchor money was a tentative move towards the acceptance of the Spanish dollar as the colonial currency but it was not successful. Unlike the token silver coinage introduced in the United Kingdom in 1816, the anchor money was struck at full intrinsic value so was not likely to remain in circulation in the colonies. Also this was the period of break up of the Spanish Empire so the continued supply and standard of the Spanish American dollar itself was in doubt.

As well as the old familiar problems with the colonial currencies of the West India Islands (which were effectively on a gold standard) and of the remaining North American colonies more problems had arisen elsewhere. New colonies including the Cape, Berbice, Essequibo and Demerara, Ceylon, Malta and Mauritius had come to Britain as a result of the Revolutionary and Napoleonic Wars and had accounted in Dutch, French or other denominations. The actual specie in circulation would have been a mixture of anything that was available,

---

7 *A coin of token value has a face value of more than its intrinsic value but is still guaranteed by the state. This differs from a private or bank token whose stated value is guaranteed only by the issuer.*
8 *The Coinage Act 1816 (56 George III, c.68). The first sovereign coins are dated 1817.*
9 *38 George III, c. 67.*

The preferred currency of the colonies.
The Spanish American dollar (this one Mexico 1810).

Anchor coins subsidiary to the dollar.

Half dollar 1822. *Quarter dollar 1822.*

Eighth dollar 1822.

Sixteenth dollar 1820.

particularly the Spanish dollar. In the ex Dutch colonies large amounts of paper currency, government and private, were in circulation and the new British administrations tried to tackle this by insisting on redemption. At the Cape this proved impossible and paper continued in issue under the British administration. By the early 1820s nearly all the circulating medium was paper. In Berbice also redemption was not possible and paper continued in issue for many years but in the neighbouring colony of Essequibo and Demerara a circulating coinage was provided. In 1798 Portuguese johannes (6,400 reis) above a certain weight were countermarked to guarantee their value and in 1808 Spanish dollars were cut and countermarked for local currency. From 1809 a series of silver coins in guilder denominations was introduced in the name of the British king to be joined by copper stivers and half stivers in 1813. In Ceylon the circulating medium when the British took over was almost entirely paper and copper. To improve the situation an extensive series of silver and copper coins in Dutch denominations was struck locally in Ceylon and later at Boulton's mint in Birmingham and at the Royal Mint.

In Mauritius the currency of account was French. Spanish dollars circulated as did Indian rupees. The Bengal rupee, referred to as the "sicca" rupee, became the practical standard.[10] In 1818, while awaiting the decision that would result in anchor money being struck for the island, a large quantity of copper pice was imported from India and in 1822 base silver tokens were struck for Mauritius at the Calcutta mint with currency values of 50 and 25 sous (i.e. the half and quarter of the Bengal rupee). As the Bengal rupee was rated at two to the "colonial dollar" these tokens would have been equivalent to quarter and eighth dollars.[11] Unlike the anchor money that arrived in Mauritius at about the same time the government tokens, being considerably overvalued, remained in circulation for many years.

In the territories that merged to form the West African Settlements in 1821 the Spanish dollar, usually rated at five shillings, was the normal currency with accounts in sterling.

The various colonies that eventually formed modern Canada (Newfoundland, Nova Scotia, Canada itself, Prince Edward Island, New Brunswick and the vast areas to the west administered by the Hudson's Bay Company) had various currency systems that would not be fully unified until the later 19th century. The different currency systems gave the dollar various rates above its proclaimed legal value of 4/6d sterling. In Nova Scotia the customary currency value of the dollar was 5/- and this "Halifax currency" gradually gained general acceptance in the other North American colonies. The provision of small change throughout British North America at this time was left largely to private enterprise and quantities of copper tokens appeared in the larger cities from about 1812.

Some of the coins struck for use in Essequibo and Demerara, in Ceylon and in Mauritius at this time are illustrated here. The story of all of them will be expanded and continued in later chapters.

Coins struck for the ex Dutch and French territories

Essequibo and Demerara countermarked and cut coins.
Countermark of 1798 on a false but acceptable johannes and a Holed dollar for three guilders currency and segment from centre for three bitts, cut and countermarked in 1808.

---

10 The Bengal "sicca" rupee was the Murshidabad rupee struck at the East India Company's Calcutta mint. It would be phased out in 1838 after the introduction of the Company's uniform rupee in 1835.

11 The French "colonial dollar" was still the money of account in Mauritius and would continue to be a unit of account until 1876. Originally the same value as the Spanish dollar it became, about 1810, a money of account only and sank to the level of two sicca rupees.

6 Pax Britannica

Royal Mint issues for Essequibo and Demerara

Two guilders, 1809   *Stiver 1813.*

Three Guilders 1816.   *One guilder 1816.*

Ceylon issues struck locally and in the United Kingdom

Forty eight stivers 1808.   *Twelfth rix dollar 1803*

Forty eighth rix dollar, Birmingham 1802   *Rix dollar, Royal Mint 1821.*

Mauritius. 1822 issue from Calcutta in French denominations

Fifty sous.   *Twenty five sous.*

85

The problems outlined above were those with which the home government had to grapple if uniformity was to be achieved throughout the colonies. Uniformity was desirable, as had always been the case, in order to regularize payments between the various parts of the Empire but the main problem within each colony was still the chronic shortage of circulating coin. As the future standard and supply of the Spanish American dollar were both subject to uncertainty it was felt that the best way to resolve all these matters was the introduction of large quantities of sterling silver and copper coins into the colonies to provide both a circulation and a currency. The Spanish dollar would be given a uniform rate throughout the colonies for concurrent circulation until sufficient sterling coins were in place.

The changes were to be made by recommendation and example rather than by Act of Parliament and a Treasury Minute of 11th February 1825 embodied the proposals in detail. Sterling would be introduced initially by making payments to British troops in UK silver and copper coins instead of dollars. The Minute noted that the dollar had generally been the prevalent current coin against which the value of other currencies, metallic and paper, had been determined and recognized that it would have to continue in use for some time while sterling was being introduced. It noted also that the rate for the dollar had not been fixed with reference to the intrinsic value of the coin. In parenthesis it must be remembered here that the rate had been fixed at 4/6d with reference to its intrinsic value in the 1704 Proclamation but since then the dollar had been debased slightly in 1728 and again in 1772. The Minute went on to state that compared to the long standing mint price of silver the dollar should now be worth 4s 3·79d and expressed the opinion that the sterling rate for the dollar should be rounded up to 4/4d. As a solution to the various problems sterling silver and copper coins would be introduced as the currency of the colonies provided that the silver was convertible at will by the holder into the standard gold coin of the UK by means of bills of exchange. This proviso was necessary because British silver was now a token coinage. The rate at which silver was converted into coin was now above both the market price and the mint price; twenty British shillings were no longer intrinsically worth a gold sovereign. As long as it was convertible into gold this token silver could be expected to remain in circulation in the colonies and retain its face value. If the rate at which bills of exchange were issued for sterling silver was about the same as the risk and expense of sending it home that also would tend to keep the coins in the colonies. The rate suggested was 3%, that is a Treasury bill for £100 in gold would be given for £103 of silver tendered. The silver would remain in the colony; the bill only would travel home. The Treasury Minute concluded with particular arrangements for specific colonies where the main coin in use was not the dollar. For the Cape and for Ceylon the rix dollar was rated at 1/6d, also convertible into UK gold at a premium of 3%. The substance of the Treasury Minute was communicated to the Commissaries in the colonies by circular letter.

An Order in Council of 23rd March 1825 then gave legal currency to British coins in the colonies generally and laid down the concurrent rate of 4/4d for the dollar and 1/6d for the rix dollar which had been suggested in the Treasury Minute. British copper coins were to be a legal tender up to one shilling only as in the UK but no limit was placed on the silver. British troops serving in the various colonies should henceforth be paid in sterling silver and copper coins and it was hoped that from this beginning sterling silver would become the currency of the Empire.

6 Pax Britannica

British coinage current in the colonies after 1825
The main denominations of the British gold standard after 1816

Sovereign 1826.

Crown 1819.

Half-crown 1826.

Shilling and sixpence of 1816.

Penny 1826.

Halfpenny 1827.　　　　Farthing 1825.

The sterling rate given to the dollar was crucial if the system was to work. The Order adopted the rate of 4/4d suggested in the Treasury Minute and based on the old (1601) mint price of silver. However, at the market rate for silver the correct sterling equivalent should have been about 4/2d. As a result sterling silver was undervalued and could not compete with the dollar in circulation. Also, the Order did not specify sterling rates for foreign gold coins. In colonies where a gold standard based on foreign gold coins prevailed (mainly the West Indies) British silver was thus even further under-rated. The erroneous rate given to the dollar and the failure of the Order to rate gold at all led to the re-export of a great deal of the imported sterling. Also, much of the sterling silver issued from the military chests was being exchanged by the paymasters for dollars or some other circulating medium and the silver returned to the chests for bills on the Treasury. Either way it was not getting into circulation in the colonies as planned. If sterling was to become the currency of the colonies the plan would have to be adjusted and it took some time to do this.

In 1827 the Treasury issued instructions that troops should actually be paid in the sterling coins drawn from the military chests and the practice of exchanging them for dollars, etc (which was very profitable for the paymasters) should cease. In the same year the premium on Treasury bills was halved to 1½% to deter the transfer home of sterling silver coins and encourage the use of bills instead.

A Treasury Minute of 19th June 1835 reduced the Army rate for the doubloon from 69/4d to 66/- which put it on a more equitable rating compared with the dollar. The dollar itself though was still overvalued at 4/4d sterling.

In 1838 a Committee of the Privy Council was appointed to look into the state of silver currency in the West Indies and at last concluded that the rating of the dollar at the mint price rather than the market price of silver was the basic cause of the problem. The bullion value of the dollar was found to be about 4/2d and the doubloon 64/- and these values were adopted for concurrent circulation with sterling. Thus the two main faults of the 1825 Order (the sterling rate for the dollar and a rate for gold) had been addressed as far as the West Indian colonies were concerned.

An Order in Council of 7th September 1838 revoked the 1825 Order for the West Indian and American colonies. A further Order in Council and Proclamation of 14th September 1838 ordered that the new rates (4/2d for the dollar and 64/- for the doubloon) should apply throughout the West Indies and British Guiana. Although the 1825 Order had been revoked for the American colonies as well as the West Indies the 1838 Proclamation, it will be noticed, was not applied to North America.

These measures succeeded in bringing sterling into circulation in the West Indies and led to their application to Mauritius, West Africa, St Helena, Malta, Gibraltar and Hong Kong during 1843 and 1844. Although it had taken many years to sort out what may seem a simple problem for the colonies most affected it must be remembered that the old mint price which had proved such a hindrance in bringing silver to the Royal Mint and in introducing sterling to the colonies was at least a fixed and stable standard to work with. The market price (which was in fact mentioned in the Treasury Minute of 1825) would always be a variable.

The British "token" silver coins introduced in 1816 had a limit of legal tender of forty shillings in the United Kingdom but the Order in Council of 1825 placed no limit of legal tender on them for circulation in the colonies. The intention had been to create a sterling silver circulation effectively backed by gold as it was exchangeable to any amount for bills payable in London. Nevertheless, the use of token silver as an unlimited legal tender was contrary to the sound principles of currency and did not have specific legal sanction. Although this had not caused any difficulty it was likely to do so in the future and the Board of Treasury looked into the matter. By 1852 it had decided that any change in respect of the West Indian colonies would be unhelpful. Nevertheless, a Treasury Minute of 12th October 1852 noted that the recent discoveries of gold in Australia had required a much larger circulation and increasing quantities of silver were being sent there. It was therefore time to put the currency of the Australian colonies on a sound basis by applying the same regulations to it as applied in the United Kingdom, particularly the legal tender limit of forty shillings for the silver coins. The Minute also proposed that the measures should be extended to the colonies of New Zealand, Ceylon, Mauritius and Hong Kong. An Order in Council and Proclamation of 16th October confirmed the new arrangements which would (and did) come into force when published in each colony.

In spite of these changes a uniform sterling currency throughout the Empire would never be achieved. The attempt to do so illustrated the futility of trying to impose an alien scheme on areas under other influences. Eventually there was an acceptance by central Government that currencies other than sterling would have to circulate in many parts of the Empire.

In general the colonies of Europe, the West Indies, Australasia and Africa did adopt sterling as their currencies, those of North America and the East adopted dollar currencies and those of the Indian Ocean used the rupee. We will look at this in more detail in later chapters.

In 1816, as we have seen, Britain adopted the gold standard. Silver, now a token coinage, was limited in legal tender to 40/- and the copper to 1/-. The main silver denominations were the crown, half-crown, shilling and sixpence, the copper consisting of the penny, halfpenny and farthing. In some of the colonies where British coinage was introduced following the 1825 Order it was found that other denominations would be useful.

In Malta many items of necessity were priced at a grano and if the existing base coin of that value was to be replaced a denomination smaller than the farthing would be required. The proclaimed rate of the farthing in Maltese currency in 1825 was three grani and the Governor strongly urged that a one-third farthing should be introduced. An Imperial third farthing was therefore struck specifically for Maltese use from 1827 (and would continue to be struck intermittently as required until 1913).

The threepence was a Maundy coin from an early date but was not part of the Imperial currency system in 1825. From 1834 however currency threepences, of the same design as the Maundy coin, were struck specifically for colonial use. In Jamaica this was a useful equivalent to the half real but it went also to other West Indian islands, to the Bahamas, to Malta, Mauritius, West Africa and St. Helena. In 1845 the threepence went into circulation in Britain itself and became part of the Imperial coinage. Many years later the Imperial silver threepence was again struck exclusively for the colonies from 1942-5 after the introduction of a twelve sided nickel-brass threepence in the UK.

The three-halfpence was a completely new denomination. It was of course half a threepence and, with the exception of Malta, went to the same colonies. Like the threepence it was introduced in 1834 but never became part of the home coinage. It was produced for colonial use until 1862.

Another Maundy denomination struck for circulation in the colonies was the twopence of 1838, 1843 and 1848. In British Guiana this passed as a half bitt (⅛ guilder). The fourpence denomination was added to the British coinage in 1836 and differed from the Maundy fourpence in showing Britannia on the reverse. This coin was useful in British Guiana as the equivalent of a bitt (¼ guilder) but was not popular in Britain itself. After it had ceased issue at home (1855) it was difficult for the colony to obtain further supplies and the denomination was struck especially for British Guiana in Imperial style in 1888.

Large quantities of British silver and copper coins were sent to Ceylon following the Order in Council of 1825. Eventually Ceylon would adopt the British Indian rupee as its currency but British copper coins continued in use for some time. As in Malta, smaller denominations than the farthing were required. From 1828 to 1839 half farthings of Imperial design were produced intermittently for Ceylon where they were equivalent to a twelfth of a fanam. This denomination continued to be struck occasionally until 1856 but from 1842 was legal tender also in Britain. The quarter farthing was also struck from 1839 to 1853 but exclusively for use in Ceylon.

Sterling denominations specially struck for colonial use

Third farthing for Malta 1827.

Threepence 1835 and three-halfpence (or penny-halfpenny) 1836.

Fourpence 1836 and twopence 1838.

Half farthing 1830.   Quarter Farthing 1839.

For use in Ceylon

In 1860 bronze coins of reduced size and weight were introduced to replace the British copper denominations.[12] From 31st January 1869 the old copper coins were no longer legal tender in the United Kingdom although they continued to be exchanged at the Mint until 1873. The colonies were allowed until June 1876 to exchange their copper coins at nominal value, a period later extended to 31st December 1877.[13] Although the Mint would not exchange copper coin from the colonies after that date it was up to each colony individually to decry copper coins by proclamation if and when it wished.[14]

---

12 *22 & 23 Vict. c. 30.*
13 *Order in Council of 24th March 1876.*
14 *Tasmania for example did so in 1875 (see Chapter thirteen).*

Bronze replaces copper

Bronze penny 1881.

Halfpenny 1901.   Farthing 1895.

Bronze third farthing for Malta 1884.

The East India Company continued to strike its own coins for its territories in the East which of course were not affected by the attempts to introduce sterling into the colonies. From 1757 its third major mint, Calcutta, joined Madras and Bombay in the production of its coins and in its administrative capacity the Company soon gained control of other mints. In the areas governed by the Company there were many different standards of rupee and in the Madras Presidency[15] the pagoda and fanam coinage was still also in use. In 1806 the Directors stated their intent that the three Presidencies of Bengal, Madras and Bombay should work towards a uniform currency for the whole of the Company's Indian territories. The exact standard required was a silver rupee of 180 grains containing 165 grains of pure silver and each of the Presidencies was expected to work towards this. In Madras production of the pagoda and fanam coinage ceased in 1812 and the Madras rupee became the money of account in January 1818. By 1833 each of the Presidencies had rupees on the required standard. It was then possible to produce a uniform rupee for all of British India in the name of William IV and this came into issue in 1835. In Bengal it had been the Farrukhabad rupee that had been brought onto the required standard. The heavier Bengal "sicca" rupee of Murshidabad which circulated in large numbers in lower Bengal and was familiar in several British colonies was never brought into line. It ceased to be legal tender in Bengal in 1838.

The new uniform coinage naturally included fractions of the rupee but gold mohurs and a few double mohurs were also struck when gold was brought to the mint. The silver rupee was the standard; the mohur was intended to pass at fifteen rupees (but see Chapter eleven). All the precious metal coins bore the portrait of the British monarch (William IV followed shortly by Victoria). A uniform copper coinage was also introduced which bore the Company's arms.

---

15 From the earliest times the Chief Factor or Head of a main Company settlement became known as its President. The various factories and ports under his control were his Presidency.

It may seem unusual that a private company should issue coins bearing a royal portrait but we have already seen in the last chapter that the same was done in the Gold Coast in 1818. Like the Company of Merchants of Africa, the East India Company was now effectively a Crown department but in India the Moghul Emperor still occupied his seat at Delhi. The use of a royal portrait here was a clear statement that the Company, backed by the Crown, was now the paramount power in India. It was a remarkable statement which appears not to have been challenged or questioned in any way.

The East India Company's uniform coinage of 1835

Mohur.

Rupee. Half anna.

Half rupee. Quarter anna (pice).

Quarter rupee. Twelfth anna.

We must now return to the historical narrative and to another matter that reflected Britain's changing attitude to the old order: free trade.

Like other colonial powers, Britain had always been keen to protect her colonial trades. At home she also protected her industries. Agriculture was the traditional foundation of wealth based on land ownership and, in 1815, still employed more people than any other industry. The Industrial Revolution which began c.1750 had already developed important manufacturing industries which, like agriculture, were considered worthy of protection. Britain's colonial trades were protected by the Navigation Acts, her agriculture by the Corn Laws and her manufactures by tariffs on foreign imports.

The Navigation Acts have already been described in some detail. Tariffs were basically taxes imposed on certain items to make their import prohibitively expensive. The Corn Laws used tariffs in a more complex manner. Their purpose was to protect British cereal growers against foreign competition but also to ensure Britain's corn supply when crops failed. Foreign corn could not be imported without payment of a heavy duty unless the price of British corn rose above a certain level. This did not fix the price of corn which still varied with the harvests but it did protect British farmers against what may have been cheaper imported grains in times of plenty. In times of great shortage when prices naturally rose, foreign corn could be imported at a nominal duty thus hopefully ensuring an adequate supply.

By the beginning of the 19th century and particularly as a result of the loss of thirteen of the American colonies it was obvious that opportunities for trade and investment existed outside the Old Colonial System. The Industrial Revolution had revealed many sources of profit other than agriculture and Adam Smith had openly questioned the old order.

Apart from increased trade with the ex American colonies there had also been a considerable increase in trade with South America. In the settled period which followed the Napoleonic War trade was also growing with Europe. In the East restrictions on trade to the territories run by the East India Company were being lifted and there was the tantalizing possibility of a more open trade with China. All of this was outside the Old Colonial System. Within the System Britain's remaining colonial possessions were not seen as hugely prosperous. The West Indies were in recession. The Cape was undeveloped and New South Wales was in its infancy as anything more than a penal settlement. The remaining North American colonies had some commercial significance and perhaps promise for the future but with the example of the United States and the ex Spanish colonies fresh in their minds the assumption of the British people was that all colonies would seek and get independence as they prospered. Realization began to dawn that the restrictions of the Old Colonial System were holding back British commercial expansion. By the 1830s it was clear that trade did not depend solely on power and Britain's manufacturers and merchants began to seek a more liberal environment in which they could expand their activities. Free trade would enable Britain to import more raw materials and food and export more manufactures than she could otherwise do. Her industries were relatively so advanced that Britain's manufacturers had no fear of a free market and unrestricted trade. Others were not so sure.

The protection of grain prices was effectively a tax on corn and therefore on bread. The industrial manufacturers were concerned that this would lead to demands for higher wages and increasingly presented the Corn Laws as benefiting only the landowning classes. Opposition to them was thus presented as a class issue and became a popular cause. Those who defended the Corn Laws feared that lower prices would ruin farmers, lead to lower agricultural wages and put Britain at the mercy of foreign producers.

Opposition grew and in March 1839 the anti-corn law league was established, campaigning tirelessly for repeal. Although the traditionalists in Government resisted for as long as they could, the Corn Laws were finally repealed in 1846 and this was a major step in the direction of free trade.

Modifications to the Navigation Acts in the 1820s and 1830s still left the Old Colonial System more or less intact but increasingly out of alignment with the spirit of the age. Free trade was now considered necessary for human progress in general. Complete free trade, some argued, would remove the need for military conflict of any sort and make colonial empires redundant. Free trade therefore became a moral cause as well as an economic goal. Britain's cultural self confidence at this time coupled to her naval and economic power carried the movement to its logical conclusion. What Britain was doing was right, not just for her but for the world.

The Navigation Acts were repealed in 1849 and by 1860 all the preferential arrangements with the colonies had gone. Although this was not an end to tariffs, for practical purposes free trade had been established.

While Britain championed free trade there were nevertheless parts of the world where the concept was not welcome. China was one of them and here Britain proved willing to impose freedom of trade through the so called "Opium Wars" which will be discussed in Chapter twelve.

Another region where free trade had sometimes to be encouraged by force was Africa. As free trade ideas gathered pace it was plain that those economies which were still reliant on the slave trade did not need to be producers of raw materials and consumers of manufactures. It would be far better for Britain's brave new world if these regimes could be replaced with others that would be prepared to produce and consume. The introduction of these principles to Africa was seen as a supplement and encouragement of Britain's anti slavery activities.

The defence of British interests around the world was not neglected but there was no specific plan for the defence of the Empire as a whole. Imperial troops were spread around the world as expediency demanded and colonial units, often volunteer, were raised as required. The function of all these troops, whether imperial or colonial, was to keep order and guard against insurrection and minor incursion. The ultimate security of the colonies depended on the Royal Navy which to all intents and purposes controlled the seas and made an external attack by another European power unlikely. However, as iron ships replaced the old "wooden walls" there was concern that technological change was undermining the effectiveness of the Royal Navy. Whole fleets with the latest equipment could now be constructed with relative ease by those with the inclination and the funds to do so. Maintaining naval superiority was becoming expensive.

Questions therefore began to be asked about how secure the Empire really was and, as the world order began to change, how safe was Britain itself? The example of Prussia's efficient army and its successes in Europe hastened the reforms of the British Army being carried out by Edward Cardwell (Secretary of State for War, 1868 to 1874). Under a policy initiated in 1861 the self governing colonies were now responsible for their own internal defence allowing Cardwell more troops to protect the homeland. It was not though until 1879, when the "Royal Commission on the Defence of British Possessions and Commerce Abroad" was set up that the whole matter of Imperial defence was first examined. The Commission completed its reports in 1882 and it was obvious that the Empire needed an integrated system of defence based on a navy with properly defended support facilities around the world. This could not work without the active cooperation of the colonies in agreeing some equitable division of costs and responsibilities and it was in this light that the first Colonial Conference was called in 1887 to discuss defence and communication.

At this first Colonial Conference the Australasian colonies agreed to assist with naval costs which until that time had been considered a purely Imperial expense and this enormous burden began to be shared. Subsequent Conferences discussed the unity of the Empire in more general terms and gained further concessions on naval costs but in peace time the other self governing colonies were reluctant to follow the example set by Australia and New Zealand.

The Boer War of 1899 to 1902 (Chapter nine) showed that against major rivals Britain's land forces were not as effective as the small colonial wars had led her to assume. This stimulated an array of reforms that gave the British Army a better preparedness for the next great struggle. Outside the United Kingdom imperial troops were still stationed at key points.

While the self governing colonies had taken responsibility for their own land forces there were still imperial garrisons at Halifax and the Cape because of their important role in imperial defence. The so-called "fortress" colonies of Bermuda, Gibraltar and Malta and many of the smaller colonies where coaling stations and repair facilities were sited also had imperial garrisons and defensive armament. Some British regiments were stationed in India together with the large Indian Army inherited from the East India Company. These various garrisons allowed troops to be deployed quite swiftly from place to place and troops from the self governing colonies had already assisted imperial forces in the Sudan and South Africa. The Empire though still depended on the Royal Navy with its network of coaling and repair facilities for its ultimate defence and the safety of its commerce. That commerce moved in British merchant ships across oceans made safe by this elaborate infrastructure.

Secure communications were a vital element of defence and from the 1850s submarine and overland telegraph cables were laid to keep the Empire connected. As far as possible, for security, this came ashore only on British territory and the last major link was that from Canada across the Pacific to Australia and New Zealand. The "All Red Line" was completed early in the 20th century and was so named because it joined the parts of the map that were now traditionally coloured red (or pink).

The period we have looked at in this chapter was a relatively settled one in which Britain was strong enough to impose her will in many minor colonial wars for what she perceived was the greater good. Deposed local rulers may have questioned "the greater good" but in the overall scheme of things in 19th century politics the rights and traditions of less advanced societies received little recognition.

It was though a period of defensive climax when Britain realized that the Empire might be vulnerable to attack and when she found (in the Boer War) that her imperial might could be challenged. A period too in which the Empire began to take an increasing role in the burden of defence. As the First World War approached the Empire was united by its defensive infrastructure, by its commerce and also by a sense of common purpose.

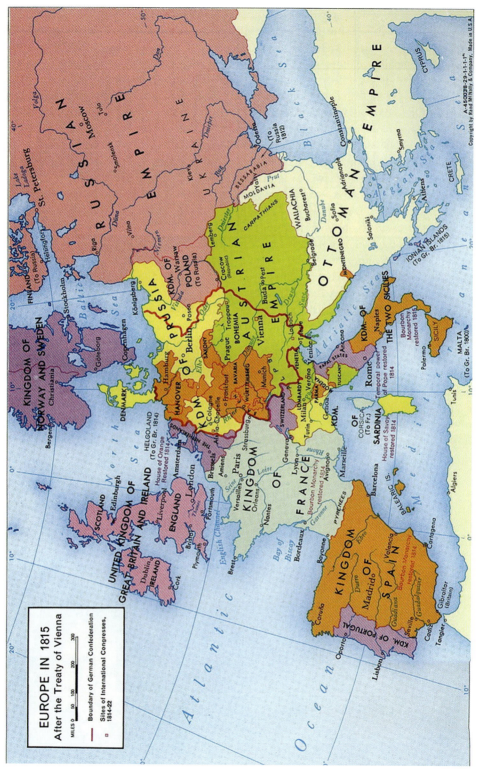

The balance of power in Europe after 1815.

7

Britain and Europe

IF we forget for a moment the territories administered by the East India and Hudson's Bay Companies it has been possible until now to look at the Empire as a single entity. It was held together not by any strict form of central administration but by the Old Colonial System. During the 19th century that system was steadily dismantled and a free trade policy adopted by Britain. Also, as British influence spread, new forms of administration such as protectorates would begin to appear. From now on, as we look at Britain's imperial activities in more detail, it is easier to do so on a regional basis and easier also to understand the coins and tokens in that way. In this and the following chapters we will therefore look at Britain's world geographically in the period from Waterloo to the First World War and at the coins for some years beyond that. A concluding chapter will bring the story together for the final years.

We have already looked at some of the broader aspects of imperial activity in the 19th century including anti slavery, free trade and the attempt to introduce sterling silver throughout the colonies. Before proceeding to our first regional look at Britain's world after 1815, which will be at home and in Europe, we must also look at her foreign policy in the years following Waterloo.

The monarch still had some influence on foreign policy and since the time of George I Britain's kings had also been rulers of Hanover. They thus had interests of their own other than purely British interests. Britain was though a constitutional monarchy and there was no distinct royal policy that was different from that of the government. Britain's foreign policy in the years following Waterloo was basically that of her Foreign Secretary. In shaping it he necessarily had to take into account the views of the Sovereign, of his colleagues in the Cabinet, of Parliament and of public opinion but his policy was based firmly on what he felt was Britain's best interests and there was little serious disagreement on what those interests were.

The core interest was the security of the homeland against the threat of invasion. Beyond that Britain's best interests arose out of her position as a maritime and commercial power so a vital interest was the protection of her overseas trade. To secure these interests the Royal Navy, already the largest in the world, was to be maintained at a strength greater than that of the combined navies of any two possible rival nations. Apart from a great navy with strategic bases it was becoming increasingly necessary to protect British citizens involved in trade all over the world, not just in the colonies. For this a strong diplomatic presence, to be backed by force if necessary, was essential.

There was also a growing body of opinion that if Britain's wealth was to grow competition and free trade were essential. These should not only be protected but encouraged, vigorously if necessary.

Relations between Britain and the United States were those of mutual distrust for most of this period although there was considerable British investment in industrial development there. Increased commercial ties with South America made it very much in Britain's interest to maintain contact with those countries as they broke away from their colonial rulers. As a colonial power and a monarchy it was difficult for Britain to openly support the new republics. She worked instead to ensure that matters would be resolved by negotiation rather than by force and also tried to ensure that the United States would not gain undue influence in the region. The strength of the Royal Navy was vital in protecting these interests.

The security of British interests in India and the routes to and from India were always major concerns. The Cape of Good Hope came permanently into British hands in 1806 and its retention was important for the protection of the main commercial route to India and the East. Britain though had always needed to be connected with India swiftly as well as safely and for this the overland route via the Eastern Mediterranean and the Persian Gulf was of vital importance, particularly for communication. The opening of the Suez Canal in 1869 increased the importance of the Mediterranean route and decreased that of the Cape.

Rightly or wrongly Russia was perceived as a likely threat to British India and to the overland route so British foreign policy was aimed at keeping her in check all along her southern border. This would lead to wars in Afghanistan and agreements with Persia but closer to home it was the Ottoman Empire that acted as a bulwark against Russian expansion. Constantinople (Istanbul) in Russian hands would threaten the overland route to India so the Ottoman Empire had to be safeguarded and, if necessary, defended. The Russian threat may have been overestimated but it was the only threat from a major power that would come overland and could not be dealt with by the Royal Navy.

These were the main interests on which Britain's foreign policy was based. Over the years it had also been shaped by the fear that France would dominate Europe and damage Britain's colonial empire.

In Europe other nations also feared French expansion and had sought to contain France and her revolutionary ideals before they could spread dangerously across Europe. In the recent wars Britain had therefore found allies in Europe and the peace settlement which followed had to satisfy all of them. Its basic aims were to remove Napoleon permanently and to contain France within her traditional boundaries.

The first Peace of Paris in May 1814 allowed for the cessation of hostilities and paved the way for the Vienna Congress which, from September 1814 to June 1815, decided how Europe should be partitioned for the future. In the meantime Napoleon had escaped from Elba and war had resumed. The Second Peace of Paris signed in November 1815 concluded matters after Napoleon's final defeat and fixed France's frontiers at where they had stood before the war. The arrangements made at the Vienna Congress were important. They sought not only to create a lasting peace and curb future French and revolutionary ambition but also to resolve matters after the dissolution of the Holy Roman Empire in 1806. The map of Europe had to be redrawn.

The states that formed the Alliance against France at the end of the war (Austria, Britain, Prussia and Russia) all had different priorities at the negotiations but all of them sought to remove the various threats that France posed to them and wanted to ensure that she should not again emerge from her traditional frontiers. With that aim in view France's neighbours were strengthened. The Austrian Netherlands were joined to the old United Provinces to form the United Kingdom of the Netherlands under the House of Orange. Most of the Rhineland went to Prussia. A Confederation of German states created a buffer between Austria and Prussia as well as making any interference with minor German states more difficult. Further south, Swiss independence was re-established and strengthened by the addition of Geneva. Savoy and Piedmont were restored to the king of Sardinia (who also gained Genoa). Elsewhere in Europe there were other adjustments to the map which, in total, were designed to satisfy all the parties involved and create a stable balance of power.

Hanover was now a kingdom rather than an electorate but Britain annexed no territory in mainland Europe as a result of the Revolutionary and Napoleonic wars and had not sought to do so. Nevertheless the final settlement of the war and the resulting balance of power enormously strengthened Britain's position. In Europe, as long as the balance of power was maintained, it freed her from all danger of invasion leaving her free to develop her commercial and imperial future. In the wider world it confirmed the most important overseas conquests made by Britain during the war.

Britain remained suspicious of France and of Russia but in the years following 1815 her principal concern in Europe was the maintenance of the balance of power agreed at Vienna. To better ensure this it was not long (1818) before France was included in the Alliance that had been ranged against her and in fact peace was maintained between the major powers of Europe for some forty years.

Some peripheral European territories did come to Britain as a result of the war, some she had had earlier and one (Cyprus) would come later. It is now time to examine these and to look at the coins and tokens that they used.

We have seen (Chapter five) that the Isle of Man, Jersey and Guernsey have never been part of Great Britain or of the United Kingdom but are self governing British Crown dependencies. They were not colonies so the coins and tokens struck for use there are not colonial. They do though differ from those of the United Kingdom so deserve some mention and we will take a brief look at them here.

The **Isle of Man** was ruled by Lords Proprietors termed the Lords of Mann (usually with two n's). From the early 15th century these had been the Stanleys, soon to be the Earls of Derby but in 1736 the title passed by inheritance to the Dukes of Atholl. In 1765 the title was purchased by the Crown and British monarchs from George III to the present day have been Lords of Mann. The coins used were mainly those that circulated in Britain but, because there were fourteen Manx pennies to the British shilling, it was necessary from time to time to produce a distinct copper coinage for small change. This was done by the Earls of Derby in 1709 and 1733, by the Duke of Atholl in 1758 and under George III in 1786, 1798 and 1813. An 1839 coinage (pennies, halfpennies and farthings in the name of Victoria) was at the same weight standard as the British copper coinage, the declared intention being that there would henceforth be twelve Manx pence to the shilling. This was enacted in 1840 and all Manx issues prior to the 1839 issue were demonetized. The Manx penny was equalized with the British coinage at twelve to the shilling and there was no further need for a separate coinage. As in the United Kingdom shortages of coins from time to time led to the use of tokens issued by both banks and private individuals.

ISLE OF MAN

Earls of Derby.
Penny 1733.

Duke of Atholl.
Penny 1858.

George III, as Lord of Mann

Penny 1786.   *Penny 1798.*

Tokens

Douglas Bank token 1811.   *Private token 1830.*

Victoria, as Lord of Mann

Penny 1839.

7 Britain and Europe

The connection with the Channel Islands goes back to the time of William the Conqueror, Duke of Normandy, who invaded England in AD1066. The Channel Islands were part of his duchy and maintained their connection to the English monarch when the rest of Normandy was lost in 1204. The main islands are Jersey, Guernsey, Alderney, Sark and Herm but the "Channel Islands" are not a single political unit. Jersey and Guernsey have been separate Bailiwicks since the 13th century, the Bailiffs being the civil heads of government. These governments came to be termed the States of Jersey and the States of Guernsey. Although Alderney and Sark have governments of their own they, and Herm, are part of the Bailiwick of Guernsey. For many years the coins and currency systems of the Channel Islands were predominantly French but during and after the Napoleonic War they all experienced a great shortage of coins in circulation.

In **Jersey** British sterling would supersede French currency as the sole legal tender in 1834. The first official coins (actually tokens) for the island are some years earlier but are nevertheless in sterling denominations. Because of the shortage of regal silver coins experienced in the islands (and in Great Britain) at this time the States of Jersey obtained approval to have a silver token coinage struck at the Royal Mint. A three shillings token and its half, the eighteen pence, were struck in 1813. They remained in circulation until 1834 when sterling was declared the sole legal tender. Some private copper tokens, also in sterling denominations, appeared at about the same time as the silver tokens but do not appear to have been struck in large numbers.

After 1834 French copper coins, of necessity, continued in circulation and were rated at 26 sous to the shilling. When copper coins were produced for Jersey in 1841 to alleviate the small change problem they were based on the same relationship (26 to the shilling). The Jersey penny (two sous) was thus one thirteenth of a shilling and showed this unusual denomination. They were also proportionately lighter than the British penny. When the copper coinage was replaced by bronze in 1866 the Jersey one thirteenth of a shilling was struck at the same weight as the British bronze penny but no change was made in the stated denomination until 1877. In that year it could simply have become the "penny" but was instead denominated "one twelfth of a shilling". Throughout these coinages there were also divisions of the main copper

JERSEY

Sterling tokens of 1813

Three shillings Bank token. *Eighteen pence Bank token.* *Jersey, Guernsey and Alderney penny token.*

JERSEY
Copper coinage

Thirteenth shilling 1861.

Twenty-sixth shilling 1844.

Fifty-second shilling 1841.

Bronze coinage

Thirteenth shilling, 1870.

Twelfth shilling 1877.

Twenty fourth shilling 1909.

Twelfth shilling 1913.

Twelfth shilling 1947.

Twelfth shilling 1957.

and bronze denomination. Initially these were the one twenty-sixth of a shilling and the one fifty-second of a shilling and from 1877 the one twenty-fourth of a shilling and the one forty-eighth of a shilling. The special bronze issues of Jersey showing these curious denominations continued into the 1960s, changes of monarch necessitating changes to the obverse portrait. From 1957 there was also a quarter shilling (threepence) struck in nickel-brass. The first decimal coins appeared in 1968.

French coins were the legal tender in the Bailiwick of **Guernsey** but British coins became legal tender alongside them in 1870. French currency was retained as the money of account until superseded by British sterling currency in 1921. Guernsey was a little ahead of Jersey in producing its own copper coins to provide small change but here it would obviously be based on the French coins in use. In Guernsey this was the liard but the coin based on it was termed a "double". The double was an ancient French denomination and the liard on which it was based was worth about one eighth of a penny sterling. The four doubles and one double were introduced in 1830, the eight doubles in 1834 and the two doubles in 1858, all of them being struck in Birmingham. The eight doubles was the Guernsey penny and was rated at 12½ to the British shilling in 1870. In Guernsey the change from copper to a lighter bronze issue took place in 1864. In 1921 the eight doubles became the exact equivalent of the British penny (240 to the pound). Although sterling became the sole legal tender in that year the two doubles (farthing) continued in issue until 1929, the one double (half farthing) until 1938 and the eight and four doubles (penny and halfpenny) until 1949 without any major change in design. In 1956 the eight and four doubles were reintroduced to a new design together with a threepence in copper-nickel. These were the last coins before decimalization.

GUERNSEY

Copper eight doubles 1834.

One double 1830.

Bronze four doubles 1893.

Ireland had been an integral part of the United Kingdom since 1801[1]. English, later British, monarchs had claimed rule of all or part of it since the Anglo-Norman invasions that began in 1169. The ruling classes were the Anglo-Irish nobility whose titles derived from feudal grants, a system alien to the indigenous population. Governing Ireland had therefore been difficult. Union was designed to protect Ireland from French ambition and to strengthen British control. It had been intended that it would go hand in hand with full Catholic emancipation for the enlarged United Kingdom, something that a continued Anglo-Irish parliament at Dublin would never have conceded for Ireland. The King though, as head of the Church of England, was bitterly opposed to the idea of Catholic Members of Parliament at Westminster and the Union went ahead without the implied emancipation. The Irish therefore saw union as a measure that had been forced upon them under false pretences.

Although Catholic emancipation was won in 1829 there were other matters concerning the Church and land tenure in Ireland that ensured that the Union would remain in contention. In 1870 the Home Government Association was formed. This became the Home Rule League in 1873 which the next year returned fifty nine members to the House of Commons. It was clear that their aim of self government within the United Kingdom would have to be addressed and in 1886 a Home Rule Bill was introduced in the House of Commons. It was defeated and a second Bill that passed the Commons in 1893 was defeated by the House of Lords. A further Bill passed the Commons in 1912 and was enacted in 1914[2]. Its implementation was postponed on the outbreak of the First World War but self rule for Ireland within the United Kingdom had been agreed.

There were though more extreme elements of nationalism in Ireland who sought to end the British connection completely and establish an independent republic. This they attempted by force in what became known as the Easter Rising in April 1916. It took some six days to subdue at considerable loss of life and the British reaction was harsh. Rebellion in wartime was a very serious matter and Britain's allies had to be reassured that the United Kingdom was secure. The leaders of the Rising were court-martialed and executed and many of their followers were imprisoned. The incident and its aftermath polarized Irish opinion. After the war Britain pushed on with the home rule agenda but an alternative republican government was established by the Sinn Féin Party in Dublin declaring Ireland to be independent. After some eighteen months of warfare talks began in London which resulted in the Anglo-Irish Treaty of 1921. This arranged for the establishment of the "Irish Free State" as a self governing Dominion within the British Commonwealth and this came into effect in December 1922. Ulster though had been given the option of remaining within the United Kingdom, and did so.

We saw in Chapter two that English rulers struck coins for Ireland from the 12th century. Silver coins were struck for Ireland until the time of Charles I and during that troubled reign a brief issue of gold coins was struck on the French pistole standard in 1646. After that, precious metal coins of England and sometimes elsewhere circulated as required and from the reign of Charles II the only regal coins struck for Ireland were of copper. Many private tokens were issued in Ireland over the years and the great shortage of United Kingdom silver coins in the early 19th century led to issues of silver tokens by the Bank of Ireland. In 1804 Spanish American dollars began to be over struck to circulate at six shillings Irish and a series of lower denominations from thirty pence to five pence Irish were struck from 1805 to 1813. The designation "Irish" stems from the fact that thirteen Irish pounds were equivalent to twelve pounds sterling making the Irish denominations different from their British counterparts.

---

1 *The Acts of Union 1800 came into effect on 1st January, 1801.*
2 *The Government of Ireland Act 1914 (4 & 5 Geo. V. c. 90).*

There were thirteen pence Irish to the British shilling and it is for this reason that a separate, lighter copper coinage had continued to be struck for Ireland. The last of these issues was that of pennies and halfpennies dated 1822 and 1823 under George IV. After the Union the differential rate was an anomaly but it was not until 1826 that it was finally abolished and sterling coins came into full use[3]. A separate Irish Free State coinage was introduced in 1928 which will be examined in Chapter fourteen.

The last Irish coins before sterling came into full use

Halfpenny 1822.   *Penny 1823.*

After England's Glorious revolution it was considered important to secure a Protestant succession to the throne. All eventualities were allowed for and this resulted in Anne succeeding William III in 1702. Two years before that her last remaining child had died and it seemed unlikely that she would have more. The Act of Succession 1701 (extended to Scotland at the time of the Union) laid down what would happen if she died childless and it was a "belt and braces" Act. The succession would pass to Princess Sophia, Electress and Dowager Duchess of Hanover, a granddaughter of James I of England and then to her Protestant descendants provided they did not marry Roman Catholics. Anne died childless as expected but Sophia had predeceased her. It was thus Sophia's son George, already Elector of Hanover, who succeeded to the throne of Great Britain as George I in 1714. So began a long association between Britain and Hanover which only came to an end when Salic law prevented Queen Victoria succeeding to the German kingdom in 1837.

The portraits and titles on the coins of **Hanover** during this period are familiar to students of British numismatics. It must be remembered though that it was the Hanoverian rulers who became kings of Britain, not the other way around. The coins of Hanover are German coins and nothing to do with Britain or the British world.

Britain's first colony in Europe was **Gibraltar** which was taken by an Anglo-Dutch force under Admiral Sir George Rooke in 1704. It had been taken in the name of Charles, Archduke of Austria, who was the Grand Alliance's nominee for the Spanish throne during the War of the Spanish succession. In the event Charles did not become king of Spain and at the Treaty of Utrecht in 1713 Gibraltar was confirmed to Britain, who had provided the main garrison.

Control of Gibraltar gave Britain an important presence in the approaches to the Mediterranean and a useful naval base. Its importance would greatly increase after the opening of the Suez Canal in 1869. From then on Britain's commerce with India, the East and Australia would pass increasingly along this route.

---

3   *The Currency Act 1825 (6 Geo IV. c.79) in force 5th January 1826.*

For the whole of the period examined in this chapter legislative and executive power in Gibraltar was solely in the hands of the Governor who was a military officer of general rank. This reflects the status of Gibraltar as a military fortress more than a civil community. Nevertheless, as trade and commerce grew, the civilian community increased and by 1815 numbered some 10,000.

In the early 19th century, as this community grew in importance, several of the merchants in Gibraltar issued tokens to relieve the shortage of small change and all of these were in Spanish denominations (quartos and two quartos) reflecting the predominant coinage in use. They are dated from 1802 to 1820. In 1815 the Governor also recommended that silver one real and two reales coins should be struck for use in the colony to alleviate the problem of small change for the garrison but no action was taken.

Although sterling was ordered to be the legal tender for payment in all British colonies in 1825 Gibraltar was so closely connected commercially with Spain that this proved impossible to enforce. In Spain, and therefore also in Gibraltar, the doubloon was rated at sixteen dollars. When the sterling value of the dollar was corrected to 4/2d (on 1st January 1843 in Gibraltar) the doubloon thus had to be rated at 66/8d (16 dollars) instead of the 64/- rate based on its bullion value laid down for most of the other colonies.

The introduction of sterling copper coins also led to some confusion. Because of its size the farthing was generally accepted in trade as a quarto. This made 48 pence equivalent to the dollar (which consisted of 192 quartos) instead of the 52 pence laid down in 1825 and 50 pence in 1843. To ease this confusion a special issue of copper coins was struck for Gibraltar in 1842 in the Spanish denominations of two quarts, one quart and half quart. Spanish coins remained in circulation for many years but it was not until 1872 that this was legally recognized by an Order in Council which gave Gibraltar a currency (that of Spain) that coincided with actual conditions. Only in August 1898 was the lawful money of the United Kingdom declared the sole legal tender for payment in Gibraltar.

GIBRALTAR
Tokens

Robert Keeling,
two quarts 1802

Richard Cattons,
two quartos 1813.

James Spittles,
quarto 1820.

Coins of 1842

Two Quarts.   Quart.   Half quart.

Important as Gibraltar became it was not the best all weather harbour and had no hinterland to supply its needs. A much better harbour was Port Mahon on the island of **Minorca** which was also more relevant to the Royal Navy's 18th century requirement to observe French movements at Toulon. Minorca was taken in 1708 during the War of the Spanish Succession, its people generally supporting the Habsburg claim. Like Gibraltar it was taken in the name of the Archduke Charles but confirmed to Britain in the Treaty of Utrecht of 1713. Minorca remained in British hands until 1782 although it was taken and held by France from 1756 to 1763 during the Seven Years War. At Versailles in 1783 it was ceded to Spain who, with French assistance, had taken it the year before. During the Revolutionary Wars it was again occupied by Britain from 1798 to 1802 but returned to Spain at the Treaty of Amiens. No coins or tokens relative to a British colonial study are known to have been produced for Minorca.

During the 18th century there is evidence to show that the British Government would have preferred to keep Minorca rather than Gibraltar but after 1815 Britain's requirements in the Mediterranean had changed. As Minorca was lost, Malta was gained and this also had a very good harbour. With both Gibraltar and Malta in British hands Britain's interests could be safeguarded at both ends of the Mediterranean.

Malta came under British control when the French garrison holding it capitulated in September 1800 after a long siege. The Treaty of Amiens which ended the Revolutionary Wars in 1802 restored it to the Knights of Malta. The British though remained, claiming uncertainty about French intentions and when war resumed the next year the British evacuation was suspended. Malta was confirmed to Britain at the 1814 Peace of Paris.

Malta's function, like Gibraltar, was that of a fortified naval base but the governors of Malta always had to take account of a much larger civilian community than did those of Gibraltar. The conflict of interests between running a naval base and the rights of the people was a constant source of friction. Malta was initially run solely by military governors as a Crown colony and although there were serious attempts to include elected members in the Council of Government the Maltese themselves had little real say in the government until the establishment of a parliament in 1921.

Malta had had its own coinage under the Knights of St John of Jerusalem based on the denominations of Sicily and Italy and this continued in use during the brief French occupation and for many years after the British arrived. Spanish dollars were also in use and the Sicilian dollar would become a major part of the circulating medium.

The introduction of British sterling in 1825 seems to have solved problems with the copper coinage, at least after the third farthing denomination began to be struck especially for Malta from 1827. This was discussed in the last chapter. The introduction of sterling silver however was more problematic. Malta was basically part of a foreign (Italian) currency area and a token silver coinage (which British silver was from 1816) was therefore difficult to accept. Even though it was imported in quite large quantities and British gold coins were brought in from 1826, sterling silver was used mainly for government payments and remittances home while the Sicilian dollar became the preferred coin in actual circulation. An Order in Council of 1855 making British coin the sole legal tender did not change the situation and the Sicilian dollar continued to circulate at 4/2d although no longer legal tender. Only in 1885 when the Italian Government announced the imminent withdrawal of non decimal coins did things change. The intrinsic value of the Sicilian dollar was less than could be obtained by exchanging it at the Italian mints so all those in circulation in Malta were hastily gathered in by the Government and transmitted to Italy. It is estimated that some 2,811,133 Sicilian dollars from Malta were exchanged in this way the holders eventually receiving 4 shillings per dollar. To replace this large withdrawal of coin efforts were made to import more British sterling which in 1886 became the sole currency of Malta. Although Malta achieved independence in 1964 sterling coins continued in use until Malta decimalized in 1972.

The only coins struck specifically for Malta under British rule were the copper third farthings of Imperial type from 1827 to 1913 (the metal being changed to bronze in 1866).

Malta third farthings

1827 (copper).   *1835 (copper).*   *1884 (bronze).*

After the opening of the Suez Canal in 1869 the importance of Gibraltar and Malta, now guarding an important commercial artery, increased considerably. The Suez Canal itself and Egypt too would soon become vital British interests but, geographically situated in Africa, these will be dealt with in a later chapter.

Another territory that came to Britain as a result of the Napoleonic Wars was the **Ionian Islands**. Under Venetian rule for many years they had changed hands more than once during the Revolutionary Wars and some had been seized by Britain over the period 1809 to 1814. At the Peace of Paris it was uncertain what should be done with them but it was plain that an independent state on the edge of the Ottoman Empire would be likely, one day, to upset the delicate balance of power being arranged at the Vienna Congress. It was therefore agreed that they should come under British protection and in November 1815 the United States of the

Ionian Islands came into being. The main islands were Corfu, Cephalonia, Zante, Santa Maura, Ithaca, Cerigo and Paxos.

Although an independent state under British protection, the High Commissioners sent out over the years to administer the Protectorate tended to treat the Ionian Islands as a colony. While British protection undoubtedly led to improvements and offered some security to the people of the islands it did not automatically extend to them the privileges enjoyed by formal colonies and the voice of their Assembly was largely ignored. As a result the relationship between the British administration and the Ionian Islanders was not generally a happy one. When Greece was recognized as an independent nation in 1832 many of the islanders felt that this was where their future should lie.

Britain's main interest in the region was stability and when Prince William George of Denmark (brother in law of the Prince of Wales) was recognized as the successor to Otto I of Greece the British Government could see no real reason why the Ionian Islands should not become an integral part of his kingdom. There were strategic arguments for continued British control and the transfer had to be agreed by Austria, France and Russia but the consensus of opinion in the Cabinet was that the islands were troublesome and expensive to run. Their transfer to a now friendly Greece would not only be in line with the wishes of the islanders but would improve stability and increase British influence in the region. The Ionian Islands passed into Greek control and out of our story in 1864.

The currency system in use when the British arrived in the Ionian Islands was based on that of Turkey with 40 paras equal to a piastre. The Spanish dollar (5½ piastres) was the coin most in use as a standard of value and for military payments. During the initial occupation a shortage of minor silver coins was overcome by importing Spanish and Sicilian fractions of the dollar and countermarking them with local values (60, 50, 30 and 25 paras) for circulation. As these simple countermarks were easy to copy a more complex countermark showing also the bust of George III soon replaced them. The coins were countermarked on the island of Zante which was the centre of British administration for the islands before the establishment of the Protectorate. These countermarked coins remained in circulation for some years.

Ionian Islands locally countermarked coin

Fifty paras overstruck on a Sicilian coin c.1813.

A supply of copper coins was requested but no action was taken until 1819 when a series was struck at the Royal Mint to the same weights and sizes as the British penny, halfpenny and farthing. These show the lion of Venice (which was still in use as the emblem of the Protectorate) with legend **ΙΟΝΙΚΟΝ ΚΡΑΤΟΣ** (Ionian State) on the obverse and Britannia on the reverse but show no denomination. Although supplied to the islands in 1819 and 1820 they were not released into circulation until 1821 when a new decimal currency system was introduced. There were now 100 oboli to the dollar and the new copper coins were given legal circulation as the two oboli (penny sized coin), obol and half obol. It was immediately realized that a smaller copper denomination was required and a quarter obol (of the same basic design as the British struck coins but somewhat cruder) was struck locally at Corfu. The larger copper denominations proved unpopular and many of them were returned to the Royal Mint for melting in 1827/28.

In 1834 new minor denominations began to be struck at the Royal Mint. These were a silver 30 lepta and a copper lepton, the lepton being one fifth of an obol. The remaining old copper coins still in circulation were demonetized in 1835 and the new coins continued in issue intermittently until 1862.

IONIAN ISLANDS
The oboli coinage

Two oboli 1819 (Royal Mint).   Locally struck quarter obol 1821.

New denominations from the Royal Mint

Lepton 1834.   Thirty lepta 1852.

In northern Europe, **Heligoland** was taken from a small Danish garrison in 1807. The previous year Napoleon had introduced his "continental system" designed to shut off all Britain's trade with Europe. When Denmark threw in her lot with France the island seemed to the British to be an ideal base from which to break Napoleon's "system" and to blockade continental ports. It succeeded admirably becoming a busy and prosperous entrepôt for the rest of the war. Denmark confirmed it to Britain at the Treaty of Kiel in 1814.

In the 1880s a newly unified Germany came to view Heligoland in British hands as a threat to her North Sea ports. She had no claim to the place, it having been formerly Danish, but the British Government was prepared to do a deal. It became part of a comprehensive agreement on British and German interests in Africa and was basically exchanged for German interests in East Africa.

Queen Victoria was not enthusiastic about the deal reminding Lord Salisbury that "… Giving up what one has is always a bad thing"[4]. Nevertheless Heligoland (German: "Helgoland") was formally handed over to Germany on 9th August, 1890. No coins or tokens specific to the British period of control are known.

---

4 *Cypher telegram from the Queen at Balmoral to the Prime Minister 12th June 1890.*

For our last European territory we move back to the Mediterranean but forward some years. By this time events had moved on in Europe, as we shall see shortly, and the Russo-Turkish War had ended in 1878. As always Britain was interested in protecting the Ottoman Empire as a bulwark against Russian expansion and the recent war had given Russia a dangerous advantage. Other European powers were also concerned at Russia's Balkan advances and met in congress at Berlin, with Russia and the Ottoman Empire, to force modifications to the Treaty of San Stefano which had ended the war. Before this congress began Britain had concluded a secret alliance with the Ottoman Empire whereby Britain would lease, occupy and administer Cyprus. This would protect the Sultan against further aggression and provide Britain with a secure base from which she could protect her increasing interests in the eastern Mediterranean as well as those of the Ottoman Empire. The agreement was signed on 4th June 1878, just before the start of the Berlin Congress, and was accepted by the other powers.

Cyprus was administered by a High Commissioner, his Legislative Council having an official majority until 1882 and thereafter an elected majority. The position of Cyprus within the British Empire and its form of government would remain unchanged until the Ottoman Empire entered the First World War on the side of Germany at which time the island was formally annexed by Britain.

The currency of Cyprus in 1878 was based on the Turkish piastre but the copper coin of that denomination in common circulation was not fixed in relation to other coins. The new British administration gave it a fixed exchange of 180 to the British gold sovereign. The High Commissioner recommended that a new coinage be struck to replace the copper piastres in circulation and this began to be supplied, from the United Kingdom, in 1879. It was in three denominations, the piastre with its half and quarter, and was struck in bronze. A variety of coins actually circulated but in 1882 British silver was admitted as a legal tender, the shilling being equivalent to nine piastres. The British half-crown denomination was never legalized in Cyprus to avoid confusion with the florin (two shillings).

By the 1890s the main coins in circulation were British gold and silver and a little French gold all rated in piastres together with the bronze piastre coinage. In 1900 an Order in Council made the British gold sovereign the sole legal tender for unlimited amounts and it was also decided to replace sterling silver coins with coins denominated in piastres. The eighteen piastres (equivalent to two shillings), the nine piastres (shilling), the four and a half piastres (sixpence) and the three piastres (fourpence) all came into issue in 1901.

The portrait of Victoria used on this initial issue of Cyprus silver coins was designed by G. W. De Saulles and was not used on any other coinage. Medal collectors though will find it familiar and philatelists may also note similarities[5]. The piastre based coinage for Cyprus was struck in the name of subsequent British monarchs until 1949. The quarter piastre was discontinued in 1926 and from 1934 the piastre and half piastre were struck on smaller scalloped flans in cupro-nickel. In 1942 both these denominations were changed to bronze, still on scalloped flans, as a wartime austerity measure and continued in that form until 1949. Of the silver denominations the three piastres was struck only in 1901 and the four and a half piastres ceased issue in 1938. An impressive forty five piastres denomination was introduced in 1928 to mark fifty years of British occupation but was struck only in that year. The eighteen piastres and the nine piastres were thus the only silver coins in issue when the metal content was changed from sterling silver to cupro-nickel in 1947. These two coins were then

---

5 For example the Jubilee Medal of 1897, the Queen's South Africa Medal of 1899 and, for philatelists, the 1897 stamps of Canada.

denominated as "two Cyprus shillings" and "one Cyprus shilling" and were reduced to the same size as the United Kingdom florin and shilling. The last of these coins are dated 1949. A decimal coinage was introduced in 1955 based on one thousand mils to the pound. Subsidiary coins only were struck, the largest being the 100 mils. Higher denominations were in banknotes issued by the Government of Cyprus. In 1960 Cyprus achieved independence.

CYPRUS

Quarter piastre 1879.

Half piastre 1879.

Piastre 1879.

Eighteen piastres 1901.

Forty five piastres 1928.

Bronze piastre 1945.

Cupro-nickel two shillings 1949.

Decimal one hundred mils 1955.

As noted earlier (Chapter three) a separate Secretary of State to deal with colonial affairs was first appointed in 1768. With the loss of the American colonies this department was abolished in 1782 and responsibility for the remaining colonies passed to the Home Office. In 1801 this responsibility was transferred to the War Office which was renamed the War and Colonial Office. The increasing importance of the colonies led to the appointment of a Permanent Under-Secretary for the Colonies within the War and Colonial Office in 1825.

It was not until 1854 that War and Colonies were separated. A Colonial Office was then created and Britain had her first Secretary of State for the Colonies. He dealt of course with colonies only. Protectorates and so on, like the Ionian Islands and Cyprus, were the responsibility of the Foreign Office and British India would (from 1858) be the responsibility of a separate India Office.

The settler colonies of Canada, Australia, New Zealand and South Africa were moved towards responsible government (i.e. government responsible to an elected assembly) and this will be discussed in the chapters relevant to each of them.

By the 1870s Europe had moved on and events had conspired to upset the balance of power arranged at the Congress of Vienna.

Greece and Belgium had emerged as new states but the first real signs of change came in 1848 when a series of revolutions swept across Europe. Of the major European powers only Britain, Russia and the Ottoman Empire were not directly affected. Trouble arose with demands for greater democracy and freedom and because of an upsurge of nationalism, liberalism and socialism. The reasons for the various revolutions were social rather than political but all of them threatened the old order. They were not coordinated and most were resolved for the time being. Nevertheless they led to the establishment of the Second Republic in France under Napoleon III and to the end of absolute monarchy in Denmark. They also encouraged ideas of national unity in the many German and Italian states.

The first major war between the great powers since 1815 was the Crimean War of 1854 – 1856. It came about because of the decline of the Ottoman Empire and the rights of France and Russia to protect Christians living within the Empire. France, with a show of force, obtained recognition that the Roman Catholic Church, under France, was the supreme Christian authority in the Holy Land. Russia felt strongly that authority should have remained with Orthodox ecclesiastics. In July1853 she thus moved into the Ottoman Empire and occupied the Danubian principalities of Moldavia and Wallachia ostensibly to protect the Orthodox Christians of that region. Britain, ever anxious to curb Russian expansion, and France, guardian of the Catholics of the Ottoman Empire, sent warships to the region.

Russia's continued occupation of the Danubian principalities led the Sultan to declare war on Russia in October 1853. The destruction of Turkish ships at Sinop and Russia's refusal to withdraw from the principalities gave Britain and France cause also to declare war on Russia in March 1854. When Austria failed to support the Russian invasion the Czar was forced to agree to withdraw his troops from the principalities leaving very little reason to continue the war but Russia would not agree to allied terms. Britain and France, anxious to remove the threat to the Ottoman Empire, combined against Russia in an attack on the Crimea aimed at taking the Black Sea port of Sevastopol.

After a long history of Anglo-French wars it was a novelty for Britain and France to be fighting on the same side, a matter that seemed particularly difficult for Lord Raglan, commanding the British forces, to come to terms with. A veteran of Waterloo and steeped in

British military history he automatically referred to the enemy (the Russians) as "the French" even when conferring with his allies which must have been intensely annoying.

It was a hard fought war with battles at Alma, Balaclava and Inkerman before Sevastopol finally fell but it resulted, as Britain wished, in the curbing of Russian ambitions in the region. Russia gave up her exclusive claim to protect Turkish Christians, the integrity of the Ottoman Empire was to be guaranteed by the major powers and Russian warships were barred from using the Black Sea.

Europe had been shaken but not yet in a way that was detrimental to British interests. The three European wars that followed Crimea though would change the face of Europe completely[6]. All of them were brief but they would lead to the unification of Italy (finally completed in 1870), to the fall of Napoleon III and the founding of the French Third Republic in 1870, and to the unification of Germany in 1871. The newly unified German Empire, led by Prussia's Chancellor Otto von Bismarck, with its powerful army and efficient government would soon become the most powerful nation of continental Europe. Until 1914 this new Europe would maintain an uneasy balance of power but Britain would have far less influence in how that was arranged.

Britain had avoided most of the political and social problems of Europe during the 19th century. She had a constitutional monarchy of long standing. Legislation such as the Reform Act 1832, the Municipal Corporation Act 1835 and the various Factory Acts had advanced political and social reform. The repeal of the Corn Laws in 1846 had dampened proletarian passions and free trade had been established. Above all Britain was rich and powerful and there seemed no reason to doubt that she would remain so.

In the 1860s the vague liberal perception was that the newly self governing settler colonies would move to independence and the Empire as it stood would be dismembered. By the 1870s public opinion, both at home and in the colonies, had moved firmly to the more conservative view that the Empire should be consolidated. It was a period of increased national awareness and pride. Britons at home and in the colonies saw their country as the home of constitutional and religious liberty, of intellectual and commercial achievement, of prosperity and trade. It was a nation with a maritime power and an imperial greatness of which they were proud and in which they felt secure.

The feelings of the time can perhaps be judged from Britain's official and public reaction to the Russo-Turkish War of 1877-1878. In her continuing defence of the Ottoman Empire and the road to India Britain made it clear that she would use force against Russia to prevent the fall of Constantinople. Although any official communications on the matter would have been couched in rather stuffier terms they would have given exactly the same message as that expressed in a popular music hall song of the day:-

> "We don't want to fight but by jingo if we do
> We've got the ships, we've got the men, we've got the money too…."

The popular feeling was that Britain could do pretty much what she wanted and the term "jingoism" had been born. What could possibly go wrong?

In Europe, Germany allied herself with Austria-Hungary in 1879 and with Italy in 1882 to form a Triple Alliance for mutual protection. Already Germany was developing her industries

---

6 *The Franco-Austrian War of 1859 set Italian independence under way. The Austro-Prussian War of 1866 began German unification under Prussia. The Franco-Prussian War of 1870-1871 founded the German Empire and led to the establishment of the Third French Republic.*

and her scientific skills. Soon Britain, traditionally basing her education system on the classics, was loosing ground to Germany in her manufacturing industries particularly in newer fields like the chemical and electrical industries and the development of the motor car. And in armaments too.

For some years insular Britain ignored this rise in German power and military capability that was changing the face of continental Europe. With her naval power and her Empire Britain was content to leave Europe alone. Without too much concern she watched Germany develop world commerce and seek colonies but when the Imperial German Navy began to expand into a battle fleet that could threaten British supremacy at sea she became seriously alarmed.

Partly because of this concern a series of agreements were signed between Britain and France in 1904, soon to be termed the "Entente Cordiale". These were aimed at settling colonial matters of mutual concern but they also spelt the end of British neutrality in Europe. In 1907 an Anglo-Russian Convention was also signed. This covered matters of mutual concern in Asia but as Russia and France had been in alliance since the 1890s it brought about a general connection between the three nations of Britain, France and Russia. This would come to be known as the "Triple Entente" and aligned these nations against those of the "Triple Alliance" (Germany, Austria-Hungary and Italy).

There were various conditions and exemptions attached to the agreements that formed the Alliance and the Entente and agreements too with other European powers but this was the general alignment of the major powers as Europe moved towards 1914. It was plain that Great Britain and Germany were the most significant of the powers involved. It was plain too that the era of Pax Britannica was coming to an end and that inevitably there would be a collision between these two powers.

For some years before 1914 tensions in Europe had been mounting and Germany was anxious to settle matters before France could again become a threat and before Russia completed the modernization of her armies. She thought it unlikely that Britain would intervene in a purely European conflict. In June 1914 the Austrian Archduke Franz Ferdinand and his wife were assassinated by Serb nationalists. Austria-Hungary made demands of Serbia which were not fully met and five days later declared war. Russia mobilized in order to defend Serbia. Germany was ready to support Austria-Hungary and welcomed the excuse to declare war on Russia. This she did on 1st August, asking France to remain neutral. France declined and on 3rd August Germany declared war on her too making it clear that she would not respect the neutrality of Belgium. So far Germany's effort to secure her position in Europe had gone according to plan[7]. She was at war with both Russia and France and confident of success on both fronts. Britain though could not countenance German control of the coasts across the Channel. On 4th August 1914, having received no assurances on German respect for Belgian neutrality, Britain declared war on Germany and the Great War had begun.

---

7 *The so called Schlieffen Plan devised by the Chief of the German General Staff in 1905. Under this plan France would be swiftly taken allowing troops to return to the east before Russia could fully mobilize.*

The Story of the Coins and Tokens of the British World

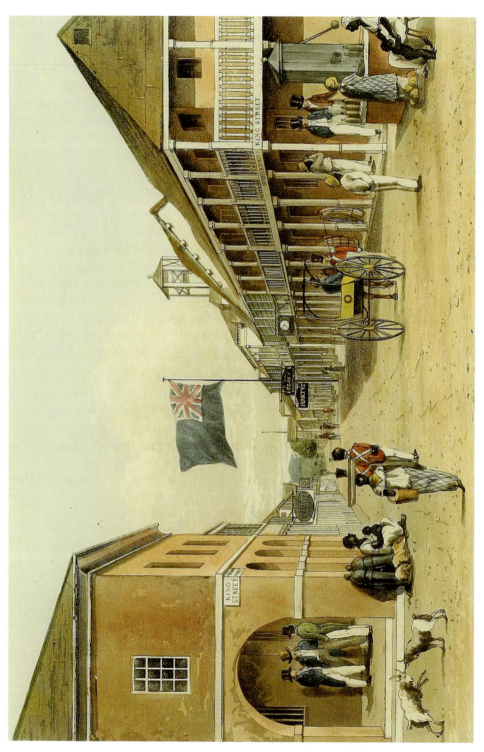

Kingston, Jamaica in 1825.

The Americas

IN this and subsequent chapters the term "nineteenth century" is flexible. In general it covers the hundred years from Waterloo (1815) to the First World War but there will be minor excursions into earlier and later periods where the narrative requires.

By the beginning of the 19th century Britain's possessions in the Americas were geographically divided into two regions. In the north were the colonies that would eventually become Canada while to the south were the tropical colonies of the Caribbean. Between them (in place of former British colonies) lay the United States of America with whom there were border and other disputes from time to time. Britain also had commercial interests in Central and South America.

We will begin our survey of British interests in the Americas with the lands that would become the Dominion of Canada and must look first at the extensive regions held by the Hudson's Bay Company. Chartered by Charles II in 1670 its first Governor was Prince Rupert, a cousin of the king, and the grant was for all the lands draining into Hudson Bay. This extensive area was named Rupert's Land and was a proprietary colony. The Company concentrated on the fur trade and for many years did little in the interior preferring to trade with the Indians who came to their trading posts on the coast of Hudson Bay.

The French also traded for furs and, even after Canada was ceded to Britain in 1763, encroached on the rights of the Hudson's Bay Company. The French worked mainly from Montreal and were far more active than the Hudson's Bay Company, travelling far inland to secure their furs. To compete with this and to keep the French traders out of its charter lands the Hudson's Bay Company had to change its tactics and also move inland. Its first inland post, Cumberland House, was built near the Saskatchewan River in 1774. By this time Montreal had been in British hands for some time and British fur traders had joined the French in competition with the Company. By 1784 the main Montreal rivals of the Hudson's Bay Company had formed themselves into the North West Company.

There was bitter rivalry between the two companies but the fur traders explored and settled as they traded. It was Alexander MacKenzie of the North West Company who, in 1789, first descended to the arctic seas by the river that now bears his name and he too who first crossed the Rockies to the Pacific four years later. Privately, Lord Selkirk (who had a controlling interest in the Hudson's Bay Company) founded the Red River Colony near modern Winnipeg in 1812. This was largely a philanthropic venture to settle Scots displaced by the Highland clearances at home but it was hoped it would provide useful supplies for the Company and thwart the expansion of the North West Company. In this way discoveries and claims were made by the fur traders in the vast areas in the north and west of the continent. The damaging competition between the two companies came to an end when they agreed a merger in 1821, the combined company taking the name of the Hudson's Bay Company.

In the same year the new combined company was licensed by Parliament to manage the North Western Territory. Its structure now combined trading rights with sovereignty under the British Crown and it had nominal control over the whole northern part of the continent apart from Canada (as it then was) and the maritime colonies to the east.

Canada itself at this time still consisted of Upper Canada and Lower Canada as arranged by the Constitutional Act of 1791. The maritime colonies were Newfoundland, Nova Scotia, New Brunswick and Prince Edward Island. Cape Breton Island was finally annexed to Nova Scotia in 1820.

When Napoleon introduced his "continental system" in Europe (in 1806) aimed at damaging Britain's trade there had to be a response. Britain issued Orders in Council banning neutral ships from using ports that did not allow British trade and imposing a blockade on those ports. As a neutral state with a large merchant fleet and much trade with France, the United States objected to these sanctions claiming them to be illegal under international law. She objected also to Britain's insistence that her navy had the right to impress British nationals serving in American ships. There were other matters too resulting from the aftermath of the War of Independence which needed to be settled, particularly Britain's support for Indian nations which restricted American expansion. Relations between the United States and Britain deteriorated until the United States declared war in 1812. As news travelled slowly the Americans were unaware that the offending Orders in Council had already been cancelled but the other grievances remained.

At this time the future of Upper and Lower Canada as British colonies was uncertain. Neither was heavily garrisoned by British troops so they relied heavily on militias for their defence. Upper Canada had seen large scale immigration from the United States since the original influx of loyalists and it was assumed there would be republican and American sympathies there. Lower Canada was largely French and, although they may have been wary of the United States, sympathies were not likely to lie staunchly with Britain.

The exact intent of the United States in declaring war at this time is uncertain. It was assumed that the conquest of Upper Canada would be a formality and there were those in the United States who felt this would be a useful bargaining chip. There were also those who saw it as an opportunity to expel Britain from the continent once and for all. What is certain is that the United States felt aggrieved and insulted by Britain's actions. In the event there was no support in Upper Canada for the American invasion and the militias of Lower Canada responded well. The war was settled by the Treaty of Ghent, agreed late in 1814 and ratified by both governments in February 1815, which restored territory taken by both sides. The war had been limited to action in North America and at sea.

After the war it was clear that Canada was not going to be absorbed by the United States and nor was either part of it about to seek independence. The war had given Canada a firm footing on which to build.

With the war behind them the United States and Britain were able to accept that there were matters of mutual interest. A major concern of the United States was the fate of the ex Spanish colonies of Latin America. Would they be allowed to remain as independent republics or would Spain attempt to recover them? Would other European nations assist Spain or attempt to make claims themselves? The United States favoured a New World unencumbered by Old World jealousies. Britain was also concerned at what may happen and for this there were two main reasons. Firstly, a reversion to the Spanish mercantile system would damage the large trade Britain had built up with South America. Secondly any Old World intervention could realign the nations of Europe and upset the balance of power so recently arranged there.

In 1823 the United States President, James Monroe, defined his country's foreign policy on the matter. Existing European colonies would not be interfered with but future attempts by European nations to colonize or interfere with any of the states in North or South America that were recognized by the United States would be viewed as acts of aggression and would require intervention. This eventually became known as the "Monroe Doctrine" and would be a long standing tenet of United States foreign policy. In the 1820s the United States knew that she did not have the power to enforce such a policy effectively in distant waters but she knew also that Britain fully approved the policy. The Royal Navy had the presence and the power to back that approval.

The years following the 1812 war were years of economic progress in both Upper and Lower Canada. Populations increased but so too did political awareness. By the 1830s there were demands for responsible government from both and conciliatory moves from the British Government. In Lower Canada though this would seriously compromise the British minority and in Upper Canada the Government was suspicious of radical views. By 1837 Louis Joseph Papineau had emerged as the leader of the French party in Lower Canada and William Lyon MacKenzie as the leader of the radical movement in Upper Canada. Both were opposed to British rule and open rebellion broke out in both colonies.

The revolts were dealt with swiftly and both leaders fled to the United States. The causes for the rebellions were investigated and found to be more deep seated in Lower Canada than in Upper Canada. The resultant report recommended reunification of the Canadas and a single responsible government. Canada would have ministers accountable to an elected Assembly and a Governor willing to act in accordance with the advice of his ministers.

Union was agreed by both Upper and Lower Canada and an Act of Union was passed by the Imperial Parliament in 1840[1]. A Proclamation brought it into force on 10th February 1841. Responsible government was a new concept for colonial rule so was brought in step by step over the next few years. The Governor would have a Council (soon known as the Ministry, the Administration, the Cabinet or the Government) who would be representative of the people and an Assembly with an equal number of members appointed from Upper and Lower Canada. These two parts of the new Province of Canada were now known as Canada West and Canada East.

The Legislature of Canada met first at Kingston in 1841. In 1844 Montreal became the seat of government. In 1849 it was decided to transfer it to Toronto for two years and then to hold sittings alternately in Quebec and Toronto (for four years in each place). In 1860 it met in Quebec but it had already been decided that Ottawa should be the permanent seat. By 1865 the Ottawa buildings were sufficiently complete for the Legislature to move there from Quebec. The choice of a capital city for Canada had been a difficult one but Ottawa was defensible and roughly equidistant from Quebec and Toronto.

The difficulty in choosing a capital city reflected the differences there would naturally be when two disparate groups were cobbled together in one colony with one Assembly. There were racial and religious rivalries and a hint yet again that the old region of Upper Canada may throw in its lot with the United States. If these difficulties were to be overcome and threats of defection or annexation avoided then self government in British North America

---
1 3 & 4 Vict. c. 35.

would have to be on a grander scale. It was in this climate that a confederation of all the provinces of British North America was suggested.

Representatives of the maritime colonies of Nova Scotia, New Brunswick and Prince Edward Island agreed to meet in 1864 to discuss federation between them. Canada also asked to attend with a view to joining such a federation. Newfoundland was interested in the idea but did not attend. The Charlottetown Conference ended with general agreement that federation was the way forward and it was decided to meet again at Quebec the following month. This time Newfoundland sent observers but took no direct part in the proceedings. The Quebec Conference of October 1864 decided the form of the new federation and the delegates returned to their provinces to submit details to their legislatures. Prince Edward Island rejected the resolutions agreed at Quebec but Canada, New Brunswick and Nova Scotia decided to go ahead.

The London Conference of December 1866 finalized arrangements between Britain and the three consenting provinces and resulted in the British North America Act which came into force on 1st July 1867[2]. The Act allowed for "One Dominion under the Crown" to be named Canada. The Province of Canada was divided into the new provinces of Ontario and Quebec which were joined to New Brunswick and Nova Scotia to form the four initial provinces of the Dominion of Canada.

Provisions were made for the eventual admission of Newfoundland, Prince Edward Island and British Columbia into the Dominion by application from the Canadian Parliament and the individual legislatures. There was provision also for the Dominion to take over Rupert's Land and the North Western Territory from the Hudson's Bay Company at some future date. It was generally felt that the undoubted resources of British North America could not be fully developed unless and until all the various provinces and territories were united. The 1867 Act and its provisions laid the foundation for that development.

Of the colonies and territories that did not join the Dominion in 1867 Newfoundland was the oldest. Although claimed by Britain from an early date the home government generally discouraged large scale permanent settlement there for many years, it being mainly a seasonal base for fishermen. It became more important and prosperous during the Napoleonic and American wars but its first resident Governor was not appointed until 1816. Newfoundland was granted self government in 1855 but did not opt to join the Dominion. Granted dominion status herself in 1907 she would not become part of Canada until 1949.

Prince Edward Island was originally part of Nova Scotia but its proprietors were granted a separate government, as St John's Island, in 1770. It was renamed Prince Edward Island, after the Duke of Kent, in 1798. Although Prince Edward Island hosted the original Charlottetown Conference her legislature was unhappy about the terms finally agreed for union and did not become part of the Dominion until 1873.

The territories under the control of the Hudson's Bay Company comprised their original Rupert's Land grant and the North Western Territory stretching to the west coast. In 1849 Vancouver Island was designated a Crown colony and leased to the Hudson's Bay Company. In 1857 the discovery of gold west of the Rockies led to a large inrush of prospectors. To secure British interests the region was removed from Hudson's Bay Company control to become, in 1858, the Crown colony of British Columbia. In 1866 Vancouver was merged with British Columbia which in 1871 joined the Dominion.

---

2 *30 & 31 Vict. c. 3.*

The Hudson's Bay Company were traders and tended to discourage settlement and development in the regions it controlled. The Imperial Government was anxious to settle the west in order to discourage possible American expansion and it would only be possible to ensure this if these regions became part of the Dominion. It was inevitable that the Company's administration would come to an end. The Company agreed that for financial compensation (to be paid by the Dominion of Canada) and various concessions it would surrender its territorial rights to the Crown to be passed on to the Dominion. The province of Manitoba was created from Rupert's Land and in July 1870 became part of the Dominion. At the same time the Dominion took responsibility for the North Western Territory[3]. The Company retained its commercial function.

The Dominion now stretched from coast to coast and as the vast prairie areas between Manitoba and British Columbia developed they coalesced (by 1905) into the provinces of Saskatchewan and Alberta. The development of these great grain producing provinces was made possible by the building of railways while steamships exported their products in ever increasing quantities to a Europe eager to consume them.

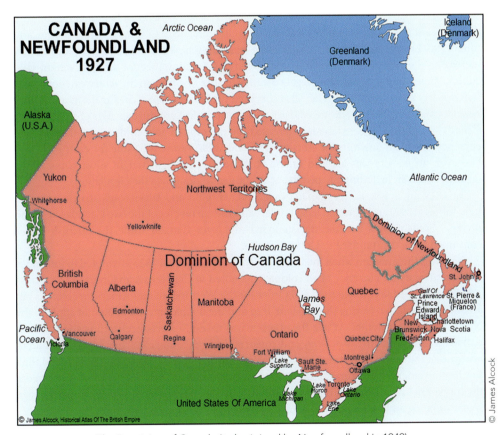

The Dominion of Canada (to be joined by Newfoundland in 1949)

---

3 *To become the "Northwest Territories" under the Dominion.*

The various territories that would eventually comprise Canada were diverse and, as would be expected, there were differing currency systems in use. Like other colonies their accounts were kept in sterling but the actual coins in use depended on what was available. The Spanish American dollar was in use everywhere. By the early 19th century this was generally rated at the Halifax rate of 5/- (five shillings) although other rates persisted for many years. As the century progressed and the United States became more influential her coins too circulated in increasing numbers north of the border. In 1785 the United States Congress had approved the use of the dollar as the new nation's currency. The Coinage Act of 1792 established the dollar as the unit of currency for the United States and noted that it would be *"of the value of a Spanish milled dollar as the same is now current."*[4] The British North American colonies therefore gave the US silver dollar the same rate as the Spanish milled dollar. In 1834 though, because of a changed gold/silver ratio, the United States reduced the weight of her gold coins and gave a specific standard to the gold dollar thus giving her a *de facto* gold standard. This and the vastly increased production of gold after the Californian discoveries all impacted on British North America and from that time rates for US gold in the British colonies were more important than the rates for Spanish silver.

In the Canadas in the early 19th century there was a general undervaluation of gold which meant that silver coins dominated the circulation and gold was exported. In May and June 1796 **Lower and Upper Canada** had passed Acts which tried to remedy this by increasing the rate for the doubloon and specifying an allowance for all light weight gold coins[5]. These same Acts also gave legal currency for the first time to the American gold eagle (ten dollars) and silver dollar. They also specified the Halifax rate of 5/- for the Spanish (and American) dollar. These measures did not solve the problem and further Acts of 1808 (Lower Canada) and 1809 (Upper Canada) increased the rates for all gold coins in circulation[6]. The currency rates laid down in the Acts of 1796 and 1808/9 were the same for each Province. However, no penalty was allowed in any of those Acts for light weight silver coins which meant that silver, including the pistareen, continued to dominate the circulation.

In 1819 an Act in Lower Canada made French gold and silver coins struck since the Revolution (1792) an unlimited legal tender[7] and the currencies of the two Canadas began to diverge. French coins became the standard of Lower Canada while the Spanish dollar continued to be the standard in Upper Canada.

This was the situation when the Imperial Order in Council of 1825 attempted to introduce sterling silver as the currency of all colonies. As noted in Chapter six an Order in Council of 7th September 1838 revoked the 1825 Order for the West Indian and American colonies but amending legislation (rating the dollar at 4/2d and the doubloon at 64/-) did not apply to the North American colonies. While the attempt was made to introduce sterling the Imperial authorities thus did little to actively and constructively encourage it. They eventually had to accept that the whole of British North America was firmly in a dollar using region and that, for the convenience of commerce, sterling would not become its currency. Before we examine the transition to a decimal currency though we must look at how the shortage of small change was now being addressed in the Canadas.

---

4   Chap 16, "An Act establishing a Mint, and regulating the Coins of the United States", April 2nd 1792, section 9.
5   36 Geo. III. c. 5 for Lower Canada and 36 Geo. III. c. 1 for Upper Canada.
6   48 Geo. III. c. 8 for Lower Canada and 49 Geo. III. c. 8 for Upper Canada.
7   59 Geo. III. c. 1.

British and Irish halfpennies were in short supply and from about 1812 (the time of the American War) tokens began to be imported to fill the gap. Although primarily imported for use in Lower Canada, which was more populous and more advanced commercially than Upper Canada at this time, these tokens found their way also to most other parts of British North America. Typical of these early types are those struck by Thomas Halliday of Birmingham and the numerous Wellington halfpennies but there were many others. Although anonymous these early tokens were of reasonable weight. Soon tokens began to appear for named issuers and some also began to be struck specifically for use in Upper Canada.

It was not long before lightweight tokens began to appear, sometimes copying the earlier issues. Some of these also came from the United Kingdom but many were undoubtedly produced in North America. Well known examples of these are copies of the Halliday tokens, the "bust and harp" halfpennies and the very crude "blacksmith" tokens. Although attempts were made to discourage the import and manufacture of lightweight tokens it would eventually be the banks of Lower Canada, not government, that took action to improve the situation.

The copper currency was in such a bad state by the mid 1830s that the banks in Montreal and Quebec were refusing to accept tokens other than by weight at scrap value. By 1836 the Bank of Montreal was issuing its own tokens to replace those it was withdrawing and these were once again of good weight. These were the "bouquet" sous, their value expressed in French, and the Banque du Peuple very soon followed with a similar bouquet token. So popular were these that they were soon imitated by a number of issuers and manufacturers and light weight copies appeared. To replace them four participating banks imported a large issue of pennies and half pennies known as "habitant" tokens because of their obverse design showing a French Canadian in winter dress. The reverse bore the arms of Montreal with a ribbon beneath carrying the name of one or other of the banks involved[8].

The next large scale issue of bank tokens would take place after the Act of Union had created the **Province of Canada**. These were issued by the Bank of Montreal from 1842 with a reverse similar to the "habitant" tokens. The obverse though now shows a front view of the bank and bears the legend **PROVINCE OF CANADA**. While the "habitant" tokens stated the denominations in French and English (e.g. **DEUX SOUS: ONE PENNY**) the new tokens show it in English only. These are clear concessions to "Englishness" in the newly united province but by the time the next major issue of tokens appeared matters again seem to have polarized. The Bank of Upper Canada tokens of the 1850s squeeze almost every symbol of Britishness into their design that it was possible to do (see illustration) while the Quebec Bank tokens revert to the habitant obverse and the denominations in French as well as English.

These issues of the 1850s were the last major issues of Canadian tokens and, like all the issues since the late 1830s, were similar in size and weight to their British counterparts. They belong to the period when the Imperial Government was still hoping that a currency based on sterling would be adopted permanently by Canada. By the 1850s though it was obvious that the currency of Canada was going to be decimal and that it was going to be based on the dollar.

---

8 These were the three chartered banks (the Bank of Montreal, the Quebec Bank and the City Bank) and the Banque du Peuple.

Canadian tokens to the 1850s

Tokens imported from England

"Halliday" halfpenny token 1812.

Locally produced tokens, 1830s

Local copy of Halliday token.

Wellington halfpenny token 1813.

Copy of imported "Bust and Harp" token (probably pre-dated to evade later legislation).

Later copy of a Halliday halfpenny retaining original date.

"Blacksmith" token (designed to look like a worn regal halfpenny).

Bouquet sou
This one of Banque du Peuple.

The "Habitant" tokens of 1837

Penny (Montreal Bank).   Halfpenny (Quebec Bank).

Province of Canada

Bank of Montreal halfpenny token 1844.

The last major token issues

Lower Canada "Habitant" penny 1852.   Upper Canada "St George" penny, 1857.

The Currency Act of 1841[9] was the first currency legislation of the newly united Province of Canada. The British sovereign and the US gold eagle with their multiples and divisions were given unlimited legal tender. Silver dollars and half dollars and French five franc coins were also legal tender to any amount. Sterling silver (which of course had been a token coinage since 1816) and the smaller fractions of dollars were limited in legal tender to £2-10-0d. Sterling was gradually becoming less relevant to Canada's commercial needs. After some discussion on the matter an Act of 1853 finally made specific provision for introducing provincial silver and copper coins based on the US gold dollar[10]. There was a delay of some years before the first Canadian decimal coins were actually struck and then they were of subsidiary denominations only. Token silver coins of 20 cents, 10 cents and 5 cents together with the one cent in bronze

---

9   4 & 5 Vict. c. 93
10   An Act to regulate the Currency, 16 Vict. c. 158. From this date Canada was effectively on a gold only standard.

went into circulation in 1858. Because the new decimal coins were divisions of the US gold dollar (itself legal tender) there was no requirement to strike a separate Canadian dollar at that time. Being struck in bronze the one cent coin was smaller and lighter than the halfpenny bank tokens in circulation which made the public reluctant to accept it. In fact the copper penny and halfpenny bank tokens continued to circulate for many years.

US gold eagle.
*The Canadian decimal coinage was subsidiary to the US gold dollar.
The Eagle ($10) was a popular denomination.*

Decimal coins introduced.
Province of Canada twenty cents 1858 and one cent 1859.

The next issue for Canada was that of 1870 and was the first coinage under the recently created **Dominion**. The silver coins were at the same token weight standard as the previous Province of Canada issue but were now of 50 cents, 25 cents (both new denominations), 10 cents and 5 cents. The new denominations were in line with US divisions of the dollar and the old 20 cents denomination of 1858 was withdrawn from circulation. Many of the old provincial cents had still not been put into circulation by1870 so no new one cent coins had to be struck for the Dominion until 1876.

Dominion coinage

Fifty cents 1881.   *Cent 1882.*

These new subsidiary coins with bank and Dominion notes now formed the main circulating medium and there was only one major innovation before the First World War. Until 1908 Canadian coins were struck at the Royal Mint in London or by Heaton of Birmingham (later The Mint, Birmingham, Ltd). In that year the Ottawa branch of the Royal Mint was opened and began to produce the Canadian coinage and Imperial sovereigns. The sovereigns were of exactly the same design as the London mint coins but for the addition of a small letter "**C**" on the reverse. It was also intended that the new mint should convert Canada's growing gold resources into dollar denominated coins and from 1912 two gold denominations ($10 and $5) were struck. Although sovereigns continued in issue at Ottawa until 1919 the Canadian gold coins ceased issue in 1914 when notes issued by the Dominion Government ceased to be redeemable in gold. Ottawa broke its ties with the Royal Mint in 1931 to become the Royal Canadian Mint under full Dominion control.

Ottawa mint $10 1913.
Canadian gold coins introduced 1912 but ceased issue with World War One.

The silver and copper coinage introduced in the 1870s continued with little change until 1920. In that year the bronze cent was reduced in size and all the silver denominations were reduced from their original sterling fineness of 925 to one of 800. From 1922 the five cents was struck in nickel on a larger flan which was then similar to the United States "nickel" in both fabric and metal content. Because of a shortage of nickel during the Second World War this was changed (in 1942) to a form of brass called "tombac" and a new flan shape (dodecagonal) was introduced so that it would not be confused with the cent. Brass was replaced by chromium-plated steel in 1944. After the war, in 1946, the five cents reverted to nickel although there was a further chromium-plated steel issue from 1951-1954. A round flan, which made the coin cheaper to produce, was reintroduced for the five cents denomination in 1963.

Although there were changes of type and monarch the other denominations suffered far less change than the five cents. The one cent was not reduced further in weight until 1980 and it was only in 1967 that rising prices led to a further reduction in the fineness of the silver coins. Patterns for the dollar were struck in 1911 but the denomination was not introduced as a currency coin until 1935. It was struck initially to celebrate the silver jubilee of George V but it began the well known series of "voyageur" dollars. The reverse depicts a canoe as used by the early fur traders and was continued as the standard reverse design for the Canadian dollar under George VI and Elizabeth II. Like the other silver denominations at that time it was struck at a millesimal fineness of 800. The reduction in the millesimal fineness of the silver coins in 1967 was from 800 to 500 but this was used only for the twenty five cents and ten cents denominations. No dollars or fifty cents were struck at that fineness before silver was replaced entirely with nickel coins at reduced weights in 1968.

Later Canadian coins

Cent 1920.

Five cents 1922.

Dollar 1935.

Fifty cents 1951

Dollar 1965.

The other provinces of British North America have similar numismatic stories to tell as they move towards decimalization and confederation. In **Nova Scotia** the currency rating of the doubloon tended to drive out silver in the early 19th century and copper was also scarce. Anonymous tokens made their appearance at about the same time as those in Canada although here there were many more named issuers of private tokens than was the case in the Canadas. Nevertheless, by 1817 there were numerous light weight tokens in circulation and in Nova Scotia it was the Provincial Government itself that took action to remedy the problem. All copper except that of the United Kingdom was to be withdrawn and a local issue of halfpence would be made to replace them. There were problems with Imperial authorization but in 1823 the Provincial Government instructed its UK agent to arrange a coinage which was probably produced in Birmingham. This was the origin of Nova Scotia's well known "thistle" coinage of halfpennies and pennies. They bore the portrait but not the name of the British monarch on the obverse and a large thistle on the reverse. The issue of 1832 continued to use the portrait of George IV but those of 1840 and 1843 show Victoria's portrait. The thistle coins were of similar fabric to British pennies and halfpennies but the next issue was different. These coins (pennies and halfpennies of 1856) were fully authorized and show the Queen's name and titles as well as her portrait. They have a floral reverse in place of the thistle and were struck in bronze. They were now smaller and lighter than their British counterparts and officially designated "tokens". It is interesting that bronze was chosen for this issue some four years before the change was made from copper to bronze in the United Kingdom and two years before it was used for the Canadian cent.

Nova Scotia would have had little problem accepting a sterling currency in the years following 1825 but was not prepared to do so unless neighbouring colonies did the same. In 1851 representatives of Canada, Nova Scotia and New Brunswick met to discuss the adoption of a uniform currency for all three provinces and agreed they should work towards that goal. Canada and New Brunswick had adopted common ratings by 1854 with $4·866 equivalent to the sovereign but in Nova Scotia British coins formed a larger part of the currency. It was decided to change to a decimal system with effect from 1st January 1860 but Nova Scotia kept her rate of $5.00 to the sovereign. This usefully allowed British silver coins to circulate as subsidiary coins in the new decimal system (the dollar was 4/-, the shilling was 25 cents) and no special silver coins were needed. The only new coins required to move onto a decimal system were therefore the bronze cent and half cent denominations (the half cent because the sixpence was equivalent to 12½ cents). The first of these are dated 1861. It would not be until after confederation that the Uniform Currency Act of 1871 extended the Canadian system to Nova Scotia and Dominion coins came into use.

Nova Scotia

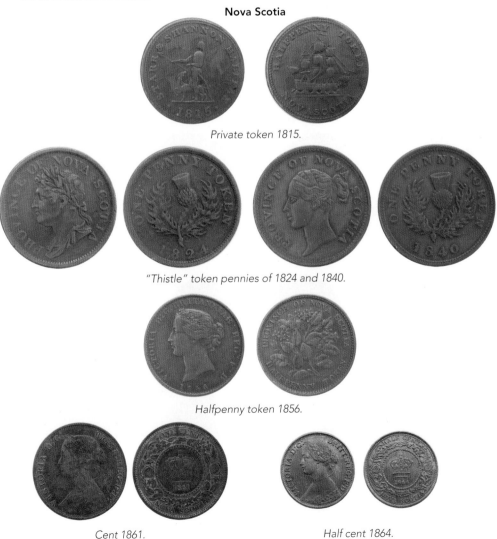

Private token 1815.

"Thistle" token pennies of 1824 and 1840.

Halfpenny token 1856.

Cent 1861.   Half cent 1864.

In **New Brunswick** various currency acts adjusted rates for the main coins in circulation with the intent always of improving matters. None of these dealt with copper coins and probably most of those in use came from neighbouring Nova Scotia. Unlike most other colonies of British North America, New Brunswick had no rash of private tokens of her own. There were complaints about the poor quality of coppers in circulation in the 1820s but this does not seem to have caused serious concern until late in the next decade. In 1840 the merchants of Saint John listed the copper coins and tokens that were acceptable, those they would take at half face value and those they would reject[11]. The Provincial Government then set about providing a copper coinage similar to that of Nova Scotia and pennies and halfpennies were struck in 1843 and 1854. There was no specific authorization from the Imperial authorities for either of these issues. The earlier pieces are designated "tokens", those of 1854 "currency".

New Brunswick moved onto the decimal system in 1860 with a subsidiary coinage in silver and bronze struck from 1861 to 1864. The denominations were 20 cents, 10 cents, 5 cents, one cent and half cent. The half cent denomination was not requested or required by New Brunswick which had different ratings to those of Nova Scotia but the Royal Mint appears to have confused the two orders. Many of the New Brunswick half cents were melted but some found their way into circulation, probably mixed with those of Nova Scotia. No further coins were struck for New Brunswick before she became a province of the Dominion but, as her currency was already aligned with that of Canada, her coins became legal tender in the Dominion from 1871.

New Brunswick

Penny token 1843.

Penny currency 1854.

Twenty cents 1862.

Ten cents 1862.

Cent 1864.

---

11 These are listed in A.B.McGullough, "Money and Exchange in Canada to 1900" 1984, p. 173. In general official British and American copper coins and the heavy British 19th century tokens were acceptable at full value. Some recently produced copies were acceptable at half face value.

After separation from Nova Scotia, **Prince Edward Island** retained the Halifax rating of 5/- for the Spanish dollar but it was not until 1813 that an Order in Council first gave currency ratings for other coins. This Order gave the British Bank of England dollar[12] a rating of 6/- but retained the 5/- rate for Spanish and other dollars. At the same time the arrangements detailed in Chapter five were made to cut and countermark Spanish dollars, the outer ring and central dump between them to circulate at 6/-. For many years coins then seem to have circulated at rates dictated by circumstance and convenience until new rates were laid down in 1849. In that year the main gold and silver coins of the day were all given full legal tender at rates well above their sterling value. Copper coins of the United Kingdom were made current up to a legal tender limit of 1/6d as were the good weight coppers of Canada, Nova Scotia and New Brunswick. The rates laid down in the 1849 Act led to sterling silver, over rated against the dollar, becoming the dominant coins in circulation.

The tokens that can be attributed to Prince Edward Island date to the 1840s and 1850s and are of a different fabric to the better coppers of the other provinces. Generally lighter, they probably passed as halfpennies but one of the few to show a denomination is designated a "cent".

Prince Edward Island passed a Decimal Currency Act in 1871. The US gold dollar became the unit of account with the sovereign legal tender at $4·866 as in Canada and New Brunswick. British silver coins with limited legal tender continued in use but their unwieldy ratings (the shilling was 24 cents) soon led to their replacement with Canadian silver coins. The only specific denomination thought necessary for decimalization in Prince Edward Island was the cent which replaced the old copper coins. This was struck in 1871 and went into circulation the next year. Although Prince Edward Island entered confederation in 1873 the provisions of the Dominion's Uniform Currency Act were not extended to her until 1881[13].

Prince Edward Island

One cent token 1855.   Token 1857.

Cent 1871.

---

12 *The Bank of England dollars were overstruck on Spanish dollars for circulation in Great Britain to relieve the great shortage of British silver coins at this time.*

13 *The Uniform Currency Act of 1871 was aimed specifically at Nova Scotia and made arrangements for Manitoba. It did not automatically apply to new provinces joining the Dominion and had to be extended to the Northwest Territories in 1875 and to British Columbia and Prince Edward Island in 1881.*

In the paragraphs above we have examined the coins and tokens in use in the colonies that formed and joined the Dominion of Canada. It must be remembered that in all of them paper currency in various forms (treasury notes, bank notes, etc) was often the largest part of the circulating currency during the 19th century but this is beyond the scope of this book. It must also be noted that in all these colonies the change to the decimal system was accompanied by a change from sterling accounting to accounts in dollars and cents.

In the territories under the control of the **Hudson's Bay Company** various accounting practices had been in use. For its main accounts the Company naturally used sterling but in its dealings with trappers and Native Americans other systems developed. One of them, the "made beaver", was in fact commodity money but soon became a unit of account. It was originally the value of a prime adult beaver pelt prepared (made up) and ready for sale. The number of pelts delivered to the Company's forts would be recorded and the person supplying them could take goods from the store to the equivalent value. Early records show that a shirt could be acquired for two made beavers, a pistol for seven. The numismatic relevance of this is that in the 1850s, in an effort to reduce bookkeeping, the Company experimented with an issue of "made beaver" tokens in brass. They were of four denominations (one, half, quarter and eighth) but do not seem to have been a great success. The issue did not become general and was restricted to the East Main District. Nevertheless, in its solely commercial role in the 20th century, the Company would again issue tokens for several of its stores and trading posts, some denominated in made beaver, others in cents.

Hudson's Bay Company

Made beaver and half made beaver tokens for East Main District. All these tokens show NB in error for MB (made beaver).

Another quite unusual issue from the territories once controlled by the Company was that of gold coins in **British Columbia**. This region became a colony in 1858, mainly because of the discovery of gold. The miners found it extremely difficult to exchange gold for the small amount of coin in circulation. Although some sterling silver was sent to the colony to ease the situation it must have seemed reasonable to Governor Douglas that some of the miners' gold should be struck into coins. He had before him the example of gold coins and tokens struck in California under similar circumstances and agreed (in 1861) to the setting up of a mint at the New Westminster Assay Office. A few specimen $20 and $10 coins were struck but the Governor called a halt. He was perhaps aware of the controversy that had arisen when the Adelaide Assay Office attempted a similar exercise a few years earlier[14]. The mint never went into regular use and the coins did not go into circulation.

---

14 See below, Chapter thirteen.

A decimal currency act came into force in Vancouver Island on 1st January 1863 and a similar act came into force for British Columbia in 1866. A new Decimal Currency Act for the combined colony was passed in 1867 and was based on the previous acts.

The bringing of all these vast territories into the Dominion brought uniformity, if a little less interest, to the coins of British North America. In fact a quick examination of the 19th century tokens and coins of the area that became Canada will initially appear quite uninteresting. Numerous copper tokens, including spurious pieces, from private issuers, the banks and the provinces themselves are followed by silver and bronze coins subsidiary to the dollar. The only interest perhaps seems to be the cut dollars and dumps of Prince Edward Island. However, a study of the various currency problems reveals that the actual circulating medium was far more diverse. Doubloons, johannes, guineas, sovereigns, Louis d'or, American gold, Spanish dollars and a variety of other silver and copper coins were all part of the total metallic circulation. While this book looks primarily at British colonial coins and tokens a study, and indeed a collection, of them cannot and should not ignore the various foreign coins current through proclamation, act, authorization or custom. They were often a major part of the circulation and are therefore a large part of the story.

Newfoundland did not become part of the Dominion of Canada until 31st March 1949. For many years colonial development was slow and until the 19th century much of Newfoundland's trade was conducted by barter. The Spanish dollar was in use and by 1811 both merchants and government were accepting it at the Halifax rate of 5/-.

The Imperial Order in Council of 1825 rating the dollar at 4/4d was accepted by the Newfoundland government who reverted to true sterling for their accounts. The commercial community though continued to rate the dollar at 5/- and thus two currency systems arose. This was further complicated when the Imperial authorities adjusted the sterling rate for the dollar to 4/2d in 1838 and Newfoundland retained the 4/4d rate. Coins other than the dollar were not officially rated until currency laws of the 1850s which were finally confirmed by the Home Government in 1857.

Shortages of small change seem to have been met by the import of various copper coins and tokens by individuals and traders. From about 1840 some tokens were being issued by local merchants and soon large numbers were being imported, particularly those of Prince Edward Island.

Newfoundland

Private token 1841.
Rutherford's of St John's.

The Decimal Currency Act of 1863 allowed for all coins to be rated in dollars and cents, the sovereign at $4·80. This made the Spanish dollar equal to 4/2d sterling. Decimal coins in all metals were authorized and public accounts were also to be in dollars and cents. The Act came into effect on 2nd January 1865 and coins of two dollars, twenty cents, ten cents, five cents and one cent went into circulation in that year. A fifty cents denomination was added in 1870. The coins were struck at the Royal Mint supplemented when necessary by issues from Heaton's Birmingham Mint.

Newfoundland's dollar was based on the gold equivalent of the Spanish silver dollar. It therefore differed from those of Canada and New Brunswick which were based on the US gold dollar. This is why Newfoundland issued her own regular gold coins (she chose the two dollars denomination) while the other provinces, where US gold had unlimited legal tender, did not need to do so. The 4/2d rate for the dollar made the new copper cent exactly equal to the British halfpenny. The general public was very slow to adopt decimal accounting and a new currency act was passed in 1887 encouraging its use.

Because of weakness in Newfoundland's economy and possible mismanagement her two main banks failed in December 1894. They had many depositors at the time and their notes were a major part of the circulation. The government guaranteed redemption of the notes at reduced rates and the banks were wound up. All this caused great hardship and the possibility that Newfoundland would join the Dominion but in the end she weathered the storm and retained her separate status. Canadian banks though immediately opened branches in Newfoundland and because of the slight difference between the Canadian and Newfoundland dollars the two currencies had to be equalized to allow their notes to circulate freely. In 1895 Canadian currency, based on the US gold dollar, thus became also the standard of Newfoundland. The whole of British North America was now on the same standard which was also the standard of the United States: a sovereign was equal to $4·866.

Nevertheless, apart from the gold two dollars which ceased issue in 1888, the separate coinage for Newfoundland continued as before. The denominations differed in one respect from those of Canada in that Newfoundland still issued a twenty cent denomination. The Dominion of Canada had replaced this with a twenty five cents coin in 1870 in line with United States practice. The continued existence of the twenty cents denomination in Newfoundland often caused confusion in Canada where it also circulated. In 1917, during the First World War, the Newfoundland coins began to be struck at the Ottawa Mint and as no new twenty cents coins had been required since 1912 the opportunity was taken of replacing it with the twenty five cents. Both this and the fifty cents denomination ceased issue completely in 1919. The smaller silver coins (ten cents and five cents) continued in issue until 1947 although the millesimal fineness was reduced from 925 to 800 with the issue of 1945. The bronze cent was reduced in size in 1938 and this also continued in issue until 1947. These later coins came mostly from the Ottawa Mint, some from London.

Newfoundland Decimal coinage introduced from 1865

Gold two dollars 1882.

Fifty cents 1899.   *Twenty cents 1882.*

Ten cents 1872.   *Cent 1865.*

Later coins.

Cent Edward VII 1904.

Twenty cents 1912.   *Twenty five cents 1917.*

Ten cents 1947.   *Cent 1941.*

SUMMARY FOR BRITISH NORTH AMERICAN COINS AND TOKENS

1763 Spanish dollar and French coins in use. Sterling accounting.

1800 Halifax rate of five shillings per dollar in general use (a few years later in Newfoundland).

1812 Tokens begin to be imported to Canada from about this time, a little later in the maritime colonies. Large issues of tokens continued to 1850s, some by banks.

1825 Attempt to introduce sterling at 4/4d per dollar by UK Order in Council.

1838 Order in Council of 1825 revoked for colonies and possessions in America and the West Indies. New Order in Council made for West Indies and British Guiana only. There was no further Imperial legislation for sterling coins in North America.

1853 Canada decides to introduce decimal coins subsidiary to the US gold dollar. Dollar accounting introduced.

1858 Province of Canada decimal coins introduced.

1860 Nova Scotia and New Brunswick adopt decimal currency but at different rates. The Nova Scotia rate of 4/- per dollar allowed her to continue using sterling silver coins as divisions of the dollar but bronze cents and half cents were introduced (1861). New Brunswick adopted the same rate as Canada and introduced her own decimal denominations in bronze (1861) and silver (1862).

1865 Newfoundland decimal coins introduced after an Act of 1863. Her dollar is different from that of the United States and Canada so a gold denomination is required as well as silver and bronze.

1867 New Brunswick and Nova Scotia join Canada to form the Dominion of Canada. Their separate coinages cease.

1870 Dominion coinage introduced.

1871 Prince Edward Island adopts decimal currency at same rate as the Dominion. She strikes her own bronze cent but continues to use sterling silver at awkward rates.

1873 Prince Edward Island joins the Dominion. The Dominion coinage and that of Newfoundland are henceforth the only coinages for British North America.

1935 Silver dollar denomination introduced in Canada.

1949 Newfoundland joins the Dominion (her last coins are dated 1947).

1968 Silver replaced with nickel for the Canadian coinage.

The main **Caribbean** colonies in the 19th century were:
Jamaica.
Barbados.
The Leeward Islands of St Kitts, Nevis, Antigua, Montserrat and the Virgin Islands.
The Windward Islands of St Lucia, St Vincent, Grenada and Tobago.
Dominica (geographically between the Windward and Leeward Islands).
Trinidad.
British Guiana (formed in 1831 from Berbice together with Essequibo and Demerara).
British Honduras (which became a colony in 1862).

The French islands of Guadeloupe and Martinique lay north and south of Dominica. Both were in British hands from time to time as a result of the French wars but both were finally restored to France in 1816. Curaçao was also in British hands during the Napoleonic war and was returned to the Dutch in the same year. As well as the main colonies there were several smaller territories and to the north-east of the Caribbean lay the Bahamas and Bermuda.

Although the Caribbean colonies were a diverse group they had much in common. As smaller colonies scattered among those of other nations and with large slave majorities they had often felt less secure than the mainland colonies to the north so had naturally tended to be more dependent on the mother country. The period from 1815 to 1914 was one of peace during which these colonies could feel territorially more secure. Nevertheless a number of circumstances combined to shake the social and economic fabric of most of them.

The main product of these colonies was sugar which was produced by slave labour. Over the years there had been an increasing market for this product in Britain, Europe and North America making the plantations extremely profitable and the sugar producing colonies very important. The recent wars though had disrupted that market and the disruption proved to be more than temporary. Napoleon's blockade of Europe had encouraged farmers there to produce sugar from beet and this unwelcome competition would not go away. The abolition of slavery deprived the planters of their traditional source of labour and they soon discovered that the emancipated slaves preferred subsistence farming to paid work on the plantations. To secure a regular work force indentured labour had to be imported, mainly from India, at some expense[15]. Britain's subsequent moves towards free trade eventually removed all colonial preferences and seriously affected the sugar producing colonies[16]. Sugar prices fell and late in the century reached crisis point when increased export bounties were placed on sugar beet by European governments. With no cheap labour and no preferential tariff the British colonies could not compete with the slave produced sugar of Cuba or Brazil. Nor could they compete with the increased production of European sugar beet.

The 19th century was thus a period of economic difficulty and decline in the British West Indies which could only begin to be reversed when crops were diversified. In 1900 though the largest product of the British West Indies was still sugar and by 1914 the Caribbean colonies, now considered the *"slums of the Empire"*[17], accounted for very little of Britain's total trade. All this was in stark contrast to developments elsewhere in the Empire and in Britain itself. Sugar had lost the importance it once had and the sugar colonies had not adapted.

The depressed state of these colonies in the 19th century together with the social effects of abolition led to hardship, disappointment and unrest. These and other problems led to tensions which occasionally erupted into quite serious disturbances. The worst of these were in British Guiana in 1856, in Jamaica (Morant Bay) in 1865 and in Barbados in 1876.

The long established sugar colonies had representative government through their elected assemblies and were proud of this long tradition. In the years following abolition the planters attempted to keep control of these assemblies by adjusting the franchise to their own advantage. Over the years however this did not prevent the election of increasing numbers of middle class coloured and Jewish members whose prime interests were commerce and business rather than plantation. There was thus no guarantee of continued support for the

---

15 *From the ending of slavery to the First World War it has been estimated that more than 400,000 "East Indians" arrived in the West Indies as indentured labourers. Many of them chose not to return home.*
16 *Particularly the Sugar Duties Act 1846.*
17 *A turn of phrase attributed to David Lloyd George. In fact Joseph Chamberlain when Colonial Secretary referred to Britain's Caribbean colonies as "the Empire's darkest slum" in the 1890s.*

plantation system within the assemblies. The home authorities though and the governors they appointed felt that the system most likely to ensure the economic survival of the sugar colonies was the traditional plantation. They thus tended to side with the planters. The various factions within the West Indian assemblies made government extremely difficult and if the plantations were to continue to provide profit, revenue and employment there would have to be stronger executive government. The example of newer colonies like British Guiana and Trinidad which had not advanced from Crown colony status was plain to see. It was largely to secure the plantation system and to attract the investment required to make it work that political change began to be considered. At a time when the white settler colonies in North America, Australasia and Southern Africa were achieving responsible government this was not an easy decision for the Home Government to take without very good reason. The catalyst for change came with the uprising at Morant Bay, Jamaica in 1865.

The rebellion (for such it was) was brutal but short. Officials and others were beaten to death and firearms plundered. The colonial authorities were mindful of the events which had created the neighbouring Haitian Republic some years earlier and of the more recent mutiny in India. Their reaction (perhaps overreaction) to what was essentially a local uprising was therefore swift and ruthless in order to prevent its spread. More than 400 of those suspected of taking part in the rebellion were executed, some without trial, many more were flogged and homes were burnt. Jamaica's handling of the rebellion was severely criticized and this led quickly to constitutional change. The Governor suggested to the Assembly that it should abolish itself to allow a stronger executive government. Knowing that this was in the planters' interests, perhaps chastened by recent events and knowing also that the British Government was prepared to act, the Assembly agreed. Jamaica lost her ancient institution without a fight and became a Crown colony in 1866.

This decision by Jamaica strongly influenced the other Caribbean colonies and by the late 1870s all of them had reverted to Crown colony government except Barbados. Following emancipation Barbados had not suffered change to the same extent as other colonies. With little spare land many of the ex slaves had little alternative but to accept paid work and, although there were other problems, the plantation system was little changed. Unlike the other sugar colonies, Barbados retained her elected assembly for the remainder of the colonial period. The others continued to be Crown colonies well into the 20th century.

There were attempts during the 19th century to group several of the colonies together for ease of administration. The main groupings would be the Leeward Islands, the Windward Islands and the colonies tied administratively to Jamaica but arrangements were fluid. The Leeward Islands, with a long history of association, were divided into two groups in 1816 but reunited in 1833. Dominica became part of the new union but would eventually (1940) be transferred to the Windwards. The Windward Islands were also formally united in 1833 although St Lucia did not join them until 1838. Barbados, the only sugar colony to have retained her elected Assembly, left the Windward Islands in 1885 to become a separate administration. In 1888 arrangements were made for Tobago to leave the Windward Islands for union with Trinidad with effect from 1st January 1889. To the west, the logwood cutters (or "Baymen") on the mainland had, for many years, been the responsibility of the Governor of Jamaica. When their settlement became the colony of British Honduras in 1862 this continued to be the case and she had a Lieutenant Governor responsible to the Governor of Jamaica. In 1884 this connection was finally severed and British Honduras became a separate Crown colony.

Although they had much in common the Caribbean colonies had differences too and attempts to form a union of all of them would never succeed. By the early 20th century there were seven administrative units in the Caribbean which would remain largely intact until after the Second World War. These were:-

Jamaica with its dependencies of Turks and Caicos and the Caymans.
Barbados
The Leeward Islands of St Kitts, Nevis, Antigua (with Barbuda and Redonda), Montserrat, Anguilla and the Virgin Islands.
The Windward Islands of Dominica, St Lucia, St Vincent and Grenada (with the Grenadines).
Trinidad and Tobago
British Guiana
British Honduras
Outside the Caribbean but in the same part of the world lay the Crown colonies of the Bahamas and Bermuda.

In most of these colonies the circulating coinage was in the unsatisfactory state described in Chapter five with cut and countermarked silver at various rates and gold (often plugged) at standards that differed across the region. The Spanish pistareen circulated freely. It was shortcomings such as these that prompted the Home Government to take action and, in 1825, to attempt the introduction of sterling silver as currency throughout the Empire.

As in North America, the erroneous rate selected for the Spanish dollar and the failure to rate the doubloon caused problems. In the West Indies though and in British Guiana the new rate of 4/2d per dollar and a rate of 64/- for the doubloon was applied by the Order in Council and Proclamation of 14th September 1838 and this generally gave the required result. Each of the colonies had its own particular currency problems and each had its own administration, even those that were grouped together in the Leeward and Windward Islands. The various measures that were taken to introduce sterling therefore differed in timing and in content in each of them. In general sterling coins were introduced from 1825 and began to replace the assortment of Spanish coins, "anchor" money and cut and countermarked coins in use. In some of the colonies this process was complete or almost so even before the remedial measures of 1838 and by the 1850s nearly all had sterling currencies. Some of the Assemblies expressed misgivings at the unlimited legal tender given to sterling silver but this was largely disregarded by the Home Government. US gold was made legal tender throughout the West Indies in 1853 and Australian gold was given legal tender status throughout the Empire in 1866. A decline in the gold price of silver in 1876 made it possible to import silver dollars to the colonies at a lower price than the 4/2d specified in 1838. To prevent the reinstatement of the dollar in the currencies where it was still legal tender most of the Caribbean colonies therefore demonetized Spanish, Mexican and Columbian dollars in the late 1870s.

We must now look at the particular problems faced by each of the colonies.

In 1825 the area that would become **British Guiana** was administered as two separate colonies and Dutch denominations were still in use. Essequibo and Demerara was a single administration and Berbice was the other. The currency of Berbice was mainly paper but we have seen (Chapter six) that this was not the case in Essequibo and Demerara. Here a coinage in guilder denominations was in issue from 1809 and in fact this continued in spite of the 1825 Order in Council designed to introduce sterling throughout the colonies. Sterling silver sent to the colony simply would not stay in circulation while the dollar was rated at 4/4d. The guilder denomination coins remained in circulation because their intrinsic value was less than their currency value and the home Government reluctantly agreed to further issues of those coins. The three guilders denomination was useful because the Spanish dollar was accepted as its equivalent in the money of account. Interestingly, although Berbice joined the other two colonies to form British Guiana in 1831 these coins continue to bear the legend "**DEMERARY & ESSEQUIBO**". Only in 1836 was the correct "**BRITISH GUIANA**" legend substituted.

In spite of the 1838 adjustment to the value of the dollar very little sterling circulated in British Guiana before 1850 and it was not until the 1870s that sterling became the main coinage in circulation. Even so old traditions died hard. As noted in Chapter six the Imperial fourpence had become popular in British Guiana where it had been equivalent to a bitt (¼ guilder). It continued to be a popular denomination among the sterling coins imported and when the supply dried up the Imperial currency fourpence of 1888 was struck specifically for British Guiana. A further fourpence, this time actually named for "**BRITISH GUIANA AND WEST INDIES**" was struck in 1891 and further coins of this denomination were struck until 1945. In 1917 this denomination ceased to be legal tender in the West Indies and the legend was reduced to "**BRITISH GUIANA**".

Accounts in British Guiana were kept in guilders until an Ordinance of 1839 changed it to dollars. This was intended as a temporary measure while sterling accounting was introduced but although Spanish, Mexican and Columbian dollars ceased to be legal tender in 1876, the dollar continued to be the money of account for the rest of the colonial period.

BRITISH GUIANA

Three Guilders 1832, still for "Essequibo and Demerary".

Guilder 1836.

Imperial fourpence 1888.

Fourpence 1891 for "British Guiana and West Indies".

Private token for British Guiana (c.1900) showing continued popular use of dollar denominations.

British Honduras differed from the other Caribbean colonies in several respects. This region did not formally become a British colony until 1862, it did not grow sugar and it did not adopt sterling as its currency. For many years the logwood cutters on this coast had been under the general oversight of the Governor of Jamaica. Logwood (mahogany) was used as commodity money but any transactions involving coin were in the currency of Jamaica. In theory sterling would thus have been introduced in 1825 and the currency should have been that of the United Kingdom from 1840. Because of its proximity to the states of Central America the settlement was clearly in a currency area outside the influence of sterling and in 1855 it was decided to keep its public accounts in dollars and reales. The dollar was rated at 4/-. In 1864 the money of account was adjusted to "dollars and cents". The fall in silver prices in the 1870s led not to the demonetization of the silver dollar (as happened elsewhere) but to the adoption by British Honduras of a silver standard. Legislation of 1887 made the dollar of Guatemala the standard for the colony and other South American dollars were rated as equal to it. The Mexican dollar was rated at 108 cents but as this led to difficulties that coin and its parts were demonetized in 1889. The silver standard not being found ideal and trade increasing with the United States the US gold dollar was made the standard of value in 1894.

In 1885 a bronze one cent coin was struck for use in the colony which was one hundredth of the silver dollar but in 1894 it became necessary to introduce coins that were subsidiary to the US gold dollar. Silver subsidiary denominations of 50 cents, 25 cents, 10 cents and 5 cents were introduced at the same weight and fineness as the Canadian coinage (which was also subsidiary to the US gold dollar). The British Honduras cent was much larger than its Canadian counterpart but for the moment continued in issue as it was. Only in 1914 was it reduced to the same weight and approximate size as the Canadian cent.

BRITISH HONDURAS (LATER BELIZE)

Cent 1888. Fifty cents 1897.

Cent 1950

Fifty cents 1954 (British Honduras). Fifty cents 1975 (Belize).

With some adjustments all these denominations continued in issue until 1980. The silver coins were struck at the sterling millesimal fineness of 925 but in 1907 the five cents was changed to cupro-nickel and struck on a larger flan. In 1942 it was changed again, to nickel-brass. The other silver denominations continued at sterling fineness until a complete change was made to cupro-nickel in 1952. The bronze cent was produced on a much smaller flan from 1954 and on a scalloped flan from 1956

On 1 June 1973, in the run up to independence, the colony's name was changed to Belize and the legend on the coins was changed to reflect this. On the reverse of the coins **BELIZE** replaces **BRITISH HONDURAS** but the coinage continued, otherwise unchanged, until just before full independence in 1981.

In **Jamaica**, by 1810, currency rates were measured against the dollar rather than the doubloon. The dollar was usefully rated at 6/8d currency which gave the Spanish American real a rate of 10d and made three dollars equal to exactly one pound currency. The doubloon was accepted at 16 dollars giving it the awkward currency rate of £5-6-8d. By 1817 though most of the doubloons and dollars in circulation had been exported for commerce and the actual currency consisted of small silver. Although some copper tokens had been issued in Jamaica in the 18th century it had until now been a prosperous colony and the smallest coin in use appears to have been the silver half real at 5d currency. When British silver and copper was introduced in 1825 the copper coins were therefore an innovation. There seems to have been little need for them and even an aversion to them. The shilling though was popularly rated at a quarter dollar giving it currency at 1/8d with other sterling silver in proportion. This meant that in Jamaica the doubloon (16 dollars) was equal to 64/-, the rate that would be specified in the Order in Council and Proclamation of 1838. This equitable rating against the doubloon gave sterling silver an advantage over the dollar and by the 1830s British shillings and sixpences formed the main metallic currency. There was though a great deal of paper in circulation by that time.

Jamaica was one of the first colonies to show concern at the unlimited legal tender of sterling (token) silver and in 1837 attempted to limit its legal tender to £5. This though was disallowed by the Home Government in 1839 by which time their new legislation concerning rates for the dollar and doubloon had come into force. A subsequent local Act decreed that from 31st December 1840 the currency of the United Kingdom should be that of Jamaica although British silver as well as gold still had unlimited legal tender. The dollar and doubloon were given their correct 1838 rates of 4/2d and 64/-. Here the silver dollar was demonetized in 1876.

By mid century Jamaica had lost much of her prosperity and smaller denominations were required. The Imperial threepence and its half, the penny-halfpenny, became popular but from 1841 the legal tender of silver coins smaller than the sixpence was limited to 40/-. British copper was legal tender up to 1/- but this was still not a popular metal for coinage. In 1869 a cupro-nickel penny and halfpenny were therefore authorized and the farthing denomination was added in 1880. Although metal content and size were adjusted in 1937 and the farthing discontinued in 1952 this distinctive coinage of minor denominations for Jamaica continued until 1969, several years after independence[18]. Jamaica became an independent Commonwealth realm in 1962 but did not introduce her own decimal currency based on the Jamaica dollar until 1969. Of the old dependencies of Jamaica, Turks and Caicos adopted the US dollar as its currency in 1969 and the Cayman Islands adopted their own dollar in 1972. Both became separate Crown colonies.

---

18 From 1937 the Jamaica coins were struck in nickel-brass and the two larger denominations were reduced in size.

JAMAICA

Penny 1880.

Halfpenny 1882. Farthing 1880.

Penny 1919.

Penny 1945. Penny 1962.

The **Leeward Islands, Windward Islands and Barbados** mostly introduced sterling coins quite quickly. In fact Grenada overrated the shilling at 2/6d in 1827 effectively driving everything but sterling from circulation at that early date. In Dominica and the Virgin Islands though large numbers of the old cut coins were still in circulation and this hindered the introduction of sterling silver. In St Lucia the traditional use of French denominations was also a problem to be overcome[19]. Although sterling coins had entered circulation they were still rated in terms of the doubloon and this naturally led to some inconvenient currency rates. The fixing of the doubloon at 64/- in 1838 was useful but did not solve the problem of awkward currency rates for sterling coins. The obvious next step was to base their currencies on sterling instead of the doubloon and between 1839 and 1864 all these colonies fully assimilated their currencies to it, Montserrat being the last to formally adopt sterling denominations. All of them demonetized the silver dollar over the period 1876 to 1882.

19 *The last of Dominica's old cut coins were removed from circulation in 1862. In the Virgin Islands the final withdrawal did not take place until 1892. St Lucia's final withdrawal of cut coins took place in 1851.*

Tobago was part of the Windward Islands group until joined to Trinidad in 1889. When sterling coins were introduced following the 1825 Order in Council Tobago did not give them currency rates as did other colonies at this time. Instead she adopted sterling denominations and gave the dollar the currency rate of 4/4d laid down in the Order. The doubloon was rated at 69/4d (16 dollars). As both of these rates overvalued the Spanish coins sterling did not remain in circulation. The remedial legislation of 1838 allowed sterling silver to become the main circulating medium. In the colonies the proclamations announcing imperial legislation were of necessity somewhat delayed. In Tobago US gold coins were made legal tender in 1854 and Australian gold in 1871. The silver dollar was demonetized in 1879.

The 1825 Order in Council was brought into force in **Trinidad** (by Proclamation of the Governor) on 1st January 1826. At that time there was a shortage of small silver but the overrating of the dollar at 4/4d led to the immediate re-export of British silver. The revised rates of 1838 did not immediately improve matters but by 1850 British coins were in general circulation. At no time though did Trinidad specifically prescribe sterling denominations of account. Government accounts were kept in both sterling and dollar currency and most private accounts continued to use the dollar and the cent. US gold was admitted as legal tender in 1853 and Australian gold in 1866. The silver dollar was demonetized in 1876.

Late 19th century tokens of Trinidad showing varied use of currency

Half stampee (one cent) token of H.E.Rapsey.   *Farthing token of J.G.D'ade.*

It will be noticed that although sterling coins came into use throughout the West Indies the Spanish dollar continued to exert a great deal of influence and currency of the United States began to do the same. Nevertheless, by the end of the 19th century all the West Indian islands and British Guiana were using sterling coins. These coins were supplied to the colonies at full face value, the profit accruing to the Royal Mint. We will examine this in more detail in Chapter nine when we look at how this was dealt with in West Africa. There, and in later chapters, we will see that some colonies took responsibility for their own issues of sterling coins allowing them to secure the profits of coinage for themselves. They did this through the establishment of Currency Boards but the coins issued under these arrangements could only be legal tender in the colony concerned and therefore had to be of distinctive design. The individual West Indian colonies were too small to make arrangements of this sort but the quantity of sterling coins imported could be reduced by the issue of Government currency notes. These began to appear in some West Indian colonies in the early 20th century but interestingly most of them were denominated in dollars. They were legal tender at the historic rate of 4/2d sterling per dollar and, together with sterling coins, formed the currency of the West Indies until after the Second World War.

By that time the notes of several of the islands had become legal tender throughout the region and something had to be done to regularize these unusual arrangements. In 1946 a West Indian Currency Conference was held in Barbados which recommended that the currency of British Guiana and all the British Caribbean islands with the exception of Jamaica and its dependencies should be unified. The unit of currency would be a British West Indian dollar of the value of 4/2d sterling and a Regional Currency Board would be established to manage it.

The British Caribbean Currency Board was duly set up in 1950 and began issuing its own notes in dollar denominations in 1951. Until 1955, the British West Indian dollar existed only as paper money and sterling coins continued to circulate with it. In that year though, the Currency Board introduced a decimal coinage to replace the sterling coins. The 50 cents, 25 cents and 10 cents were struck in cupro-nickel, the 5 cents in nickel-brass and the 2 cents, cent and ½ cent in bronze. The 4/2d rate for the dollar was continued making the one cent denomination exactly equivalent to a British halfpenny. The new coins bore the legend **BRITISH CARIBBEAN TERRITORIES EASTERN GROUP** but only remained in issue until 1965. It was during this period (in 1961) that the British Virgin Islands, part of the Leewards group, left the arrangement and adopted the US dollar as its currency.

Decimal divisions of the British West Indian dollar

Fifty cents 1965.   *Two cents 1965.*

This was now a period of political change as some of the colonies moved to independence and the old Currency Board was superseded (in 1965) by the East Caribbean Currency Authority. The British West Indian dollar was replaced at par with the East Caribbean dollar. This continued to be pegged to sterling at 4/2d until 1976 after which it was pegged instead to the United States dollar. The end of the old sterling rate for the dollar laid down in 1838 is a fitting place to bring our story of the British West Indies coins to a close.

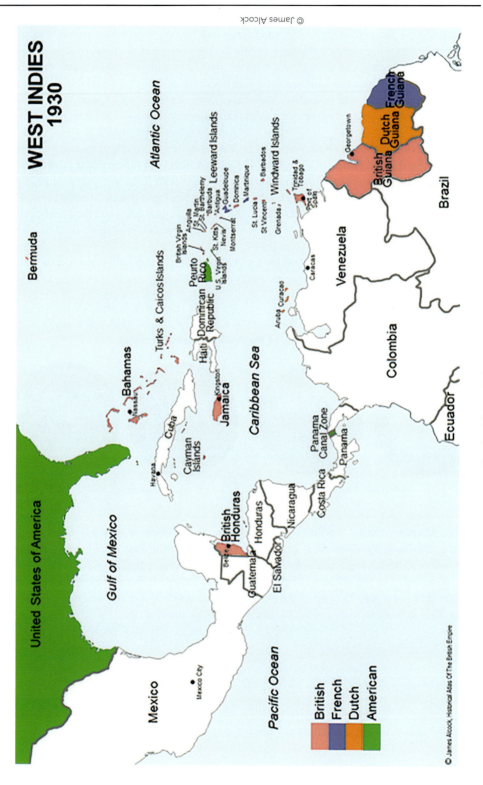

The Caribbean Colonies

SUMMARY FOR
BRITISH WEST INDIES COINAGE

1800 Cut, countermarked and plugged coins in use.

1825 Attempt to introduce sterling at 4/4d per dollar

1838 Dollar rate adjusted to 4/2d. Doubloon rated at 64/-.

1850 Sterling well established in most colonies by this time but not until about 1870 in British Guiana.

1869 Jamaica adopts cupro-nickel versions of the bronze sterling denominations.

1876 Decline in price of silver led to demonetization of the dollar in most colonies by 1882 (but not in British Honduras).

1887 British Honduras adopts the silver dollar of Guatemala as its standard.

1894 British Honduras adopts US gold dollar as its standard and introduces subsidiary decimal coins.

1950 British Caribbean Currency Board (BCCB) established for Leeward Islands, Windward Islands, Barbados, Trinidad and Tobago and British Guiana. Jamaica and its dependencies were not part of this arrangement. The common currency is the British West Indies dollar represented initially by paper money only.

1955 BCCB introduce decimal coins subsidiary to the British West Indies dollar to replace the sterling coins in circulation.

1962 Jamaica becomes independent as a Commonwealth realm but continues to use sterling coins until decimalization in 1969.

1965 BCCB superceded by East Caribbean Currency Authority (ECCA). East Caribbean dollar replaces the British West Indies dollar at par and BCCB decimal coinage ceases. (The ECCA would issue its own decimal coins in 1981).

1973 British Honduras changes its name to Belize. Its coinage continued as before and was never associated with the East Caribbean dollar.

1976 The East Caribbean dollar ends its historic peg to sterling.

Beyond the Caribbean and outside the sphere of the East Caribbean dollar were the Bahamas and Bermuda. In the **Bahamas** the currency in 1825 was mainly Spanish. The currency rates then assigned to British coins were based, as in the Caribbean colonies, on the 4/4d laid down for the Spanish dollar in the 1825 Order in Council. As happened elsewhere sterling disappeared from circulation as soon as it was issued. By 1828 large importations of the Spanish pistareen were driving other coins (gold and silver) out of circulation too. When the corrected rates for the dollar and doubloon were brought in the Bahamas legislature almost immediately (November 1838) enacted that sterling should be the local money of account. In private transactions there was some reluctance to give up the dollar or the old currency ratings but by 1850 British coins were well established. Speculative importations of

US silver fractions and Mexican dollars in the 1870s threatened the continued use of British coins until, in 1881, the Bahamas followed the lead of other colonies and demonetized the silver dollar. More sterling silver (with unlimited legal tender) was brought in to replace them. The Bahamas' main commercial partner though was the United States and although British silver remained the main subsidiary circulation it was generally accepted that the US gold dollar was, in practice, the local standard of value. In 1966 the Bahamas adopted a decimal currency with its dollar pegged and exactly equal to that of the United States.

The currency of **Bermuda** in 1825 was similar to that of the Bahamas. However, on the introduction of sterling the shilling gained popular acceptance as a quarter dollar as had also happened in Jamaica. As the doubloon was 16 dollars this put the shilling (at 64 to the doubloon) in an almost exactly correct relationship to it and it was the dollar rather than sterling silver that disappeared from circulation. Following Britain's amending legislation of 1838 Bermuda enacted that the currency of the islands should be the currency of the United Kingdom with effect from 1st January 1842. The silver dollar was demonetized in 1876 and the doubloon in 1882 leaving sterling as the sole legal tender. In spite of her geographical position and trading pattern the pound sterling continued to be the official currency of Bermuda until she adopted a decimal currency in 1970. Her dollar was not pegged to that of the United States until 1972.

Also in the Americas sit (geographically) the Falkland Islands but these are best left to the beginning of the next chapter where, together with parts of Africa, we will look at all the Atlantic islands.

9

Africa and the Atlantic

BEFORE examining mainland Africa we will look at the Atlantic islands which for our purposes are the Falkland Islands, St Helena, Ascension and Tristan da Cunha.

The Falkland Islands were within the region confirmed to Spain by the ancient Treaty of Tordesillas. Spain therefore did not relinquish her claim of sovereignty when both France and Britain made their own claims through settlement in the 18th century. The French came to a financial agreement with Spain and withdrew but Britain maintained her claim by an assumed right of prior discovery[1]. Britain saw the islands as a useful base for whaling and for ships bound for the Pacific but saw them also as a threat to her shipping if they should be occupied by another power. Nevertheless, without relinquishing her claim, Britain left the Falklands in 1776 as part of a world wide plan to reduce military expenditure where possible. By 1820 the South American republics had rejected Spanish rule and in that year an American privateer licensed by the new government at Buenos Aires (the United Provinces of the River Plate) made a claim to the islands on their behalf. In 1828 the United Provinces granted East Falkland to a private venture hoping that a colony could be established and an attempt by that venture to assert a sealing monopoly led to the detention of three American sealing vessels. The American response was to send a ship of her Brazil Squadron to investigate. USS "Lexington" evacuated most of the settlers, destroyed much of the settlement and declared the islands free from all government. Britain decided it was time to revive her claim before any other power became established. In December 1832 HMS "Clio" arrived and declared sovereignty. The Captain demanded and received the surrender of a small military detachment from Buenos Aires and despite strong protests from the United Provinces British sovereignty was asserted and maintained.

Development was slow but settlers began to arrive from Britain in 1841. Ten years later the Falkland Islands Company was incorporated to develop the colony and early in 1852 received its Royal Charter. Cheviot sheep were introduced. Ships bound to and from California during the gold rush years provided a welcome boost to the colonial economy and, until the opening of the Panama Canal in 1914, Port Stanley was a busy ship repair facility on the route to the Pacific. By the time of the First World War coaling and communication facilities also made the Falkland Islands an important link in Britain's naval organization.

---

1 *The English navigator John Davis was driven among islands described as "never before discovered" in 1592. Earlier maps though show that the islands were certainly discovered before that, probably by the Portuguese, and Spain must have known of their existence. They had not however been settled so British (and French) claims to the Falklands were similar to their claims to islands not settled by Spain in the Caribbean.*

In the early years coins were not plentiful in the Falkland Islands and in 1844 the Governor was left with no alternative but to issue paper money in order to make payments. The few coins in use were mainly Spanish dollars and doubloons but the corrected rate of 4/2d for the dollar and the rate of 64/- for the doubloon were not introduced until 1849. There was a gradual introduction of sterling coins and by 1890 the circulating medium was almost entirely British silver and copper. No coins were struck specifically for the Falkland Islands during this period.

The various territories that came to be dependencies of the Falkland Islands were little more than sealing and whaling grounds and (later) bases for scientific observation and Antarctic exploration. These were South Georgia and the South Sandwich Islands (discovered by Captain James Cook in 1775), the South Orkney Islands, the South Shetlands and Graham's Land (later "Graham Land"). All of these were declared dependencies of the Falkland Islands in 1908 but none of them have a numismatic history.

St Helena was in the hands of the East India Company until 1834 although it was not until 1836, when the new governor arrived, that the handover could be put into effect. It had been a calling point for the Company's ships from Europe and all over the East and, as would be expected in such a place, a variety of coins circulated. The Spanish dollar was a favourite but silver and copper coin from India, Chinese cash and anything else that could be pressed into circulation and had a chance of staying in the island was welcome. Accounting had always been in sterling and the Company had produced two issues of coins in sterling denominations for the island, one in 1714 the other in 1821[2].

East India Company issues for St Helena

Threepence 1714.

Halfpenny 1714. *Halfpenny 1821.*

After handover to the Crown, St Helena declined in importance. With the Cape firmly in British hands, the subsequent introduction of the steamship and the opening of the Suez Canal in 1869 the colony's original function lost its importance. However, in 1840 a Vice Admiralty Court was established to deal with vessels detained while engaged in the slave trade and for many years the island was a depot for processing liberated Africans. All of this brought some prosperity to the island.

In 1830 the Spanish dollar was rated at 4/2d and the doubloon at 64/-. At this time St Helena was still administered by the East India Company so Imperial legislation did not apply. It will be noted that these are exactly the rates that would eventually be fixed for the West Indies and British Guiana in 1838 but in 1834, when St Helena passed to the Crown, the Imperial rate for the dollar was still 4/4d. St Helena therefore had to change to this erroneous

---

2 For the period of East India Company control see Peter R. Thompson, "The East India Company and its Coins", 2010. The 1714 issue was struck at Madras and consisted of a silver threepence and the halfpenny and farthing in copper. The 1821 issue was of halfpennies only and was struck at the Soho Mint in Birmingham.

rate until the amending legislation was extended to the island in 1843. All foreign coins except the dollar and doubloon were then demonetized and replaced with sterling through the Commissariat. The silver dollar was demonetized in 1879 (because of the fall in the price of silver) and in 1880 the doubloon was also demonetized. This left only United Kingdom gold, silver and copper coins as legal tender. At the same time the legal tender limit for silver was fixed at 40/- as was the case in the United Kingdom.

Because of its isolated position St Helena provided a secure quarantine for those that Britain preferred to keep out of circulation. Between 1900 and 1902 it became the home of some 6,000 Boer prisoners of war but its most famous prisoner arrived many years earlier. On 15th October 1815 HMS "Northumberland" arrived off Jamestown and two days later her principal passenger was ferried ashore. It was hoped this was a place where Napoleon Bonaparte could be kept securely. So important was this matter that it was considered necessary to occupy any uninhabited islands within striking distance to deny their use to France in any attempt at escape. Ascension Island was occupied by British forces in October 1815 for this reason and Tristan da Cunha in August 1816. Napoleon had escaped custody before (from Elba) and no chances were being taken this time[3].

Ascension Island was administered by the Admiralty until it became a dependency of St Helena in 1922. **Tristan da Cunha** was initially administered from Cape Colony. It would become a dependency of St Helena on 12th January 1938. No currency coins were struck specifically for either of these territories.

On the continent of Africa British interests fall into three regions; West Africa, Southern Africa and East Africa. In this chapter we will look at the first two of these regions. Egypt and the Suez Canal were not part of the 19th century Empire but Britain accrued considerable economic and strategic interests there. On grounds of chronology and geography these are best examined with East Africa in the next chapter.

Beyond the Barbary coast **West Africa** was the first part of the continent to attract English adventurers and we have seen in previous chapters that the slave trade became the main reason for English (later British) activity there. In 1807 Britain banned her slave trade and from that time her interest in West Africa was changed. Sierra Leone was failing as a commercial enterprise and became a Crown colony on 1st January 1808. It was soon the centre of Britain's anti slaving activities. The Gold Coast forts which had been used for slaving continued to be run by the Company of Merchants Trading to Africa and were maintained with grants from the Government. They either had to be put to other uses or abandoned. Although the African Company adapted as far as it could to the new moral climate it had been founded to facilitate slaving and was obviously an outmoded institution. It was finally abolished by an Act of Parliament in 1821 and its forts, possessions and property passed to the Crown. The forts it had administered on the Gold Coast and the trading posts on the Gambia River were joined to Sierra Leone to form one administrative unit under the Governor of Sierra Leone at Freetown.

The main purpose of Britain's West African settlements at this time was to facilitate the work of the Royal Navy's Preventative Squadron. Only the Gambia was considered commercially viable and the British Government soon planned to abandon the Gold Coast completely. The "notes" for the Gold Coast forts, which we must remember were rented from

---

3   *Napoleon died in St Helena in 1821 and was buried in a secluded valley of his own choosing. His original tomb, beautifully maintained, is still there but in his will his preference was to be buried beside the Seine. His remains were removed from St Helena in 1840 and taken to Paris.*

local rulers, were originally in the hands of the Fante but early in the 19th century fell into the hands of the Ashanti. Although they lived inland with their capital at Kumasi the Ashanti were masters of the Gold Coast. The coastal peoples, mainly the Fante, were traditionally considered to owe them allegiance and, from time to time, the Ashanti staged punitive expeditions to the coast to remind them of this. Although not aimed at the European forts these attacks did cause major disruption to normal trading activities. In 1826, at Dodowa, one such attack was halted by a British-led alliance of coastal people and the notes for the forts passed into British hands. The value of the Gold Coast forts to Britain was open to question but she now owned them by right of conquest. If they were to be of any commercial value it was essential that some sort of agreement should be reached with the Ashanti to secure inland trade.

In 1828, rather than abandon them completely, the remaining Gold Coast forts were put back into the hands of private merchants. Like the African Company before them this Committee of Merchants received a parliamentary grant to maintain them although, for legal reasons, the forts continued to be dependencies of Sierra Leone. In 1831 these merchants agreed a treaty with the Ashanti and the coastal peoples which laid the foundation for peace on the Gold Coast for some years. This created a climate in which legitimate trade could flourish. In fact so successful were these merchants that by 1843 the British Government felt the necessity of taking direct responsibility and appointed a Governor for the Gold Coast responsible to the Governor in Chief at Freetown. The Ashanti though had made their agreement with the Committee of Merchants, not with the British Government. They were not happy with the expansion of British interests beyond the forts; a matter we must return to shortly.

Also in 1843 the Gambia was given its own government and separated from Sierra Leone. From 1850, when a growing Gold Coast was itself separated from Sierra Leone, British interests in West Africa thus comprised the three separate colonies of Gambia, Sierra Leone and Gold Coast. Legitimate trade between these colonies and other coastal states began to grow and Lagos, further east, was the seat of much of this. The slave trade still flourished there and it would not be long before the Consul appointed to oversee British interests at Lagos was urging direct control. The interests he oversaw were commercial more than philanthropic but Britain's moral stand against the slave trade was ample justification for interference. Lagos, a thriving commercial centre, became Britain's fourth West African colony in 1861.

The regions beyond Lagos which would one day become Nigeria had already attracted the attention of British merchants. Foremost among these was Macgregor Laird although his pioneering voyage of 1832-1834 was not a commercial success. It would be some years before he was again involved in the Niger trade, mainly for palm oil brought down from the interior. By the late1850s Laird had trading posts at Aboh, Laird's Port (Onitsha) and Laird's Town (Lokoja) as well as an ironclad steamer to supply them. This ship was subsidized by the British Government and also supplied up river mission stations. When Laird died in 1861 his company was wound up and the mission stations were subsequently supplied annually by the Royal Navy. Other traders though were working the Delta and would soon move further inland.

Although trade was increasing in the Niger Delta some doubt was being expressed at home about the continued usefulness of Britain's West African colonies. In the liberal climate of the day there was a general aversion to annexation and intervention in foreign lands and the main reason for Britain's presence in West Africa (policing the abolition of the slave trade) was fast disappearing. Nevertheless the Governor of the Gold Coast had built on the agreements made by the Committee of Merchants with the Fante, a "Bond" being signed by many of their leaders in 1844 recognizing British authority. The Ashanti were having none of this. The abolition of the slave trade had seriously affected their economy and they now felt isolated and shut off from the coast. Once more they began to appear in force in the coastal regions, in 1863 inflicting several defeats on British led forces before withdrawing north in triumph ahead of the rains. Trade was brought to a standstill at a time when Britain's very presence in West Africa was being questioned at home.

In 1865 a Parliamentary Select Committee was called to examine a report on the region and decide, mainly on grounds of trade, whether the West African colonies were of any further use to Britain. There were commercial interests in the region but the most promising was the trade of the Niger Delta, an area as yet outside colonial control. The Committee decided it would be in Britain's best interest to abandon all the colonies except Sierra Leone but nevertheless adopted a proposal that all four colonies should, for the time being, be cobbled together once again and administered from Freetown. The Gambia, the Gold Coast and Lagos would each have an Administrator responsible to the Governor in Chief of the West Africa Settlements (who was also the Governor of Sierra Leone). This would give greater central control over local government and when dealing with problems such as the Ashanti. The new arrangements came into force on 19th February 1866. It was agreed that there should be no further extension of colonial rule in West Africa and that most of the colonies should eventually be given up. A special case was argued when the remaining Dutch forts on the Gold Coast were taken over in 1872 as a tidying up exercise. Innocuous as this seemed it again stirred up trouble with the Ashanti who had a claim to the Dutch fort at Elmina. In 1873 they descended on the coast to make good their claim, again disrupting trade. By that time the political mood in Britain had swung to one of consolidating the Empire and it was decided to deal with the Ashanti once and for all. To do this Sir Garnet Wolseley was appointed Governor and British troops dispatched. This overwhelming force cleared the Ashanti from the coast, destroyed Kumasi and made agreement with the Asantehene based broadly on that of 1831.[4] To consolidate the British position, Gold Coast and Lagos were detached from the West Africa Settlements and constituted a single administration, the Gold Coast Colony, in 1874. Sierra Leone and Gambia continued to be called "West Africa Settlements" until they were separated from each other in 1888.

This is the way things stood in British West Africa when events began to unfold that would change imperial attitudes and perceptions completely. Until this time the colonies that formed the West Africa Settlements had been little more than the coastal ports and forts. The areas inland and upriver from these were under British protection or unofficial jurisdiction but the area and extent of this protection was not specified. In general it included the areas that traded with the coastal colony but it had never been considered necessary to stake out the exact borders. They were variable and depended largely on political convenience. On the west coast of Africa Britain had worked this way for many years more or less undisturbed by other European powers.

In 1876 Leopold II, King of the Belgians set out under the guise of philanthropy to obtain a rich portion of Africa for his country. In fact he obtained it for himself but the region would eventually become the Belgian Congo and Leopold's activities opened the eyes of others to the fact that vast areas of Africa were as yet unclaimed by the colonial powers. Soon Britain,

---

4   The Asantehene was the King of the Ashanti. There would be two more brushes with the Ashanti. In 1896 the Asantehene and members of his family were exiled to the Seychelles (St Helena was perhaps considered too close). In 1900 the Governor of the Gold Coast, pointing out that the Asantehene was unlikely to return, demanded the king's sacred symbol of office, the golden stool, causing deep resentment. Ashanti was formally annexed to Gold Coast Colony on 1st January 1902.

France, Germany and the Belgian Crown were involved in a race for influence and control throughout the continent to secure the riches of trade and mineral resources while Portugal sought to retain what she had. This "Scramble for Africa" changed the old ways forever and the emphasis now was on retaining and expanding Britain's interests rather than giving them up. Their extent had to be strictly delineated before international agreements could be reached on who owned what and the political map of Africa began to take on a strange appearance. Borders were agreed in terms of latitude and longitude for the convenience of the colonial powers instead of being based on the rivers, mountain ranges and so on that had traditionally divided the peoples of Africa.

In West Africa matters were largely settled by the Berlin Conference of 1884-1885 organized by Bismarck. Germany was new to the imperial scene and the fact that the conference was held in Berlin is a measure of her swift rise in influence. German claims to Togoland and Cameroon were recognized and there was general agreement on the borders between German, French and British interests. By that time though there was a growing realization in London that a more formal protection was needed for British interests on and around the Niger.

A Protectorate was declared over the coastal regions of the Niger and Oil Rivers in 1885 and in the next year the Royal Niger Company (previously the National African Company) was granted a Royal Charter[5]. It set about developing its own and British interests up river. It was instrumental in keeping large areas of the Niger basin out of French and German hands but in 1899 was bought out by the British Government. The areas taken over from the Company became the Protectorate of Northern Nigeria, the original Niger and Oil Rivers area becoming the Protectorate of Southern Nigeria. Lagos (now a bustling trading centre) had been separated from Gold Coast Colony in 1886 and would be joined to Southern Nigeria in 1906. Northern and Southern Nigeria were united to form the Colony and Protectorate of Nigeria on 1st January 1914, its seat of government at Lagos.

The term "colony and protectorate" was now used quite freely to describe the original settlements and the hinterlands which had been formally attached to them. By 1914 the scramble for Africa was over and the colonial powers had agreed their relative spheres of influence.

The principal coin in circulation in **Sierra Leone** in the early years of colonial administration was the Spanish dollar popularly rated at 5/-. The doubloon (16 dollars) thus passed at £4. As trade grew there was a shortage of small change and an 1822 request for copper coins resulted in a proposal to send out local copper coins which were divisions of the dollar. Only recently had anchor money silver coins been put into circulation in several British colonies and copper "cents" would have been a useful addition to the series. The fiftieth and one hundredth dollar denominations were struck but the scheme was abandoned and most of the coins melted.

"Anchor" money and proposed copper divisions

"Anchor" half dollar 1822.　　　　　　　　The fiftieth dollar (two cents) of 1823.

---
5 The term "Oil Rivers" was a general term applied to parts of the Niger Delta where palm oil was traded.

As elsewhere, sterling was introduced in 1825 and the overvaluation of the Spanish dollar at 4/4d kept British coins out of circulation. Spanish dollars were regularly cut into quarters both officially and unofficially and light and clipped quarters were soon a problem. The Sierra Leone Council attempted to remedy the situation by countermarking full weight quarters with a crowned **WR** stamp, the initials being those of <u>W</u>illiam IV <u>R</u>ex. The attempt failed because the quarter could be subsequently clipped without damaging the countermark and also because false stamps were soon in use. In 1839 the cut coins were demonetized. The presence of the cut coins as well as the over-rating of the dollar meant that dollars and doubloons were still the main coins in circulation at that time. The amended rate of 4/2d for the dollar and the rate of 64/- for the doubloon were applied by Order in Council of June 1843 to "*Sierra Leone, the River Gambia, Cape Coast, and elsewhere on the western coast of the continent of Africa*". French five franc pieces in silver and twenty franc pieces in gold were given legal tender at the same time. The fall in silver prices led to the dollar (but not the five francs) being demonetized in 1880. British sterling coins came into general use and would continue to be used until a distinctive British West African coinage, still in sterling denominations, was introduced early in the 20th century.

The Gambia, always closely associated with Sierra Leone, had a very similar currency history. Here though the proximity of the French settlements tended to give the Gambia a much larger circulation of French five franc pieces. As in Sierra Leone Spanish dollars were cut into quarters to provide small change and to discourage their export but in the Gambia the cutting of five franc pieces was also common. After demonetization of cut money in Sierra Leone much of that which had not been redeemed found its way to the Gambia where cut money continued in use until 1843.[6]

Cut and countermarked coins in West Africa

Cut and countermarked quarter dollar for Sierra Leone. *Cut quarter of a French five francs from Gambia.*

Until 1874, when it was separated from the West Africa Settlements and combined with Lagos, the laws concerning currency on the Gold Coast were generally those of Sierra Leone. In 1875 the legal tender rates of coins in the new **Gold Coast Colony** were proclaimed and were naturally those already in force - those proclaimed for Sierra Leone, etc in 1843. On the Gold Coast however there had been a long tradition of using uncoined gold by weight (the ackeys and takus noted in Chapter five) and this was still in use in 1874. It continued in use until gold dust and nuggets were finally demonetized in 1889. The Spanish dollar had already been demonetized (1880) because of the fall in the gold price of silver and in Gold Coast Colony the French five franc piece had been demonetized at the same time. By the 1890s sterling silver was the main circulation but copper coins were not in use. The threepence was the smallest denomination in circulation and cowries were still used for some smaller transactions.

---

6 David Vice, "*The Coinage of British West Africa & St Helena 1684 – 1958*" 1983, p.63.

The Gold Coast Proclamation of 1875 was specifically applied also to **Lagos** (which was now part of Gold Coast Colony) as was the demonetization of foreign silver in 1880. Sterling came into general use but in Lagos this included some copper coins.

When British merchants first began trading to the area that became **Nigeria** it was largely unknown to Europeans and did not enjoy any form of metallic currency. The cowry was in general use but was cumbersome for large payments as were the trade goods used for barter. In 1858 Macgregor Laird introduced a supply of copper tokens which would have been useful in lieu of cowries for small payments. With its value expressed as a fraction of the dollar and of the sterling penny this token would have been a useful common denominator for both currencies. At one four hundredth of a dollar and one eighth of a penny it represented the correct exchange rate between the two, a dollar being 4/2d. Sterling silver came into general use but in the Niger region, as in some other parts of West Africa, copper coins found little acceptance with the ethnic peoples. Because of this the Governor of Lagos had noted the need for a subsidiary coinage in something other than bronze for that region. Already cupro-nickel denominations from the penny downwards were in issue in Jamaica where there was a similar dislike of copper and bronze. Nigeria got a penny in cupro-nickel and tenth penny in aluminium in 1907. As aluminium proved unstable in the local climate the metal used for this denomination was changed to cupro-nickel from 1908. A halfpenny was added to the series in 1911. These coins bore the legend **NIGERIA – BRITISH WEST AFRICA**.

Beginnings of coinage in Nigeria

The Macgregor Laird token of 1858 (eighth penny, four hundredth of a dollar). *Gilruth Brothers token probably used in Lagos in 1870s (issuer unidentified).*

Nigeria tenth penny 1908 (aluminium). *Penny 1908 (cupro-nickel).*

By the later 19th century British silver coins were being imported into West Africa (and other colonies around the world) in increasing quantities. This had indeed been the intention of the legislation of 1825. Its export to the Crown colonies was handled by Crown Agents and encouraged by sending it free of the charges of packing, freight and insurance. It was possible for the Mint to do this because the silver coins were "token" in value but were charged to the colony at the full rate of £1 (i.e. one sovereign) for each 20 shillings of silver. The difference covered the costs but when the price of silver fell from the 1870s large profits began to accrue to the Mint. Colonies that became self governing had slightly different arrangements but sterling silver was still supplied at 20 shillings to the sovereign.

In 1897 the Governor of Lagos suggested that his colony should share in this profit. While this seemed reasonable and a committee was set up to examine the matter the Treasury felt that profit sharing could lead to over estimates of the silver required by the colonies. This in turn could lead to problems at home if large quantities of surplus coins (token in value) were sent back. The idea of profit sharing was therefore dropped. The alternative, which was eventually adopted for West Africa and some other sterling using colonies, was for the colony to take full responsibility for its own issues of silver and retain all the profit. To make this work each colony involved would need its own distinctive sterling coins which would not be legal tender elsewhere. For West Africa it was decided that a single such coinage would be legal tender in all the British possessions on the coast (Gambia, Sierra Leone, Gold Coast and Nigeria) and the West African Currency Board was constituted in 1912 to complete the arrangements and manage the coinage.

The British West Africa silver coinage was in four denominations; two shillings, shilling, sixpence and threepence. The first of these were dated 1913 and they began to replace the sterling silver in circulation in that year. The base metal coins (the penny, half and tenth already in issue for Nigeria) did not immediately become the responsibility of the Board but from 1912 these denominations dropped the **NIGERIA** part of the legend and could be used throughout British West Africa. At times the amount of coinage required by the Board exceeded the capacity of the Royal Mint and some coins were struck at The Mint Birmingham Ltd, by King's Norton Metal Co. Ltd, by Gaunt and Sons Ltd and at the Pretoria Mint in South Africa. The areas of German West Africa in Togoland and Cameroon which came to Britain after the First World War also adopted British West African currency. After the war the price of silver would rise making it unprofitable for the Board to coin in that metal. As in the United Kingdom the fineness of the silver was reduced to 50% in 1920 but in the same year it was decided that the four silver denominations should be struck in brass. The threepence was changed again (to cupro-nickel) in 1938 to produce a larger coin which could bear a security edge to deter forgers. The metal used for the penny, half and tenth was changed to bronze in 1952.

The last of the West African Currency Board coins were dated 1958 as the various territories moved towards independence. Nigeria, which achieved independence in 1960, made a further issue of the same denominations in 1959 but with the new legend **FEDERATION OF NIGERIA.** The shilling of this coinage continued to be struck after independence in 1961 and 1962.

West African Currency Board

Silver shilling 1914.   Brass two shillings 1938.   Cupro-nickel penny 1936 (Edward VIII).

Federation of Nigeria two shillings 1959

Britain's interest in **Southern Africa** began at the Cape of Good Hope. From the early 17th century the East India Company discussed, planned and even attempted to establish a supply base there for ships bound to the East but in the end were beaten to it by the Dutch. The Cape was still in Dutch hands when the Stadtholder of the United Provinces, William V of Orange, was turned out of his country by republican allies of France and fled to London in 1795. From London William conducted a government in exile and, *inter alia,* instructed Dutch colonial governors to surrender to British forces in order to keep those colonies out of French hands during the Revolutionary War.[7] The letter of instruction to the Cape arrived in June 1795 and came with the British force sent to take control in the name of the Stadtholder. Unsure whether he should obey this or support the new Batavian Republic established in the Netherlands, the Governor resisted. Eventually terms of capitulation were agreed and Britain took control of the Cape in September 1795. It was returned to the Dutch in 1803 following the Peace of Amiens but, with war resumed, the Cape was finally forced to surrender to a British fleet in January 1806. It was now obvious that the Cape had to be kept out of French hands and in 1814 it was confirmed to Britain by Anglo-Dutch treaty. This was endorsed at the Vienna Congress the next year.

Cape Colony was seen as a useful strategic base and for many years this was all that Britain required of it. The area taken over though was ill defined. Its hinterland was farmed by the hardy descendants of European emigrants, mainly Dutch, who had spread inland and for whom Britain now had responsibility. While the "Cape Dutch" of the central colony generally came to terms with the change of ownership the inland farmers had become almost a different race of herders and hunters. No longer Dutch but not at all keen to be British these people were known as "Boers". Their customs and beliefs put them in immediate conflict with the liberal attitudes of their new colonial masters. Boer and Briton found each others' beliefs totally incomprehensible.

The story of British expansion in Southern Africa is partly that of an imperial administration attempting to impose its rule and its principles on Boers who were intent on maintaining their freedoms. Superimposed on that is the three way struggle between British imperialism, the Boer and the native African for control of the land, its pasture and, later, its mineral wealth. It is a much larger story than that of the coinage but one that must be told if we are to see the coins and particularly the tokens in their true light.

The area occupied by the Boers extended east as far as the Great Fish River where, as a pastoral people, they had begun to dispute territory with the Bantu. The term "Bantu" was a general term applied to the peoples of tropical Africa including the Zulu, Xhosa, Matabele, Mashona, Bechuana, Basuto, Swazi and many more. It did not apply to the Khoikhoi and Bushmen of the western Cape with whom the Dutch had first come into contact. The Khoikhoi at this time were usually referred to as "Hottentots"; the Bantu as "Kaffirs", both terms being considered derogatory in later years. The Bantu at the Great Fish River were the Xhosa. By the time Britain took permanent control at the Cape there had already been three "Kaffir Wars" between Boer and Xhosa and the fixing of the eastern limit of the colony was a pressing matter. The fourth and fifth Kaffir Wars (1811-1812 and 1818-1819) attempted a military solution but if Bantu expansion was to be checked at the Great Fish River more settlers were required. Immigration from Britain was seen as the solution and in 1820 some 5,000 settlers, eager to leave the problems of post war Britain behind them, arrived in Algoa Bay at British

---

7 *The instructions sent to Dutch colonies, ships at sea and elsewhere are known as the "Kew Letters". They were sent from Kew Palace where the government in exile had been set up.*

Government expense. They would be largely responsible for their own defence against marauding Bantu and therefore for the security of the frontier. The 1820 settlement scheme was not an unqualified success. The area was more suited to pastoral farming than the arable farming for which the settlers were equipped. There were initial crop failures and many of the new settlers eventually drifted to the towns. Nevertheless a significant English element had been added to the predominantly Dutch population of Cape Colony and the language of law would soon become English. A border of sorts had been claimed in the east beyond which the British and Cape governments recognized Bantu rights even if the Boer did not.

The Khoikhoi were the main indigenous people of Cape Colony and over the years some of them had intermarried or formed less formal relationships with settlers producing a mixed race of Afrikaans speakers. Descendants of these migrated inland like the Boers but went mainly to the north. In the colourful and somewhat direct language of the day one such mixed race group was termed "Bastaards" and settled in the area north of the western Cape. About 1813 officials of the London Missionary Society, considering it more dignified, persuaded them to change their name to "Griquas" and their main settlement at Klaarwater became Griqua Town. In 1834 Griquas in the region were granted some autonomy and this more or less confirmed the northern limit of Cape Colony.

The London and other missionary societies active in Southern Africa presented the gospel of liberty and proclaimed the brotherhood of man. Their ideals were in line with British humanitarian thought and represented the onward march of European philanthropy. For the pastoral Boer whose neighbours were often hostile Bushmen or Bantu these were uncomfortable concepts. He was also resentful of a British administration that extended the restrictions of modern law and order to his lands and protected Bantu rights in the east. Immediately after the sixth Kaffir War of 1834-1835 large numbers of Boers, not ready for the changes that were being imposed upon them, left Cape Colony in what became known as the first Great Trek. They sought freedom from British rule, not confrontation with it and their trek took them north. They crossed the Orange River seeking new lands where they could live in their own manner. Some moved on beyond the Vaal but numbers of them turned east and, outflanking the Fish River border, moved towards the rich pasture of the Zulu, perhaps the most powerful of all the Bantu races.

The Great Trek was not a peaceful exodus to unoccupied lands. The Boer and the Bantu both hungered for land and for the same reasons. Both were pastoral people and both wanted grass and water for their stock. Knowing that the Bantu would not give this up easily the Boer was ready to fight for it. In spite of their limited numbers they succeeded remarkably well. In Natal they came into contact with the Zulu under the paramount chief, Dingaan. Thinking they had achieved agreement with him to settle in the region a group of Boers including their leader were slaughtered while visiting Dingaan's kraal and many more lost their lives in the surrounding country. This was avenged at what became known as Blood River when the Boers with modern weapons and tactics were able to inflict a decisive defeat on the Zulu. The next year, 1839, the Boer republic of Natalia was set up centred at Pietermaritzburg and the Boers were soon assisting elements of the Zulu in Dingaan's overthrow. The Zulu though had not gone away and the two races were uneasy neighbours.

In the lands north of the Orange and Vaal Rivers the Boers encountered the Matabele (often termed Ndebele). Like the Zulu, the Matabele were a military people with well organized impis and the Boer had to fight hard for his new land. Tales of small groups of laagered Boers risking everything they had in the world, not least their wives and children, against the massed attacks of the Matabele impis make stirring reading. The Matabele though were not writing their side of the story. Subject to fierce Boer counter-attacks they mourned their dead and were driven north where they would become the strongest native power between the Limpopo and the Zambesi. South of the Limpopo the Boer could claim his land by right of conquest.

The British authorities were unsure what to do about British subjects (the Boers) who had left the colony, renounced their allegiance and founded independent communities. An Imperial Act of 1836 applied the criminal law of the Cape to British subjects in adjoining territories up to latitude 25° S.[8] The authorities had no doubt that the emigrant Boers were British subjects and therefore subject to the law. The Boer didn't think so and beyond the Orange River was left pretty much to his own devices. It was the new Boer republic in Natal that caused most concern. If the Boer was allowed access to Port Natal (later "Durban") it would be easy for him to make alliances with other nations and the port would be open to foreign trade.

As early as 1824 British traders from the Cape had obtained a grant of land from the Zulu paramount chief, Chaka, and established trade with him around Port Natal. When Dingaan became paramount chief in 1828 their continued presence became uncertain but the British Government ignored requests to take responsibility for the region as a colony. When Dingaan mounted his attack on the first Boer settlers the British settlement was also broken up and the few British traders who later returned to Port Natal recognized Boer rule from Pietermaritzburg. In order to secure the port British troops were sent there and in 1843, after some confrontation with the Boers, Natal was declared a British colony. The Boers of Natalia decided not to contest this further. Still not prepared to submit to British authority and still not at peace with the Zulu, many of them moved off into the high veldt to join their colleagues north of the Orange River.

Britain now had two colonies in Southern Africa (Cape Colony and Natal[9]) and was claiming legal jurisdiction over "British" subjects north of the Orange River. At this point we will take a short break from the historical narrative and look at the money in use in Southern Africa up to this time.

Its position and function attracted a variety of coins to Cape Colony including the ubiquitous Spanish dollar. In 1806 though there was a shortage of coin in circulation and the Dutch authorities had mostly been using paper money denominated in rix dollars. This had depreciated to the extent that a Spanish dollar (worth about 4/2d sterling) passed for 2½ or 3 rix dollars. Nevertheless, the new Governor proclaimed currency rates for the various coins in circulation which brought the paper rix dollar up to a par of 4/- sterling. His proclamation also attempted to retain specie in the colony by prohibiting the export of gold and silver currency. The colonial authorities though were forced to continue the Dutch practice of issuing paper in order to make payments and by 1825 the paper rix dollar had depreciated to 1/6d. There was hardly any metallic currency in the colony when the Imperial Order in Council of 1825 introduced sterling silver as the general circulation of all British colonies. Because of the special situation at the Cape a sterling value of 1/6d was formally placed on the paper rix dollar before British silver was introduced. In Cape Colony these could be exchanged for sterling silver coins but could also be exchanged directly for bills on the Treasury in London on the same terms as silver (£103 in paper rix dollars or silver coin would buy a bill for £100 in gold). Sterling denominations came into use for public accounts at the beginning

---

8 *The Cape of Good Hope Punishment Act 1836 extended British jurisdiction (not sovereignty) up to 25°S. There was though no means of enforcing it beyond the Orange River at that time.*
9 *For some years Natal was annexed to Cape Colony but was separated from it in 1856.*

of 1826. Unlike many of the other colonies British coins came into use at the Cape immediately after 1825. Foreign coins were hardly seen and the Spanish dollar posed no threat to the introduction of sterling silver. The last of the paper rix dollars were withdrawn in 1841.

The first coinage struck specifically for use in Southern Africa was a small one for use in and around Griqua Town. Apart from the genteel suggestion that they should call themselves Griquas an Inspector of the London Missionary Society felt that, as they had no circulating medium, the Griqua community would benefit from a coinage to encourage trade. Four denominations were struck and are assumed to be denominated in pence. They are of 10 and IIII in silver with a ½ and ¼ in copper and bear the legend GRIQUA TOWN. They were to be used to pay employees of the London Missionary Society and so find their way into circulation. Struck in England about 1815 the silver coins probably disappeared from circulation quite quickly. The copper pieces are often well worn and may have remained in circulation a little longer.[10]

Griqua Town halfpenny c.1815.

No separate currency regulations were made for the new colony of **Natal** but in practice her currency was the same as that of Cape Colony. British coins were the medium of exchange although silver and copper were scarce.

The Boer, when he needed them, used the same coins as the colonists. As coin use increased issues of tokens, for various reasons, were made and we will examine some of these later. First though we must return to the historical narrative.

Throughout the Empire (as in the lands administered by the East India Company) the man on the spot often felt he knew far better how to deal with matters than a remote authority in London. Colonial governors though could not always see the bigger picture and communication was slow. An urgent course of action that was not in line with central policy sometimes seemed sensible and the outcome often had to be accepted by the Home Government. After the sixth Kaffir War of 1834-1835 the Governor at the Cape had created a new province beyond the eastern border of Cape Colony. The Province of Queen Adelaide was agreed with the Bantu and provided a great deal of security on the border. In this case though the arrangements were very soon disallowed by London and this was one of the factors that contributed to the Great Trek. Although Natal was reluctantly made a special case the British Government was strongly opposed to Imperial expansion at this time. Nevertheless when the seventh Kaffir War began in 1846 there was uncertainty on how best to manage British affairs throughout Southern Africa and the next year a new governor was appointed for Cape Colony. He was a popular appointment both in London and the Cape and had very clear ideas on how to proceed. Sir Harry Smith was a soldier and this was not his first visit to the Colony. In the sixth Kaffir war he had fought alongside Boers against the Bantu and had then governed the ill fated Province of Queen Adelaide being very critical of its subsequent

---

10 The main reference for these is H. A. Parsons, "The Coinage of Griqualand" in Spink, Numismatic Circular 1927. For a more recent review of all the evidence see Peter R. Thompson, "The Early Griqua Coins" in Coin News, May 2007.

demise. By 1847 the Governor of Cape Colony was also High Commissioner for the whole of Southern Africa so Sir Harry came with responsibility for British interests throughout the region. His view was that the best way to deal with troublesome people was to rule them and he set about this by claiming new regions to secure the eastern Cape, similar to the arrangements of the 1830s. In the north he extended Cape Colony fully to the Orange River. In 1848 he proclaimed the area between the Orange and Vaal Rivers to be subject to the Queen naming it the Orange River Sovereignty. As an old friend of the Boers he felt that here and eventually beyond the Vaal as well they would be happy to return to the fold under his leadership. The old borders had gone and Bantu as well as Boer, Khoikhoi and Griqua were British subjects.

The British Government viewed all this with apprehension. They reluctantly recognized the Orange River Sovereignty and acquiesced in the new colony of British Kaffraria which Smith had created in the east hoping that these would ensure stability. When the eighth Kaffir War began in 1850 it was obvious that this was not the case and before it ended Sir Harry Smith was recalled. In the new Orange River Sovereignty an uneasy peace had been maintained but it was clear that it could not be retained without troops and expenditure. With a new governor in place at the Cape it was time to negotiate. The Sand River Convention of 1852 agreed that emigrant Boers beyond the Vaal should have the right to govern themselves without British interference. In 1854 the Bloemfontein Convention withdrew British sovereignty north of the Orange River. The two Boer republics of the Zuid-Afrikaanche Republiek (or "Transvaal") and Orange Free State were conceived and the Boer at last had the freedoms he had longed for.

Cut off from the sea the Boer Republics posed little threat to Cape Colony and Natal and would probably have been left undisturbed but for three major developments. Although the Orange River had been seen as a natural border to Cape Colony the discovery of diamonds and then gold changed imperial thinking very swiftly. The Scramble for Africa completed the trilogy. By the end of the century British claims in Southern Africa had not only moved beyond the Orange River. They had crossed the Vaal, the Limpopo and even the Zambesi.

Diamonds were discovered from the late 1860s in the lands of the Griquas and in Orange Free State and this immediately attracted population and capital. Griqualand West was soon a British colony and would eventually (1880) become part of Cape Colony. "New Rush" developed rapidly as the centre of diamond mining and in 1873 was renamed Kimberley. One of the farms on which diamonds were discovered was named de Beers after the family who owned it and this was one of the many claims eventually purchased by a young man not long out from England. Over subsequent years Cecil Rhodes gradually monopolised the mining and marketing of diamonds in Southern Africa using the name of the original farm for his company. In 1888 De Beers Consolidated Mines Limited was formed and Rhodes effectively controlled the industry.

Britain now saw herself as the paramount power in Southern Africa and therefore the ultimate arbiter between Boer and Bantu. It was, for example, to prevent Boer incursions that Basutoland requested and obtained British protection in 1868. In fact Britain was now seeking some sort of unified state in Southern Africa under her dominion. Although diamonds were improving the economy of the Orange Free State, the Transvaal was financially weak and under threat from the Zulu. On instructions from London and after discussion with its President, the Governor of Natal annexed the Transvaal in 1877 and took over its administration. This was done on the assumption that the majority of her population and government would welcome British rule. There were official objections but on the promise of self government Transvaal accepted the annexation. In the same year the Permissive Confederation Act was passed which allowed any of the communities of Southern Africa to confederate under British dominion if they so wished. Although none took it up at this time the concept of "South Africa" as a Dominion, similar to that of Canada, was now established.

A major obstacle to confederation was the continued independence of the Zulus with their traditional, powerful and effective military organization. Like the Boer, the Zulu had no intention of giving up his independence. Zululand lay between Natal and the Transvaal and as long as her traditional lifestyle was allowed to exist was seen as a threat to both of them. The Zulus were invited to permanently disband their impis, accept a British Resident and adopt a more peaceful if less colourful way of life. They ignored the invitation and preparations were made to impose British suzerainty upon them.

The Zulu War of 1879 achieved what it set out to do but at enormous and unexpected cost. The first major contest between the Zulu impis and the British forces sent to impose control took place at Isandhlwana with the loss of 800 British lives and 500 of their allies. The line was only just held at Rorkes Drift. Nevertheless the Zulus had also suffered, and continued to suffer, enormous losses and in the end accepted their new overlord. British Residents were appointed to the districts although Zululand was not formally annexed until 1887.

In the Transvaal there was no sign of the promised self government and an opportunity to move peacefully towards confederation was lost. The Transvaal rose in revolt and here Britain did not have her own way. The First Boer War (1880-1881) led to the recognition once more of an independent Transvaal State soon again to be named the Zuid-Afrikaanche Republiek (Z.A.R.)

Just a few years later large quantities of gold were discovered in the Z.A.R. and both the Boer Republics could now enjoy an unfamiliar prosperity. As the Scramble for Africa gathered pace the continued independence of these republics; flourishing, potentially hostile and with a diminishing need for confederation (except perhaps between themselves) began to concern the British authorities. Germany had successfully laid claim to part of South West Africa in 1884 and it was important that the land between this and the Boer Republics was secure. It was important too to ensure that the Boer Republics did not establish links to the sea through Portuguese territory to the north.

The lands to the west of the Boer Republics and north of Griqualand West were mainly in the hands of the Bechuana (Tswana). The region was of no commercial significance except as the traders' (or "missionary") road to the north but it lay between German interests in the west and the Z.A.R. To secure this "buffer" region for Britain a force was sent north from Capetown and the whole region up to 22°S was claimed as a British Protectorate. The southern part of this became the colony of British Bechuanaland in September 1885 and would become part of Cape Colony ten years later. The huge area north of the Molopo River, too large to administer directly, continued to be the Bechuanaland Protectorate.

Various companies and individuals were now seeking mining concessions in Mashonaland to the north of the Bechuanaland Protectorate. The Mashona were a peaceful people over whom the Matabele claimed sovereignty and it was rumoured that their land contained rich deposits of gold. It was to stake claims in this region for Britain and for himself that Cecil Rhodes (already wealthy from his diamond interests) negotiated rights with Lobengula, king of the Matabele. Armed with this concession he applied for a Royal Charter which was granted in1889. The British South Africa Company was formed to contain Boer expansion and develop British interests in the region north of the Bechuanaland Protectorate. In return for extensive powers of government and other rights the British South Africa Company would secure huge areas of Southern and Central Africa for Britain during the period of the "Scramble". The British Government was happy for private enterprise to stake British claims where Portugal, Germany and the Boer may otherwise have done. Happy too that it should be done without direct control and without cost to the taxpayer. It would not be long before there were some who felt there should have been rather more control over Rhodes and his Company.

Rhodes' original concession from Lobengula was understood by the Matabele to be for mining rights only. The Royal Charter was granted in spite of serious doubts about the legality of this agreement and gave the Company far more than Lobengula had assumed. Rhodes' intention became clear to the Matabele when his pioneers who trekked north from Bechuanaland arrived at what would become Salisbury in September 1890. They came with a 500 strong force of armed police and had been promised farms as well as mining claims. The region would soon be known as Rhodesia.

The Matabele felt they had been tricked into surrendering rights in Mashonaland but took no action against the pioneer column or subsequent settlement. Their king knew that the assegai and massed impis were no match for modern weapons. In Mashonaland though large finds of gold did not materialise and if the Company was to remain solvent settlers would have to be attracted to develop farming. The continued presence of the warlike Matabele who still claimed the Mashona as a subject people discouraged this. In 1893 Matabele warriors entered Mashonaland and carried out a punitive attack on their subject people, killing many of them. This was the excuse the Company needed to mount an attack on the Matabele. It may seem incredible that a private company with limited manpower should consider such a move but, as Hillair Belloc's Captain Blood would famously say,

> "Whatever happens we have got
> The Maxim Gun, and they have not."[11]

The Company's force had five Maxim machine guns and the result of the Matabele War of 1893 was as expected. The Company entered Bulawayo in November 1893, the Matabele and their king melted into the country and large farms were granted to the victors. Rhodesia was doubled in size. The last of the Matabele impis would rise again in 1896 but after this Second Matabele War[12] it was clear that the European with his resources and expertise would be the dominant race in Southern Africa for many years to come. By the closing years of the 19th century the Bantu warrior had been forced to give up his military and predatory traditions and had become the farm hand, the mine worker and the city labourer. The subsequent struggle for domination would be between Briton and Boer.

The gold discoveries in the Z.A.R. had attracted many immigrants. To the Transvaalers these were all foreigners ("uitlanders"). Soon these outnumbered the Boers and to give then the vote would mean putting the future of the Transvaal into the hands of foreigners. Britain, still very keen on confederation, would have welcomed change and therefore supported the demands of the Uitlanders, many of whom were British, to be given the franchise. Cecil Rhodes felt the same and so too did his close confidant, Dr Leander Starr Jameson (the Company's Administrator in Rhodesia). By the end of 1895 a plot had been devised whereby

---

11 Hillair Belloc, "The Modern Traveller", 1898.
12 The Second Matabele War is often termed a "rebellion". The Mashona, finding their new masters no better than the Matabele, rebelled at the same time and hundreds of settlers lost their lives.

an armed revolt by the Uitlanders would threaten the overthrow of the Transvaal Government. A force from Rhodesia under Jameson would then enter the Transvaal to restore order and bring it into confederation. The "Jameson Raid" began on 29th December with a force made up mainly from the Company's Police. The Uitlanders though had not risen and did not rise. On 2nd January Jameson and his force surrendered and were imprisoned at Pretoria.

The Jameson Raid had far reaching effects. It left Rhodesia without an armed police force at a critical time. Cecil Rhodes who (amongst other things) was Prime Minister of Cape Colony had to resign that position. It hardened the attitudes of the Boer Republics against confederation, led them into an alliance with each other and encouraged them to seek contacts elsewhere, particularly with Germany. If British paramountcy was to prevail the Boer would now have to be coerced. With Transvaal refusing to budge on Uitlander rights Britain began to send troops to the Transvaal borders. Her refusal to remove them led to a state of war being declared. On 11th October 1899 Britain was at war with the Boer Republics and the Second Boer War had begun.

Britain had become used to winning her colonial wars though not all of them without cost. No adequate preparations were made to take on the Boer whose forces anyway were irregular commandos. No heed was taken of how those commandos had dealt with the Zulu and the Matabele or of how they had forced the issue in the First Boer War. The might of the Empire would suffice. Nevertheless, the war was not over by Christmas as some had assumed and massive reinforcements were needed before it could be brought to a conclusion. These came not only from the United Kingdom but from Australia, Canada and New Zealand and troops were also raised in Cape Colony and Natal. Although the Orange Free State was annexed (as Orange River Colony) in May 1900 and the Z.A.R. (as Transvaal Colony) in September the Boers melted into the country and continued the fight. By the time peace was at last agreed in May 1902 Britain had spent more than £230 million on finally securing Africa's diamonds and gold. The human cost was also large. More than 70,000 lives, Allied, Boer and African, had been lost in the war.

In spite of all the years of bitterness culminating in a vicious war the long sought confederation did finally come about. Cape Colony had enjoyed self government since 1872 and the Colony of Natal since 1893. Transvaal Colony was granted self government in 1906 and the Orange River Colony in 1907. The South Africa Act 1909 allowed for these four self governing colonies to become provinces of the Union of South Africa on 31st May 1910. Orange River Colony reverted to its previous name and became Orange Free State Province, the others retaining their old colonial names as Cape Province, Natal Province and Transvaal Province. Special arrangements were made for the Bechuanaland Protectorate, Basutoland[13] and Swaziland[14] which came under the care of the High Commissioner but were expected to join the Union at some later date. The Rhodesias[15] remained separate and continued to be run by the British South Africa Company but the 1909 Act allowed that these too could become part of the Union in the future.

Nyasaland sat geographically between Southern Africa and East Africa. With the aim of

---

13 Basutoland was a Crown colony from 1884 until it became independent in 1966.
14 Swaziland had been under the administration of Transvaal and continued to be so when Transvaal became a British colony after the Boer War. In 1906, when Transvaal was granted responsible government, Swaziland became the responsibility of the High Commissioner.
15 The area north of the Zambezi was known as Northern Rhodesia from 1897. Southern Rhodesia comprised Mashonaland and Matabeleland and would become a self governing colony in 1923. Northern Rhodesia was a protectorate.

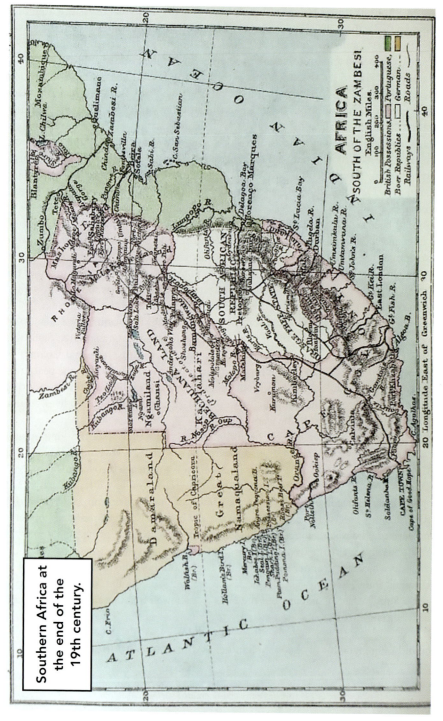

Southern Africa at the end of the nineteenth century.

developing the region, where missionaries had been active for some years, the African Lakes Company began operating in 1878. Because of increased British activity and to limit Portuguese claims a protectorate (the Nyasaland Districts Protectorate) was formally declared in 1891. Two years later this was renamed the British Central Africa Protectorate and in 1907 the name was changed again to the Nyasaland Protectorate. It was never envisaged that Nyasaland would become part of the Union of South Africa and in later years it would be associated instead with the Rhodesias[16].

With the creation of the Union of South Africa in 1910 as a Dominion of the British Empire political union between the two European races had been achieved. The strength of that union was uncertain but in 1914 South Africa entered the First World War along with the other Dominions when war was declared.

We have seen that British coins came into general use in **Cape Colony** and **Natal** without difficulty. An Order in Council and Proclamation of 10th November 1866 extended the legal tender status of Sydney Mint sovereigns and half sovereigns to various colonies including the Cape of Good Hope and Natal. The same Proclamation allowed for gold coins of future branches of the Royal Mint also to be proclaimed legal tender provided they were of the same denominations struck in London. The Royal Proclamation came into effect in Cape Colony in January 1867 and in Natal the next month. The British Coinage Act of 1870 was applied to the Cape and Natal by Order in Council and Proclamation of 29th November 1881. This came into force in the Cape and Natal in February 1882 and the currency of both these colonies was then based on sterling gold with unlimited legal tender. Under the provisions of the Act the legal tender limit of subsidiary coins was fixed at forty shillings for silver (still of course "token" in value), one shilling for bronze pennies and sixpence for the smaller bronze denominations.

When the southern part of **Bechuanaland** became a Crown colony in 1885 all the laws then in force at the Cape were applied to it. As the Coinage Act of 1870 had already been adopted by the Cape it therefore applied equally to British Bechuanaland.

An 1891 Proclamation by the High Commissioner for Southern Africa[17] provided that the coinage to be used in the Bechuanaland Protectorate would be that in use at the Cape. The British South Africa Company adopted the same standard for its areas of control and administration at the same time. British Central Africa (**Nyasaland**) was in part administered by the Company and also used sterling coins.

By the time of the Second Boer War British coinage was thus the normal coinage for the whole of British Southern Africa. British coin was also in use in the Boer Republics but the **Z.A.R.** produced its own regular coinage from 1893 [18]. These were at the same weight and standard as British coins as laid down in the Coinage Act of 1870 and in the same denominations from the pound (or "*pond*") to the penny. Only the Royal Mint and its branches could strike the "sovereign" but in any case the Republic would not have wanted to use such a royalist term for its equivalent gold coin. The crown and half-crown were denominated as 5 shillings and 2½ shillings, probably for the same reason. All the Z.A.R. coins bore the portrait of President Kruger. The **Orange Free State** never had a distinctive currency issue and used both British and Z.A.R. coins. After the war British coinage regulations applied to the new colonies.

---

16 The Federation of Rhodesia and Nyasaland was formed in 1953 from the self governing colony of Southern Rhodesia and the protectorates of Northern Rhodesia and Nyasaland. The Federation officially ended on 31st December 1963 as these three territories were prepared separately for independence.
17 The General Administration Proclamation of 10th June 1891.
18 Although the first Z.A.R. coins are dated 1892 production did not begin until 1893.

Production of the Z.A.R. coins of course ceased when British forces took Pretoria in 1900 but they were declared legal tender in Orange River Colony in 1900 [19]. From 1911 they were legal tender throughout the new Union of South Africa and remained in circulation until the 1930s.

A branch of the Royal Mint was opened at Pretoria in 1923 to produce Imperial sovereigns and half sovereigns from the Witwatersrand gold. It is interesting to note that the Royal Mint had ceased the regular issue of sovereigns in 1917 but they continued to be struck at Pretoria until 1932[20]. The Pretoria sovereigns and half sovereigns carry the mint mark "**SA**" on the reverse.

The opening of the Pretoria Mint in 1923 was also the occasion of the introduction of the Union's own distinct coinage in sterling denominations. Although British silver coins had already been reduced in fineness to 50% because of the increased price of silver the **Union of South Africa** silver coins introduced in 1923 were of 80% silver. Only in 1951 would they be reduced to 50% and they remained at that level until the Union coinage ceased in 1961. In that year South Africa became a republic, left the Commonwealth and ceased using sterling coins.

SOUTH AFRICA
Some of the British coins in use c.1900.

Sovereign 1899 (this one of Melbourne mint)

Halfcrown 1893.

Penny 1881.

Some Z.A.R. denominations

Pond 1892.

Penny 1892.

Two and a half shillings 1897.

---

[19] It is interesting to note that the Z.A.R. coins, the regular coinage of the Transvaal, were not officially declared legal tender in Transvaal Colony until 1906.
[20] Britain came off the gold standard in September 1931 but South Africa retained it for a further fifteen months.

9 *Africa and the Atlantic*

Union of South Africa coins

Two and a half shillings (halfcrown) George V 1923.

George VI Penny 1942.

Halfpenny 1959.

Southern Rhodesia did not begin to strike her own distinctive coins until 1932. Here the silver coins were initially at sterling fineness, were reduced to 50% silver in 1944 and were cupro-nickel from 1947. This coinage continued until 1954 after which coins in sterling denominations were struck for the combined territories of Rhodesia and Nyasaland. When that Federation was dissolved at the end of 1963 what had originally been Southern Rhodesia became simply "Rhodesia". Unusually, Rhodesia's new coins show the denomination in sterling and cents thus stating their relationship to both the pound and the rand of the new South African Republic.

SOUTHERN RHODESIA

Halfcrown 1951.

Penny 1934.

Rhodesia and Nyasaland.
Halfcrown 1957.

Rhodesia.
Two shillings/twenty cents 1964.

169

The tokens of Southern Africa mostly appeared later than those of British North America and elsewhere and are often not as well produced. Some are in "white metal" and subject to corrosion. Nevertheless, many of them illustrate the social and political history of the region in a way that coins can never do and we will now look at some of them.

Among the earliest tokens of Southern Africa are those of Natal where the main commercial centre was Durban. Originally Port Natal, the town was renamed in 1835 in honour of Sir Benjamin D'Urban, a popular governor of Cape Colony. A shortage of small change resulted in several businesses producing tokens and those of Blackwood Couper & Co. are typical. They were general merchants and shipping agents and issued tokens of a shilling, sixpence and threepence dated 1861. These tokens continue the use of the form "D'Urban" which had largely fallen out of use by this time and interestingly remind us of the contemporary style of colonial architecture by depicting the company's premises on the reverse.

Several tokens belong to Kimberley, a "frontier" town in its early days, and the region around it. The hostelry issuing tokens named for "The" Hotel has not been positively identified. Was it *the* best there was in Kimberley or were the tokens issued before a name had been decided? Values of 2/6d, 1/- (shilling) and 6d are known, their relatively high value indicating pre payment tokens of some sort.

The diamond mines employed many immigrant workers. Soon these were housed in compounds and were often paid in tokens which could only be used in the company store. These are very functional and are often uniface. Those for Bultfontein Diamonds struck in brass are probably early examples as Bultfontein was taken over by De Beers about 1888. Those used at the De Beers mines are known in brass and in white metal. The white metal tokens are known with different shaped segments cut out of them which identify those used at different mines. Those with a dumbbell cut out of them are attributed to Bultfontein under De Beers, those with a small half moon segment are attributed to the Dutoitspan mine and those with no cut are attributed to Wesselton. The De Beers tokens are of 2/6d, 1/-, 6d and 3d.

A Capetown token of early style is interesting because of its similarity to a Tasmanian token. The Capetown halfpenny was issued by Marsh & Sons; Importers while the Tasmanian firm of H. J. Marsh & Brother issued a very similar halfpenny in Hobart. Were the two issuers related?

The Bechuanaland Border Police were raised as an Imperial mounted force in 1885 to patrol the vast areas of the Protectorate and keep its borders secure. Their task at times must have seemed a lonely and thankless one but, routine patrols apart, this unit would participate in several significant incidents. In 1890 many of its members were recruited into the British South Africa Company's Police to accompany the pioneer column to Salisbury. In 1893 they formed the core of the southern column that was dispatched to assist in the Matabele War. Having reached Bulawayo some of its members accompanied the force that was sent (unsuccessfully) to capture the Matabele king[21] and some remained posted to Matabeleland after the war. Late in 1895 some were persuaded to join the ill fated Jameson Raid into the Transvaal. On occasion though the Bechuanaland Border Police (BBP) found time to relax in their canteen for which tokens exist dated 1893. Three denominations are known, the shilling, the sixpence and the threepence of which the shilling is illustrated opposite.

Further north, in British Central Africa, the company owned by Eugene Sharrer issued tokens in several denominations. Those from 2/8d down to a 1d have been recorded. Sharrer arrived in Blantyre in 1889 and became involved in coffee planting, river traffic and trade. The tokens were for use at his Kubula Stores and are particularly interesting as they were made from vulcanite.

Opposite are just some of the tokens that illustrate the history of Southern Africa but we must now move on. Beyond Lake Nyasa lay other British interests that looked not to the Atlantic and Home but to the Indian Ocean and to the East.

---

21 They accompanied but were not part of the disastrous Shangani patrol which was ambushed and annihalated when trying to arrest Lobengula.

9 Africa and the Atlantic

Early Durban token

Blackwood Couper & Co. threepence 1861.

Kimberley token

"The" Hotel. Good for 2/6d.

Some diamond mine tokens

Bult Diamonds two shillings.   De Beers brass shilling.   De Beers Bultfontein half-crown.   De Beers Dutoitspan half-crown.

The Marsh halfpenny tokens

Port Nolloth, Cape Colony

Marsh & Sons Capetown.   Marsh & Brother, Hobart.   Bracteate trader's token threepence. F. W. Dreyer, 1890s.

Grahamstown, Cape Colony

Morris's Hotel penny 1872.

Bechuanaland.

Bechuanaland Border Police canteen shilling.

Central Africa

Two shillings.   Four pence.
Kubula Stores Blantyre. Vulcanite tokens.

171

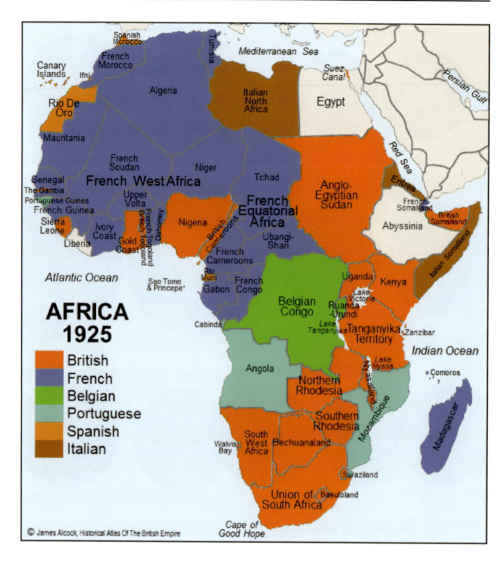

Africa after the First World War.

10

Egypt and East Africa

EGYPT was part of the Ottoman Empire and would remain so until the start of the First World War. Britain was primarily concerned for its security because, like much of the Ottoman Empire, Egypt lay on the overland routes to India.

For many years the building of a canal which would join the Mediterranean to the Red Sea had been contemplated and in the 1850s the Frenchman Ferdinand de Lesseps obtained a concession from the Khedive to construct and operate such a waterway. When the Suez Canal was finally opened in 1869 the shares of its Company[1] were mainly in the hands of French investors and of the Khedive. In financial difficulties, the Khedive sold his shares to the British Government in 1875. This gave Britain a measure of control over this new gateway to India but it also increased her interest in Egypt.

As Egypt strove to modernize, her debt increased alarmingly and in order to protect their bondholders the European Powers took control of financial affairs. Britain and France were soon exercising a "Dual Control" which inevitably affected most aspects of administration, including taxation.

The resentment that many Egyptians felt at this foreign control came to a head in a military inspired revolt which, in 1882, led Britain to send in a force to restore order and safeguard assets. The Egyptian army was met and defeated at Tel el-Kebir on 13th September allowing Britain to restore the authority of the Khedive. For some years after this defeat Britain had to supervise an Egyptian army whose effectiveness had been destroyed.

To her assets in Egypt Britain had thus added an involvement in administration and then a military responsibility. International assistance had been requested to deal with the disturbances of 1881-1882 but only Britain had taken effective action. France therefore lost much of her influence in Egypt, a state of affairs that she did not fully accept until the Entente Cordiale of 1904. Officially the Khedive still ruled under the Suzerainty of the Ottoman Empire and British administration was advisory. It was also assumed to be temporary but would continue beyond the First World War.

With responsibility for Egypt came (reluctantly) some responsibility for the Soudan (modern: "Sudan") which had been part of Egypt since 1820. Here the slave trade still flourished and the Khedive had appointed Major-General Gordon as his Governor-General at Khartoum to deal with that and other issues. Gordon had resigned in 1880 but with the

---

1 *This was the Compagnie Universelle du Canal Maritime de Suez (English: "Universal Suez Ship Canal Company"). Often referred to simply as "The Suez Canal Company".*

Egyptian army in disarray after the events of 1882 a Mahdist revolt against Egyptian rule soon broke out in the Sudan. Gordon was asked to return, his task now to evacuate civilians and troops loyal to the Khedive so that Egypt could abandon the Sudan completely. He felt he should first find a competent authority to which he could hand over the country and remained in Khartoum to attempt this. He was soon under siege and the relief of Khartoum became a popular cause for the people of Britain. Bowing to public pressure the Government organized an elaborate relief expedition which arrived in Khartoum on 28th January 1885. Just two days earlier, after a siege of ten months, the city had fallen and Gordon had been beheaded.[2]

The Sudan was then left to the Mahdists but in Britain the avenging of Gordon's death became a popular jingoist demand. There was also the unfinished business of the slave trade but these were not the reasons why Britain began to seek control in the Sudan. As the Scramble for Africa quickened Egypt would be under threat if the Upper Nile fell into the wrong hands. So too would Britain's awakening interests in East Africa.

By the mid 1890s Egypt's finances were far more stable and her army greatly improved. It was time to begin the re-conquest of the Sudan. An Anglo-Egyptian force under the leadership of Major-General Kitchener (Sirdar of the Egyptian army) began the campaign in earnest in 1896 and in September 1898 the Mahdists were defeated at Omdurman. The next year the British and Egyptian governments set up a joint rule of the whole of the Sudan, Kitchener becoming its Governor General. Anglo-Egyptian control would continue with a few minor hitches until Sudan became independent on 1st January 1956.

In 1914 the Ottoman Empire entered the war on the side of Germany. From her position of administrative and military strength Britain immediately declared Egypt to be a British Protectorate. The suzerainty of the Ottoman Empire was thus terminated, the Khedive of Egypt was deposed and a Sultan appointed. Egypt was a British Protectorate from December 1914 until February 1922 and although she then became an independent kingdom there would be a British presence there until 1956.

For many years before the Suez Canal was opened a regular steamship service ran between Suez and Bombay, passengers, mail and small items of cargo from Europe travelling overland from Alexandria via Cairo. On this important route lay Aden which was of no great commercial importance but was a useful coaling station. By 1838 the British Government was anxious to take control and a disagreement with the local ruler furnished the excuse for the East India Company to take Aden by force in 1839. It was administered by the East India Company until 1858, the year in which all the Company's responsibilities passed to the Crown. It then continued to be part of the Indian Empire until it became a Crown colony in 1937. From an early date the Directors of the East India Company saw the potential of Aden as an entrepôt for the region and in 1850 made it into a free port. The importance of Aden grew and would grow further after the opening of the Suez Canal in 1869.

As we have seen in Chapter seven colonies were the responsibility of the Colonial Office while protectorates were generally under the Foreign Office, at least until they became established. All areas east of the Cape of Good Hope were the responsibility of the East India Company until that responsibility passed to the India Office in 1858. Along with the administrative expertise of the East India Company the India Office therefore inherited a number of territories outside mainland India. Several such territories (Aden was one of them) therefore remained under India Office control for some years before being transferred to the

---

2 *The exact circumstances of Gordon's death are uncertain - his head may have been severed later. The entire garrison of Egyptian and loyal Sudanese troops (some 7,000 in total) had been slaughtered. The relief expedition returned to Egypt from the Sudan in safety.*

Colonial Office or elsewhere. As new territories came to Britain there were thus different ways in which they could be administered.

To secure Aden it was important that adjoining areas should also be under some sort of control. By the time the India Office took over, the island of Perim at the entrance to the Red Sea was already part of the Aden Settlement. In the 1860s and 1880s further areas of land were purchased securing the port and a water supply and these became part of the Settlement. The Kuria Muria Islands far to the east were ceded to Britain by the Sultan of Muscat in 1854 and these were attached administratively to Aden in 1868. Throughout the period of British control agreements were made with the rulers of various tribal states in the hinterland behind Aden so this area of British influence (soon termed the Protectorate) was of varied extent. Administration of the Protectorate was minimal and ill defined. Only in 1927 was it decided that the Protectorate would be the responsibility of the Colonial Office rather than the Foreign Office, Aden itself continuing to report to India for another ten years.

In 1834 the East India Company made a survey of the island of Socotra which lies off the Horn of Africa. It was seeking suitable locations for coaling and watering steamships between Suez and India. So accurate was the survey that the chart produced remained in use as the British Admiralty chart for the island until superseded by a metric version in 1987. Socotra was not selected as a coaling station but it was not in Britain's interest that it should fall into the hands of others. In 1876 the Sultan of Qishn, who controlled Socotra, agreed that no foreign power would be granted interests there and ten years later the whole Mahra Sultanate of Qishn and Socotra came under formal British protection to become one of the states of the Aden Protectorate.

This was now the period of the "Scramble" and in the Horn of Africa Britain's main rivals for territory were France and Italy. The Somali coast opposite Aden began to come under British protection from 1884 as treaties of friendship and protection were made with tribal states in the region. Initially this area was administered by Residents from Aden and was thus ultimately under the India Office. It passed to the Foreign Office in 1898 and to the Colonial Office in 1905. The Somaliland Protectorate lay between French Somaliland to the north and Italian Somaliland to the south and was usually referred to as "British Somaliland" to distinguish it from those other territories.

No British coins were struck specifically for **Aden** or **British Somaliland** and no tokens of relevance have been recorded. Some states of the Aden Protectorate issued their own coins from time to time but, as Aden was administered from India, British Indian coinage was soon the legal tender of the Settlement itself. Rupees and subdivisions were first shipped to Aden from India in April 1839.[3] British Somaliland was not commercially significant. Its connection with Aden, supplying much of the garrison's mutton, and its traditional trading pattern ensured that here too British Indian coins became current.

For much of its commerce the whole region depended on the use of the main trade coins of the day. The rupee of India would find a natural place in this scheme of things but the dollar sized coins of Europe and Spanish America had already done so. One that had found particular favour in the Arab lands for many years was the thaler (dollar) of Maria Theresia, Archduchess of Austria from 1740 to 1780. By the time of her death the coins bearing her portrait had achieved a particular reputation for reliability and fineness from the Levant to the Yemen. After her death the demand for these coins was such that the Gunzburg mint continued to produce them, initially from remaining dies and then from new dies still bearing the date

---

3 *Major F. Pridmore in SNC July/August 1957, p. 307.*

1780. Maria Theresia thalers were soon the preferred form of payment throughout the region known today as the "Middle East" and the Austrian mints met the demand for them for many years. Over the ensuing 160 years many millions of them would be struck for use in north eastern Africa and Arabia with no change of date, legend or type.[4] No activity in the region, military or commercial, could expect to succeed without a supply of these coins and it has been noted that the invasion fleet which left Bombay late in 1838 bound for Aden carried ten boxes, each containing 4,000 Maria Theresia thalers.[5] They were not a legal tender in Aden but were considered by many to be the real standard of value and were in frequent use for payments in the Aden and Somaliland protectorates until the 1960s.

When India achieved independence in 1947 the British Indian coinage ceased and it was necessary to find an alternative currency for Aden. It seemed sensible that the currency of the nearby British territories in East Africa (the East African shilling) should be that which replaced the rupee and this came into effect in 1951.

In British Somaliland the East African shilling had already come into general use during the Second World War but here also it did not finally replace the rupee as the sole legal tender until 1951. The East African coinage will be examined below.

During the First World War huge numbers of troops were sent to **Egypt** which acted as a useful base from which they could come and go from Gallipoli, France and other theatres of war. They came from Britain, from the Dominions and from India bringing with them British sterling and British Indian rupees which entered circulation. Soon too there was an increased need for local coinage.

The coins struck for Egypt while under British protection began in 1916 and, with minor adjustments, continued the existing currency system of piastres and tenths subsidiary to an Egyptian pound. In 1914 Egyptian banknotes had become legal tender and were no longer convertible into gold. Under the Protectorate the Egyptian pound was therefore effectively the pound note.[6] There were one hundred piastres to the pound and ten milliemes to the piastre. Calcutta, Bombay and the two Birmingham mints of Heaton and King's Norton all struck coins for the Protectorate giving some indication of the large numbers required. They differ from earlier Egyptian coins in showing dates and denominations in both English and Arabic. The denominations struck were the half millieme in bronze, the two, five and ten milliemes in cupro-nickel and the two, five, ten and twenty piastres in silver. In 1916 only there was also a small issue of the hundred piastres (pound) in gold. These coins were in the name of Sultan Hussein Kamel until his death in 1917. His successor, Sultan Ahmad Fuad, is named on a single issue of silver denominations dated 1920 which were the last to be struck under the Protectorate. His later coins were struck as King of Egypt after Egyptian independence so are not part of our story.

4 *After the First World War Austria-Hungary had ceased to exist and the new Republic of Austria claimed the succession right to the Vienna mint. Although it was generally accepted that this included the monopoly right to strike the Maria Theresia thaler the Italians had long argued that they also had a right to coin it (Milan and Venice had struck the coin when still part of the Austro-Hungarian Empire). In 1935 Italy secured the right to strike the Maria Theresia thaler, primarily to fund her operations against Abyssinia (Ethiopia) and production began at Rome. The deal with Austria covered a 25 year period during which the output of the Vienna mint would be restricted. This seriously reduced the supply available to the international community. The fact that the coin was not the legal currency of Austria or any other country allowed the Royal Mint to begin striking the Maria Theresia thaler in 1936. Paris, Brussels and Utrecht soon followed suit while Bombay and Birmingham would later supplement Royal Mint production. In 1960 the Italian contract expired and Vienna sought and regained the Austrian monopoly. By this time the Maria Theresia thaler had lost most of its commercial importance but it is still struck when required at the Vienna Mint, still at the original standard and still dated 1780.*

5 *Major F. Pridmore in SNC July/August 1957, pp 305-308.*

6 *The Egyptian pound had always been worth a little more than the sovereign (pound sterling) which was equivalent to 97½ piastres.*

The **Sudan** in general used the coins that were in use in Egypt. A few coins were struck locally after 1884 but none of these form part of our story.

Coinage for Egypt as a protectorate

Ten milliemes 1917. *Ten piastres 1917.* *Five piastres 1920.*

The trading networks of East Africa were centred on Mombasa and Zanzibar. From about 1700 Zanzibar had been in the hands of the Imams (later: "Sultans") of Oman who found it easier to control than mainland Mombasa. It had since grown into a bustling centre of commerce trading mainly with the Arab world and with India but Zanzibar was also the largest slave emporium on the east coast of Africa. In the 1830s the Sultan of Oman, with whom Britain enjoyed good relations, moved his main seat from Muscat to Zanzibar where traders from British India were welcome. A British Consul was appointed in 1841.[7] After the death of Said bin Sultan in 1856 his dominions were divided between two of his sons. When the deal was finally completed (with British mediation) Zanzibar and Oman became separate Sultanates. Zanzibar included several islands and a lengthy strip of the adjacent East African coast. There were trading routes stretching far inland along which slaves and ivory travelled to ports on the coast and to Zanzibar but the vast area traversed by these routes was little more than a vague sphere of Zanzibari influence.

Missionaries and explorers (David Livingstone the foremost amongst them) had brought the horrors of the slave trade through East African ports to public attention and for some years Britain had been attempting to curtail the slave trades of the Arabian Sea. This had achieved little real success but in 1873 a more comprehensive treaty to ban the slave trade was agreed with the Sultan of Zanzibar. Even this though did not attempt to ban slavery within his dominions. Slavery was part of the social and economic structure of the region and was not abhorrent to the laws or religion of Islam so abolition itself was a difficult matter. Britain's view though was that the old ways would eventually have to go. There could be no argument in favour of slavery or of the slave trade. The British Government and the Royal Navy set about the task of abolishing East African slavery and in the process the region was steadily secured for British trade, investment and settlement.

On the East African mainland Carl Peters, founder of the Society for German Colonization, arrived in 1884 and began making treaties in lands nominally subject to the Sultan. The loss of Khartoum in 1885 and the Egyptian withdrawal northwards was seen by Otto von Bismarck

---

7   Atkins Hamerton had been the East India Company's Agent at Muscat and followed the Sultan's court to Zanzibar. Here he had the dual role of British Consul (responsible to the Foreign Office) and Political Agent of the Bombay Government.

as British weakness in the region and the Kaiser was persuaded to declare a protectorate over the areas claimed by Peters. In August 1885 German warships arrived off Zanzibar to demand recognition and, on British advice, the Sultan agreed to this. By late 1886 the two European powers had reached agreement that the inland regions should be divided between them and on the extent of the territory to be left to Zanzibar. The Sultan was to keep the islands and a strip of coast ten miles deep while British and German spheres extended inland as far as Lake Victoria. To this the Sultan had little choice but to agree. The northern part of this extensive inland area would be the British sphere and would soon become the East Africa Protectorate, later Kenya. The southern part would become German East Africa, later Tanganyika.

Both the spheres of interest agreed in 1886 were shut off from the sea by the Sultan's coastal strip and agreements were soon reached with Zanzibar concerning this. The northern part of the strip was leased to the newly formed British East Africa Association in 1887 while the southern part was leased and then sold to the German East Africa Company. This allowed the development of the port at Mombasa by the British and of Dar es Salaam by the Germans leading eventually to a decline in the importance of Zanzibar.

The European "Scramble for Africa" now centred on the obscure region to the north and west of Lake Victoria. The southern part of this region was home to the Baganda who were still independent under their Kabaka. Buganda would eventually form the nucleus of the British protectorate of Uganda and was coterminous with the sources of the Nile.[8] Further north, in southern Sudan, Egypt had founded the province of Equatoria to safeguard the Upper Nile but in 1885 had abandoned the Sudan to the Mahdists. While an attempt had been made to rescue Gordon at Khartoum the Khedive's Governor of Equatoria, much further south, was left to fend for himself. Eduard Carl Oscar Theodor Schnitzer, better known to history as Emin Pasha, moved his headquarters south to Wadelai in what is now northern Uganda but had no intention of abandoning Equatoria.

Apart from Emin Pasha and the Baganda this strategic area was a political vacuum to which no colonial power had made formal claim. It was the hub of a wheel whose spokes were the Sudan (and thus Egypt), Ethiopia, British and German East Africa and the Congo Free State of Leopold II. Having been ignored for some years Emin Pasha was suddenly the centre of attention. Relief expeditions were planned and launched which were thinly disguised attempts to gain control of Equatoria while the Baganda also became a focus of attention. Although Leopold II of the Belgians showed interest the final race for control of the region was between Britain and Germany.

The expedition that located Emin Pasha in April 1888 was that led by Henry Stanley (famous for an earlier expedition to locate a certain Dr. Livingstone). Stanley's expedition was funded mainly by the British businessman William Mackinnon who was the main force behind the founding of the British East Africa Association. As Stanley was still legally in the employ of Leopold II his relief expedition had to start from the Congo but Mackinnon had asked him to conclude whatever treaties he could in the region of the Nile Lakes committing those who signed them to British protection. Leaving the Congo in February 1887 Stanley experienced enormous difficulties crossing Africa before finally locating Emin Pasha in April the next year. Stanley was disappointed to discover that the Pasha, like Dr. Livingstone before him, had no desire to be rescued. What he wanted was ammunition and supplies that would allow him to remain in Equatoria and this, the exhausted relief expedition could not provide. It would be another year before Stanley could persuade Emin Pasha to accompany him to East

---

8 *Only in 1862 was Lake Victoria identified as the source of the Nile by the British explorer John Hanning Speke.*

Africa. On the journey they were met by Germans and escorted to Bagamoyo in German East Africa where they arrived on 4th December 1889.

With an interest in the security of the Upper Nile it was important to Britain that other Powers did not gain too much influence in the region. There was thus some concern when Emin Pasha announced that he would throw in his lot with his countrymen and work for the German East Africa Company to assist them in securing the Nile Lakes region. There was concern too at the activities of the German imperialist Carl Peters who was busy making treaties in the same region, also for the German Company.

The Germans on the ground were clearly winning the race to claim Buganda and the Nile Lakes but behind the scenes the British and German governments were already negotiating on broader issues. In 1890, as part of a much larger agreement, it was decided that the region should be a British sphere of influence. The agreement between the two nations covered various interests in Africa but the key to the resulting treaty was Heligoland in the North Sea. As Germany constructed the Kiel Canal and began expanding her fleet it was vital to her that Heligoland should not remain in British hands. The Anglo-German Treaty of 1st July 1890[9] allowed for the transfer of Heligoland to Germany, recognized British rights to the whole of northern East Africa (thus securing the Upper Nile and Egypt), agreed that Zanzibar should be under British protection and delineated the German spheres of influence in East, West and South West Africa.

The British East Africa Association had been granted a Royal Charter as the Imperial British East Africa Company in 1888 with William Mackinnon as its President. He had high hopes for his organization which he modelled on the old East India Company and its Charter gave it full rights of government. Like the Royal Niger Company (chartered in 1886) and the British South Africa Company (to be chartered in 1889) its purpose was to develop British interests in its designated region without charge to the Treasury. The Association had already made a number of agreements with local rulers in the British sphere of influence beyond the coastal area leased to it by the Sultan of Zanzibar. When Stanley arrived on the coast with Emin Pasha in 1889 he had with him a bunch of the treaties that Mackinnon had asked him to obtain but even before that the Company felt it wise to push on into the interior, trying to thwart German advances. The agreements made with East African rulers (and throughout the continent in this period) were usually very simple documents and it is doubtful if many of those who appended their marks to them were fully aware of all the implications. Nevertheless, it was these that would now form the basis of the Company's claims around the Nile Lakes and elsewhere and the Anglo-German Treaty of 1890 would negate any German agreements in the region.

Mombasa was the centre of the Company's administration but the Imperial British East Africa Company now had legal title to lands far into the interior and beyond Lake Victoria. To secure their rights the Company sent a force under Captain Frederick Lugard to inform the Kabaka of British rights and impose some sort of rule over Buganda and its vassal states. This, with some bloodshed and the help of the Maxim gun, he eventually managed to do but it was clear that the Kabaka was not entirely happy with the outcome. Uganda would be a troubled region for some years.

If Buganda ("Uganda")[10] was to be of any use to the Company, trade would have to be developed but the cost of portage from the Lakes to the sea was prohibitive. Only high value commodities like ivory were worth transporting and if trade was to flourish roads, even a

---
9 *Usually known as the Heligoland-Zanzibar Treaty.*
10 *Buganda was the immediate kingdom of the Kabaka. The term Uganda was soon used to describe Buganda and its vassal states. The extent of the Uganda Protectorate would grow over the years.*

railway would have to be built. In July 1891 it became clear that the British Government would not guarantee the cost of building a railway to Lake Victoria and the Company found itself heavily overextended. It decided to retrench and in December that year Lugard was instructed to abandon Uganda and return to the coast.

Initially the British Government was in favour of withdrawal although it was recognized that France would be likely to step in (with implications for the security of Egypt). Public opinion though, based on maintaining British honour and prestige, forced a re-think. The Company was persuaded to remain in Uganda until the British Government assumed control in March 1893. Uganda formally became a British Protectorate on 18th June 1894.

Some two years after handing over Uganda the Company sold all its remaining assets to the Government, surrendering its Charter and also its concessions from the Sultan of Zanzibar. Its brief period of administration was over and the East Africa Protectorate came into being on 1st July 1895. This, and the Uganda Protectorate, passed from Foreign Office to Colonial Office administration in 1905.

As a British protected state from 1890 Zanzibar had a Consul General who reported to the Foreign Office. British control of Zanzibar was further strengthened after a disputed succession in 1896 triggered one of the almost inevitable colonial wars of the time. At 0902hrs on 27th August 1896 the first shots of the Anglo-Zanzibar war were fired at the Sultan's palace from Royal Navy ships. With the distinction of being the shortest war in recorded history it ended 38 minutes later at 0940hrs. Nevertheless lives had been lost and a beautiful building destroyed. The offending Sultan sought and found refuge with the German Consul. His successor had a better understanding of what was required in the brave new world. A final decree abolishing slavery in Zanzibar was issued on 6th April 1897 for which the new Sultan would be knighted by Queen Victoria. The old ways were gone. In 1913 responsibility was transferred to the Colonial Office and a British Resident appointed.

Agreement was reached with Italy in 1891 on the extent of Italian interests to the north. With this and the Anglo-German agreement of 1890 the extent of British interests in East Africa was more or less settled. British imperialists, like Cecil Rhodes, had long dreamed of a tract of British territory from the Cape to Cairo with a railway running its entire length. The establishment of German East Africa blocked these plans and French imperialists still thought in terms of a territory stretching from the Atlantic to the Red Sea, or at least as far as the Nile. The French had not been as closely consulted in the division of East Africa as they would have liked but objected strongly when Britain leased part of the Egyptian province of Equatoria to Leopold II of the Belgians in 1894. The lease was designed to block any French move to the east. The French objected on the quite reasonable grounds that Britain had leased territory that she did not own and began to plan a claim of their own.

While the Anglo-Egyptian reconquest of the Sudan was nearing completion under Kitchener word reached him that a European led party had raised a flag at Fashoda, in the south. Fresh from his victory at Omdurman he set off to investigate and found that a French force had indeed laid claim to this part of the Sudan. Kitchener challenged their right to be there but the matter was referred to their respective governments without coming to blows. Their respective governments found the matter difficult to resolve and the "Fashoda Incident" of 1898 brought Britain and France perilously close to war. In the end though, diplomacy triumphed. The French withdrew without a fight and in March 1899 it was agreed that the division between French and British interests would be the watershed between the Nile and the Congo.

There was now no major threat to the British in East Africa but the region had been acquired mainly to keep other nations out, not because it was rich in resources. The Uganda and East Africa protectorates were products of the "Scramble" rather than reasons for it. If they were to be profitable, or at least pay their way, it was time to consolidate and the first task was to establish proper communications between the interior and the coast. The first road suitable for wheeled vehicles (ox carts) did not reach Lake Victoria until 1896. By that time the Government had decided to go ahead with a railway and this reached the shores of Lake Victoria in 1901. This large investment together with the cost of administration gave some urgency to the matter of development.

The interior of the East Africa Protectorate contained an extensive highland region which was not densely populated and, with its temperate climate, seemed ideal for European style farming. As much of this region was not under active cultivation it could officially be designated as "waste" or "unoccupied" land and arrangements were made to grant it to European settlers. The Crown Lands Ordinance of 1902 allowed settlement to begin in earnest. Areas already actively occupied by the Kikuyu, Masai and others were reserved for their continued use but new grants were made only to Europeans, many of whom came from South Africa. The region became known as the "White Highlands" and was the basis for the commercial development of what would become Kenya.

The Uganda Protectorate was very different. Here, population was relatively dense and African farmers were ready to produce cash crops (particularly cotton) for export.[11] European settlement was not encouraged because it was not necessary for Uganda's development and at first there was little Crown ("waste") land that could be granted.

These developments allowed both protectorates to become self supporting by the time of the First World War. The different patterns of European settlement resulted in the East Africa Protectorate becoming a colony (as "Kenya") in 1920 while Uganda remained a protectorate until independence in 1962.

As may be supposed from the historical summary the coins in use in East Africa were various but the Maria Theresia dollar was the normal standard of value. This was marginalized by the Indian rupee during the second half of the 19th century which gradually became the normal currency of use. The coins of the East African Currency Board, established in 1919, would eventually circulate throughout the region but before we examine that we must look first at each of the protectorates.

Usual trade coins in Middle East and East Africa

Maria Theresia dollar dated 1780.   *The British Indian rupee which gradually superseded it.*

---

11 *This was encouraged in Uganda by the British Cotton Growers' Association.*

In **Zanzibar** the Sultan issued coins of his own in the 1880s in both pice (divisions of the rupee) and riyals (the riyal itself being a dollar sized silver coin) but neither of these was continued. With its connections to Muscat and the Arab world the Maria Theresia dollar continued to be popular in Zanzibar but by 1890 the British Indian rupee and its subdivisions had become the normal currency. The Sultan's pice struck in the 1880s were similar in weight and size to the British Indian quarter anna and circulated, like the quarter anna, at 64 to the rupee.

In 1908 the rupee was officially acknowledged as the unit of currency, the Zanzibar rupee being the same standard as the rupee of British India.[12] Its division into annas and pice though was abolished in favour of a division into 100 cents and a subsidiary coinage of twenty cents in nickel with a one cent and ten cents in bronze was struck. This followed the recent decimalization of the rupee in East Africa discussed below. In the same year Government notes were successfully introduced in multiples of the rupee but the new Zanzibar coins did not go into general circulation. Serious concerns were raised about their suitability and eventually they were returned to the United Kingdom and sold to the Royal Mint for their scrap value. There were no further issues of these minor denominations of 1908 and very few survive. No specific Zanzibar rupee coin was struck, supplies of British Indian rupees being adequate.

The coins in use in Zanzibar thus continued to be the British Indian rupee and the old Zanzibar pice supplemented by the coins in use on the East African mainland. The British sovereign, as in India itself, was fixed at 15 rupees giving the rupee an exchange rate of 1/4d (one shilling and fourpence) sterling.

In January 1936 Zanzibar adopted the currency of the East African Currency Board, taking on the East African shilling as its currency in place of the rupee. From about 1927 the rupee in Zanzibar had been rated at 1/6d sterling so at the time of changeover the rupee was equivalent to 1½ East African Shillings. Shillings and cents of the East African Currency Board remained the currency of Zanzibar until 1966.

From its base at **Mombasa** the Imperial British East Africa Company issued coins dated 1888 and 1890. The original concession to the British East Africa Association from the Sultan of Zanzibar gave it "*….the right to establish a bank or banks anywhere in his Highness' territories above mentioned, with the exclusive privilege of issuing notes….*". The "territories above mentioned" constituted the coastal strip leased from the Sultan. In its Founders' Agreement, which formed the basis of its Charter application, the Company called for the right "*…to establish banks, issue notes, and coin money…*". The Charter itself empowered what was now the Imperial British East Africa Company to "*create banks*" making no mention of notes or coins.[13] Nevertheless the Sultan's concessions for the coastal strip gave the Company the authority and sovereign powers of the Sultan (who had already issued coins for Zanzibar). For the British sphere of influence beyond the coastal strip, the Charter granted all powers necessary for the purposes of government.

The coins struck for the Company were silver rupees and bronze pice dated 1888 and smaller silver denominations (half rupee, quarter rupee and two annas) dated 1890. Some of the pice were struck at Calcutta, all the other coins being struck by Heaton of Birmingham. These coins were on the same standard as British Indian coins and remained in circulation alongside them in East Africa for some years after the Company ceased to exist. The legend

---
12 *Zanzibar Currency Decree, No 3 of 1908.*
13 *The original concession to the Association was dated 24th May 1887, Article VII dealing with banks and notes. The Founders' Agreement was dated 18th April 1888 and the Charter, 3rd September 1888. The Sultan's concession was renewed (for the newly chartered company) on 9th October 1888 with no change to Article VII.*

"**MOMBASA**" which appears prominently on these coins refers to the Company's main seat of administration on the coast. The coins circulated throughout East Africa although the use of coin was not widespread in the interior until the building of the railway.

The Company was never financially strong enough to open a bank or issue notes.

Imperial British East Africa Company, Mombasa

Rupee 1888.

Half rupee 1890.

Quarter rupee 1890.

Two annas 1890.

Quarter anna 1888.

The term "**British East Africa**" is confusing as it is sometimes used to refer to all British interests in East Africa. We have seen though that the East Africa Protectorate (later Kenya), the Uganda Protectorate, Zanzibar and Tanganyika (the last of which came to Britain after the First World War) all had separate political identities. Nevertheless, apart from their geographical location, there was much that they shared in common. Both East Africa and Uganda had been administered by the Imperial British East Africa Company until taken over by the Foreign Office as protectorates. Both of them also passed to Colonial Office control in 1905. Throughout East Africa the common coinage was based on the British Indian rupee.

When their territory passed to the Foreign Office the coins of the Imperial British East Africa Company (IBEAC) continued in circulation together with British Indian coins. The first new coin required for the **East Africa Protectorate** was an issue of bronze pice dated 1897, 1898 and 1899 to supplement the coins already in circulation. An Order in Council of 1898[14] formally recognized the Indian rupee as the unit of currency and confirmed the actual coins then in circulation. These were the various denominations of British Indian coins, the IBEAC coins and the newly introduced pice (quarter anna) of the East Africa Protectorate. It was not long though before proposals were made for change. It was suggested that the decimal system in use in Ceylon (a rupee divided into a hundred cents rather than into annas and

---

14 *The East Africa (Currency) Order in Council of 18th May 1898.*

pice) would be more logical and convenient. The introduction of paper money was considered an urgent need for those who had to remit large sums and for travellers. The existing currency system had come about because East Africa's trade was mainly with the Arabian Sea but, as settlers began to arrive and exports to Europe increased, there were suggestions that a connection with sterling may be more suitable.[15]

Following a review, the East Africa and Uganda (Currency) Order in Council of 1905 allowed for changes to be made. The rupee was confirmed as the standard unit of currency for both protectorates but, as suggested it was now to be divided into 100 cents. A local Currency Board was established and a new subsidiary coinage was struck, the fifty cents and twenty five cents in silver, the ten cents and five cents cent in cupro-nickel and the cent and half cent in aluminium. The new decimal coinage was struck from 1906 although the half cent was not introduced until 1908 and the five cents not until 1913. As in British West Africa aluminium proved unsuitable and from 1909 the two lower denominations were struck in cupro- nickel. A single coinage sufficed for both protectorates and bore the legend "**EAST AFRICA & UGANDA PROTECTORATES**". The new coinage was subsidiary only, the supply of the rupee denomination from British India and the remaining IBEAC rupees being sufficient. The sovereign, which had passed for some time at 15 rupees, was made legal tender for that amount. From its offices in Mombasa and Kampala the local Currency Board began issuing notes redeemable in silver rupees. When sufficient quantities of the new subsidiary coins were in circulation the old annas and pice denominations were withdrawn and demonetized. From June 1910 the coinage of the two protectorates consisted of British Indian and IBEAC rupees, their associated halves and quarters (which circulated as fifty and twenty five cents) and the new subsidiary coins from fifty cents down to the half cent.

An interesting feature of the new coins is that, like those of British West Africa, the cupro-nickel denominations have a central hole. As cupro-nickel had a similar appearance to silver the hole was a useful, perhaps necessary, indication that the coins were of lower value but for those who had clothes without pockets coins were not a particularly convenient form of exchange. The central hole would allow the coins to be strung together for easy carriage and thus encourage the use of coin in preference to trade goods. This joint coinage for the East Africa and Uganda Protectorates continued in issue until 1919.

Government coinage for East Africa and Uganda (subsidiary to rupee)

East Africa Protectorate pice 1899.

East Africa and Uganda Protectorates fifty cents 1906.

Cent 1907 (aluminium).

Ten cents 1907.

---

15 Sir Charles Eliot, "The East Africa Protectorate", 1905, p.206.

After the First World War much of German East Africa came to the United Kingdom as a League of Nations mandate and was named Tanganyika Territory. The East Africa Protectorate became the Colony and Protectorate of Kenya while Uganda continued to be a protectorate. Provision now had to be made for coinage for a much larger area.

Late in 1919 the **East African Currency Board** was established in London to provide for and control the supply of currency to Kenya, Uganda and Tanganyika. One of the first things it had to tackle was the steeply rising price of silver which resulted in an increase in the sterling value of the British Indian rupee. Silver, measured against gold, was increasing steadily in value and the rupee was now worth considerably more than its historic rate of 1/4d sterling. This was a problem that had to be addressed.

The first step taken by the East African Currency Board was the issue of a one rupee note with unlimited legal tender in May 1920. The new note was designed to replace the rupee coin and thus provide some stability but this was not enough. In spite of East Africa's position on the shores of the Indian Ocean and its connections with India the time was now considered right to tie the East African currency to sterling rather than to the rupee. This was a difficult time to make changes, mainly because of the fluctuating price of silver so the change was not as simple as it might have been.

A start was made in 1920 when the rupee could be conveniently rated at two shillings (one florin) sterling. A new coinage came into issue, the main coin (and primary unit) being the florin at ten to the pound sterling. Like the rupee it replaced, and to which it was equal, the florin was divided into one hundred cents. The fifty cents coin was now officially denominated "Fifty Cents – One Shilling" and there was also a twenty five cents coin in silver. Although the florin was the same weight and size as the British Indian rupee all the East African silver coins were now 50% silver.[16] The silver coins were supplemented by the ten cents, five cents and one cent in cupro-nickel. Although the one cent was reduced in size all the other denominations, apart from the new florin, were substantially unchanged from the previous East Africa & Uganda Protectorates issue except that they now bear the simpler legend "**EAST AFRICA**". Florin notes replaced the recently issued one rupee notes.

So far, so good but hardly had the florin been introduced than the price of silver began to fall. This was financially disastrous for the Board which was committed to redeeming rupees at two shillings. Part of the solution was to issue a new coinage in 25% silver this time based on the shilling rather than the florin. The florin coinage was thus of very brief duration (June 1920 to the end of 1921) and the shilling became the unit of the East African Currency Board from 1st January 1922.

In other colonies and protectorates that adopted sterling, as in the home country, the shilling was a division (one twentieth) of the pound. In East Africa there were always twenty shillings to the pound sterling but it was the shilling that was the primary unit of account, not the pound. Like the florin it replaced and the rupee before that, the East African shilling was divided into 100 cents. The new shilling's subsidiary coins were the "Fifty Cents – Half Shilling" in 25% silver and the ten cents, five cents and one cent in bronze. All these denominations began to be struck in 1921 to prepare for the change from the florin to the shilling at the beginning of 1922. The lower denominations were now in bronze to distinguish them from the earlier cupro-nickel coins. Currency notes in multiples of the shilling were also issued.

The East African shilling remained at par with the British shilling, being backed by sterling securities. It was though always a larger coin than its British equivalent. This was because at

---

16 Although British silver coins were also reduced to 50% fineness in 1920 the British Indian rupee was not reduced in fineness until 1940 (see Chapter eleven).

the time of its introduction it was worth more than the "Fifty Cents – One Shilling" of the preceding florin coinage and it was felt that a larger coin was necessary.

After 1922 the only significant alteration to the East African Currency Board coinage was the introduction of cupro-nickel in place of 25% silver for the shilling and its half in 1948. There were of course changes of portrait and legend with changes of monarch and from 1942 the ten cents and five cents denominations were struck on thinner flans.

As we have seen, Zanzibar adopted the coinage of the East African Currency Board in 1936 and in 1951 it was adopted also by British Somaliland and Aden. The coinage of the Board ceased in the early 1960s as the various territories that used it moved towards independence and opened their own central banks. The Board's responsibilities for currency finally ceased in 1966.

East African Currency Board

Florin 1920.

Cupro-nickel cent 1920.

Shilling 1922.

Fifty cents 1924.

Bronze ten cents 1933.

Bronze five cents 1941.

Shilling 1952.

Fifty cents 1963.

SUMMARY FOR BRITISH EAST AFRICAN COINAGE

Later 19th Century	Rupee generally replaces Maria Theresia dollar as main currency in use and normal standard of value.
1888	Imperial British East Africa Company coinage introduced (rupees and divisions as in British India).
1897	Bronze pice issued for East Africa Protectorate to supplement coins in circulation.
1898	British Indian rupee formally recognized as unit of account for East Africa and Uganda Protectorates.
1905	Rupee confirmed but now to be divided into one hundred cents. Sovereign confirmed at fifteen rupees (as in British India). A local Currency Board was established with offices in Mombasa (East Africa) and Kampala (Uganda).
1906	New decimal coins introduced subsidiary to the British Indian rupee.
1919	East African Currency Board (EACB) established in London to provide currency for enlarged area (now including Tanganyika).
1920	New coinage introduced linked to sterling. The florin of one hundred cents replaced the rupee as the main unit.
1922	Shilling (of one hundred cents) becomes the main unit of currency. It is at par with the British shilling.
1936	Zanzibar adopts the currency of the EACB.
1951	Aden and British Somaliland adopt EACB currency.
1966	EACB's responsibilities end.

East Africa had belatedly adopted a sterling based currency. Beyond it, as we move into the Indian Ocean, we also move firmly into the rupee using area and this will be the subject of our next chapter.

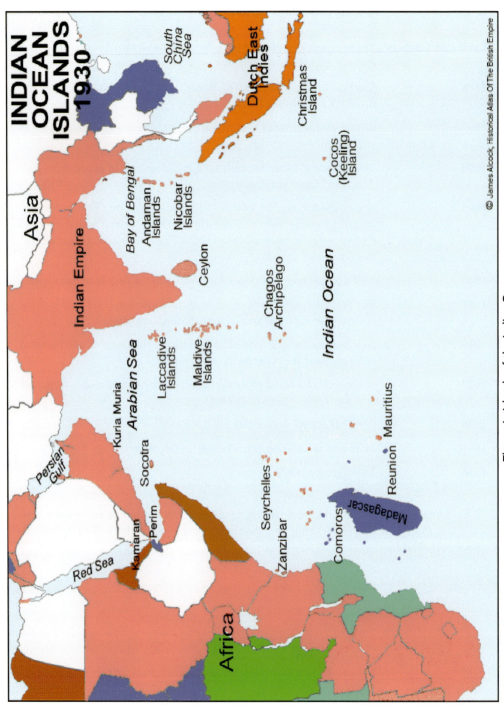

The main islands of the Indian Ocean

11

The Indian Ocean

APART from India itself the territories that claim most of our attention in this chapter are Burma, Ceylon, Mauritius and the Seychelles. Before we examine each of them however we must take a brief look at the Persian Gulf to which Britain attached a great deal of importance and we must not forget the many smaller islands of the Indian Ocean in which Britain developed interests over the years.

At the beginning of our period the whole of the Indian Ocean was the preserve of the East India Company whose primary interest in the Persian Gulf was trade. At first this was with Persia (modern Iran) through the port of Jask. Later the Company also used Gombroon (Bandar Abbas) and then Bushire but it soon also had a factory at Basra in Turkish Arabia. From there it was not long before an overland route through Baghdad and the Mediterranean was established as an artery of communication between India and London. The overland routes allowed swifter communication concerning commercial and political matters than the sea route round the Cape but this particular route could only function if the Persian Gulf was safe for navigation. It was for this reason that the East India Company and the British Government attached so much importance to effective control of the seas of the Persian Gulf.

The notion of controlling an eastern sea was not unrealistic in the 18th century. Most of the Eastern states were largely self sufficient and had not needed to develop naval power while European East Indiamen were not simple trading vessels. They were equipped and manned to hold their own against all comers and nowhere in the East could they be matched for firepower and sophistication. When necessary they could be backed by ships of the Royal Navy so only a rival European nation could thwart such a plan. So important was this last consideration that during the Napoleonic Wars the Persian Gulf factories, normally subordinate to the Company's Bombay Presidency, were placed directly under the Governor General of India in order to deal more effectively with any French threat.

A lesser but constant threat to trade in the eastern seas was that of piracy. Not all the Company's trade moved in powerful East Indiamen, particularly the "country" trades (anything other than the direct trade with Europe). Any armed opposition to free trade tended to be viewed by European nations as "piracy" although many of those who practiced it viewed it more as an enforcement of their own rights and freedoms. In the early 19th century the Qawasim of the eastern Gulf were a particular menace not only to trade but to the overland dispatches that came via Basra, often in smaller "country" ships. The Qawasim operated mainly from the ports of Ras al-Khaima and Sharjah and competed with the Omanis and others for a share of the increasing trade of the Persian Gulf and Arabian Sea. Their methods of "competing" included demands for tribute, the capture and ransom of ships (sometimes British or under British protection) and the murder of their crews all of which could only be classed as piracy by the British. At this time the Arabs of what came to be called the "Pirate Coast" were often referred to collectively in British records as the "Joasmi". The Qawasim were considered to be the main offenders but their methods of armed commerce were common to all the "Joasmi Pirates".

From the early 19th century these coastal Arabs became inspired by the Wahhabi, a relatively new Islamic movement in the Arabian Peninsula, and their commerce raiding at sea increased. Action had to be taken to subdue them and major expeditions were mounted against them in 1809 and 1819. These involved Government forces as well as those of the East India Company and in the latter expedition Ras al-Khaima was practically destroyed. In January 1820 agreement was reached with most of the maritime Arab rulers that there would be no further attacks on seaborne trade.

The General Treaty of 1820 sought to pacify the seas while avoiding British involvement in the complicated internal affairs of the signatory states. In both these aims it generally succeeded although it soon fell to the British Resident in the Gulf to police the treaty by overseeing its observance and settling matters arising between signatories. The Treaty covered acts of piracy, which were strictly defined, but did nothing to prevent disruption to shipping as a result of declared wars. To address this problem a truce was arranged between the Arab rulers in 1835 the object of which was the prevention of all hostile activities at sea for a fixed period. After twice being renewed a perpetual truce was agreed in May 1853. It was these truces that allowed the "Pirate Coast" to become known as the "Trucial Coast".

The British Resident was still the final arbiter but the Treaty on piracy and the Perpetual Truce were maritime agreements designed only to pacify the seas. They did though weaken the power of the Ottoman Empire which was still the nominal ruler of most of the Arabian Peninsula and it was perhaps this as much as anything else that made treaties with Britain acceptable to the Wahhabis and desirable to the Sheikhs of the coast. Similar agreements with Bahrain, Qatar and eventually Kuwait brought these also into the British sphere of influence in the later 19th century and the Sultan of Muscat had been in treaty agreement for many years.[1]

In forming agreements with these various states Britain had recognized their right to make them. This effectively recognized their independence, not only from the Ottoman Empire but from Persia, who had long standing claims to islands on the Arabian side of the Gulf, including Bahrain. Nevertheless in the late 19th and early 20th centuries Britain extended her influence along the entire coast from Kuwait to Oman with further agreements giving her preferential rights over the affairs, mineral rights and (later) oil exploration rights of the various states and restricting their dealings with other Powers. Britain had achieved control of the seas and a great deal of influence on the Arabian shores of the Persian Gulf without major wars or formal annexations but in doing so had disregarded Persian and Ottoman claims.

Britain would have liked Persia, as the main sovereign power of the region, to remain strong, independent and on friendly terms. In addition to the Resident for the Persian Gulf at Bushire the Company, later Britain herself, usually had an envoy at the Shah's court in Teheran. There were a few spats between the two countries including the Persian War of 1856-1857

---

1   The Anglo Omani agreement of 12th October 1798 was a Treaty of Friendship between the Sultan and the Government of British India, the catalyst for it being the French invasion of Egypt in that year.

over diplomatic issues and a perceived threat to India (of which more later) but otherwise relations were generally tolerable. Nevertheless Persia still maintained her claims to Bahrain (and would do so until 1970).

The Ottoman Empire nominally extended over the Arabian Peninsula to the shores of the Persian Gulf. In Europe the Ottomans had traditionally enjoyed British support for the purpose of containing Russian ambitions but Britain paid little heed to Ottoman claims on the Gulf shores south of Kuwait.

In the period before the First World War there were thus conflicting claims and interests in the region by the Persians, the Ottomans, the British and others. By and large though, Britain policed the seas while the states involved lived with their differences and got on with life.

The way in which Britain had secured her interests in the **Persian Gulf** ensured that she had no responsibility for coinage in any of the Gulf States. Few of the states with which Britain had treaty relations had any coinage of their own until well into the 20th century relying until then on Ottoman and Persian coins and the usual trade coins of the day. As elsewhere in the region the Maria Theresia thaler was a favoured and respected coin but was gradually displaced by the rupee of British India and its subdivisions.

British India was never a British colony. It was part of the Indian Empire whose separate status can be clearly illustrated from coins. A British penny of George VI bears the obverse legend **GEORGIVS VI D: G: BR: OMN: REX F: D: IND: IMP**. In its expanded form this would be Georgius VI, Dei Gratia ("George VI, by the Grace of God"), Britanniarum Omnium Rex ("King of all the Britains"), Fidei Defensor ("Defender of the Faith"), Indiae Imperator ("Emperor of India"). This gives him three separate offices. As King of *all* the Britains (the United Kingdom and the British Dominions beyond the Seas.) he was the head of the British Empire. As Defender of the Faith he was head of the Church of England. As Emperor of India he was ruler of British India and suzerain of the princely states. Although it could be formally defined as being part of the British Empire the Indian Empire was a separate unit within it. A rupee of British India at this time bears the much shorter obverse legend **GEORGE VI KING EMPEROR** using his Indian title only.

Titles on British and British Indian coins

British penny 1944.   British Indian rupee 1944.

How did Britain's unusual relationship with India come about? In earlier chapters we have seen how the East India Company built on the basic grants of the early firmans and became ever more involved in local affairs as its trade and influence grew. India at this time was not a single political entity. Moghul rule, direct or indirect, extended over most of the sub continent but the many disparate states that comprised that empire had an ever changing pattern of alliances and disputes. It was in this environment, under Moghul paramountcy, that the Company operated and developed its various interests.

The 18th century quarrels between Britain and France spanned the world and soon extended to India. This compelled the Company to develop and extend its local alliances and to build its armies into a formidable fighting machine. Also, the 1740s saw British Crown forces deployed in India for the first time to assist the Company in dealing with the French and their allies. This was an indication of how important India had become to Britain and eventual success against the French greatly increased the influence, prestige and responsibilities of the East India Company.

By the 1750s the Company thus enjoyed considerable influence in several parts of India. Already, a general firman agreed with the Moghul Emperor at Delhi (known as "The 1717 Firman") had placed the Company in a position of advantage throughout Moghul India. Its provisions were jealously guarded and in Bengal it gave the Company the right to move its goods free of customs. Inevitably the Company's servants interpreted this to their maximum advantage and soon much of Bengal's trade was moving duty free under Company passes for which fees were paid. The Nawab was losing much of his revenue and the Company was unable to curb the excesses of its own servants.

So bad had matters become that in 1756 a new Nawab decided to expel the Company from Bengal and revoke the terms of the 1717 Firman within his territory. This he did in June of that year but he had chosen a bad time to make his move. After some successes against the French and their allies in southern India the Company was in no mood to meekly accept the loss of valuable privileges in Bengal. There were land and naval forces at Madras that could be sent north.

Calcutta was recaptured with little resistance early in 1757, the Nawab agreeing immediately to reinstate the terms of the Firman and to pay compensation. The Company though wanted more and had the power at hand to obtain it. The Nawab's army was met and defeated at Plassey in June 1757 and a new Nawab, the Company's own nominee, was appointed. Such was the Company's influence in the years after Plassey that by 1765 the Moghul was willing to grant it the diwani (superintendence of the revenue) for the whole of Bengal, Bihar and Orissa. This did not give the Company sovereignty but it did give it the civil administration of the entire region.

In the later 18th century there was also a major expansion of the territories administered from Madras and it was the collection of revenues in all these vast areas, not military conquest, which forced the Company to elaborate a system of government in India. The settlement of the revenues and the judicial and civil organization that ensured its collection formed the basis of that government. With revenues as well as commerce to protect there was a constant need to secure borders through treaties and the elimination of real or perceived threats leading inexorably to territorial expansion and increased influence.

The period in which the Company was extending its interests coincided with a weakening of the control which had made the Moghuls the paramount power in India. Paramountcy was not a precise concept but for centuries there had been a general assumption that without it India would not enjoy the blessings of internal peace. A paramount power bore no allegiance to any overlord and assumed the power to interfere in the internal government and foreign affairs of the various lesser states under its influence.

For the moment the East India Company still acknowledged the Moghul Emperor as its overlord in India. With Moghul decline though the Company, with its increasing armies paid for from local revenues, was soon a serious contender for the paramountcy. A private company may not have seemed an obvious alternative to Moghul rule and neither the Directors in

London nor the British Government intended that it should. Nevertheless by the end of the 18th century the Marathas were the only force that stood between the Company and paramountcy and by 1819, after a series of Maratha wars, circumstances and attitudes had changed. The East India Company, with Government backing, now considered itself and was generally considered to be the paramount power in India.

In its rise to power the Company was not left entirely to its own devises. There was a general feeling in London that it was not proper for a private company to administer large parts of India and concern too at the lack of control over the private activities of its servants. The British Government also felt it was entitled to some of the revenues raised, not least because the Company's gains had been assisted by Crown forces.

Direct British Government involvement in Indian affairs began with the Regulating Act of 1773 which appointed a Governor General in Bengal. It allowed for Crown appointees to the Governor General's Council and for a judiciary in Bengal that was independent of the Company. The India Act of 1784 strengthened the position of the Governor General in India and appointed a Board of Control in London with detailed supervision of most of the Company's affairs. Between them the Regulating Act and the 1784 India Act brought the Company under Government control and made it little more than a department of the British Government. This laid the basis for the Company's government in India until the 1850s. The British Government continued to be uneasy about the involvement of a commercial enterprise in administration but through the various Charter renewals the Company lost the last of its commercial interests and by 1834 had become an administrative organization only.

A major concern for the Company was the security of what can now be termed "British India" and the area of most concern was the North West Frontier. It was from here, through Afghanistan, that major invasions had come in the past and it was by this route that Russia would come if, as was suspected, she coveted India. Russian overtures to Afghanistan and her increasing influence over Persia were thus viewed with deepest suspicion as the "Great Game" was played out between the British and Russian Empires for supremacy in this part of the world.[2]

From its position of power in the 1830s the Company assumed that a quick invasion of Afghanistan to install a friendly ruler would be little more than a formality and that this would secure the North West Frontier once and for all. It was therefore decided to mount a major expedition to depose the existing Amir at Kabul (Dost Mahomed) and reinstate a previous ruler (Shah Shuja). Kandahar was occupied in April 1839 and Shah Shuja installed at Kabul in August. It was soon discovered that he was not a popular ruler and would need a large British force in permanent support. In 1841 rebellion broke out in Kabul which the British could not contain. They opted to retreat from the Afghan capital, leaving the city in January 1842. The force which left Kabul consisted of 4,500 troops, 700 of them British, and perhaps 10,000 camp followers. This cumbersome column very soon came under attack and seven days later only one Briton (Surgeon William Brydon) and a few sepoy stragglers arrived at Jalalabad. The retreat from Kabul was a major catastrophe and a serious blow to the Company's prestige. A large military column had been annihilated by enemy action and the effects of the bitter cold. At the end of the day Dost Mahomed was back in office, Shah Shuja had been assassinated and the North West Frontier had not been secured.

The Company proved strong enough to recover from this reverse quite quickly. Sind was annexed in 1843 and the Punjab taken in 1849 bringing the whole region up to the Afghan

---

2 *The period of the "Great Game" is generally taken as being from the Russo Persian treaty of 1813 (when Russia encroached on Persian territory) to the Anglo Russian convention of 1907 (when British and Russian spheres of interest in Asia were agreed).*

hills under British control. In Afghanistan Dost Mahomed did not prove to be an implacable enemy and from 1855 was in alliance with the British. This alliance was tested in March 1856 when Persian troops occupied Herat, a small state on Afghanistan's western border. Herat was important to Afghanistan and to Britain because it lay on the main route from Persia (and Russia) into Afghanistan and India. The Governor General had no intention of risking an overland expedition into and through Afghanistan so soon after the disastrous retreat of 1842 but the war he waged on the Persian coast (1856-1857) did force the Persians to withdraw from Herat. Dost Mahomed stuck by his alliance with the British for the rest of his life (he died in 1863) thus bringing calm to the North West Frontier at a crucial time for British India.

By the 1850s there was some unease in India about the nature, speed and direction of the various changes being introduced under East India Company rule. These included the "doctrine of lapse" under which any state could be annexed by the paramount power if there was no legitimate heir. States that were judged to be governed incompetently could also be taken over and under this last provision Oude (Awadh) was annexed in 1856. There was naturally great resentment among the ruling classes affected and there were soon rumours in the army and elsewhere that Christian conversion was planned.

The spark for the Indian Mutiny is supposed to have been the use of cartridges for use with the new Enfield rifles. They were rumoured to be greased with both beef and pork fat and the normal firing drill required them to be bitten open before loading, a practice deeply offensive to both Hindus and Muslims. The Mutiny began in earnest after men of the 3rd Light Cavalry were disciplined and disgraced for refusing to handle them. There had been previous mutinies in the Company's armies but that which began at Meerut on 10th May 1857 and spread quickly to Delhi and beyond was something very much bigger. It was widespread and violent, more akin to a revolt than a mutiny, and seen by many Indians as a holy war. It did not though extend to the whole of India where there was still little concept of national identity at this time. There were large regions that did not wish to involve themselves in revolt and some that actively supported the paramount power in suppressing it. This support came not only from parts of British India but also from some of the independent states of Rajputana. Although there were large scale massacres of Europeans British forces eventually proved strong enough to suppress the rebellion and re-establish control although some of the reprisals were as brutal as the Mutiny itself. For these and for the general conditions which had led to the revolt the Company was severely criticised.

As we have seen above, British Government involvement in India began with the Regulating Act of 1773 and the Company, steadily shorn of its trading activities, became little more than a British Government department. By 1834 it was clear that sooner or later responsibility would have to be transferred to the Crown and the Company's last Charter renewal of 1853 was open ended, allowing a transfer when convenient. The events of 1857-1858 were the catalyst and resulted in the swift transfer of government to the Crown. The India Act of 1858 received royal assent on 2nd August and took effect on 1st September. The government of India which had been vested in the East India Company in trust for the Crown was henceforth vested directly in the Crown and the Queen was proclaimed in major Indian cities on 1st November, 1858. The Governor General (Lord Canning) received the additional title of Viceroy and in London the President of the Board of Control (Lord Stanley) became the first Secretary of State for India.

The Moghul Emperor was accused of complicity in the Mutiny and divested of an office which had been little more than symbolic for many years. Even before the Mutiny it was understood that his successor would leave the ancestral palace and lose his traditional grandeur but the fact that Moghul rule had ended was brought home to Bahadur Shah Zafar with a brutality that seems unnecessary even in the heat of the moment. After capture, the three princes thought most complicit in the revolt (two sons and a grandson) were stripped and shot in full public view and their naked bodies left outside Delhi's Red Fort for all to see. It was a shocked old man who was exiled to Burma where this last of the Moghul Emperors would die in 1862.

Queen Victoria took a great interest in her new dominion and was personally concerned at the deep seated problems that had led to the Mutiny. It was a matter of great pride to her when the Crown's position in India was consolidated by the Royal Titles Act 1876 and subsequent Proclamation which granted her the additional title of Empress of India. This new title appeared almost at once on her Indian coins but was not to be used in the United Kingdom where it was felt it would be inappropriate. Nevertheless the Queen herself tried to insist that it be used on the new Jubilee coinage introduced in the United Kingdom in 1887. On that occasion her request was ignored but when the "veiled head" portrait was introduced in 1893 the **IND· IMP·** title appears on the British coinage for the first time. It would be used by subsequent monarchs until 1948.

British half-crown of 1893 introducing the IND· IMP· title

The Mutiny showed that a large gulf had developed in some parts of India between the Company and those they ruled. That rule passed immediately to the Crown and conciliation began almost at once with the Queen's Proclamation of 1st November 1858. Religious toleration would be observed. There would be racial equality in official appointments. Ancient rights and customs would be respected. Rebels would be pardoned unless convicted of the murder of British subjects. In India it was the Crown's "…*earnest Desire…to administer its Government for the benefit of all Our Subjects resident therein*…." The massacres and reprisals though had soured relations and conciliation was a lengthy process. The fine words of the Proclamation had to be translated into something more tangible. The "doctrine of lapse" was renounced which guaranteed the continued existence of the remaining independent states. The rulers of those that had supported the paramount power were rewarded with titles and grants. The Government of India now concentrated on material improvements in communications, public services and administration. Social change was left well alone although a European style education was encouraged. Perhaps wisely the Indian army was radically reformed, the proportion of British troops being increased. By the end of the 19th century some attempt had been made to attract Indians into the higher ranks of the Civil Service but no such progress had been made in the army. The independent states would retain that status (although their external affairs were in the hands of the paramount power) until India herself became independent in 1947.

The currency system of **British India** was based on the silver rupee. There were sixteen annas to the rupee and an anna was four pice. The smallest silver coin was generally the two annas (eighth rupee), denominations below that being in copper. The one pice was often denominated "quarter anna". The gold mohur was not legal tender but generally passed for fifteen rupees.

We have seen (Chapter six) that a uniform coinage for the whole of "British India" in gold, silver and copper was introduced by the East India Company in 1835. The Act which introduced it required the precious metal coins to bear the head and name of the reigning monarch but when William IV died in 1837 it was not immediately possible to produce sufficient obverse dies for new coins in the name of Victoria. The Act therefore had to be amended to allow coinage to continue in the name of William.[3] When the uniform coinage was first introduced it was intended that the date shown on the coins (1835) would represent the date of this major alteration to the coinage and would not be changed until new coins should be ordered to be struck. The currency coins of William IV are therefore all dated 1835 even though they continued to be struck for some years. The name and portrait of Victoria was finally introduced to the coinage in 1840-1841. The rule that the date shown on the uniform coinage represented the era of an alteration results in all the Company rupees and fractions in the name of Victoria being dated 1840. A new denomination, the silver two annas, uses 1841 which was the date of its introduction and her mohurs have the same date for the same reason.

The copper coins (half, quarter and twelfth annas) which bore the Company's arms instead of a portrait did not need to be changed so continued to be dated 1835. A new copper denomination, the half pice, is dated 1853. The "era dating" rule breaks down a little with the copper issues because mints began striking them at different dates. The Calcutta-struck half and twelfth annas are dated 1845 and 1848 respectively and quarter annas struck at British mints are dated 1857 and 1858. The above remarks refer to the currency issues. The period of machine struck coinage is a period when patterns and proofs of other dates sometimes exist.

When the Crown took over in 1858 it again took some time to produce the new dies required. The Company's uniform coinage with fixed dates therefore continued in issue until it could be replaced by British Indian coins in 1862. Because of limited capacity at the Indian mints and an increasing coinage requirement the Birmingham mint of Ralph Heaton and Sons was contracted to strike quarter annas in 1857. James Watt & Company was similarly contracted in 1860 and this British struck copper coinage also continued in issue until 1862, all in the name of the Company. James Watt's coins could not carry the date of his contract as India had already passed to the Crown by that time. They therefore have the fixed date of 1858.

The first British Indian (as opposed to East India Company) currency coins are dated 1862. They are all in the same metals and at the same weight and standard as the Company coins they replaced. The Queen's portrait is now a crowned bust and the reverse legend is entirely in English (the Company's uniform coinage had included the value in Persian). The copper coins now also have the Queen's bust on the obverse.

The habit of "era dating" died hard and coins continued to be issued bearing the date 1862 for some years. At the Bombay mint a system of privy marking was used (on the rupee denomination only) to indicate the actual year in which each coin was struck. The mark consisted of dots on the reverse, each dot presumed to indicate one year. An 1862 rupee with seven dots would actually have been struck in 1869/70 and one with twelve dots in 1874. The

---

3   *The original Act was Act XVII of August 1835 by the Honourable the Governor General of India in Council. The ammending Act was Act XXXI of November 1837.*

dots were mainly above the lower flower of the design although one or two dots sometimes appear below the upper flower. Regular yearly dating for the British Indian coinage began in 1874.

The 1862 "Government" coinage, like the Company's coinage before it, was struck at the three mints of Calcutta, Bombay and Madras. In May 1869 the Madras mint ceased operations, the other two mints being considered to have sufficient capacity for the coinage.

Continuation of the Company's uniform coinage and introduction of the Government coinage

East India Company

Mohur 1841

Rupee 1840

Half rupee 1840

Quarter rupee 1840

Two annas 1841

Half pice 1853

Quarter Anna 1858

British Indian coinage introduced 1862

Mohur.

Rupee.

Half rupee.    *Quarter rupee*    *Two annas.*

Half anna.    *Quarter anna.*

Half pice.    *Twelfth anna.*

Bombay rupee with privy date marking.

The silver rupee, as the standard of British India, had unlimited legal tender as did the half rupee. The smaller silver coins and the copper were legal tender up to one rupee. However, the gold coins allowed by the Act which introduced the uniform coinage in 1835 were not to be legal tender in any of the Company's territories. This was not an attempt to remove gold from circulation but the Directors of the Company had been strongly in favour of monometallism for many years and silver had always been the standard of Moghul India.

The gold coins allowed by the 1835 Act were the two mohurs, the mohur, half mohur and quarter mohur and these were to be struck on request for the convenience of those who brought gold to the mints. The suggested rate was fifteen rupees to the mohur but as they were not legal tender these gold coins, like any other commodity, would pass at whatever they fetched in the market place. In the event the two mohurs and one mohur were the only gold denominations struck under the Company although for Victoria the two mohurs is known only as a proof. Under the Crown (after 1862) the mohur continued as the only gold denomination in general production.

Although still not legal tender it was generally assumed that gold would be a useful part of the currency of British India and there were various attempts to encourage its use. In 1841 the treasuries were authorized to accept the gold coins allowed in the 1835 Act at the fixed rate of fifteen rupees per mohur. Initially this caused little problem but with gold discoveries in California and Australia the fixed rate available in India began to attract large quantities. From 1st January 1853 the Indian treasuries ceased to accept gold coins. Gold could still be brought to the mints for coining but the certificates for gold deposited could be discharged only in gold coin.

In 1864 the Government of India agreed to receive British and Australian sovereigns at the treasuries at ten rupees (half sovereigns at five rupees) and there were soon official suggestions that these should be made legal tender. In 1866 a Commission[4] was appointed to look into this and other aspects of the currency and reported in favour of gold becoming a legal tender part of the currency. The Commission suggested denominations of fifteen, ten and five rupees. By 1868 the sovereign had been revalued at the rate of ten rupees four annas, the half sovereign in proportion, which made them unsuitable for the intended system. A Government notification though declared that gold coins struck under the Act of 1835 would be received according to their stated value and the mohur, at fifteen rupees, was still in intermittent issue. All that was required to comply with the recommendation of the Mansfield Commission was therefore the introduction of gold coins of ten and five rupees. These were authorized by Act XXIII of 1870. Small numbers of both denominations were struck but very little gold was brought to the mint for coining and by 1875 the question of a legal tender gold coinage for India had been dropped for the time being. Once again the only gold coin in issue was the mohur for the convenience of those bringing gold to the mint.

Gold coins authorized in 1870

Ten rupees.   *Five rupees.*

---

4 *This was the "Mansfield Commission" chaired by Sir William Mansfield.*

Queen Victoria became the Empress of India on 1st May 1876 and from 1877 the title used on the British Indian coins changes from **VICTORIA QUEEN** to **VICTORIA EMPRESS.** There was otherwise no alteration to the coinage although very soon after the change of title the half anna, considered too cumbersome, ceased to be issued for currency.

Change of title

Rupee 1876 "Victoria Queen".   Rupee 1877 "Victoria Empress".

From about 1873 the world price of silver began a sustained decline. As India was on the silver standard her overseas payments, measured mainly in gold, rose steeply and this marked the beginning of a difficult period for her currency. The British Indian mints were open to free coinage meaning that they were obliged to accept bullion from the public for coining. This attracted increased imports of silver and the rupee, which had been close to 2/- sterling in 1873, stood at only 1/3d in 1893. The Government was keen to stabilize its value but as long as the mints were open to the free coinage of silver the rupee could not be made to circulate above its intrinsic value. By Act VIII of 1893 the Government thus closed the mints to free coinage, retaining the right to strike rupees itself at the fixed gold price of 1/4d if they were required. The purpose of the Act was to stabilize the gold value of the rupee by restricting its supply with the intention of introducing a gold standard. The same Act also brought to an end the free coinage of gold and the last of the mohurs allowed by previous Acts are dated 1891. In fact the value of the rupee continued to fluctuate, at one point dropping to 1/1d and for several years only the smaller silver denominations (and copper coins) were struck. By 1898 though the market rate was very close to 1/4d and it was decided to make the sovereign legal tender at fifteen rupees. Act XXII of 1899 at last put India on a gold standard but it was an unusual arrangement. The rupee was now fixed at one fifteenth of a sovereign (that is, 1/4d sterling). Nevertheless it retained the weight and fineness laid down in 1835 and (quite unlike subsidiary coins elsewhere in the world) continued to be legal tender to any amount. There was no obligation on the Government to convert rupees into gold. British India therefore did not have a gold standard like that of the United Kingdom but had developed instead what amounted to a "gold exchange standard". By careful management the rate of 1/4d sterling for the rupee was maintained until 1917. Throughout this time there was little public demand for a gold coinage and plans for a gold mint in India were dropped in 1902.

There were of course changes of portrait for Edward VII (1901-1910) and George V (1910-1936) although the coinage itself remained largely unchanged. In 1906 bronze replaced copper and a new denomination (the one anna in cupro-nickel) was introduced. To avoid any confusion with silver coins it had a scalloped edge.

Later monarchs

Edward VII rupee 1903.

Cupro-nickel one anna introduced 1906

George V rupee 1911.

During the First World War it was considered advisable to coin bullion reserves into legal tender coin. As the price of silver was now rising a gold coinage was planned for this purpose and it was agreed in 1917 that a branch of the Royal Mint, similar to those set up earlier in Australia and Canada, should be set up in Bombay. As a temporary measure coins of fifteen rupees and of the same weight and fineness as the sovereign were struck at the Bombay mint. When the Royal branch mint was set up within the existing Bombay mint compound this coinage ceased and sovereigns began to be struck in August 1918. These were the same as the Royal Mint sovereigns but were distinguished from them by the small letter "**I**" (for "India") on the reverse. Neither of these gold coins was struck in large numbers and the Royal branch mint was closed in April 1919.

First World War gold

Fifteen rupees 1918.   Sovereign 1918.

From 1916 silver prices rose strongly and in 1918 the silver two annas was replaced by a cupro-nickel coin. As with the anna of 1906 this coin was given a different shaped flan (in this case square) to avoid confusion with silver. To further conserve silver two new denominations in cupro-nickel, the eight annas (round) and four annas (scalloped) were introduced in 1919 as temporary replacements for the half and quarter rupee. These were struck until 1920 (eight annas) and 1921 (four annas).

During the war the rupee had been struck in huge numbers but with peace came a slackening of trade which created a surplus of coins in circulation. In 1923 production of the rupee was therefore suspended for an indefinite period of time. The post war period was a difficult one for many currencies including sterling. The United Kingdom came off the gold standard after the First World War. It attempted to return to it (as a gold bullion standard rather than a gold specie standard) in 1925 and finally abandoned it in 1931. India had her own currency problems but some sort of peg to sterling was important. While the United Kingdom was on the gold standard a peg to sterling was also a peg to gold but between 1919 and 1925 sterling itself varied against gold. From 1917 the price of silver rose steeply and then in 1920 began to fall. This caused the sterling exchange rate of the rupee to vary considerably exceeding 2/10d in 1920 and dipping below 1/3d a year later. In 1925 the United Kingdom returned to a gold standard and twenty shillings sterling was again equal to a gold sovereign. A Royal Commission was appointed to examine India's currency problems and recommended a gold bullion standard for India similar to that adopted by the United Kingdom. However, the resulting Currency Act of 1927 allowed only a modified version of that recommendation and rated the rupee at 1/6d sterling. This was once again a sterling and gold exchange rate but only because the United Kingdom was on a gold standard. When the United Kingdom came off the gold standard in 1931 India had to decide whether to follow sterling or gold. In the event the links with sterling were considered so great that India adopted a sterling exchange standard and retained the rate of 1/6d sterling for the rupee.

With the Currency Act of 1927 the sovereign and half sovereign lost their legal tender status in India becoming bullion only. As before, the silver rupee and half rupee had unlimited legal tender, the quarter rupee and other coins being legal tender only up to one rupee. Throughout this difficult period it had not been considered necessary to resume production of the rupee denomination. Only in 1940 when war once more created a demand for more coins did rupees again begin to be struck for currency.

At the change of reign in 1936 Edward VIII had abdicated before any coins were produced in his name for India so those of George VI followed those of George V. When rupees again began to be struck in 1940 so urgent was the need that the dies for them were prepared from specimen punches dated 1938 and 1939. These rupees were still at the standard laid down in 1835 but most countries using silver coins, including the United Kingdom, had already been forced to reduce their fineness. It was not long before India followed suit and in 1940 the fineness of the rupee and its subdivisions was reduced to the same fineness as United Kingdom silver coins (50%).

A wartime innovation was the introduction of a square half anna in nickel brass in 1942. The bronze denominations (quarter anna, half pice and twelfth anna) had continued in issue but in 1943, due also to wartime exigencies, a new one pice (quarter anna) coin with a large central hole was introduced and the smaller denominations discontinued.

In 1946 the minting of the 50% silver coins was suspended. Half and quarter rupees in nickel were introduced in that year and rupees in 1947. The design of these new nickel coins was radically changed to show an Indian tiger on the reverse and these would be the last British Indian coins before independence.

The last King Emperor

Rupee 1944.

Cupro-nickel two annas 1939.

Quarter anna 1939.

Wartime pice 1943.

One anna 1946.

Nickel rupee 1947.

Although the Government of India was able to exercise control over the currency of British India it had little control over such matters in the many independent states under its suzerainty. Some of these continued to produce their own coins. After the exile of the last Moghul, the takeover by the Crown and the guarantees for their future existence many of these states began to include references to the Queen on their coins and some began using her portrait.

In contemporary records and publications these states are nearly always referred to as "Native States" which indeed they were. These were the ancient states of India which had existed for hundreds of years before intruders like the Moghuls and the European trading companies had arrived. Later, the term "native" (with a small "n") came to have derogatory connotations, particularly in a colonial context, and the term "Princely States" came into use. In the period under discussion though, they were the Native States of India and not all their rulers would have described themselves as mere "princes".

The **coins of the Native States** were at various standards and subject to varying degrees of control. This resulted in fluctuating exchange rates and other inconveniences all of which were of concern to the Government of India. Attempts were therefore made to reduce the quantity of Native State coinage finding its way to the treasuries. In 1870 it was declared that where mints had been closed or had been inoperative for five years their revival could not be permitted. Two years later it was resolved that under strict conditions certain coins of the Native States could be legal tender in British India and eventually Act IX of 1876 defined those conditions. To achieve legal tender status the coins (whether gold, silver or copper) would have to be identical in weight and fineness with the coins of British India and be struck at British Indian mints. They had to be different in design to the previous coins of the State and have their values inscribed in English. The States agreeing to these conditions also had to agree not to issue coins on their own account for a period of thirty years.

As the Native States retained responsibility for their internal affairs, including coinage, handing over production of their coinage to the British Indian mints was entirely optional and only six states took up the offer, one of them not until 1908. The coins produced for them had the same obverse designs as the British Indian coins with a distinctive reverse for each State.

Alwar had rupees struck dated intermittently from 1877 to 1891.

Bikanir had rupees dated 1892 and 1897, a quarter anna dated 1895 and a half pice dated 1894.

Dewas Senior Branch and Dewas Junior Branch had quarter annas and twelfth annas dated 1888.

Dhar had a quarter anna, half pice and twelfth anna all dated 1887.

Sailana had quarter annas dated 1908 and 1912.

Some Native States coins

From local mints. With portrait or name of Victoria (وکٹوریا)

Bharatpur rupee 1858. Bindraban rupee 1859.

Bundi rupees 1869 and 1901.

Kuchawan rupee 1863.

11 The Indian Ocean

Kutch five kori 1865. *Kutch hundred kori 1866.*

Kutch three dokda 1888. *Radhanpur rupee 1881.*

From the British Indian mints

Alwar rupee 1891. *Bikanir rupee 1892.*

Dewas (Senior Branch) quarter anna 1888. *Dhar half pice 1887.*

Sailana quarter anna 1912.

Because of the currency problems of India in the later 19th century various other states came to agreement with the Government that the British Indian rupee would be their sole legal tender. In these states arrangements were made to withdraw their own distinctive coins at an agreed rate of exchange. Native State coinage did continue but of some thirty four states issuing their own coins in the 1870s less than ten were doing so by 1947.

Tokens would never form a major part of the currency of India but some uses should be mentioned. An early issue was that of copper rupees struck for use in the Andaman Islands. Situated in the Bay of Bengal these remote islands were an ideal place for a secure convict settlement and a new one was founded there, just after the Mutiny, in 1858. The settlement was for lifers and long term prisoners many of them becoming "self –supporter convicts" who, under certain conditions, were paid for surplus produce. There was soon a great shortage of currency and it is recorded that this was dealt with at first (1860) by the issue of cardboard tickets which passed for a rupee.[5] The experiment being a success the Superintendent of the settlement applied to Calcutta for copper token rupees to be struck and his request was approved. There were two issues of these dated 1861 and 1866. Both have the reverse legend **ANDAMAN TOKEN ONE RUPEE.** Both have obverses showing the Queen's portrait, the earlier piece showing her with coronet (an obverse used for the Straits Settlements), the later showing her crowned as on the 1862 rupee. Both of these were officially but clumsily holed right through the bust presumably so that prisoners and others without pockets could carry them on a string. It was a utility currency in every sense of the word. In the end officialdom felt this currency was a threat to discipline and the tokens were withdrawn in 1870.

Another use for tokens was to pay wages on the tea gardens of Assam. This region had come under East India Company control from the 1820s and became part of British India with the handover to the Crown in 1858. The exciting discovery that tea could be grown here as easily as in China resulted in hundreds of gardens (plantations) being established by the end of the 19th century. Much of the labour required had to be brought in and came mainly from Bengal on long term contracts. Paying them created a need for large quantities of small value coins which were not readily available in the hills of Assam. To avoid the cost and inconvenience of carriage many planters therefore adopted the use of tokens. These were usually to the value of a particular task, perhaps a day's pay. A single three annas token could then be used in lieu of at least three legal tender coins (a silver two annas and two copper half annas), the tokens eventually being redeemed in bulk. It is known that tea garden tokens were in use by the 1870s and they probably continued to be used until about the time of the First World War.

A few other enterprises in India also issued tokens to suit their own particular circumstances and British army units sometimes used metallic tokens in their canteens and coffee shops. A whole series of canteen tokens appeared during the Second World War so that change could be given at a time when small denomination currency was scarce.

When drought hit Bihar and parts of Bengal in 1873 the Lieutenant Governor determined to use all the resources at his disposal to ameliorate the usual consequences of such a disaster. Huge quantities of rice were imported from Burma and public works were put in hand to relieve the effects of the famine. Brass rupee tokens dated 1874 were struck at the Calcutta Mint to pay those employed on the famine relief works and could be used to buy grain at a fixed price from Government stores. Similar tokens were struck in copper for use in South India in the famine of 1876. These bore the legend **"RELIEF ½ SEER TOKEN"** and were exchangeable for a half seer of rice.[6]

---

5   F. Pridmore "Coins of the British Commonwealth Part 11 Asia", p.122.
6   *A seer was just over two pounds (a little less than one kilo). Half a seer was presumably equivalent to the unit of work for which the token was given.*

Examples of Indian tokens

Andaman rupee 1861.   Kanan Devan Hills Produce Co Ltd, Travancore. Four annas 1890s.

Tea Garden tokens

Anniepore three annas, Sylhet 1870s.   Satghas Estate 1883. No stated value.

Canteen tokens

XVIII Hussars coffee shop two annas (late 19th century).

Buckingham & Carnatic Mills   The Apollo Mills

Famine relief token

Rupee 1874 for use in Bengal and Bihar.

SUMMARY FOR
BRITISH INDIAN COINAGE

Currency system: One rupee = sixteen annas. One anna = four pice.

1835	East India Company establishes a uniform coinage for the whole of its territories in India.
1858	Administration passed to Crown.
1862	British Indian coinage introduced.
1870	First attempt to limit the coinage of the Native States.
1876	Facility to strike Native States coins at British Indian mints to same specifications as British Indian coins. Six states eventually have coins struck under these arrangements.
1877	"Empress" replaces "Queen" as Victoria's title on the coins.
1899	Gold standard but silver rupee continues to have unlimited legal tender. Rupee fixed at fifteen to the sovereign.
1906	Copper denominations changed to bronze.
1918	Gold fifteen rupees coin introduced at same weight and fineness as the sovereign.
1918	Branch of Royal Mint established at Bombay to strike sovereigns. Striking of fifteen rupees coin ceases.
1919	Royal branch mint at Bombay closed. No further gold coins struck for British India.
1919-1925	Period when the sterling rate for the rupee varied considerably. A period also when the United Kingdom left the gold standard (1919) and adopted a gold bullion standard (1925).
1927	India adopts a sterling exchange standard. Gold coins no longer legal tender. Rupee stabilized at 1/6d.
1931	United Kingdom abandons gold standard. Rupee pegs to sterling (at 1/6d) rather than to gold.
1940	Millesimal fineness of the rupee reduced to 500 from the original standard of 1835.
1946	Silver coins begin to be replaced with nickel.
1947	Last coins of British India. Independence 15th August.

To govern India the British had always relied on the acquiescence of the people and on the support of Indian soldiers. The various areas which came into British hands had previously been run in dictatorial style by their various rulers. From the monarch down to the village officer the authority of the immediate superior was absolute and usually regarded with implicit obedience. As the East India Company gained control it therefore expected (and largely got) the obedience of those immediately below it and of those below them. The Company could never have governed these vast regions in any other way and nor could the Crown. It was a state of affairs that survived the Mutiny but it would only survive as long as there was no sense of national identity in India.

By the 1890s the old Presidency system of administration developed under the East India Company was largely obsolete. The Presidency civil services were combined into a single Indian Civil Service by 1889 and the three Presidency armies were finally combined under one Commander in Chief in 1895. The supreme Government of India had been developed from that of Bengal and Calcutta continued to be the seat of the Governor General and of the Commander in Chief. Every summer, from about 1864, the machinery of government removed itself to the coolness of the hills at Simla, a lengthy journey before the railway was completed in 1903. Nevertheless, it was not entirely convenient for the whole of India that the permanent home of the supreme Government should be in Bengal.

The first ruling British monarch to visit India was King George V who attended the great Durbar held at Delhi in 1911 to celebrate his coronation. Here, on 12th December, the king himself announced that the capital of his Indian Empire would be moved from Calcutta to a more central location, the spot on which he stood. It would be many years before the buildings of "New Delhi" were completed but the administration was moved to Delhi almost immediately in 1912.

Under the Crown there was a growing awareness that India was, or could become, one nation and nationalist ideals began to be voiced. The first meeting of the Indian National Congress took place in Bombay in 1885 and the All-India Muslim League was founded in 1906. At first their demands were simply for a greater share in government for Indians (Congress) and better education (Muslim League). The British Government tried to address their concerns with the Indian Councils Acts of 1892 and 1909 under which provincial governments were given more powers and their legislatures became more representative. Inevitably this was not enough. Soon there were demands for responsible government like that enjoyed by the settler colonies and eventually a call for full independence. We will look at the events leading to 1947 in Chapter fourteen.

In the mean time there were ongoing concerns for the security of the North West Frontier. The First Afghan War had done little to resolve matters and when Russia sent a mission to Kabul in 1878 the old fear of foreign influence again came to the fore. Britain demanded the right also to send a mission and when the Afghans refused entry the Second Afghan War began. In this war (1878-1880) British forces achieved some success. The Treaty of Gandamak (May 1879) accepted British control of Afghan foreign policy, a British minister at Kabul and British control of the passes into Afghanistan. There was a setback in September when the mission installed at Kabul was massacred and hostilities resumed. Kandahar though was the region that was of most importance to British India as it controlled the important routes between Herat and India. In February 1880 it was decided that its Governor, Sher Ali Khan, should be recognized as an independent ruler effectively breaking up Afghanistan.[7] With Kandahar and the most important passes under British control Kabul could be left more or less to its own devises.

---

[7] *This decision was formally made public at a Durbar in Kandahar on 15th March (Memorandum 132 dated Kandahar, 25th March 1880).*

What appeared to Calcutta to be a successful conclusion was soon criticized from London. In April 1880 Gladstone's Liberal government displaced Disraeli's Conservatives and the Viceroy was soon informed of London's displeasure. It appeared to the new Secretary of State for India that unwelcome liabilities had been assumed (Kandahar and the lines of communication) and that a State which Britain had wanted to be independent and strong had been reduced to anarchy. What was now required was the withdrawal of British troops to India in an honourable and seemly manner after stable government in Afghanistan had been secured. Reluctantly, the agreement with Sher Ali Khan of Kandahar contracted in the name of the Queen would have to be *"scrupulously respected"* unless and until he could be persuaded to take a pension.[8] A new Viceroy, better informed on the new government's views, was already on his way and, arriving in the summer, took up his office at Simla rather than Calcutta, the first Viceroy to do so.

The period of the Second Afghan War produced an unusual numismatic item at **Kandahar**. A copper falus of the period, almost certainly part of the local coinage, has a British style reverse of a crown within a wreath. Dating is never very clear on these coins but they seem to belong to AH 1296 (December 1878 to December 1879) the year in which British troops arrived in Kandahar. This was a little before British recognition of an independent Kandahar State but they had already recognized Sher Ali Khan as Governor of the city. These coins are likely to be honorific in the same manner as some of the coins of the Native States of India at this time which named the Queen.[9] It is interesting that at his formal recognition as ruler of the Province in May 1880 Sher Ali Khan requested that the Political Resident state verbally his right to coin money. This had not been mentioned in any letter from the Viceroy and the Resident duly obliged.[10]

The new Viceroy soon came to agreement with Abdul Rahman who was to be the new Amir of Kabul. By the end of 1880 Sher Ali Khan had dutifully requested and accepted retirement to India and his short reign in Kandahar came to an end. Afghanistan could once again attempt unity (under Abdul Rahman) while Britain retained control of her foreign affairs and would protect her against foreign aggression. British and Indian troops could return to their garrisons in India in the honourable and seemly manner suggested.

Kandahar

Local falus c.1879.

Britain's accord with Russia (the Convention of 1907) further reduced the risk of war in the region. For Persia, as far as commercial developments were concerned, the Convention agreed a Russian sphere of influence in the north of the country and a British sphere in the south eastern provinces with a "neutral" zone between them. For Afghanistan the Russians

---

8 *Letter to the Governor General of India in Council from the India office, London, 21st May 1880. Sher Ali Khan was formally confirmed as the Wali of Kandahar on 11th May 1880 (Memorandem 204 dated Kandahar 19th May 1880).*

9 *F. Pridmore, "The Kandahar Falus or Paisa", SNC December 1976, P.455.*

10 *Memorandum 204 (see footnote 8)*

accepted that political relations with the Amir would be conducted through the British Government. The integrity of Persia and Afghanistan was respected but neither was consulted on these arrangements. The rights of smaller countries still received little recognition in the deliberations of the great.

The North West Frontier was thus stabilized to some extent but large numbers of Britain's troops, perhaps one third of her standing army, continued to be garrisoned in India. Together with the Indian Army itself this was an enormous military resource all paid for out of Indian revenues but it was not only available for the defence of the Indian Empire. When war came in 1914 there was no doubt that the Army in India was also available for British and Imperial defence.

Trade with **Burma** (modern Myanmar) from the East India Company settlements in mainland India had begun in the 17th century and was centred mainly at Syriam in the Irrawaddy delta. Much of this business was in the hands of country traders seeking teak, rubies and lac but Burma was also important as an inland route towards China along the Irrawaddy River. There were attempts to exclude the French and to protect British interests from time to time but the Company enjoyed no exclusive rights in Burma and trade was intermittent. During the 19th century though, a number of wars would attach the whole of Burma, piece by piece, to British India.

The first of these wars was the result of conflicting claims in eastern Bengal where there had been several border incidents over the years. The Governor General was anxious to secure India's eastern border and knew that a more defensible limit would be the hills to the east of Arakan which had once been an independent state but was now part of Burma. The king of Burma was also anxious to settle his claims once and for all and laid plans for an ambitious invasion of Bengal through both Arakan in the south and Manipur and Assam in the north. When these plans turned to action the British reacted vigorously in both theatres, declaring war in March 1824. As a diversion they also mounted a direct attack on Burma through Rangoon which had now replaced nearby Syriam as the main commercial centre. Assam was secured and Arakan and Rangoon taken with relative ease. Tenasserim, to the south of the Irrawaddy delta, was also taken but there was hard and protracted fighting along the course of the Irrawaddy River before the First Burmese War could be brought to a close at Yandabo, just below the Burmese capital at Ava. Here, on 24th February 1826, the Burmese agreed to give up Arakan and Tenasserim adding most of Burma's Bay of Bengal coast to British Indian control. She agreed also to give up her claims to Assam, Cachar and elsewhere in the north. The cost to Burma in lost territory, financial indemnity and loss of self esteem was enormous and although a commercial treaty was arranged it was not long before problems arose including the perceived insult and abuse of British subjects.

In 1851 the Government of India dispatched a naval squadron to Rangoon to investigate one such incident and when demands were not immediately satisfied its commander recommended war to resolve what should have been a trivial affair. Hostilities began in January 1852 but the Second Burmese War did not begin in earnest until reinforcements had arrived in April. Martaban, Rangoon and Bassein were soon in British hands but there was no sign that the Burmese were ready to accept terms and the rainy season had begun. It was clear that the cost of such an expedition could only be recouped by cession of territory and it was decided that the whole of Lower Burma should be annexed. The extra troops thought necessary for this arrived in Rangoon in September and by 20th December the annexation of the province could be announced. By March 1853 the Burmese were ready to talk but in fact never signed the proffered treaty. It was thus a ceasefire only that ended the Second Burmese War in June 1853.

For some years this new region proved difficult to control but trade, revenues and population were soon increasing. In 1862 all the annexed territories (Arakan, Tenasserim and Lower Burma) were grouped together as a single province of British India designated as "British Burma". By now of course British India was under the Crown rather than the Company.

Various points of friction arose between the now land locked Burmese Kingdom and British Burma including fears that the Burmese were becoming a little too friendly with the old enemy, France who already had interests in Indo China. Such was the way things stood that little excuse was needed to annex what remained of Burma and the Third Burmese War began in 1885. After a quick advance to Mandalay (the new capital), Upper Burma was formally annexed on 1st January 1886. Burma's last king, Thibaw, was exiled to India. Upper Burma was now added to the British Indian province of "British Burma" the whole becoming simply "Burma". Pacifying the country took a little longer but was generally completed by 1895. Burma was given its own Lieutenant Governor, subject to the Governor General at Calcutta, in 1897. It would remain part of British India until 1937 and would achieve independence in 1948 (Chapter fourteen).

The currency of Burma was that of British India. For a few years after 1886 Burmese coins recently struck at Mandalay continued in circulation, the kyat being equal to one rupee. Apart from the years of Japanese occupation during the Second World War British Indian currency continued in use until Burma's own notes and coinage were introduced after independence.

Ceylon is the term used on the British colonial coins and tokens of present day Sri Lanka. It is used also in contemporary publications and documents. In fact for many years colonial Ceylon, first in Portuguese hands, then Dutch and eventually British, was restricted to the coastal regions, the kings of Kandy remaining independent until 1815.

In 1795 Ceylon was in Dutch hands but the Stadtholder of the United Provinces had been forced to flee his country by allies of France. There was thus concern that Ceylon, with its excellent harbour of Trincomalee, would become a base from which the French could threaten India. The British Government was naturally anxious to remove that threat. When the Stadtholder wrote his letters from Kew Palace suggesting the surrender to Britain of Dutch overseas territories, Bengal and Madras were immediately informed of how things stood.[11] An expedition was swiftly mounted from Madras and took Trincomalee in July 1795. The Dutch in the island were not willing to submit without argument but their last stronghold (Colombo) capitulated in February 1796 and the administration of Ceylon passed to the East India Company's Madras Presidency. The abrupt change in administration and the introduction of the revenue system of Madras led to serious unrest and a Governor and Commander in Chief for Ceylon was appointed by the British Government in 1798. For the moment he still had to report to the Governor General at Calcutta but by 1801 the British Government had decided that, if it could be retained by international agreement, Ceylon should become a Crown colony rather than a Presidency of the East India Company. The Treaty of Amiens in 1802 confirmed Ceylon to Britain and it duly passed under the control of the Secretary of State for War and the Colonies. Only when the last King of Kandy was deposed in 1815 and his dominions were also vested in the British Crown did the whole island come under British rule.

---

11 The "Kew Letters" of 1795 articulated the Stadtholder's attempt to retain Dutch overseas territories by passing them temporarily to Britain for the duration of the war. See also Chapter nine.

We have seen (Chapter six) that when the Company took responsibility for Ceylon the circulating medium was almost entirely paper and copper and that Dutch denominations were continued. There were four doits (or "challies") to the stiver, four stivers to the fanam and twelve fanams to the rix dollar. The stiver was often termed a "pice". The rix dollar was not a coin at this time but a unit of account.[12] Copper coins were struck locally from 1801 and at Matthew Boulton's mint at Birmingham from 1802 denominated in fractions of a rix dollar. The forty eighth was the equivalent of the stiver and was struck both locally and in Birmingham. Larger denominations were struck locally and smaller denominations in Birmingham. The largest of the copper denominations was the twelfth (the fanam). The smallest was the one-hundred-and-ninety-second (the challie). The Birmingham struck coins continued only until 1804, locally struck coppers continuing until 1816. Silver coins began to be struck locally in 1803 and were awkwardly denominated in multiples of the stiver. The forty eight stivers was in fact the rix dollar but there was also a twenty four stivers (half rix dollar) and later a ninety six stivers (two rix dollars). These silver coins continued in issue until 1809. The locally struck coins were first produced by private contractors but in 1811, to reduce costs, a mint under the immediate inspection of the Government was opened which continued the local copper coinage without change until 1816. The Government mint was under the direction of Anthony Bertolacci, a civil servant who was Acting Auditor General.

In 1814 a shortage of coins in circulation led to the striking of silver fanam tokens (one twelfth of a rix dollar) which are tiny compared to their chunky copper equivalent. These continued to be struck into 1815. In that year a new copper coinage of two stivers, one stiver and half stiver denominations was struck at the Royal Mint. A silver coinage of rix dollars was also planned but not actually struck for currency until 1821, also at the Royal Mint. A further shortage of coins in 1823 led to the importation of Madras rupees and quarter rupees which were countermarked with a crown giving the rupee a local rate of 1⅓ rix dollars and the quarter rupee a rate of four fanams.

Coinage for Ceylon before 1825

Locally struck copper coins

Twelfth rix dollar 1803.   Forty eighth rix dollar 1801.

---

12 A Proclamation of 8th June 1796 gave currency to all Dutch copper coins, the stiver to pass at 48 to the rix dollar. The Madras star pagoda was rated at 180 stivers. Interestingly the British halfpenny and farthing were rated at one stiver and half a stiver respectively indicating that these coins were familiar in Ceylon and Madras at that time. The Arcot rupee struck at Madras was considered equivalent to the rix dollar.

Coinage for Ceylon before 1825

Supplemented by Birmingham struck coins 1802-1804

Forty eighth rix dollar 1802.

One- hundred-and-ninety-second rix dollar (challie) 1802.

Locally struck silver coins

Ninety six stivers 1808. Forty eight stivers 1808. Twenty four stivers 1808.

Fanam struck 1814-1815.

Royal Mint issues

Two stivers 1815. Rix dollar 1821.

Emergency issue

Madras rupee and quarter rupee countermarked for use in Ceylon.

The Imperial Order in Council of 1825 applied to all colonies of which Ceylon was one. Public accounts which had previously been in rix dollars, fanams and pice (stivers) were now changed to pounds, shillings and pence. Large quantities of British silver and copper coins were sent out including eventually the smaller denominations of half farthings and quarter farthings introduced specifically for use there (as noted in Chapter six). When the half farthing became legal tender also in the United Kingdom in 1842 its reverse design was altered slightly with the addition of a shamrock and thistle to the motif below the date. The motif on the quarter farthing which was never legal tender in the United Kingdom did not change.

India of course was not a colony, was in no way affected by the 1825 Order in Council, used the silver rupee as its standard and greatly influenced the currencies of the Indian Ocean, including Ceylon.

For some years Ceylon used sterling as required by the 1825 Order with the rix dollar rated at 1/6d and the Spanish dollar at 4/4d. The sicca rupee (i.e. that of Bengal) was to pass at 2/1d and those of Bombay and Madras were to pass at 1/11d. In 1833 though, all these rates were reduced. Some years ahead of similar moves in other colonies the rate for the dollar was reduced to 4/2d. At the same time the rate for the sicca rupee was fixed at 2/- and that of other British Indian rupees at 1/10d. Nevertheless its proximity to India clearly placed Ceylon in the rupee using area and, for various reasons, most of the sterling silver brought in was being re-exported. By 1836 there was a new uniform British Indian rupee and, although lighter than the sicca rupee, this was now rated at 2/- in Ceylon. This overvalued the British Indian rupee relative to sterling and in practice led to its adoption as the standard of value. British gold coins were made legal tender in 1852 and Australian gold four years later but this had little effect. Unofficially the silver rupee of British India had become the local standard of Ceylon.

General practice became official on 18th June 1869 when an Order in Council and Proclamation revoked the 1825 Order and subsequent legislation on coinage as far as it related to Ceylon and established the British Indian rupee and its silver fractions as the sole unlimited legal tender. There was some debate however before the public accounts were changed from sterling to rupees on 1st January 1872. There would also be some innovation. The subsidiary copper coinage was to be in decimal divisions of the rupee rather than in annas and pice and an extensive copper coinage (five cents, cent, half cent and quarter cent) was struck at Calcutta from 1870. With these in circulation all the old copper coins were demonetized in 1874. In 1892 the decimalization of the rupee was extended to silver coins which were "token" in nature. Denominations of fifty cents, twenty five cents and ten cents were struck at the Royal Mint at a millesimal fineness of 800 and this allowed the fractions of the rupee to lose their unlimited status. The rupee was now the only unlimited legal tender. The half and quarter rupee and the decimal silver coins were legal tender up to five rupees and the copper coins up to half a rupee.

The huge copper five cents, about the same weight as the old British pre-1860 copper penny, was struck for currency only until 1892. The quarter cent, at the same weight as the old quarter farthing, was struck until 1904. Both these copper denominations were demonetized in 1909 although a much smaller cupro-nickel five cents was then introduced. The new coin was on a square flan to avoid confusion with the silver coins.

In 1919, because of the general rise in the price of silver after the First World War, the millesimal fineness of all the Ceylon silver issues was reduced to 550. The copper half cent was not struck after 1940 and in 1942, due to metal shortages in the Second World War, the copper cent was replaced with a lighter version in bronze. Also in 1942 the five cents was struck in nickel brass at a slightly reduced weight. In 1943 the silver denominations were replaced with nickel-brass coins, the new ten cents coin (now with a scalloped flan) not appearing until 1944. A new denomination, the two cents also appeared in 1944, also in nickel brass on a scalloped flan. There were no further changes to the coinage before independence in 1948.

Ceylon. Decimal divisions of the rupee

Five cents 1870.　　　　　　　　　　　Fifty cents 1892.

Cupro nickel five cents 1909.

Twenty five cents 1920.　　　　　　　　Cent 1925.

Bronze cent 1943.

SUMMARY OF CEYLON COINAGE

1801 Ceylon Government begin issue of locally struck coins denominated in fractions and multiples of the stiver. Rix dollar (48 stivers) was the unit of account.

1802-1804 Some of the lower denominations machine struck in Birmingham.

1814-1815 Small silver tokens for one fanam (twelfth rix dollar) struck locally to alleviate shortage of coins in circulation.

1815 Copper stiver coinage struck at Royal Mint.

1816 Locally struck coins cease.

1821 Silver rix dollar denomination struck at Royal Mint.

1823 Madras rupees and quarter rupees countermarked to pass at 1⅓ rix dollar and ⅓ rix dollar to ease a shortage of coin.

1825 Sterling coins introduced. Rix dollar rated at 1/6d.

1869 1825 Order in Council revoked for Ceylon and the British Indian rupee becomes the unit of currency.

1870 Copper coins subsidiary to the rupee introduced (decimal system).

1892 Token silver decimal divisions of the rupee introduced.

1919 Silver content reduced from a millesimal fineness of 800 to 550.

1943 Silver denominations changed to nickel-brass.

1948 Independence.

The tokens of Ceylon add interest to its numismatic history. Experiments with coffee planting led to successful cultivation by the 1830s and it was soon a major factor in the economic development of Ceylon. A devastating leaf disease[13] destroyed much of the coffee production in the 1870s and resulted in many planters turning their attention to tea. Most of the labour for these plantations came from southern India and conditions of employment were governed by the Service Contracts Ordinance (number 5 of 1841) with subsequent amendments. These protected pay and conditions, allowing labourers to sue planters for non payment of wages but they also laid down very strict rules of conduct. Like the tea gardens of Assam mentioned above the coffee and tea plantations of Ceylon were often far from supplies of coin and employed large numbers of workers. To pay these workers, quantities of small value coins would be required so many of the plantations and mills began to use tokens equivalent to a task or a day's work. The usual rate for a job or a journey was 4½d which was often considered equal to a day's pay. A common denomination for these tokens is thus 4½d, the popular equivalent of three fanams. After 1869, when the decimal rupee was introduced, the exact equivalent would have been 18¾ cents and tokens now appear showing values of 18, 18½ or 19 cents. Not all the tokens bore denominations, it being fully understood that they

---

13 Hemileia Vastatrix.

were equal to one task. Daily payment avoided the possibility of being sued for non payment but it also made it easy to refuse payment in cases of absence or misconduct. The tokens would be exchanged periodically (usually weekly) for legal tender coin and this would be handled by the kanganies ("gangers" or "overseers") who arranged the labour, paid initial advances and so on. As copper coins became more plentiful it is likely that tokens had gone out of use in Ceylon by about 1890.

Examples of Ceylon tokens

Pilo Fernando tokens for 4½d and 2¼d.

4½d token of D.V.Guneratne of Colombo.   19 cents token of J.P.Jayatilleka.

Lee Hedges & Co token for Colpetty Mills 1867. No stated value.

Mauritius ("Île de France" under French rule) was a constant threat to British India as long as it remained in French hands. It was a base from which French privateers and warships could harass British trade and from which attacks could be mounted on British India itself. Neighbouring Île de Bourbon ("Réunion" today) and Rodrigues Island were also in French hands. In 1809 a small force from Bombay took Rodrigues and in July 1810 Bourbon surrendered to a force from Madras. An attack was then mounted on Mauritius to remove the French threat once and for all. Mauritius was in British hands from December 1810 until independence in 1968. Rodrigues was administered from Mauritius during that period but the Île de Bourbon was returned to France at the Congress of Vienna in 1815.

As a British colony the Navigation Acts were soon applied and by the 1820s sugar was the predominant product. Britain had abolished her slave trade in 1807, some years before Mauritius was taken, so separate arrangements had to be made for the new colony. For some years the planters were strong enough to ignore slave trade legislation and slaves were still being imported in the late 1820s. Eventually the planters of Mauritius accepted more than £2 million in compensation for some 68,000 slaves which gives an idea of the scale of the plantation economy in 1835. With emancipation came the need for a new source of labour and, as with the Caribbean colonies, this would be indentured labour from India. The large numbers imported and the fact that many chose to stay in Mauritius led, by the 1860s, to close commercial ties with India. Much of the traditional food and clothing for the indentured labourers was imported from India and Indian firms soon appeared in Port Louis. This was one of the factors which forged strong links between Mauritius and the rupee using area. The opening of the Suez Canal in 1869 reduced the strategic importance of Mauritius. Its connections with southern Africa, Europe and Australia became less important, those with India more so.

Chapter six tells the story of what happened to the coinage and currency of Mauritius immediately after the British takeover and it will be remembered that the old French "colonial dollar" remained the currency of account. We noted also that large quantities of copper pice were imported from India in 1818, that "anchor" money was sent to Mauritius and that "token" silver coins of 50 and 25 sous were struck in Calcutta in 1822. A notice of December 1824 rated the current dollar at two sicca rupees, the British sovereign at five current dollars and the Spanish dollar at 108 cents but it is important to remember that the current (or "colonial") dollar had become a unit of account only. We must now look at what happened when the Imperial Order in Council of 1825 was applied in Mauritius.

The purpose of the Order was to introduce sterling silver and copper as currency and a local Ordinance of 25th November 1825 which came into force on 1st January 1826 attempted to do this. Four shillings of British money was declared the equivalent of one current dollar of the colonial money of account. British silver and copper was the only legal tender but various other coins were to be accepted by the public offices at stated sterling rates. The rates laid down in the Ordinance were not fixed in a consistent manner and, as was the case in many other colonies, sterling was undervalued relative to other coins. The Spanish doubloon was rated at £3-9s-4d and the sicca (Bengal) rupee at 2/1d. The Spanish dollar was rated at 4/4d as required by the Imperial Order of 1825. The overvaluation of foreign coins and the continued popular valuation of the "colonial dollar" at two rupees would lead to problems but in the mean time, in the years up to 1828, large quantities of British silver and copper were imported.

The British copper coins allowed the pice imported in 1818 to be collected in and returned to India. It also had to be decided what should be done with the 50 and 25 sous base silver coins struck in Calcutta in 1822. A Proclamation of 11th May 1831 called them in at their circulating value (the 50 sous at a quarter of the "colonial dollar"). Rather than melt them they were re-issued in August, the 50 sous to circulate at 8d, the 25 sous at 4d which was close to their intrinsic value. The 50 sous was now one sixth of the "colonial dollar" instead of a quarter.

By this time the overvaluation of the doubloon had attracted large numbers and in 1836 the Colonial Government reduced its rate to £3-6s-0d. This led to strong protests from those who held them but it was in line with the new Army rate laid down by the Treasury in 1835.

Smaller denomination French silver coins were overvalued not only against sterling but also against the five franc piece. The local Ordinance which came into force at the beginning of 1826 rated the one franc coin at 10d and the two francs at 1/8d while the five francs was rated at only 4/-. This was obviously considered unimportant at the time but by 1837 French one and two franc coins, imported for profit, formed about two thirds of the coinage in circulation in Mauritius. An Ordinance of March 1838 ironed out the difference making five one franc coins equal to 4/- and five two franc coins equal to 8/-.

In 1835 the new uniform rupee was introduced in British India and was rated at 1/11d in Mauritius. This, the Spanish dollar (still rated at 4/4d) and the doubloon (at £3-6s-0d) all kept sterling out of general circulation, most of that issued being returned to the Commissariat to purchase bills on London. As we have seen before, this was a problem common to many colonies where sterling was undervalued making other coins a cheaper tender for payment. The legislation introduced in the West Indies in 1838 to correct this problem was extended to Mauritius in 1843, the doubloon then being rated at 64/- and the Spanish dollar at 4/2d. At the same time the uniform rupee of British India was rated at 1/10d but continued for some years to be the most popular coin in circulation, usually accepted at 2/-.

The gold discoveries around the world and increased income from sugar led to a period in which sterling was the main coinage in use. In 1852 sterling coins in Mauritius became current in exactly the same manner as in the United Kingdom with gold the only unlimited legal tender and silver limited to forty shillings.[14] As the gold price of silver fell in the 1870s the question arose whether Mauritius should retain sterling or establish a rupee standard. As Mauritius was clearly in the rupee using area it was decided in 1876 that its standard should indeed be the silver rupee. At last the old concept of the "colonial dollar" worth two rupees could be done away with and with effect from 1st January 1877 the British Indian rupee became the sole unlimited legal tender together with its subdivisions. Subsidiary "token" coins in silver and bronze were authorized to be legal tender up to five rupees and these would follow the example set in Ceylon by being decimal divisions of a rupee consisting of 100 cents. As a temporary measure British bronze coins were to be legal tender up to half a rupee at the rate of four cents to the penny.

The decimal divisions of the rupee were the twenty cents and ten cents in silver and the five cents, two cents and one cent in bronze. An immediate difference will be noticed between the bronze coins of Mauritius and the much heavier copper coins of Ceylon. Mauritius was familiar with the United Kingdom bronze coinage introduced in 1860 and her coins were struck at the Royal Mint and at Heaton's mint in Birmingham. It is inconceivable that anything other than bronze would have been used. The copper coins of Ceylon were introduced earlier at a time when the old United Kingdom copper coins were still in use there and were struck at Calcutta.[15] The copper five cents of Ceylon was thus almost twice the weight of its Mauritian bronze equivalent although they were both one twentieth of a rupee.

Like the British bronze coins, those of Mauritius changed little over the next hundred years apart from changes of royal portrait. The silver ten cents was struck only until 1897, a new cupro-nickel version with a scalloped edge appearing in 1947. The silver twenty cents was struck until 1899. The main circulating coins continued to be the British Indian rupee and its subdivisions but in 1932 a decision was taken to replace this with a separate Mauritian rupee which would be pegged to sterling instead of to the Indian rupee. In fact it was pegged at the same rate as the British Indian rupee (1/6d) but in 1934 a separate Mauritian rupee began to be struck. From the same year distinctive half and quarter rupees were also struck

---

14 *Australian gold became legal tender in Mauritius in 1856.*
15 *The new United Kingdom bronze coins were introduced in 1860 and the old copper coins ceased to be current there on 31st December 1869. Those in circulation in the colonies were accepted (in London) until 31st December 1877.*

for Mauritius. It will be noted that when the separate Mauritian rupee was introduced its divisions were not entirely decimal. Half and quarter rupees continued the tradition of using British Indian coins of those denominations. Only the minor coins of Mauritius are denominated in cents.

In 1946 the silver content of the half and quarter rupee was reduced to 50%. The rupee denomination was not in issue at that time but in 1950 all the silver denominations were changed to cupro-nickel. The cupro-nickel and bronze coins of Mauritius continued unchanged for some years beyond independence.

The Seychelles were surrendered to British forces in 1810 by their French inhabitants and, like Mauritius, were confirmed to Britain after the war. They were administered as a dependency of Mauritius until 1903 when Seychelles became a separate Crown colony. As a dependency the coinage from 1810 to 1903 was the same as that of Mauritius even though the Seychelles were not always as closely aligned to the rupee using area. The first separate Seychelles currency was Government paper money issued from 1914 but British Indian and Mauritian coins continued to be used until 1939. In that year the first separate coinage was struck for the Seychelles and consisted of rupees, half rupees and twenty five cents in 50% silver. Cupro-nickel coins had replaced all of these by 1954. A ten cents in cupro-nickel on a scalloped flan was also introduced in 1939 and this was replaced by a smaller version in nickel-brass in 1953. Five cents, two cents and one cent bronze coins similar to those of Mauritius were introduced in 1948 for the Seychelles. The bronze two cents denomination ceased issue for currency in 1968. In the 1970s cupro-nickel coins of ten and five rupees were introduced, the five cents became a much smaller coin in aluminium on a scalloped flan and the one cent coin also changed to aluminium. The Seychelles would achieve independence in 1976.

MAURITIUS AND THE SEYCHELLES
Mauritius

Fifty sous and twenty five sous re-issued at 8d and 4d in 1831.

Subsidiary to British Indian rupee

Twenty cents 1877.   Ten cents 1889.

Five cents 1897.   Two cents 1877.

Mauritius rupee

Separate Mauritius rupee introduced 1934.   *Five cents 1971.*

The Seychelles

Two cents 1968.

Separate rupee introduced 1939.   *Cupro-nickel rupee 1966.*

The various other small islands of the Indian Ocean whose names are underlined in red on the maps of the day all have their story although most contribute little to the numismatic history of the region.

The Danish East India Company laid claim to the Nicobar Islands in the mid 18th century. Although no permanent settlement was made it was not until 1868 that Danish claims to the islands were sold to Britain. They then became part of British India and in 1872 were united with the neighbouring Andaman Islands under a Chief Commissioner at Port Blair. Apart from the earlier Andaman tokens noted above, the coinage of the Andaman and Nicobar Islands was that of British India.

The northern Laccadive Islands came into the hands of the East India Company through the Treaty of Seringapatam which concluded the Third Mysore War in 1792. Other islands of the group (which lay off the south west coast of India) were left in the hands of the rulers of Cannanore. In 1877, because of non payment of tribute, the remaining islands were taken over by the Government of British India. Here too the coinage in use was that of India.

To the south of the Laccadives lie the Maldive Islands. These were ruled as a sultanate which came voluntarily under British protection in 1887. In return for an annual tribute

Britain took responsibility for defence and foreign affairs, the Governor of Ceylon having immediate responsibility. As the Sultan retained control of internal affairs there was no British involvement in the coinage which was based on the larin with Indian and Ceylonese coins providing the larger denominations. The Maldives became fully independent in 1965.

The Amirante Islands were administered as part of the Seychelles which were themselves a dependency of Mauritius. When the Seychelles became a separate colony in 1903 the Chagos Islands were separated from them and continued to be administered as a dependency of Mauritius. In 1965 they were detached from Mauritius to form part of the British Indian Ocean Territory.

The Cocos (Keeling) Islands were first sighted by Captain William Keeling of the East India Company's "Red Dragon" in 1609. Many years later Captain John Clunies-Ross of the "Borneo" was sufficiently impressed with the islands to suggest that they could be a place of importance in the eastern trade. In December 1825 he called there to plant trees and vegetables and to stake a claim by nailing up the Union Flag. The owners of his ship were Hare and Company of London (John and Joseph Hare and perhaps others) who imported colonial produce and they agreed to the plan. When Clunies-Ross returned two years later with his family, some apprentices and a few useful artisans he was surprised to find that Alexander Hare (a brother of the London Hares) had already taken possession. This Hare was a colourful character who we will meet again in our next chapter. He had heard from Clunies-Ross himself of the attractions of the Cocos (Keeling) Islands and had arrived with what seemed very much like his own private harem, anxious to find somewhere for them to reside in safety. Clunies-Ross, eager to develop trade, and Hare, seeking only seclusion, soon fell out but in 1831 Hare left to attend to interests elsewhere and Clunies-Ross took possession of all the islands. Several generations of the Clunies-Ross family then ruled the Cocos (Keeling) Islands in such a manner that they were often referred to as "kings". Their main business became the export of coconut products. In 1857 Britain formally annexed the Cocos (Keeling) Islands and John George Clunies-Ross was appointed Superintendent. In 1878 the administration of the islands passed to the Governor of Ceylon and in 1886 to the Straits Settlements. In that year Queen Victoria granted ownership of the islands to the Clunies-Ross family in perpetuity. In 1903 they were formally annexed to the Straits Settlements so that the laws of that colony could be extended to them but the Clunies-Ross family continued to govern.

As the Cocos (Keeling) Islands were run largely on feudal lines, money was of little use. To facilitate store payments sheepskin tokens (or notes) in values from five rupees to one eighth rupee were issued during the later 19th century. These were superseded by similar notes in paper and in 1913 a new series of tokens, this time in "ivory", was issued in denominations from five rupees down to five cents, now using decimal divisions of the rupee. These remained in use until the 1950s.

Cocos (Keeling) Islands

Five rupees and fifty cents tokens 1913.

The Clunies-Ross family also developed interests in Christmas Island, nearly 550 miles east north east of the Cocos (Keeling) Islands. Here though, large deposits of phosphate were discovered and the island was annexed by the British Crown in 1888. Phosphate production began in 1890 and Christmas Island was administered by the Colonial Office through the Straits Settlements. So that a legal system could apply Christmas Island was formally annexed to the Straits Settlements in 1900.

Eventually both Christmas Island and the Cocos (Keeling) Islands would be transferred to Australia. For the moment though, with Alexander Hare and the Kings of Cocos on stage, our next chapter moves to a different part of the world if not to a different world entirely.

12

East of India

WE begin this chapter in the Malay Peninsula where, in the early 19th century, the territories under British control were those in the hands of the East India Company. In the 1780s a "country" trader by the name of Francis Light persuaded the Governor General at Calcutta that a settlement at **Penang** would be of the greatest advantage to both Britain and the Company. Because of the restrictive trading practises in China an entrepôt somewhere east of India was thought desirable. Penang could also be a useful naval base for the protection of Madras and Bengal and from which control could be exercised over shipping in the Malacca Strait. Through his trading connections and local knowledge Francis Light was also convinced that the area was ripe for development and his influence with the Sultan of Kedah was such that he knew a Company settlement would be welcome. Appointed to head the enterprise as the East India Company's first Superintendent for Penang, Francis Light set sail with a founding fleet from Calcutta in the summer of 1786. At a small ceremony in August the settlement was named Prince of Wales Island after the heir to the British throne, the future King George IV.

The first task was to clear sufficient land to make a settlement and for this the sepoys who came with the founding fleet and labour from Kedah would be used. The fleet brought with them a supply of tokens struck at the Calcutta Mint which are uniface and bear only the balemark of the Company. In catalogues these are sometimes referred to as "pice" (probably because they were struck in India) but sometimes as "cents" (because the standard of value in the trade of the Malay Peninsula was the Spanish dollar). They were probably designed to be used as work tallies for the building of George Town and Fort Cornwallis and as such could have been assigned any convenient value.

The axes that came with the founding expedition proved far too soft to fell the hardwood trees of Penang so Francis Light dispatched one of his vessels to Malacca to buy decent local axes. He did not though sit idle in the three weeks while the "Eliza" was away. Each morning he loaded guns on his two remaining ships with assorted small change and an occasional rupee and fired them off into the trees. The ensuing scramble to find them ensured that by the time the "Eliza" returned with the new axes the undergrowth at least was all cleared away. Or so the story goes. The uniface tokens may well have formed part of Light's "shrapnel".

In the end Penang did not become a great naval base or a major centre for the China trade but commercially it grew at a steady rate. The rank of Superintendent was changed to Lieutenant Governor in 1800 after a portion of the mainland opposite George Town had been acquired. This was named Province Wellesley and provided security and support for the main settlement at Penang. In 1805, during the French wars, it was again planned to establish a British naval base at Penang. Because of this its status was raised to that of an East India Company Presidency equal in status to Bombay and Madras but subordinate to the Governor General in Bengal. Penang now had its own Governor with a staff which included a young Assistant Secretary on his first posting, Thomas Stamford Raffles, who we will hear more of later. The naval base though did not materialise, leaving Penang with an expensive and top heavy administration for some years.

It was not long before a regular coinage based on the Spanish dollar was struck for Penang (Prince of Wales Island) at the Calcutta Mint. The copper coins are dated 1787 and are of cent, half cent and tenth cent denominations. The silver coins are of half dollar, quarter dollar and tenth dollar and are dated 1788. The reverse of these coins is an attempt to render the name "Prince of Wales Island" phonetically into Arabic. This coinage seems to have been sufficient for Penang for some time. The silver coins are quite rare but many die varieties of the two larger copper denominations are known. This indicates that these particular denominations were a substantial issue probably over a number of years even though the date remained unchanged. By about 1800 a shortage of small change led to the appearance of large and crude tin cents which show a variety of initials assumed to be those of Lieutenant Governors and East India Company officials.[1] The copper and tin coinages for Penang are nearly always referred to in the records as "pice" but it is also clear that in Penang this term referred to the hundredth part of the Spanish dollar and should properly have been "cent".

By 1809 forgeries of the tin coins were becoming a problem and a request was made for a new copper coinage to be supplied. Copper cents ("pice") and halves dated 1810 were produced at the new Tower Hill mint in London and arrived in Penang in 1812.[2] These coins are named for "Pulau Penang" (Penang Island) instead of "Prince of Wales Island" and further issues (now including the double pice) came from the Madras mint in 1825 and 1828.

In the interests of uniformity throughout its territories the East India Company was soon attempting to introduce the rupee as the standard for Penang in place of the dollar. The Governor resisted this for some time but by the 1820s the rupee had entered Penang in quite large numbers and the Bengal sicca was customarily rated at half a dollar. This in fact over rated the rupee and was causing exchange problems which had to be sorted out. After a lengthy enquiry and a revaluation of the rupee the Governor decided to drop his opposition to a change of standard and adopt the Directors' view. With effect from 1st May 1826 the Bengal sicca rupee became the money of account and standard of value for all government transactions. The Spanish dollar would continue to be received into and paid from the Company's treasury at its intrinsic value of 210 rupees 8 annas per hundred dollars. The copper coins in circulation had to be re-valued as fractions of the rupee, the cent (pice) becoming the 48th part of the Bengal sicca rupee. None of the Madras struck coins (dated 1825 and 1828) arrived in Penang before the change so the three denominations were officially double pice, pice and half pice of the rupee when they went into circulation[3].

---

1 For further details on the tin coins see F. Pridmore, "Penang Tin Pice, c. 1800 – 1803" in SNC February, 1977, pp 46-47
2 The 1810 coinage for Penang was the first coinage to be struck at the new Tower Hill mint.
3 For a detailed treatment of the Penang coinage see F. Pridmore, "Coins and Coinages of the Straits Settlements and British Malaya 1786 to 1951," pp 9 – 27.

PENANG

The uniface work tallies

The example on the right has old scratches as if fired from a ship's gun!

The first coins

Silver half dollar.

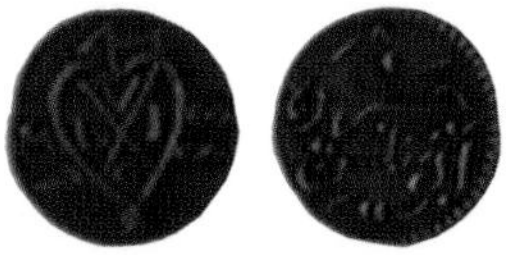

Silver tenth dollar.

Copper cent.

Copper half cent.

Tin cent

With initials A & C (probably Penang officials Anderson and Clubley) 1809.

Pulo Penang coinage

Cent 1810, Royal Mint.

Double pice 1828 struck at Madras

Dutch **Malacca** lay some distance to the south of Penang and in August 1795 was surrendered to a force from Madras which had with it a copy of the Stadtholder's letter from Kew. This required the admission of British forces to the town and harbour as friends and allies but the Dutch Governor could not agree with British demands for full control. There was thus a few days' delay before matters were brought to a head by the landing of British troops when, with little means to resist, the Dutch surrendered without casualties on either side. At the Peace of Amiens in 1802 Malacca was to be returned to the Dutch but war had resumed before any change could be made. When peace finally came it would be some time (September 1818) before the Dutch actually returned to take over. During the British occupation the East India Company administered Malacca but no coins were specifically struck for the territory. Rupees and Dutch coins comprised the main circulation. In trade, as at Penang, the Spanish dollar was the standard of value.

Knowing its tenancy was temporary the Company set about destroying Malacca's effectiveness by trying to attract its people and its trade to Penang. In 1807 the demolition of the fortifications was begun with the intention of abandoning the place or at least making it unusable when the Dutch returned. Much of what happened next in the Malay Peninsula and beyond was the brainchild of Thomas Stamford Raffles. By 1807 he had risen to the senior rank of Secretary at Penang and had no doubt been involved in the discussions on the future of Malacca. The next year, for his own health, he went to Malacca where systematic demolition had begun. He realized at once the importance of an established settlement in the trade and politics of the region and prepared a comprehensive report recommending that Britain should retain Malacca rather than destroy it. His report appears to have been sent direct to the Governor General at Calcutta as well as through his immediate superior, the Governor at Penang. Lord Minto read it and was impressed. The policy of dismantling and evacuating Malacca was reversed and plans made to retain it if circumstances allowed. Raffles saw that the established trade at Malacca was a key to influence in the eastern seas and when he obtained leave from Penang in 1810 he went in person to Calcutta to impress his views on Lord Minto. Here the possibility of taking Java from the Dutch was discussed.

Java was another of the Dutch settlements in the East that Britain was keen to take in trust for the exiled Stadtholder. However, not all the Dutch governors were eager to comply and Java would have to be taken by force. In the late 1790s, with problems to be dealt with in India, the British were not in any position to challenge the Dutch in Java and there was soon a fresh Dutch fleet at Batavia with direct orders from their new master, Napoleon, to defend it against British attack. It was not until the important base of Mauritius had been taken from the French in 1810 that an attack on Java could sensibly be considered and it was only in that year that Lord Minto received authority to proceed. Raffles was appointed "Agent to the Governor General with the Malay States" for the specific purpose of planning the Java expedition and chose Malacca as his base. From here he not only made detailed plans for the passage and invasion but was also able to develop a web of intrigue with Malay rulers and princes in Java and elsewhere.

Minto's instructions from London concerning Java were to subdue the Dutch government, destroy the fortifications, distribute the arms and military stores to the Javanese chiefs and then leave. What Raffles and the Governor General planned was far more. As the "men on the spot" they knew better. Simply destroying the fortifications and walking away, they thought, would not work and in any case would endanger the lives of the Dutch who remained. Their plan was to present the British Government and the East India Company with a *fait accompli* in which Java had become a permanent British possession. Java was taken by force in August and September 1811 and none other than Thomas Stamford Raffles (who had accompanied the attacking force) was appointed to his first Lieutenant Governorship. He set about governing Java as a regular British (East India Company) territory but kept many of the Dutch officials in office to do so. While Raffle's vision for the administration of Java could hardly be faulted some of his reforms were controversial and the authorities in London were not pleased with the situation that had been created.

As administrators in Java the East India Company had responsibility for the provision of coinage and for this there was an immediate need. This was met by use of the existing Sourabaya mint and the employment of its Dutch mint master, Johan Zwekkert. The Company's coinage for Java continued to use Dutch denominations. It was initially in half stivers and doits dated 1811 with the one stiver denomination added later. From 1813 silver and gold coins were also produced at Sourabaya and tin doits were produced at the Batavia mint in an attempt to remedy a shortage of small change. The coins produced during the short period of Company administration are thus varied and interesting. The copper coins carry the heart shaped balemark of the United East India Company surmounted with a letter "B", the significance of which is not known.[4] The silver and gold coins have legends in Arabic and Javanese, the gold coins also bearing a Christian date. All the Sourabaya struck coins are marked with Zwekkert's initial.

Java under the East India Company

Copper coins

Half stiver 1812.　　　Doit 1812.

Tin.

Doit 1814.

Silver and gold

Rupee 1815.　　　Gold half rupee 1816.

---

4 Could it stand for "British" as opposed to "Dutch" Company? The tin doits from the Batavia mint show a plain United Company balemark.

Lord Minto had assured Raffles that if Java were taken over as a British colony and a Crown Governor appointed (as had been the case with Ceylon) he would have the Residency of Bencoolen. In the event the Company would be required to hand Java back to the Dutch at the end of the Napoleonic War but it took some time for them to arrive before the transfer could take place on 19th August 1816. By that time Raffles had already been relieved to take up his duties at Bencoolen but illness demanded that he first return to England. This gave him a chance to explain his handling of the government and revenue of Java to the Directors who were unhappy at some aspects of it. Favourably impressed by his account they changed the title of Resident at Bencoolen to Lieutenant Governor especially for his appointment and he arrived back in the East as *Sir* Stamford Raffles having been knighted while he was in England.

Whatever his title there was no disguising the fact that **Bencoolen** in Sumatra was the least attractive of the Company's settlements. Raffles arrived to take up his new responsibility on 22nd March 1818 just after a series of earthquakes had devastated the place. On 7th April he wrote to his friend, John Marsden, "*This is, without exception, the most wretched place I ever beheld…*" although characteristically he goes on to say "*We will try and make it better…*"[5] The term "we" included his new wife who had suffered badly from seasickness at the beginning of the voyage out, had given birth to a daughter off the Cape of Good Hope and had then accompanied Raffles on his arduous familiarization tours around his new administration.

Bencoolen had been the East India Company's consolation prize when it was expelled from Java all those years ago in 1682. Along the coast pepper plantations had been established and a coinage of fanams and cash, struck in Madras, had been in use for many years (Chapter two). In this period Bencoolen was subject to the Company's Madras Presidency but in 1760, in an effort to improve its security, it was itself given Presidency status. Bencoolen now reported directly and independently to the Directors in London but the cost of administration was so high that it was again reduced to a Residency in 1785. Because of developments in India Bencoolen was from then on subject to the Governor General in Bengal rather than to Madras. Requests for a new coinage had already been made to both London and Calcutta and it was in Bengal that the next coinage for Sumatra was struck. It consisted of silver coins dated 1783-1784 and copper coins dated 1783. The silver coins were of two sukus (half dollar) denomination and were struck at the Calcutta mint. The copper coins were of two kepings denomination and came from John Princep's private mint at Fulta. The keping passed at four hundred to the dollar making the two kepings the equivalent of a half cent. All subsequent coins for Sumatra were in copper and from the Soho mint in Birmingham. The first of these were coins of three kepings, two kepings and one keping dated 1786, 1787 and 1798. These are similar in style to the Fulta two kepings. In 1804 a new obverse design substituting the arms of the Company for its balemark was introduced on coins of four kepings, two kepings and one keping. A second issue of the 1804 coins was struck in 1823 on thinner, lighter flans but still carrying the earlier date.

Sir Thomas Stamford Raffles was a remarkable Lieutenant Governor who set about governing the Company's Sumatra settlements, as he had governed Java, in a very enlightened manner. To do this he acted very much on his own initiative, leaving himself open to criticism from some quarters. He introduced much social change but his period of office coincided with falls in demand for both pepper and spices and his plans to increase trade and revenue came to nought. This incurred losses for the Company for which he was criticised but history will remember his time at Bencoolen for a different reason.

---

5 *Letter from Bencoolen, 7th April 1818.*

SUMATRA FROM ABOUT 1780

Coins struck in India

Two sukus 1784 struck in Calcutta.

Two kepings 1783, Fulta mint.

Initial Birmingham struck issue

Three kepings 1786.

Two kepings 1787.

New design from Birmingham.

Two kepings 1804.

Light issue of 1823 (still dated 1804)

Four kepings.

Two kepings.

Keping.

After familiarizing himself with his new administration Raffles set off to visit his immediate superior, the Governor General at Calcutta. He felt this was his last chance to state his views on the vital importance to Britain of the Eastern Archipelago. The Marquis of Hastings was now in office and, unlike his predecessor, was somewhat wary of this energetic imperialist. Nevertheless he listened to what he had to say. With Java and Malacca back in Dutch hands the supremacy of the eastern seas was again in contention. The Dutch were busy re-establishing themselves throughout the east and excluding the trade of other nations. The only British (East India Company) bases were at Penang and Bencoolen. Neither of these could safeguard the routes to China and the east or act as a major emporium of eastern trade. A new base somewhere near the southern end of the Malacca Strait would immeasurably strengthen Britain's position and secure her eastern trade. The Governor General agreed to appoint Raffles as his Agent to sail south and seek a suitable spot that was not already in Dutch hands.

With the Dutch busy consolidating their position Raffles knew that he had little time to spare but his connections and local knowledge gave him a clear idea of exactly where he would find such a place. The island of Singhapura was nominally subject to the Sultan of Johore who was himself under Dutch influence. Nevertheless, it had a good harbour, plentiful supplies of fresh water and timber and there was not a Dutchman in sight. When Raffles came to an anchor on 28th January 1819 he knew this was exactly what he was looking for. The next day he landed, made a provisional treaty with the local ruler and raised the Union Flag. As far as the Sultan of Johore was concerned Raffles discovered that there was a succession dispute that could be used to advantage. A fuller treaty was signed on 6th February with the person that he (Raffles) was happy to recognize as the rightful incumbent. The treaty recognized Singapore as British and it was immediately opened for trade as a free port. Right from the start this was a commercial venture designed to secure British trade and break the monopoly of the Dutch. Raffles left it in the care of a Resident and, after attending to other business in the region, returned to his post at Bencoolen. Because of the manner of its founding Singapore was initially subject to Raffles at Bencoolen.

The claim to Singapore was immediately contested by the Dutch who considered it to be within their sphere of influence. It was viewed with jealousy by the Lieutenant Governor of Penang who felt a new port could only damage his own settlement. At home the Directors were reluctant to take on additional responsibilities and the British Government did not want a colonial dispute that could upset the balance of power in Europe. In Bengal though the Governor General could see the advantage of a new British port and was happy to wait and see what would happen. Dutch objections were referred to the British and Dutch Governments at home and while negotiations dragged on Singapore flourished. Trade and business, anxious to escape the restrictions of the Dutch ports, increased at a staggering rate and it was clear that whatever the outcome of negotiations in Europe Singapore was there to stay.[6]

Raffles now suffered personal tragedy and in 1822, having lost three of his children to illness, he made known his intention of returning to Europe. Before doing so he paid a final visit to Singapore where he made detailed plans for the town and its constitution. Now that he was leaving, Singapore's dependency on Bencoolen was no longer appropriate and it became a Residency subject directly to Bengal. Raffles finally left Bencoolen in April 1824

---

6 *In its first 2½ years it is recorded that 2,889 ships called at Singapore with a total tonnage of 161,515 (letter from Raffles to Thomas Murdoch, 12th April 1822). By late 1822 nine European mercantile houses were in business and land prices were rising rapidly.*

and, by the time he arrived in Plymouth, Singapore had become part of a complex Anglo-Dutch agreement for the whole region. The Treaty of London, signed on 17th March 1824, agreed Dutch and British spheres of influence. Malacca would pass again to the East India Company and Dutch claims to Singapore would be dropped. This gave Britain full control of the Malacca Strait. In return, Bencoolen would pass to the Dutch giving them full control of the Sunda Strait. The remaining Dutch interests in mainland India would pass to Britain. The treaty came into effect on 1st March 1825.

Although Raffles was unwell (he would die in July 1826) he was satisfied that his plans had come to fruition. His energy together with his knowledge of the language, customs, trade, politics and people of the region had served him well, provided Britain with a secure route to China and founded what was already a major emporium of eastern trade.

As a thriving entrepôt **Singapore** needed a coinage. Its burgeoning trade naturally attracted a variety of coins and by 1823 the Resident felt it was necessary to clarify the situation. In November of that year he declared the Spanish dollar to be the legal currency of the settlement. Various rupees and the Dutch guilder would, with their subdivisions, be legal tender up to five dollars until a suitable subsidiary coinage could be produced. For small change a variety of coins were in circulation, the commonest being the Dutch silver two stivers and copper doit (quarter stiver). The Resident suggested a subsidiary coinage in silver and copper to replace these Dutch coins and circulate throughout the region. Dies were made for these at Calcutta in 1824 and some patterns produced but objections were raised and the coins did not materialize. Various small denomination coins therefore continued to circulate. As a dependency of Bencoolen the Sumatran copper coins naturally formed part of that circulation, the one keping of that series being similar in size and weight to the Dutch doit. It is clear from various correspondence that Raffles was very keen to introduce a British style coinage for the region and that he brought this to the attention of the Directors in London. It would seem also that his efforts in this direction resulted in the Company's decision to order the large light weight issue of Sumatran coins in 1823 (still dated 1804). It is most likely that many of these were intended for use in Singapore and elsewhere.[7]

By the early 1830s the demand for small change throughout the islands was such that the merchants of Singapore began to import large quantities of tokens (see overleaf). These came from Birmingham and elsewhere and were of one keping and sometimes two kepings denominations. Many have the distinctive obverse design of a fighting cock while others copy the Dutch doit and the East India Company's Sumatran one keping coins. These tokens had no fixed relationship to the dollar, passing at various rates in the market place. Nevertheless, no serious attempt was made to replace them with an official small change for some years and the tokens continued to be imported until the 1850s.[8]

---

7   *In a letter from Bencoolen dated 26th December 1821 Raffles notes that "…the extensive circulation of a British copper coinage throughout the archipelago" would be a great advantage (Memoir of the Life and Public Services of Sir Thomas Stamford Raffles, Vol. 2, p. 206). This and other correspondence is noted by F. Pridmore & D. Vice, in SNC September 1980, pp 303/4. They also note a reference to ten tons of copper coins intended for Bencoolen being landed at Singapore in November 1824.*

8   *For details of the merchants' tokens see F. Pridmore "Coins of the British Commonwealth Part 2 Asian Territories", pp 147-175 and (for a fuller treatment) "Coins and Coinages of the Straits Settlements and British Malaya 1786 to 1951", pp 68-143. These works are updated by joint papers by F.Pridmore and D.Vice in SNC 1980, pp 302/4 and 1981, pp 3-6.*

Typical Singapore merchants' tokens

Merchant copy (1830s) of light issue Sumatra keping.   "Island of Sultana" type.

Birmingham copy (1830s) of Dutch quarter stiver. Imported for use as a token.   A "cock" token (the most frequently used obverse type).

In 1826, following the recent Anglo-Dutch agreement, Malacca and Singapore were added to the Penang Presidency to form the **Straits Settlements.** To reduce costs this Presidency was downgraded to Residency status in 1830 and attached to Bengal. The Straits Settlements remained part of British India for some years passing directly under the Governor General in 1851. As with India itself, ultimate responsibility passed from the Company to the India Office in 1858 by which time Singapore had become by far the most important of the Straits Settlements. By that time also there was some concern that as an appendage of India the affairs of the Straits were not being properly addressed. One of those concerns was the currency. As part of British India the Company would have liked the Straits to use its uniform coinage for day to day transactions but could only insist that the rupee was the official standard and should be used for government accounts. The Straits Settlements though were firmly in the dollar using area and their increasing trade was mainly with regions other than India. There were several reasons for dissatisfaction at the way India governed the Settlements but it seems to have been the Copper Currency Act of 1855 that brought matters to a head.[9] We will look at this in a little more detail when we come to the coins but by July 1856 there were calls for the Straits Settlements to separate from India and become a Crown colony. By 1860 a transfer had been agreed as there seemed little reason why the Straits should continue to be governed from India. It took some time to sort out the detail but responsibility for the Straits Settlements finally passed to the Colonial Office on 1st April 1867.[10]

The policy towards the Malay States had always been one of non intervention. The Straits Settlements were coastal commercial bases whose trades were mainly outside the Peninsula. They had never been seen as centres from which influence should be extended into the Malay States where alliances could lead to unwanted responsibilities or even to conflict with Siam.

---
9   *British Indian Act XVII of 1855.*
10 *Under the Straits Settlements Act 1866 (29 & 30 Vict c. 115)*

There is no doubt that the British presence in the Settlements deterred Siam from encroachments in the Peninsula and as the century wore on Siam began to be seen by Britain as a useful buffer between French interests in Cochin China and her own perceived sphere of interest further south. Also, in spite of the policy of non intervention, British trade and influence had spread and the merchants of the Settlements were keen to develop commercial opportunities inland. By 1870 attitudes were therefore beginning to change and it was possible to envisage Britain as the paramount power in the Malay Peninsula just as she was in India. The Colonial Office and the Straits Government knew that in some regions trade was badly affected by rivalries between Chinese societies who sought to control the developing tin industry. They thought also that some of the Malay States would welcome a measure of British intervention to restore law and order. When Sir Andrew Clarke was appointed Governor of the Straits Settlements in 1873 his instructions were to seek a solution and make recommendations. The appointment of British Residents to States who consented to such an arrangement was specifically suggested as a way forward.

The State of Perak, which bordered Penang, was suffering the uncertainties of a succession dispute as well as serious unrest among the Chinese tin miners in the Larut district so it seemed likely that Perak at least would accept such an arrangement. As the man on the spot Sir Andrew felt that it was important to act at once rather than report and await instructions. Wasting no time he therefore called a conference which took place at Pangkor, a small island off the coast of Perak, in January 1874. The resulting treaty (or "engagement") led to the appointment of a British Resident for Perak who would be deferred to on all matters except those touching Malay religion and custom. To better control piracy, Pangkor and an adjoining coastal strip of land known as the Dindings were ceded to the United Kingdom and became part of the Straits Settlements. The Pangkor Engagement laid the foundation for agreements with other states, the Residency system being extended almost at once to Selangor and Sungei Ujong (a minor state within the Negri Sembilan) and eventually to Pahang and the whole of the Negri Sembilan. The system was not an immediate success as many Malays were not happy with the full implications of British control. Nevertheless these States comprised the entire Malay Peninsula between Penang and Malacca and in 1895 agreed to join together as the Federated Malay States.[11] A Resident General was now appointed to oversee the individual State Residents and took up his office at Kuala Lumpur in Selangor.

Johore (modern "Johor") covered the whole of the southern Peninsula between Malacca and Singapore. In 1885 a treaty between Britain and Johore recognized the ruler as Sultan and formalised relations between the two countries. It was agreed that Johore would retain full control of internal affairs and that Britain would take control of foreign affairs. There would be no Resident like those of the states further north but the Sultan agreed in principle to have a British advisor. Johore did not join the Federated Malay States in 1895 and in the event a General Advisor was not appointed until 1910. Initially there was little interference in the way Johore was run but in May 1914 a new treaty gave the General Advisor greater control of internal affairs.

The area north of the Federated States was increasingly considered by Britain to be within her sphere of influence. Siam however still claimed suzerainty and it was not until March 1909 that all Siamese rights in Kedah, Kelantan, Trengganu and Perlis were formally transferred to Britain. Here, Advisors rather than Residents were appointed. These states were not tied to each other and did not join the Federated Malay States but became, like Johore, Protected States.

---

11 The Treaty of Federation was drawn up in 1895 and signed on 1st July 1896.

By 1914 "British Malaya" thus consisted of:-

The Crown colony of Straits Settlements which comprised Penang (with Province Wellesley), Malacca, Singapore and the Dindings (including Pangkor).

The Federated States of Perak, Selangor, the Negri Sembilan and Pahang.

The Protected (Unfederated) States of Kedah, Kelantan, Trengganu, Perlis and Johore.

The Governor of the Straits Settlements whose seat was at Singapore served also as Britain's High Commissioner for the Malay States.

British Malaya continued to be the mixture of administrations outlined above until the Second World War augured irrevocable change. It became an important part of the Empire not only because of its strategic position but for the tin and then rubber that it produced.

We have seen that by the 1830s a mixture of coins was in circulation in the **Straits Settlements.** Penang had its own copper coins struck until 1828 which had been designed to be divisions of the dollar but were now officially divisions of the rupee. These were beginning to circulate throughout the Settlements. The use of Dutch coins in Malacca was gradually dying out and large numbers of tokens were being imported to Singapore for use there and in the ports to which she traded. In Penang, in 1826, the East India Company had introduced the Bengal sicca rupee as the standard in place of the dollar and with the founding of the Straits Settlements in that year this applied also to Malacca and Singapore.

The rules laid down in 1826 did not demonetize the dollar. They established the rupee as the coin of account and standard of value but the dollar continued to be received and paid at the Straits Treasuries at its intrinsic value (210-8-0 sicca rupees per 100 dollars). Government accounts were kept in rupees while the merchant classes were free to conduct their business in dollars. The legal situation though was altered by the Indian Act XVII of 1835 which made the Company's new uniform rupee the sole legal tender for British India. The Straits Settlements was part of that administration and on 15th January 1836 the Governor was instructed to comply and make the Company's uniform rupee the sole legal tender. This signalled the beginning of a long contest between the East India Company who wanted a uniform coinage throughout its territories and the commercial community of the Straits who knew that use of the dollar was vital to trading success. To comply with the instructions of 1836 the rupee of account in the Straits had to be changed from the Bengal sicca (at 210-8-0 per hundred dollars) to the new Company rupee (at 222 per hundred dollars) and the old pice in circulation would have to pass at 45 to the rupee instead of 48. All this made official accounting quite complicated but of more concern to the merchants was the fact that the use of the dollar and the Dutch guilder was to cease. The protests from the Singapore Chamber of Commerce were such that in 1839 the dollar was quietly allowed to continue in use as before and to be paid and received at the Treasuries at 222 rupees. Round one had gone to the trading community who were able to ignore the official standard as they had done since 1826. Even so, the dollar was no longer a legal currency and the Indian Government took no steps to make it so for the remaining years of their administration.

By 1842 there was a great need for a suitable copper coinage to replace the merchants' tokens and other minor coins and the Straits Governor requested a coinage of cents, halves and quarters subsidiary to the dollar. The Bengal Government responded by sending Indian copper coins which had an awkward exchange rate with the dollar and did not pass into general circulation. It was then reluctantly agreed that a special copper coinage would have to be authorized and these began to be struck at Calcutta in 1845. It was not though until 1847, when legislation had exempted the Straits from British Indian Acts concerning copper coinage, that the first shipment arrived in the Straits. These new copper coins (cent, half cent and quarter cent) continued in issue until 1862 bearing the legend **EAST INDIA COMPANY** and dated 1845. Like the coins of India itself these were of fixed date and there was insufficient capacity at the mints to change the designs immediately after the transfer from Company to Crown in 1858.

The cent denomination was about the same weight as the old Penang cent (pice) that had been in issue from 1810 to 1828 and this new coinage was an official recognition that the dollar was the popular currency of the Straits Settlements. A copper coinage with a guaranteed relationship to the dollar (unlike the tokens) was readily accepted but none of this altered the legal situation. The rupee was still the sole unlimited legal tender.

In 1852 the Acting Governor of the Straits brought attention to the fact that the dollar was an illegal currency and voiced his view that the legislation allowing the special copper coinage in cents was flawed. He recommended that the rupee and its subdivisions should replace dollars and cents in practice as well as by law. There were immediate local objections and the matter appeared to have been shelved but early in 1854 the Supreme Government in Bengal sent orders to Singapore showing that this was not so. Among other things dollars received at the treasuries were not to be reissued but sent to Calcutta for re-minting. It was recognized that the dollar circulated by custom but it was felt that Indian copper coins could and should be exact divisions of the dollar as well as of the rupee. This being the case the 1845 cents halves and quarters would no longer be required so production would cease. In 1855 an "Act to Improve the Law relating to the Copper Currency in the Straits" was passed by the Indian Government which laid down the rates for the various Indian copper coins and made them legal tender. The pice (quarter anna) was to pass at 140 per dollar, the other coins in proportion. Large numbers of Indian copper coins were sent to the Straits in 1855 and 1856 to make the new system work.

As had happened before, the Indian copper coins at their awkward rates did not go into general circulation. There was huge public outcry at this further attempt to install the coins of British India as the normal currency of use leading, as we saw earlier in this chapter, to suggestions that the Straits would fare better if it were separated completely from British India. In 1857 the Directors in London were moved to write to the Governor General in Bengal that he really needed to listen to people in the Straits and sort matters out. His new legislation for the Straits copper currency should be reconsidered in light of the special circumstances of the case.[12] Above the Directors' signatures, this somewhat scathing letter signs off:- *"We are, Your affectionate friends,"* in the usual manner but it had the desired effect. The 1845 cents, halves and quarters were soon again being struck in quantity in Madras as well as Calcutta, the new supplies arriving in the Straits by the middle of 1858. Dollars continued to be accepted and issued by the treasuries. There was no further attempt to oust the dollar from the Straits Settlements but no move either to make it legal.

Most of the coins we have examined so far in this chapter belong to the East India Company. Foreign coins have been mentioned and we have noticed the tokens used in Singapore but we have seen nothing that could be defined as "colonial". From 1858 though the India Office was responsible for the whole of British India to which the Straits Settlements were attached and the coinage becomes official if not yet colonial.

By 1862 the Indian mints were in a position to change all their coin designs to reflect the change of responsibility from Company to Crown and new coins were struck for the Straits Settlements at Calcutta. These were exactly the same in weight, size and denominations as the

---

12 Letter from London to the Governor General of India in Council dated 14th January 1857.

1845 dated coins that they replaced but instead of the Company's name bear the legend **INDIA-STRAITS**. Again they were of fixed date and continued in issue, dated 1862, until the Straits was transferred to the Colonial Office. Although the dollar and its copper subdivisions were now the main circulation in the Straits Settlements, Indian coins remained legal tender and the rupee continued to be used for Government accounts.

The reluctance to grant legal status to the dollar in the Straits Settlements stemmed from the fact that neither the Indian nor the British Government could guarantee the standard or supply of a foreign coin. So far the Mexican dollar had maintained the old standard and was freely available but only a British dollar would be any guarantee of this for the future. For this reason the commercial community sought the introduction of such a coin. In Hong Kong, where the Mexican dollar replaced sterling as the legal tender in 1863, there were similar concerns and it was agreed that a mint could be opened there under Royal Mint supervision in 1866 to coin Hong Kong dollars at Mexican weight and fineness. This "British" dollar and subsidiary Hong Kong coins were welcomed in the Straits Settlements where they soon came into circulation.

The final change from the rupee to the dollar in the Straits Settlements took place on 1st April 1867. The Legal Tender Act was passed by the local Legislature on the same day that the Straits Settlements passed from the Indian to the Imperial Government and became a Crown colony. It repealed all laws making Indian coins legal tender and declared the Hong Kong dollar to be the standard. Together with those of Spain, Mexico, Peru, Bolivia and any others subsequently declared of equal standard this was to be the sole legal tender. The copper cents, halves and quarters were legal tender up to one dollar and a proposed subsidiary token silver coinage would be legal tender to two dollars. By this time the British Government had accepted that their plan to introduce sterling throughout the colonies was unsuitable for many of them. This new colony was obviously in a dollar using area and could be supplied from the Hong Kong Mint so the Home Government supported the adoption of the dollar as the legal standard currency of the Straits Settlements.

Unfortunately the Hong Kong mint was closed in 1868 after only two years of operation as it was not working to full capacity and arrangements had to be made to strike the proposed subsidiary coins for the Straits elsewhere. Production of token silver coins at a millesimal fineness of 800 began at the Royal Mint in 1871 in denominations of twenty cents, ten cents and five cents. A fifty cents denomination was added in 1886. Royal Mint production of silver coins was frequently supplemented by the Heaton mint in Birmingham and from 1909 many of the silver coins came from Bombay. Copper cents, half cents and quarter cents were struck by Heaton in 1872 after which most of the copper coinage was struck at Calcutta. There was one issue of copper coins from James Watt's Soho mint in 1875 and one from the Royal Mint (struck in bronze) dated 1884. In 1887 a grained edge was added to the copper coins to deter forgery. All of these subsidiary coins bear the legend **STRAITS SETTLEMENTS.**

Another problem caused by the early closure of the Hong Kong Mint was the resultant absence of a "British" dollar and calls now increased for this to be remedied. On 10th January 1874 an Order of the Governor in Council added two new dollars to the list of those that were legal tender. The United States trade dollar and the Japanese yen were both classed as having the same fineness and intrinsic value as the Hong Kong dollar but this was not a permanent solution. Following a review of the currency in 1890 all previous laws regulating legal tender were repealed and a new law introduced. The Mexican dollar now replaced the Hong Kong dollar as the standard against which other dollars should be measured. The only coins considered equal to it and also having unlimited legal tender were the United States trade dollar, the Japanese yen and the Hong Kong dollar.[13] Legal tender limits for the token silver coins and the copper remained unchanged at two dollars and one dollar respectively.

In the 1890s the gold price of silver was falling causing problems for countries on a silver standard. We saw in the last chapter that India took strong measures to stabilize her currency at this time and the Home Government were concerned at what should be done for the eastern colonies (the Straits and Hong Kong). In 1893 the Governor of the Straits Settlements appointed a special committee to look into the problem. It could not agree on whether a gold standard should be adopted (much of the colony's trade was with other silver using countries) but it did recommend the issue of a British dollar to circulate in the Straits and other eastern possessions. At about the same time Hong Kong was reporting a great shortage of Mexican dollars due to price fluctuations and it was clear that if neither of these colonies was going to move to a gold standard something would have to be done to guarantee the supply and standard of the legal tender coin. It was therefore agreed in 1894 that a British Colonial dollar should be struck at Mexican weight and fineness. Official records always refer to this coin as the "British dollar" although it is often referred to elsewhere as the "British trade dollar". Coining of this began at Bombay in 1895 and a United Kingdom Order in Council of 2nd February 1895 made it legal tender in the Straits Settlements.[14] The Mexican dollar was still the standard of the Straits Settlements and those now stated as being equivalent to it were the new British dollar, Hong Kong dollars of 1866-1868 and the Japanese yen. The Hong Kong half dollar is dropped from the list of legal tender coins and in 1898 the Japanese yen was removed from the list.

It is important to remember that although British influence spread throughout the Peninsula the Acts, rules and regulations concerning the currency applied only to the Straits Settlements. Nevertheless, with slight modifications the changes of the 1890s were adopted by Johore and the Federated Malay States and it was important that future changes should be acceptable to them.

In 1903 it was finally decided to adopt the gold standard but to do this the currency had to be under full local control. This meant the production of a new Straits dollar distinct from those of Mexico and Britain and which could be pegged to gold at a rate chosen by the colony. The new coins began to be struck at Bombay in 1903 and were initially at the same weight and fineness as the British dollar. By 1904 sufficient quantities had arrived to allow it to be declared the standard for the Straits Settlements and all the old dollars (Mexican, Hong Kong and British) were demonetized. The number of Straits dollars produced could now be controlled in order to fix a suitable rate against gold. In 1902 the gold price of the dollar had dropped as low as 1/6d and it was intended that the new dollar should be pegged at 2/-. The price of silver though began to rise and in 1906 it was finally pegged to gold at 2/4d. It was confidently expected that the change to a gold standard would put the Straits currency on a firm footing for the foreseeable future but a continuing rise in the gold price of silver made further changes inevitable.

In 1907, as its bullion value continued to rise, the weight of the Straits dollar had to be reduced by a quarter to ensure that it continued to be a token coin at the fixed rate of 2/4d and was not sent to the melting pot. At the same time the fifty cents coin was upgraded to a "half dollar" and given unlimited legal tender, its millesimal fineness being increased from 800 to 900 and its weight reduced to match the new dollar. The old fifty cents coins were demonetized

---

13 Order in Council of 21st October 1890. The Hong Kong half dollar was included in the list of coins which had unlimited legal tender because it was struck at the same standard. It should not be confused with the fifty cents coin which was part of the token silver series struck in 80% silver and had limited legal tender.

14 It was also legal tender in Hong Kong and Labuan.

on 1st January 1909. Later that year the subsidiary silver coins (below fifty cents) at the original 800 millesimal fineness began to be withdrawn to be replaced with similar coins with a fineness of 600.

The striking of the various denominations was intermittent and for the first few years of George V (1910-1936) they continued to use the name and portrait of Edward VII. The first coins to bear the portrait of George V (some of the subsidiary silver coins) are dated 1916. The First World War stimulated a further rise in the price of silver and a rise also in the price of copper. In 1918 it was decided that both the weight and fineness of the dollar and half dollar would have to be reduced yet again and a millesimal fineness of 500 was adopted for these. The smaller silver coins retained their weight but their millesimal fineness was reduced from 600 to 400. In 1919 the weight of the cent was reduced considerably and it was struck in bronze on a square flan. The only striking of either of the smaller "copper" denominations after 1916 was an issue of the half cent, also in bronze on a square flan, in 1932. In 1920 the five cent denomination was struck in cupro-nickel but by this time the price of silver was at last beginning to fall. The last adjustment to the coinage of the Straits Settlements was when it was decided in 1925 to increase the millesimal fineness of the minor silver coins from 400 to 600 to reflect this fall in price. No dollars or half dollars were struck after this decision was taken and the first minor coins at the increased fineness are dated 1926. The cupro-nickel five cents also reverts to a silver coin from that date. Although none are dated later than 1935 the coins of the Straits Settlements continued in issue until 1938 by which time plans were well under way for a currency for the whole of Malaya.

STRAITS SETTLEMENTS

Official units of account

1826, Bengal " sicca" rupee.

1836, new uniform rupee.

1867, Hong Kong dollar (and equivalents).

East India Company copper coins 1845 (dollar system)

Cent..   Half cent.   Quarter cent.

"British India" copper coins 1862 (dollar system).

Cent.   Half cent.   Quarter cent.

Crown colony subsidiary coins.

Cent 1872.   Half cent 1872.   Quarter cent 1884.

Fifty cents 1896.   Twenty cents 1898.   Ten cents 1879.

Other legal tenders.

US trade dollar 1877.

Japanese trade dollar (1875).

British dollar 1901.

Straits dollar 1903.

Later coins.

Reduced weight dollar 1908.

Fifty cents (now "half dollar") 1908.

George V dollar 1920.

Bronze cent 1919.

The story of the Straits coinage may seem complicated but in summary it is really quite simple. The copper coinage introduced in 1845 by the East India Company was continued by the Indian Government in 1862 and then under the Colonial Office from 1872 with little change until the First World War. The subsidiary silver coinage was introduced in 1871 and changed little except in fineness for the rest of our period. The standard coin was the Mexican dollar, a specific Straits dollar having to be struck when it was decided to adopt the gold standard.

The currency of the Crown colony (paper as well as metallic) came into extensive use throughout the Malay Peninsula in the 20th century. In consequence the Federated Malay States felt entitled to and applied for some of the profits that arose from the issue of the Straits currency notes. In September 1933 a Commissioner was appointed to look into the matter with a view to introducing a currency for the whole of British Malaya. He reported that Malaya (the Colony together with the Federated and Unfederated States) was a single economic unit and that the coins and notes of the Straits Settlements already formed its legal tender.

His recommendations, which were accepted, were that a Currency Commission for Malaya should be set up with the duty of issuing and managing a pan-Malayan currency. The currency would be jointly and severally guaranteed by the participating governments. Unlimited legal tender should be restricted to currency notes and the dollar and half dollar (which had almost disappeared from circulation) should be reduced to the status of subsidiary coins. By 1938 all the steps necessary for the unification of the currencies of the Straits Settlements and the Malay States had been completed and the new system came into effect on 21st October. The participating governments comprised the whole of British Malaya and were the Straits Settlements, the Federated Malay States (Perak, Selangor, Negri Sembilan and Pahang) and the States of Johore, Kedah, Kelantan, Trengganu and Perlis. Brunei, which will enter our narrative when we move to Borneo, also became a participating State.

The coins of **British Malaya** continue the style of the Straits Settlements coinage but now bear the name and portrait of George VI (1936-1952) on the obverse. They are in minor denominations only and the reverse legend is changed to **COMMISSIONERS OF CURRENCY MALAYA**. The twenty cents, ten cents and five cents dated 1939 were initially at the increased millesimal fineness of 750. These, together with any of the older silver coins of the Straits still in circulation, were legal tender up to two dollars. The cent and half cent of this coinage were legal tender up to one dollar and currency notes were the only unlimited legal tender.

It is interesting to note that although Malaya was occupied by the Japanese from 1942 to 1945 quantities of the silver coins and the bronze cent were struck from 1943 in anticipation of a resumption of British control. The silver coins from 1943 are at the reduced millesimal fineness of 500 and the cent was at reduced size and weight. After the Second World War these all went into circulation but it was soon decided to remove silver altogether from the Malayan coinage. This was in line with practice in the United Kingdom and the "silver" denominations struck from 1948 are in cupro-nickel.

Changes to the administrative arrangements of the Far Eastern colonies after the war led to the substitution of the Commissioners of Currency, Malaya by the Commissioners of Currency, Malaya and British Borneo. The new Board of Commissioners came into being in 1952 so the new coins use the name and portrait of Elizabeth II and change the reverse legend to **MALAYA AND BRITISH BORNEO** but, apart from the addition of a fifty cents coin, the denominations and appearance of the coinage remain unchanged.

Commissioners of Currency Malaya

Twenty cents 1943.

Cent 1941.

Malaya and British Borneo

Fifty cents 1961.

We now move back in time and further east to the island of Borneo. There is no doubt that the ambitions and excesses of individuals lent a great deal of colour to the early period of colonial expansion, not least in the territories that came to be ruled by the East India Company. By the early 19th century improved communications and increased Government control had checked this to some extent but east of India individualism still thrived. We have seen the huge influence Raffles had in the occupation of Java and the founding of Singapore but there were others who, acting under little restraint, expected to have enormous influence and hoped for huge reward, not always under the umbrella of British Imperialism. One such was Alexander Hare who we have already met in the Cocos (Keeling) Islands.

When Java was taken from the Dutch in September 1811 other Dutch interests in the Malay Archipelago were also surrendered to British control and Residents were appointed to them. Bandjarmasin on the south coast of Borneo had been abandoned by the Dutch in 1809 on economic grounds so was not one of them but in 1812 its Sultan appealed for British assistance to control piracy. In response to this Raffles appointed Alexander Hare as Resident. Hare was apparently one of Raffles' informants at Malacca when the Java expedition was being planned and had a detailed knowledge of the eastern seas. He appears to have been well acquainted with the Sultan of Bandjarmasin from whom he managed to obtain a personal grant of some 1,400 square miles of territory. Here he founded the state of **Maluka** which he ruled for some years producing his own coinage of doits. His rule though was controversial as was the role of Raffles in the venture. Unlike other territories Maluka had not been obtained from the Dutch by conquest but from the local Sultan by personal grant to Alexander Hare. Raffles was keen to secure a permanent British presence in the region that would not have to be handed back after the Napoleonic War and naturally made no objection to his friend receiving the grant. Maluka was sparsely populated and to improve this Hare requested immigrants from Java. Raffles was happy to oblige, sending convicts from Javanese jails and others who opted or could be induced to go. By this time there was already some unease about the nature of the entourage Hare was gathering about him which included increasing numbers of young women and illegitimate children. Enemies of Raffles, both English and Dutch, would later accuse him of running an inter island slave trade and procuring for his debauched friend but in fact there were strict rules concerning which prisoners could be transported and guidelines concerning those who went voluntarily. After the Dutch returned to Java and the eastern seas in 1816, they almost immediately made a new treaty with the Sultan of Bandjarmasin but initially Hare was left alone in his independent kingdom.

In June 1818, from his recent posting at Bencoolen, Raffles wrote to the new Dutch Governor General at Batavia informing him that Hare had offered his territory, granted by the Sultan of Bandjarmasin, to the British Government. The British Government appears not to have been interested and Raffles was soon setting his sights on Singapore. This left the Dutch free to expel Hare from his kingdom which he probably left early in 1819 with his extended family.[15] Because of his unusual lifestyle he found scant welcome anywhere he tried to settle, first in Java, then in Lombok and later at the Cape. From the Cape he took his family to the Cocos (Keeling) Islands in 1826 as we saw in the last chapter.

The coins struck by Hare in Maluka make no claim to be British colonial. Although he was sent as Resident to Bandjarmasin his coins were struck in his personal capacity as the ruler of Maluka. They find a place in this book because of his connections with Raffles and the East India Company and because of his nationality. He would not though be the only Briton to achieve personal rule in Borneo and nor would he be the only such ruler to issue coins.

MALUKA.

Doit 1813. *Another variety (this perhaps a contemporary copy).*

On the north coast of Borneo the Dutch had far less influence than in the south and there had been East India Company contacts in the past. It was here, in 1839, that one James Brooke arrived to seek his fortune. Invalided from the Company's army some years earlier, he was at a loose end with an inheritance that allowed him to purchase a schooner. His clear intention was to set himself up in some way through settlement and trade but when he first arrived his immediate task was to bring a gift of thanks from the merchants of Singapore to the Rajah Mudah (heir apparent) of Brunei. This was for the return of the crew and cargo of a wrecked British ship but when Brooke arrived in Sarawak to meet him the Rajah Mudah was dealing with local unrest. Brooke was able to render some slight assistance before returning to Singapore. A few months later he was back offering further assistance but certainly expecting some sort of concession in return. Officially the Rajah Mudah appointed him as Resident with a right to stay in the country and seek profit. Unofficially the Rajah Mudah had granted him the lands around Kuching and Brooke was soon dealing successfully with piracy and banditry. In return for these services he was confirmed as Governor of Sarawak with the fullest powers in September 1841. Brooke was soon styling himself "Rajah" and in 1842 he was confirmed in that title by the Sultan. It was soon agreed also that the title and position would descend to his heirs in perpetuity.

---

15 The Dutch seem to have given him time to complete the construction of a 400 ton ship, the "Borneo", of which Clunies-Ross was later the Master.

Brooke declared open trade and attempted to bring all his subjects under the rule of the laws that he himself was writing. Piracy he tackled head on seeking and getting assistance from the Royal Navy. For this and for the methods he used to maintain law and order he would later be criticized by Liberal governments at home and denied the British protection that he sought for his state. Nevertheless, after a trip to the United Kingdom Brooke had returned to Sarawak in 1848 as "Sir" James with the offices of Governor and Commander in Chief for Labuan and British Consul General for Borneo. (Labuan had been granted to Britain by the Sultan of Brunei late in 1846 to serve as a naval and trading base. Initially occupied as a naval station it became a Crown colony in 1848).

Sarawak was not recognized by Britain as a state independent from Brunei until 1863 and did not attain British protection during Sir James's lifetime. Sir James was succeeded by his nephew, Charles Johnson Brooke, in 1868. He in turn was succeeded by his son, Charles Vyner Brooke, in 1917. Under the rule of the "White Rajahs" the territory of the state grew, largely at the expense of Brunei. In 1888 Sarawak at last came under British protection. The Brooke family ruled Sarawak until it was occupied by the Japanese in 1941. Immediately after the Second World War Charles Vyner Brooke announced his intention of ceding Sarawak to the Crown and, although there was local opposition to this, it became a Crown colony on 1st July 1946.

The coins of **Sarawak** have the same status as those of Maluka. The standard throughout Borneo was the Spanish dollar but the first "coin" introduced by Brooke was a doit, very similar to the tokens of Singapore. In fact it shares a reverse die with them giving the spurious AH date of 1247 and naming it as a "keping". The obverse shows a badger (or "brock", derived from the crest of the Brooke family arms) and is dated September 24th 1841 to commemorate the date of his official appointment in Sarawak. In his initial code of laws published in 1842 Brooke notes (paragraph 7) the necessity *"to settle the weights, measures, and money current in the country, and to introduce doits, that the poor may purchase food cheaply"*.[16] This indicates that although the reverse legend states it to be a keping Brooke's intention was that it should be a doit. They probably date to about 1842 and the fact that a shop of English merchandise had been opened in Kuching by 1844 indicates that currency of some sort was in use. It is likely that Singapore tokens also circulated in Sarawak as they did throughout the eastern seas.

Subsequent coinages, bearing the Rajah's name, title and portrait began in 1863 and closely follow the coins of the Straits Settlements. For James Brooke there is a cent, half and quarter, the cent being 100th of the dollar. All three denominations are at the same weight and size as the coins of the Straits Settlements as Brooke intended them to be. The first coins in the name of Charles Johnson Brooke are dated 1870 and continue the coinage of his predecessor in the same three denominations. Because of complaints from Singapore that quantities of Sarawak (and other) copper coins were circulating in the Straits Settlements the issues of cents from 1892 to 1897 are of a new design with a central hole. They maintain the same weight, the purpose of the central hole being to deter their use outside Sarawak. Silver coins of fifty cents, twenty cents, ten cents and five cents with a millesimal fineness of 800 began issue in 1900 and these too match the subsidiary coins of the Straits Settlements in weight and fineness. From January 1906 only the Straits dollar was accepted as the current standard unit.

Subsidiary coins were struck intermittently for Sarawak as and when required and the first in the name of Charles Vyner Brooke are dated 1920. In fact several new coins bear that date because silver and copper prices had risen considerably. Twenty cents, ten cents and five cents coins were struck at a reduced millesimal fineness of 400 but were followed almost immediately

---

16 *This is noted by F. Pridmore, "Sarawak Currency" in The South Australian Numismatic Journal, July 1957, p.17.*

by an issue of ten cents and five cents coins in cupro-nickel. No copper coins had been struck since 1897 and the cent is now also struck in cupro-nickel. All these, silver and cupro-nickel, are dated 1920. The next issue is dated 1927 and was of all denominations from the fifty cents to the cent. The fifty cents and twenty cents retain the millesimal fineness of 400 but although the price of metals had fallen the ten cents and five cents coins continued to be struck in cupro-nickel. Copper was again used for the cent from 1927 although it was now at reduced weight and size compared to those of 1897. A copper half cent was struck in 1933. The 1937 cent is the latest dated Sarawak coin although records show that this denomination continued to be struck until 1942 and was presumably in issue until the Japanese invasion of 1941. All the coins of Sarawak are attributed to Heaton & Sons which became The Mint Birmingham Ltd in 1889 although prior to that date none of them have the distinctive **H** mintmark.

After the Second World War Malayan coinage came into use and Sarawak was one of the participating States in the setting up of the Board of Commissioners of Currency, Malaya and British Borneo in 1952.

RAJAHS OF SARAWAK.

James Brooke

Doit 1842.

Cent 1863.

Half cent 1863.

Quarter cent 1863.

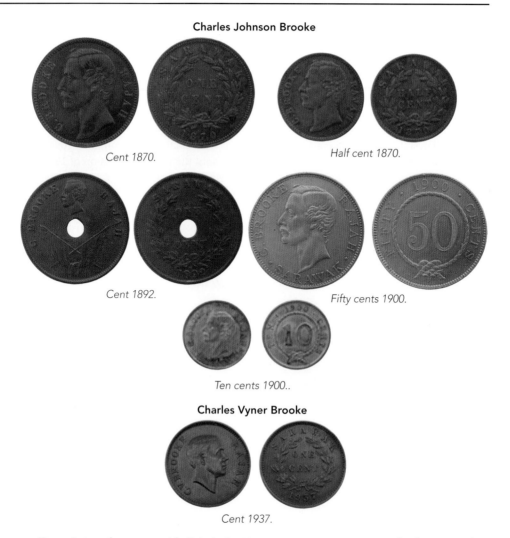

Charles Johnson Brooke

Cent 1870.

Half cent 1870.

Cent 1892.

Fifty cents 1900.

Ten cents 1900..

Charles Vyner Brooke

Cent 1937.

Brunei signed a treaty with Britain in 1847 to encourage commercial relations and to suppress piracy. It became a British protectorate in 1888. By that time Brunei had lost much of its territory to the Dutch, to Sarawak and, more recently, to British North Borneo and was little more than an enclave on the north coast of Borneo. In 1906 a British Resident was appointed to advise the Sultan on all matters of administration except those affecting the Muslim religion giving Brunei similar status to a Federated Malay State. Brunei was occupied by the Japanese from 1941 to 1945. The Residency system ended in 1959 when Brunei became a self governing State under British protection. It achieved independence on 1st January 1984.

By the 1880s the currency of Brunei consisted of silver dollars and the copper coins of Sarawak and North Borneo. The Sultan made his own issue of copper cents in 1887 which were struck in Birmingham to the same specifications as those of the Straits Settlements but the currency of the Straits gradually came into general use. In 1938 Brunei was a participating State in the establishment of the Commissioners of Currency, Malaya and also participated in the setting up of the Commissioners of Currency, Malaya and British Borneo which oversaw the new coinage of 1952.

Just off the coast of Brunei was **Labuan** which had been a Crown colony since 1848. In 1889, in a bid to reduce expenditure, it was decided to entrust the administration of Labuan to the British North Borneo Company (which we will look at below). It continued to be a Crown colony and this unusual arrangement lasted until the end of 1905 when the British Government decided to resume direct control. On 1st January 1907 Labuan was formally annexed to the Straits Settlements and became a separate Settlement within that colony in 1912. It was occupied by Japan from 1941-1945 and was joined to the colony of British North Borneo in 1946. Labuan never proved a great commercial success and no coins or tokens were struck specifically for use there. Silver dollars, Straits Settlements small silver pieces, and the copper coinage of the Straits, Sarawak and British North Borneo all passed current. As a colony, the British dollar became a specific legal tender when it was introduced in 1895 and after joining the Straits Settlements her currency history is identical to and part of that of the Straits followed by British Malaya and then Malaya and British Borneo.

To the east of Brunei and Sarawak and north of the main Dutch claims lay the region that became known as **North Borneo.** In the 1860s this region began to attract western interest and at that time was still nominally subject to the Sultan of Brunei. In 1865 he granted concessions there to the United States Consul at Brunei. The concessions were for administration and revenue collection which would allow development of the region for profit and in return for them the Sultan would receive an annual subsidy. The concessions were soon sold on to American merchants in Hong Kong who established the American Trading Company of Borneo. This Company failed and by 1875 the concessions had passed into the hands of Baron von Overbeck, the Austrian Consul-General at Hong Kong. Von Overbeck needed capital to proceed and was soon in partnership with Alfred Dent who was prepared to provide it. Dent was a member of the commercial house of Dent Brothers and Company of London who had extensive interests in the East and von Overbeck had previously worked for the family in Hong Kong. This new finance allowed the Sultan of Brunei to receive his subsidy and in 1877 he formally ceded the whole of his northern territory to von Overbeck and Dent. However, his right to do so was in question because of claims to some of that territory by the Sultan of Sulu. Von Overbeck, representing the partnership in Borneo, dealt with this by signing a similar agreement with the Sultan of Sulu at the beginning of 1878, also in return for a subsidy. This second agreement had been reached with the assistance and advice of the British Acting Consul General in Borneo, William Hood Treacher. He was careful to ensure that the agreement prevented the concession being transferred to other than British subjects without the consent of the British Government. Rather than sell on the concessions as von Overbeck and Dent had planned to do, it was therefore agreed to apply for a Royal Charter to develop the region themselves. This they did in 1878. Von Overbeck withdrew from the enterprise and Dent formed a Provisional Association to manage affairs while the application was considered.

The last of the great Chartered Companies (the Hudson's Bay Company) had only recently surrendered its territorial rights to the Dominion of Canada so when the application was made the very concept of a chartered company was outmoded. Nevertheless, a Royal Charter for North Borneo would create an area of undoubted British interest and remove the risk of it falling into the hands of a foreign power all at little cost to the Treasury. It would also allow some government control over the Company which would not be the case if a Royal Charter was denied. The application therefore received lengthy and careful consideration before a charter was finally granted in 1881. It differed from earlier Royal charters in that the Crown assumed no sovereignty over North Borneo. It therefore did not grant powers of government to the Company but simply recognized the concessions already granted by the Sultans. The monopoly of trade automatically granted in the earlier charters was now specifically disallowed and this set the tone for subsequent charters elsewhere.[17] The old charter system had been reinvented to extend British influence in a way that recognized the new concept of free trade.

The official recognition given by the Royal Charter to the concessions granted by the Sultans of Brunei and Sulu led at once to Spanish and Dutch reaction. Spanish opposition was on the grounds of her suzerainty over Sulu and thus over all lands subject to the Sultan of Sulu while the Dutch focused on the interpretation of the Anglo-Dutch agreement of 1824 dividing interests in the eastern seas. Agreement was reached with Spain in 1885 when Spanish supremacy over Sulu was recognized on condition that she dropped all claims in North Borneo. Dutch protests were largely ignored as Borneo was not specifically mentioned in the 1824 agreement and there had been British interests there for many years. It was not until 1891 that an Anglo Dutch Convention would define the border between British and Dutch interests with some precision. It was partly because of international interest and the growing importance of the region for British trade that North Borneo, Sarawak and Brunei all came under British protection in 1888. Border disputes between them were also a factor in bringing their foreign affairs under British control.

With the granting of the Royal Charter Dent's Provisional Association was dissolved and the British North Borneo Company began operations from its headquarters at Sandakan. It had a Court of Directors in London and a Governor in Borneo. We have seen that the Company had no monopoly of trade but from the beginning it opted not to trade at all. It derived income solely from the business of government including the farming of various revenues, the sale of land, duties on imports and royalties on exports. It encouraged plantation ownership to develop the economy. Tobacco, which grew quickly from planting to harvest, became a major crop on newly cleared lands and Chinese labour was brought in to work the new plantations.

An additional source of income for the **British North Borneo Company** was the issue of currency, both paper and metallic. The currency was based on the Mexican dollar of 100 cents but from 1905 was based on the dollar of the Straits Settlements. The concessions from both the Sultans included the right to coin money and patterns conforming in weight to the cent, half and quarter struck probably in 1878 indicate that Dent was very keen to exercise that right.[18] With a Royal Charter pending nothing came of these early patterns and the first coins issued by the Chartered Company are copper cents dated 1882 and half cents dated 1885. Both denominations continued unchanged until 1907 and bore the legend **BRITISH NORTH BORNEO Co.** They were at the same weight as those of the Straits Settlements and Sarawak and circulated freely throughout the region. The profits from coinage were significant in the early years and were increased by the fact that the Company's coins were legal tender also in Labuan and Brunei.

A publication of 1893 gives an interesting insight into coinage use at Sandakan at that time. "*What is known as the chit system in China is usually adopted in North Borneo, no one ever thinks of carrying about the cumberous silver dollars of Mexico and Japan which are current, and instead, whenever anything is bought, all one does is to give the shop-keeper an I.O.U. for its value. At the end of the month these are brought in for payment. There is very little small silver*

---

17 For the Royal Niger Company in 1886, the Imperial British East Africa Company in 1888 and the British South Africa Company in 1889 already noted in Chapters nine and ten.
18 F. Pridmore, "Are They Pattern Coins for British North Borneo?", SNC September 1979, p.378.

currency, and our transactions of less than a dollar are conducted in North Borneo Cents. They are packed in rolls of 50 which are very cumbersome and weighty." The writer goes on to remark that British North Borneo notes issued by the Treasury were far more convenient to carry.[19] Her observations refer primarily to currency use by Europeans in Sandakan; much of the country's internal trade was still carried on through barter. The Treasury maintained cash reserves equal to one third of the value of notes in circulation and, over the years, issued notes in various denominations from 25 cents up to 25 dollars.

Cupro-nickel five cents and two and a half cents coins were introduced in 1903. The next year a cupro-nickel cent was introduced even though the copper cent (acceptable throughout the region) continued in issue until 1907. There was no cupro-nickel half cent. A silver twenty five cent denomination was introduced in 1929 with a millesimal fineness of 500. The cupro-nickel and silver coins all have the changed legend **STATE OF NORTH BORNEO** which is the form used by the British Government to describe the territory in the Protectorate Agreement of 1888. Although the copper coins continued to use the old legend until they ceased issue in 1907 this official title is used for all coins introduced subsequent to the Protectorate Agreement. All the Company's coins are from the Heaton mint in Birmingham and show the **H** mintmark. They were struck intermittently as required until 1941.

The Japanese occupation from 1941 to 1945 was followed by the surrender of the Company's rights to the Crown in 1946. The State of North Borneo now became the Crown colony of British North Borneo. The coinage of British Malaya came into general use followed by that of Malaya and British Borneo in 1952.[20]

British North Borneo Company

Cent 1891.   Half cent 1891.

State of North Borneo

Five cents 1903.   Two and a half cents 1920.

---

19 Mrs W. B. Pryer, "A Decade in Borneo." Her husband had been the British North Borneo Company's Resident at Sandakan but in the 1890s was the Manager of the British North Borneo Development Corporation.
20 North Borneo was often referred to as "Sabah". In 1963, when various territories were combined to form Malaysia, the name became official.

SUMMARY FOR MALAYA and BORNEO COINAGES

Malay Peninsula

1787/8	Copper and then silver coins struck at Calcutta for Penang. Spanish dollar is unit of account.
c. 1800	Local coinage of tin "pice" begins.
1812	New copper coins struck for Penang at Royal Mint arrive (dated 1810). Further issues dated 1825 and 1828 struck at Madras.
1826	Bengal sicca rupee becomes unit of Government account in Penang. Malacca and Singapore joined to Penang to form Straits Settlements.
1830s–1850s	Merchants' tokens imported into Singapore in large numbers.
1836	Company's new uniform rupee declared to be the unit of account and sole legal tender.
1845	Copper coins subsidiary to the dollar struck in Calcutta (commercial community continued to use the dollar). Legend "EAST INDIA COMPANY".
1858	Administration of Straits Settlements passes from East India Company to Government of British India.
1862	Government copper coins replace the Company coins of 1845. Legend "INDIA -STRAITS".
1867	Straits Settlements becomes a separate Crown colony. Dollar becomes sole legal tender.
1871	Silver coins subsidiary to the dollar introduced. Struck at Royal Mint and in Birmingham. Legend "STRAITS SETTLEMENTS".
1872	Crown colony copper coins begin for "STRAITS SETTLEMENTS". Same weights as issues of 1845 and 1862,
1895	British dollar introduced at Mexican weight and fineness and made legal tender in Straits Settlements.
1903	Straits dollar introduced at same weight and fineness as British (trade) dollar. Intention to peg it to sterling and adopt gold standard. British (trade) dollar demonetized in Straits Settlements 1904.
1906	Straits dollar pegged to sterling at 2/4d.
1907	Straits dollar struck at reduced weight.
1939	"**COMMISSIONERS OF CURRENCY MALAYA**" coinage introduced for whole of Malaya (Straits Settlements, Federated and Unfederated States) and for Brunei.

Island of Borneo

Maluka

c.1812-1818   Coinage of doits by Alexander Hare for Maluka.

Sarawak

c.1842   James Brooke introduces a doit coinage for Sarawak.

1863   Brooke introduces a decimal copper coinage. Same denominations and weights as the Straits Settlements coins.

1900   Silver coins (same denominations, weights and fineness as the Straits Settlements coins) introduced in Sarawak.

1906   Straits Settlements dollar adopted as the sole standard for Sarawak.

North Borneo

1882   British North Borneo Company introduce copper cent. Half cent introduced 1885. Same weights as Straits Settlements coins.

1903   Larger cupro-nickel denominations introduced. Legend "**STATE OF NORTH BORNEO**".

1914   Legal tender status of Straits Settlements silver coins announced.

1929   One silver denomination (25 cents) introduced.

****

Malaya and British Borneo

1952   Commissioners of Currency, Malaya superseded by Commissioners of Currency, Malaya and British Borneo. First coins dated 1953. Legend "**MALAYA AND BRITISH BORNEO**". This coinage was for the whole of British Malaya, British North Borneo, Sarawak and Brunei. Last coins dated 1962.

Mention has already been made of the plantation system in North Borneo using significant numbers of immigrant labour. The ground rules for their employment were laid down in the Estate Coolies and Labourers Protection Proclamation of 1883. Many of the plantations were remote from Sandakan so to facilitate payments to the workforce and provide a currency for use in the estate shops employers began to introduce tokens. Some of these can be securely dated to the 1890s and the first of them may be a little earlier. "The Token Ordinance 1903" laid down the rules under which they could be issued and used.[21] Any employer of 100 or more labourers could circulate monetary tokens under certain conditions. They were required to carry a mark of value, five dollars being the maximum denomination allowed. They could only be paid to labourers under contract and had to be redeemable in current money or goods in certain circumstances. They had to be authorized by the Governor and registered at the Treasury at Sandakan. No employer could issue more than 10,000 dollars in token currency and a registration fee of 5% of the issue was due. One sample of each token issued had to be deposited in the Treasury and also in the nearest District Office. In the case of a business failure redemption of tokens was a first charge on assets. The regulations laid down in this Ordinance are interesting as they give an indication of the problems that must have arisen from the unregulated use of tokens.

---

21 *Ordinance XVIII dated 1st October 1903. This was amended slightly by Ordinance VII of 1906 and Notification 102 of 1912.*

The Ordinance defined a token as a "coin or article" and paper as well as metallic tokens were issued. No denomination higher than one dollar is known but it is unlikely that all the tokens issued have survived particularly any early examples in paper.

In 1915 it was decided to phase out the use of tokens but nothing seems to have come of this because the same scheme was again put forward in 1920.[22] At least one fifth of each issuer's authorized holding was to be withdrawn each year, the tokens to be destroyed or deposited at the Treasury thus abolishing their legal use by the end of 1924.

North Borneo tokens

Labuk Planting Co Ltd dollar. Many of the early tokens give the value in Chinese as well as English which draws attention to the fact that much of the plantation labour was Chinese.

London Borneo Tobacco Co half dollar.

Rotterdam Borneo Company dollar. (A Dutch company established in British North Borneo).

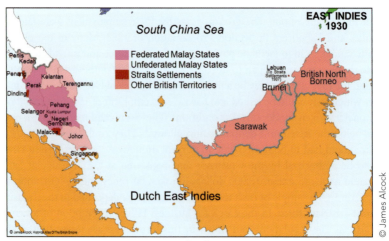

East of India.

---

22 Gazette Notifications 257 of 1915 and 207 of 1920.

We now turn our attention to China where for centuries there had been restrictions on trade with foreigners. The Chinese were wary of allowing free access to the European trading companies fearing, perhaps with good reason, that they would cause mischief and interfere unduly in Chinese affairs. The Portuguese had been allowed a settlement at Macau since the mid 16th century but apart from that European trade was effectively limited to the port of Canton (modern, Guangzhou) and had to be arranged through a select group of merchants, the Co-Hong. All official contact had to be through these Hong merchants who were responsible to the authorities for the behaviour of the foreigners with whom they dealt. There could thus be no direct contact between the traders and the authorities and business had to be conducted under a strict set of rules. Permanent residence at Canton was not allowed, the staff at the British factory removing to Macao at the end of each trading season. In this way the Chinese hoped to keep foreigners at arm's length while squeezing as much profit as they could from their trade.

The East India Company had extended trade to China at an early date hoping to find markets for British goods and by 1715 was established as the main European organization trading at Canton. They had found there was little interest in their rolls of English cloth but China had silks and teas that would be profitable in western markets. This created an adverse balance that had to be paid in silver. As its China trade developed the huge amount of silver required was a constant concern for the Company but a solution of sorts was soon at hand. India was a major source of opium and the Company was careful to maintain a strict monopoly of its production and sale. All this was legal and the sales provided a useful proportion of Indian revenues. Much of it found a ready market in China but when its import there was forbidden the Company stopped carrying it. Instead, at the annual auctions at Calcutta the opium was sold to "country" traders for export in the full knowledge that it was bound for China. The "country" ships landed it clandestinely receiving silver in return, usually arranged through their agents at Canton. The profits from this and other "country" trades were mostly paid into the Company's Canton treasury in return for bills payable in London thus providing a useful source of silver exactly where it was required. The Company, taking no direct part in illicit importation, maintained the high reputation it had at Canton for honesty and integrity while its sales of opium at Calcutta steadily increased and its China trade came onto a sound financial basis.

At the beginning of the period examined in this chapter the East India Company was losing its trade monopolies and being transformed into a solely administrative organization. The last of those monopolies, British trade with China, came to an end in 1834. By that time "country" traders working the ports of the East were already active at Canton but their numbers now increased and they were free to take part in the direct trade to Europe. The basic system of control at Canton did not change but while the Company had accepted the system with little complaint the independent traders found any form of regulation irksome. Most of them had already been involved in clandestine trade and from the 1820s that had been centred on the anchorage at Lintin Island, some 50 miles SSE of Canton. Here opium and other goods were openly transshipped into small Chinese vessels for delivery in various creeks and inlets, circumventing the controls at Canton. As the market for opium in the Canton region became saturated the "country" ships began a coastal trade taking it further afield and soon fast opium clippers, specially designed for the trade, were making two, even three, voyages a year from Bengal. Coastal ports were sometimes supplied under contracts arranged at Canton but some ventures were speculative, designed to test and develop the market. For all this to happen local officials had to be complicit in it and the Chinese were losing control of their foreign trade.

The East India Company had led British trade at Canton and their absence left a huge gap. The British Government tried to fill that gap by appointing a Chief Superintendent of the trade of British subjects in China. The first appointment to the post was Lord Napier who came with proposals to alter the system. The Chinese had no intention of changing anything and were wary of an official rather than a commercial appointment. Foreign embassies had always been treated as inferiors coming to pay homage to the Celestial Empire and it surprised and enraged Napier to be treated in the same way. He had come to enlighten them on the theory and practice of international law and he represented the most powerful nation in the world.

Arriving from Macao without the customary pass Napier was kept at arm's length in the time honoured way and was unable to deliver his proposals direct to the Viceroy. His refusal to leave or to work through the Co-Hong led to threats, a stoppage of British trade and a retaliatory attack on the Bogue forts by British frigates.[23] In the end Napier was forced to leave Canton, returning to Macau under Chinese escort without delivering his letter and without any sort of commercial treaty. He and the Government he represented had been humiliated which in the atmosphere of the day was sufficient cause for war.

A major "country" firm in the 1830s was that of William Jardine and James Matheson who would own some of the best and fastest of the opium clippers. It was this firm that emerged as the leader of the British community at Canton when the East India Company left. Lord Napier died of a fever shortly after his return to Macau but his treatment at Canton prompted Jardine, Matheson and others to petition the king (William IV) for some sort of action to avenge his humiliation. It was clear that free trade would not come about by negotiation. The mere threat of serious military action, it was argued, would open trade with China. The British Government though was not ready to go to war over a trade in which opium played a major part.

The trade at Lintin was already greater than the legitimate trade at Canton and the "Jardine party" continued to believe that the threat of force would open the whole trade with China. They based their opinion on contacts made in their illicit trade but had little conception of the deep seated need of the Chinese for isolation. On his part the Emperor of China had no perception of the tenacity of these traders or of the immense power they could summon in the name of Pax Britannica and free trade. When in 1838 the Emperor appointed a special envoy to bring these foreigners to heel there was thus no hope of any mutual understanding.

The envoy was Lin Tsê-hsü or Commissioner Lin as he came to be known to the Europeans. As Governor General of Hu-Kuang he came with some experience of dealing with illicit drugs in his own jurisdiction and determined on very strict action to end the traffic at Canton. Arriving there in 1839 he demanded the surrender of all opium in the store ships at Lintin and elsewhere. The traders would then be required to enter into a bond never to bring opium again under pain of the extreme penalty under Chinese law. The Co-Hong were reminded of their responsibilities in ensuring the surrender of the opium and informed that some of them would be selected for execution if this did not happen in three days. The next day Commissioner Lin issued an edict forbidding all foreigners to leave for Macao which they were about to do, the season being over. This amounted to a detention at Canton which was something that had never happened before. The traders offered just over a thousand chests but Commissioner Lin was very different from the officials they had been dealing with. He put the factories under close siege ordering all Chinese staff to leave and demanded that one of the leading traders be sent to him. While this was still being debated the two senior Hong merchants appeared in chains pleading that Lin's terms should be met and it seemed that if extreme violence was to be avoided all the opium would have to be surrendered.

---

23 *The Bogue forts guarded the final approaches to the Whampoa anchorage and Canton. No foreign vessels of war were allowed above the forts.*

It was at this juncture that the British Superintendent of Trade (now Captain Charles Elliot) arrived from Macau. His standing instructions were to protect the interests of British merchants engaged in the legitimate trade at Canton. Like the East India Company before him he was to have nothing to do with the opium trade but it was this that was now causing all the fuss at Canton. Believing that British lives and property were at stake he felt official intervention was necessary and in this way embroiled the British Government in the affairs of the opium traders.

Elliot decided that all British subjects should surrender their stocks of opium to the Crown to be delivered to Commissioner Lin. As the Crown's representative he would guarantee that they would be indemnified later on. Under the circumstances the traders were happy to receive this guarantee of payment and collected together some 20,000 chests worth more than £2 million. This was delivered to Commissioner Lin at Chuenpee (the site of one of the Bogue forts) and destroyed in pits of water, lime and salt over several days. When all the chests had been delivered the siege of the factories was lifted and the foreigners allowed to leave. The British merchants were instructed to sign the bond agreeing never to deal in opium again which, because of its provisions, they did with some reluctance.

Commissioner Lin had swiftly achieved all that he set out to do. He named several of the major British opium traders who would no longer be allowed to trade at Canton and assumed that the legitimate trade would resume with the new season. In this though, he was mistaken. The destruction of so much opium had increased prices and the coastal trade hardly faltered. The traders were not likely to place themselves again under Chinese control at Canton and Whampoa and for the moment would have to trade from Macau, Lintin or some other convenient anchorage. As the ships began to arrive for the new season's tea Elliot directed them to anchor between the mainland and an unimportant island to the south. The island was sparsely populated and generally known as Hong Kong. Until he knew the response of the British Government to what had happened this is where the tea would be loaded and the Americans would act as commission agents at Canton. This was not at all the outcome that Commissioner Lin had expected and he took what steps he could to force trade back to Canton. An unfortunate incident in which a Chinese was killed in a fight with British sailors worsened the situation. In spite of the Portuguese presence at Macao, where British wives and families resided, there was concern that the Chinese may act there as they had at Canton. For safety Elliot ordered the evacuation of all British subjects to the merchant ships anchored off Hong Kong Island. Short of food and water and vulnerable to attack by Chinese fire ships, the British communities that had grown up around the legitimate trade through Canton and the illicit trade at Lintin awaited some reaction from their home Government and wondered what might become of them.

In London, the imprisonment of the foreigners at Canton, the huge indemnity promised for the opium and the evacuation from Macao was too much to ignore and some action would have to be taken. In an age of enlightenment a war which appeared to support an illicit trade would be difficult to justify but no one could be allowed to treat British subjects in such a manner. The whole business of opium therefore had to be played down and the argument made that the opening of trade would benefit China as well as Britain.

The necessary expedition was assembled in India and by the end of June 1840 a large fleet of warships and transports had arrived at the Hong Kong anchorage. A full scale invasion of China was clearly out of the question. The plan was to blockade the major ports, take an island or two and appear in force at the mouth of the Pei-ho River. Here, close to his capital, they could make demands directly of the Emperor. These demands would be for an open trade, for a fixed emporium for British traders and for compensation for destroyed property (the opium), the cost of the expedition and unpaid debts. The blockade would continue until the demands were met. The Chinese lacked any means to resist such a force and after negotiation, a little fighting and a failed treaty (Convention of Chuenpee, January 1841) had to concede to all the demands. The Treaty of Nanking (August 1842) ceded Hong Kong to the British Crown as the fixed emporium. Five ports were opened to foreign trade where there would be no Hong merchants, where permanent residence would be allowed and where British consuls could be appointed to deal directly with Chinese officials. Compensation totaling 21 million dollars was payable over several years.[24]

Hong Kong began to be settled by British traders in 1841 after the Convention of Chuenpee ceded it to Britain. When that was repudiated by the British and Chinese Governments the cession of Hong Kong was in abeyance until the Treaty of Nanking confirmed it in August 1842. Ratifications were finally exchanged in Hong Kong on 6th June 1843 and Britain had a colony that, as a free port, could hardly fail to prosper.

The first Anglo-Chinese War of 1839-1842 inevitably became known as the first Opium War but this was not the end of the story. The Chinese were still reluctant participants in open trade and illicit opium imports continued to increase. A second Opium War of 1856-1860 led to the opening of more "treaty ports" to foreign trade and to the legalized import of opium.[25] The terms agreed to end the war were ratified at the Convention of Peking (Beijing) in 1860 which also added Kowloon, on the Chinese mainland, to the colony of Hong Kong. The New Territories (mainland and islands beyond the colony) were leased from China in 1898 for a period of 99 years. Apart from the Japanese occupation during the Second World War the whole of this territory continued to be a Crown colony until 1983 when its status was changed to a British Dependent Territory. It was eventually agreed that when the lease for the New Territories expired the whole of the territory should revert to China and the handover took place on 1st July 1997.

Hong Kong was naturally within the currency area of China where silver was the standard. For centuries the only actual coin in day to day use there had been the base metal cash. Silver, which was relatively scarce, did not circulate by tale but was melted into ingots called sycee which could be used for larger payments and were guaranteed by their individual issuers. Although the standard measure for silver at the Canton customs was a tael of about 580 grains of fine silver, a sycee could be of any weight. Theoretically 1,000 cash were equivalent to a tael of fine (sycee) silver but in practice the rate varied and was often much more. When foreign silver began to enter China through trade, mainly in the form of Spanish American dollars, it was at first made into sycee but gradually the coins themselves began to be accepted as being of uniform weight and fineness. By the time Hong Kong was founded the Chinese had accepted the dollar of 416 grains as a standard and 1,000 of these passed for 717 taels at Hong Kong.

---

24 The original Treaty ports were Canton, Amoy, Foochow, Ningpo and Shanghai. The form and spelling of Chinese names used in this book are the romanized versions most often found in contemporary western records. For place names modern equivalents based on the Pin-yin System of romanization are noted in the gazetteer or in the text.

25 Although the Company lost its last trading monopoly in 1834 it still retained the monopoly of opium production in India and this passed to the Crown in 1858. The argument in favour of legalizing opium imports to China was that it would allow some control over the trade and provide the Government of China with income. The sales of opium continued to be an important source of British Indian revenue until at least the 1880s by which time China was producing opium herself. By 1906 China was producing most of the world's opium and in 1907 it was agreed that British Indian imports of the drug would cease over a ten year period.

In March 1842 the Chief Superintendent of trade proclaimed certain coins to be deemed legal tender within Hong Kong and it was natural that the Mexican dollar should be the focus of his attention. The dollar was to be the equivalent of 2¼ East India Company rupees and also equivalent to 1,200 Chinese cash. A further Proclamation (on 27th April) made the dollar the standard for both government and mercantile transactions but both these proclamations predate the Treaty of Nanking. After the treaty and its ratification Hong Kong became subject to the British legislation of the day and it will be remembered that an Order in Council of 23rd March 1825 with subsequent amendments had introduced sterling to all the colonies with no limit of legal tender specified for the token silver. It was therefore necessary to revoke the local proclamations concerning the dollar and establish British token silver at 20/- per gold sovereign as the official currency of Hong Kong. This was done by Royal Proclamation following an Order in Council of 28th November 1844. The dollar was rated at 4/2d, the rupee at 1/10d and there were 288 cash to the shilling. Government accounts now had to be kept in sterling but the currency of trade was the full weight silver dollar and nothing would persuade the Chinese to accept token silver as an unlimited tender in its place. In 1852, following the gold discoveries in Australia, it was assumed that the East would adopt a gold standard and sterling silver was limited in legal tender to 40/-.[26] This brought the currency of Hong Kong fully into line with that of the United Kingdom with the sovereign as the only unlimited legal tender. Nevertheless, China (and therefore Hong Kong) remained firmly attached to silver and the Mexican dollar became the standard coin of the colony. Although Government accounts were kept in sterling all other business was in dollars and, under pressure from the colony's Governor, an Order in Council of 9th January 1863 and Royal Proclamation accepted the inevitable. The Mexican dollar and others of equivalent value were made the sole unlimited legal tender and currency of account. Hong Kong was now officially outside the currency area of the United Kingdom and arrangements were made to strike a coinage subsidiary to the dollar at the Royal Mint for local circulation. The bronze denominations were the cent (one hundredth of a dollar) and mil (one thousandth) and many of these were struck in Birmingham.[27] Multiples of the cent were to be struck in silver with a millesimal fineness of 800 although only the ten cents denomination was struck at this time. The subsidiary silver was limited in legal tender to two dollars, the bronze to one dollar. The mil or "cash" (one thousandth of a dollar) was inevitably seen as a rival to the Chinese cash (one thousandth of a tael) and proved difficult to put into general circulation perhaps because of its very small size. Like the Chinese cash it had a central hole.

At the beginning of 1864 the arrival of the new subsidiary coins from England in the British ship "Louisa" was announced.[28] With recognition that Hong Kong was outside the sterling area came pressure to introduce a British dollar equivalent to that of Mexico so that control could be exercised over its quality and supply. This led to the opening of the Hong Kong Mint to great acclaim at 11 am on 7th May 1866 and the introduction of the Hong Kong dollar. This was at the same standard as the Mexican dollar and was struck at a millesimal

---

26 An Order in Council and Proclamation of 16th October 1852 brought Australia, New Zealand, Ceylon, Mauritius and Hong Kong into line with the United Kingdom with a 40/- legal tender limit on silver coins. It came into force in Hong Kong by a Government Notification of 1853. Australian gold coins became legal tender in Hong Kong in 1856.
27 A Government Notification of 26th October 1866 states that silver ten cent pieces, **bronze** cents and **copper** cash had been received from the Royal Mint (Hong Kong Government Gazette, 27th October 1866). A later notification (of 1868) refers to the mils as "bronze" but the Hong Kong (Coinage) Order of 1895 still refers to the cents **and** mils as of "copper or mixed metal". Although they all appear to be of bronze it seems there was a facility for either metal to be used for the Hong Kong cent and mil. The same is true of official references to the Straits copper coinage (e.g. the Order in Council of 21st October 1890 which notes "copper or mixed metal" for the cent and its fractions).
28 At a meeting of the Legislative Council on 4th January 1864 (Hong Kong Government Gazette 16th January 1864).

fineness of 900. A half dollar was also struck at the same fineness and exactly half the weight. A Proclamation by the Governor of 15th September 1866 declared the Hong Kong dollar to be equivalent to that of Mexico and therefore legal tender (with the half dollar) to any amount. The opening of the Hong Kong Mint allowed the subsidiary coins also to be struck locally instead of in England. In the short period that the mint was open (1866-1868) only silver coins were struck, previous supplies of the cent and mil being adequate. The subsidiary denominations struck were the twenty cents, ten cents and five cents.

To be successful the Hong Kong dollar would have to find general acceptance in the trade of China. To assist in this an assay of the new coins was arranged at Canton and took place on 24th October 1866. One hundred dollars were submitted for assay by the Chinese process and a simultaneous assay was carried out by the Superintendent of the Assay Department of the Hong Kong Mint who had brought the coins and his own equipment to the event. The dollar was found to contain exactly 90% of pure silver (the same as the Mexican dollar) and it was therefore proclaimed that 111 taels, 1 mace and one candareen of the new Hong Kong coinage was equivalent to 100 taels of Hai-Kwan sycee silver. The Hong Kong dollar would be a valid tender in payment of Chinese government dues at Canton and the Viceroy forwarded his findings to Peking. In April 1867 the Board of Foreign Affairs at Peking agreed that the Hong Kong dollar could pass on equal terms with that of Mexico but warned Canton that this would only be the case as long as the standard was maintained and if the trading classes were not averse to using it.[29] In general trade it had taken the Chinese many years to accept the Mexican dollar in place of sycee and naturally they did prove reluctant to accept this new version. The Hong Kong dollar therefore initially passed at a small discount and did not achieve the wide circulation that had been hoped. The Hong Kong Mint was therefore underutilised and attempts were made to attract other business. The Opium Wars had opened ports in the north to European trade and here it was still preferred to accept silver by weight rather than by tale. The British Minister at Peking felt that although China would accept customs payments in Hong Kong dollars the Chinese were not ready for full scale use of the coin. Because of this patterns were produced at the Hong Kong Mint in 1867 for a tael, much heavier than the dollar, which it was thought might be more acceptable in Shanghai and the north. Several examples of these were sent to Peking to be shown to the authorities there but the British Minister repeated his opinion that the Chinese were not ready for any sort of silver coin of their own.[30] Failure to interest the Chinese in large scale use of the Hong Kong dollar or the tael resulted in a somewhat hasty decision to close the Hong Kong Mint in 1868. The mint machinery was subsequently sold to Japan where the new Meiji Government was attempting to modernize the coinage and where it was installed at the Osaka Mint.

The closure of the Hong Kong Mint ended the issue of the Hong Kong dollar and half dollar although both remained legal tender to any amount. Production of the subsidiary coins once again became the responsibility of the Royal Mint subcontracted when necessary to the Birmingham mints. Striking of silver coins resumed in all three denominations (twenty, ten and five cents) in 1872 still at the millesimal fineness of 800. The cent resumed issue in 1875 but no further issues of the mil denomination were struck, there being large quantities still remaining in store at Hong Kong.

By 1882 the amount of subsidiary silver being ordered by Hong Kong was steadily increasing but this was not only because of increased demand within the colony. By this time

---

29 *Notifications 171 and 182 of 1866 and Notification 77 of 1867 (all published in the Hong Kong Government Gazette) refer to the Canton assay and subsequent remarks.*
30 *R.N.J. Wright, "The Hong Kong Mint Taels – A Reappraisal" in SNC November 1980, p.396.*

the Hong Kong dollar, whose production had been halted, was fully accepted by the Chinese as equal to that of Mexico and this increased the popularity of the subsidiary silver coins. In China, where coin use was increasing, there was no national unit of currency between paper money and the base metal cash so the smaller Hong Kong silver coins, of consistent and reliable quality, filled a gap even though they were of only token value. They began to disappear into southern China in increasing numbers. There was of course profit in issuing subsidiary coins into circulation at full face value so although their subsequent export often led to shortages in the colony it was not seen by the colonial authorities as altogether a bad thing. From London came warnings that eventual redemption of large numbers of worn coins could cause problems but Hong Kong pointed out that they had a duty to meet the needs of the colony. They had no control over what happened to their coins after they were issued and were not actively encouraging their export to China. As the subsidiary silver was only legal tender up to two dollars they felt there was little danger of large scale redemption. The Royal Mint therefore handled ever increasing orders and in 1890 the range of subsidiary coins was increased by the addition of a fifty cents denomination. This was at the same millesimal fineness (800) as the smaller coins and like them its legal tender limit was just two dollars. At this stage the Hong Kong half dollar at the higher millesimal fineness of 900 was still a legal tender for any amount.

As was the case in the Straits Settlements the absence of a "British" dollar was now sorely felt in Hong Kong. The solution was the introduction of the British (trade) dollar as noted above in the section on the Straits. It was at exactly the same weight and fineness as the old Hong Kong dollar. The United Kingdom Order in Council of 2nd February 1895 (the British Dollar Order, 1895) was followed on the same day by the Hong Kong (Coinage) Order, 1895. This revoked all previous laws concerning the coinage and confirmed the Mexican dollar as the standard coin of Hong Kong. The Hong Kong dollar and the new British dollar were equivalent to it and all three coins had unlimited legal tender. The Hong Kong half dollar is not listed and therefore ceased to be a legal tender. The subsidiary silver coins continued as before to be legal tender up to two dollars and the "coins of copper or mixed metal" up to one dollar.

In 1890 the Canton mint had begun to strike a European style dollar and subsidiary silver coins in the same denominations as those of Hong Kong. Soon, other Chinese mints had followed suit and from 1905 attempts were made to bring all of them on to the same weight and standard. The issue of these coins reduced the requirement in China for the subsidiary coins of Hong Kong which were soon finding their way back to the colony in large numbers. In fact after 1905 no subsidiary silver coins needed to be struck for Hong Kong until 1932 and between 1906 and 1918 the Hong Kong Government operated a policy of withdrawing those it received as revenue. The one cent denomination continued to be struck intermittently when required but was reduced in size and weight in 1931.[31] When a new issue of subsidiary silver was finally required (the five cents of 1932 and 1933) it was at the same weight and fineness as earlier issues but these would prove to be the last of Hong Kong's subsidiary coins to be struck in silver.

The British dollar continued to be struck for use in Hong Kong when required. It came mainly from Bombay but some were also struck at Calcutta and at the Royal Mint in London. Many of these were held as the necessary surety for the private banks who issued notes. The public had developed a preference for bank notes rather than the heavy dollars, a preference that the banks encouraged as paper was easier to handle, store and transport than were silver coins. Because of the preference for them the bank notes passed at a small premium but in the

---

31 A Proclamation of 13th November 1931 gave the reduced weight cent legal status from 1st December.

late 1920s the price of silver fell. The note issuing banks became reluctant to import silver dollars and the supply of notes (dependent on the amount of silver reserves) became limited. The premium for notes over silver dollars therefore increased and in September 1929 peaked at an alarming 20%. The rate for bank notes against other currencies did not keep pace with the fall in the price of silver and the bank notes of Hong Kong, which were not legal tender, were parting company with the bullion that guaranteed them. The fluctuating premium was a major concern as was the great fall in the price of silver. In 1920 the dollar had stood at well over 4/- sterling but by 1930 had fallen to 1/4d. For much of 1931 it would be less than a shilling. The question therefore arose; should Hong Kong remain on the silver standard? The various options were examined and the obvious conclusion reached. Economically Hong Kong was attached to China and her silver standard could not be abandoned unless China did so first. By 1931 it was known that China was considering change but in Hong Kong nothing could be done other than to plan for the event.

China did not act until the price of silver had at last begun to rise. On 4th November 1935 she called in all privately owned silver to be exchanged for bank notes of unlimited legal tender. China had abandoned the silver standard and adopted a managed currency. Hong Kong acted almost at once with the Dollar Currency Notes Ordinance on 9th November the purpose of which was to introduce a Government one dollar note with unlimited legal tender to replace the silver dollars. This was followed by the Currency Ordinance passed at one sitting of the Legislative Council on 5th December 1935 and given assent the next day. This provided for the establishment of an Exchange Fund to take over the silver then held against bank note issues. In return the banks received Certificates of Indebtedness of the Hong Kong Government. The fund would also take over private holdings of silver dollars, subsidiary coins and bullion in return for Hong Kong currency. The Fund could hold gold, silver, foreign exchange or securities and would be used by the colonial Treasurer to regulate the exchange value of the currency of Hong Kong. Bank notes, like the Government notes of the November Ordinance, were given unlimited legal tender and Hong Kong, like China, had a managed currency.

With the changes of 1935 the British dollar ceased to be struck in that year but continued to be legal tender for any amount until 1st August 1937. Until that time it could be exchanged for dollar notes at par but was subsequently of bullion value only. As noted above, the last subsidiary coins in silver for Hong Kong were struck in 1933. The next issue was of ten cents and five cents in cupro-nickel declared current by a Proclamation immediately after the passing of the Dollar Currency Notes Ordinance on 9th November 1935. Counterfeit cupro-nickel coins soon made their appearance and in 1937, in line with advice from the Royal Mint, they were replaced by coins in pure nickel on larger flans that could carry a security edge. The ten cents continued to be struck until 1939, the five cents and the bronze one cent until 1941.

Hong Kong surrendered to Japanese forces on Christmas Day 1941. During the occupation, which lasted until August 1945, the Japanese issued paper money only and systematically removed the metallic currency to assist in their war effort. After the resumption of colonial rule, paper money continued to be issued until a new coinage could be produced. The first post war coins were the nickel-brass ten cents introduced in 1948 and five cents which began issue a year later. These were supplemented with a cupro-nickel fifty cents coin in 1951. The one cent denomination was not reintroduced after the Second World War.

Hong Kong was Britain's last major colony, her colonial coinage continuing into the 1990s. The final phase of that coinage, from the accession of Elizabeth II in 1952 to the hand over to China in 1997, is best left until our final chapter.

HONG KONG

Royal Mint issues on dollar standard

Cent 1863.

Mil 1865.

Ten cents 1863.

Hong Kong mint

Dollar 1868.

Half dollar 1866.

Later coins

Twenty cents 1888.

Five cents 1901.

Fifty cents 1894.

Cent 1901, (Heaton mint).

Fifty cents 1905.

Five cents 1932.

Ten cents 1937.

Fifty cents 1951.

We should not leave British interests in the East without a brief look at the development of the treaty ports opened up to western trade by the Anglo-Chinese Wars. We have seen (Chapter six) how Britain sought to increase her trade and influence through informal empire of this type and China was assumed to have enormous potential. Nevertheless, the free trade principal ensured that Britain did not have exclusive rights in the treaty ports system and soon the United States, France, Germany, Japan and other nations also had treaties with China.

Restricted areas within the treaty ports, termed "concessions", were leased by the Chinese Government to the various foreign powers who could then sub-let plots within them to businesses and individuals. The highest authority in such a concession was the Consul who had a high degree of autonomy over his own nationals. Britain did not appoint consuls to all of the treaty ports but in 1861 appointed a Minister to Peking for direct contact with the Chinese Government. It was to this Minister at his Legation in Peking that the various British consuls reported when necessary and from whom they could expect guidance. The Chinese did not like the system of free trade and diplomatic relations that had been forced upon them by what came to be termed "unequal treaties" but the consular network built up in China soon gave the British an air of permanence and legitimacy. This and the backing they could call on from the Royal Navy ensured that they became the predominant foreign community in many of the treaty ports, particularly in Shanghai. Britain's formal imperial presence on the coast of China was limited to Hong Kong and a small naval base at Weihaiwei[32] in the north but until the Second World War Shanghai was commercially more important to Britain than was Hong Kong itself. In general there was some disappointment at the volume of trade opened to Britain through the treaty ports but this was soon supplemented by investment and other interests.

---

32 Weihaiwei was leased from China in July 1898 primarily to check Russian moves in the region. It was initially administered as a naval base but passed to the Colonial Office in 1901. It was returned to China in October 1930.

Typical of the ships that carried settlers to Australasia in the later 19th century the "Dunedin", after conversion, carried the first successful cargo of frozen meat from New Zealand to London in 1882. (Image in public domain.)

13

Australasia and the Pacific

WE have seen in earlier chapters that penal colonies and convict labour made initial development possible and free settlement viable in New South Wales. The presence of officials and military units together with free settlement and convicts who had served their time led in due course to a situation where those who were free outnumbered those who were not. The discovery of the rich lands beyond the Blue Mountains increased Sydney's importance and by 1815 it was clear that New South Wales was not just a penal settlement but a developing colony. All of this led to a move away from direct military government with the New South Wales Act of 1823 which we have already noted in Chapter six. Before resuming our main story it may be useful to take a brief look at those who went there and there is no better place to begin than with the convicts for whom the colony was founded.

Some of the convicts arriving in their new surroundings may have been happy to sever old connections but most of them had left loved ones at home for whom they were concerned. Wives, children and elderly relatives often suffered great hardship when families were torn apart in this way and there were many petitions to the Home Office, some of them quite heartrending, seeking pardons for convicts or pleading to go with them to New South Wales. Petitions came also from parishes offering to send wives or families who had been thrown onto their assistance to ports of embarkation. Nearly all these petitions were ignored. It would have been impossible to accommodate and maintain the numbers involved and, whoever it hurt, transportation was not intended to be pleasant.

On arrival in New South Wales convicts were assigned to the Governor and were "on the store" which meant they were victualled by the Government. The usual sentence was seven years but fourteen years was given for more serious offences and some were transported for life. In the later years of transportation some came with ten year sentences rather than fourteen. Whatever the sentence it was never intended that convicts should return to the United Kingdom at the end of it but that they would settle permanently in New South Wales. To encourage them to stay Governors were empowered to grant land to deserving and industrious convicts when they were discharged from servitude and this became quite normal practice.

In the early years Government officials were assigned convicts "on the store" as part of their salary and could either employ them directly or allow them to work elsewhere in return for a fee. This practice did not cease until the 1820s but increasingly convicts were able to be assigned to free settlers and to ex-convicts. To reduce costs it was in the Government's interest to get as many convicts as possible onto private assignment and eventually "off the store". Free settlement and assignment was therefore encouraged and this allowed some convicts at least to learn useful skills before their own time expired and they became free. Those not assigned to settlers were used by the Government to improve Crown land, build roads and construct the buildings required for new settlements. This work was generally considered much harder than assignment and on occasion was used specifically to make transportation a more effective deterrent. Government employment was also the lot of re-offenders, often in newly established or isolated settlements like Norfolk Island. The general aim though was to keep the number of unassigned convicts to a minimum and many were assigned as soon as they arrived.

Convicts of good character could be granted a "ticket of leave". This did not make them free but allowed them to work on their own account and kept them "off the store". Pardons (which did restore freedom) could be granted to convicts for a variety of reasons, often for bravery or for services rendered to the government. An absolute pardon granted complete freedom but a conditional pardon required the ex-convict to remain in the colony until the full term of his or her original sentence had been completed. Expirees and those who had received an absolute pardon were free to return to the United Kingdom as best they could but only in very unusual cases were passages arranged by government. In fact the grants of land which ex-convicts were offered, the availability of work if they did not take a grant and the rates of pay offered in New South Wales gave them little incentive to return home. Family members were sometimes brought out for ticket of leave convicts and ex-convicts who could show that they were able to support them. This was an inducement to good behaviour and a further incentive for expirees to remain in the colony. Over the whole period of transportation it is unlikely that many more than 5% of the convicts ever returned home, numbers being higher in the early years.

Governor Macquarie (in office 1810 to 1821) was progressive. He saw New South Wales as a developing colony rather than just a penal settlement and felt that convicts who had completed their sentence should have the same standing as free settlers. The free settlers did not agree, feeling that ex-convicts should be excluded from social life and from any sort of office. At home, crime was rising after the Napoleonic War and there was some doubt as to whether transportation, assignment and grants of land were really an effective deterrent. Lord Bathurst (Secretary of State for War and Colonies) felt he should be better informed and in 1819 sent John Thomas Bigge as his Commissioner to New South Wales to look into matters.

When they were completed Bigge's reports made several important recommendations most of which were acted on sooner or later. Taken together, these were fundamental in shaping the future of the colony. The New South Wales Act of 1823 heralded the end of autocratic rule and allowed for a separate administration for Van Diemen's Land (modern "Tasmania"). A period of greatly increased discipline for convicts was ushered in including the use of chained road gangs. More convicts were dispersed on assignment but for those who misbehaved or re offended there were new strictly penal settlements. Bigge had noticed that the lands granted to ex-convicts were often too small to be viable and were frequently sold to capitalists so grants to ex-convicts and to settlers without funds were restricted. Pastoralists with capital were encouraged with grants commensurate with their investments and with options to buy more land besides. The wool industry, already successful, was encouraged in every way.

Until this time land grants had been free in return for a quit rent which was remitted under certain conditions and rarely collected. As more settlers began to arrive changes were possible and from January 1831 free grants ceased. Crown land was now to be sold by auction with a minimum price of 5/- per acre.

There was ample evidence that assignment of convicts was both economical and reformatory but the British Government chose to ignore this in the interests of even greater severity and deterrence. In 1841 assignment was abolished. The settlers were annoyed at losing a useful source of labour and government expenditure was increased but by this time transportation itself was coming to an end.

The settlers who came voluntarily to New South Wales were seeking financial reward and often a social standing that for one reason or another they were denied at home. The government naturally favoured those with capital who would provide employment for the convicts and develop the land. At first the number of free settlers was small and they were often quite unsuited to the task of building a colony. As the colony developed though, there was a growing need for immigrants of more humble origin to satisfy the growing demand for labour. While emigration to North America was relatively cheap it was difficult to attract immigrants to New South Wales and this led to several schemes to encourage them. Large land companies were formed in the 1820s to attract tenant farmers and the profits from the land sales which began in 1831 were specifically allocated to assist immigration. Soon the number of free immigrants arriving was greater than the number of convicts.

While the initial story of New South Wales is about convicts and settlers we should not forget the growing numbers who were being born there. Using the analogy of the coins and notes in use, settlers from the United Kingdom were sometimes referred to as "sterling" while those who were born in the colony were "currency" lads and lasses. Soon they were full grown and initially there was some surprise that the sons and daughters of convicts should turn out so well. The native born though were soon demanding a fair share of the only land they knew. For the coins, as we shall see below, sterling and currency soon became pretty much the same thing. In the minds of men though, the distinction would remain for many years.

As settlement spread inland the authorities were anxious to retain control and in 1829 a limit was set beyond which settlement should not take place. The limit of settlement was approximately 150 miles from Sydney and consisted of nineteen counties which would become known as the "Old Settled Districts". Outside this region settlement was unlawful. Nevertheless there was good grazing land beyond the limit and there was money to be made from wool. Sheep runs were soon established well beyond the nineteen counties but those who settled there had no title to their land. The only title they did have was a label that would soon resound all the way to the British Parliament. They were "squatters", originally a disparaging term but soon an influential group of settlers who had no problem with the label.

Initially squatting was a hard life. Without title to their claims there was little incentive to improve land or homesteads. Drought, floods and disease struck indiscriminately and there was no protection if trouble flared between squatters or with the Aborigines. The squatters naturally sought security of tenure but only when an annual license fee was introduced in 1836 was there any sort of legal recognition. The license gave them protection against all comers but only year by year. The Crown still had title to the land and could sell it if it so wished. The "upset" price of land (the minimum payable at auction) was increased to 12/- an acre in 1839 and to £1 an acre in 1842 so when a purchase scheme was offered to the squatters in 1844 it was angrily rejected. By this time they could rightly claim to be the life blood of the colony and any scheme to buy the enormous acreage required for grazing was seen as an unfair burden. They were also the major overseas supplier of wool to the London market. With the British press on their side, they lobbied Parliament[1] who in due course passed the

---

1 See Hansard 13th March 1844 vol 73 cc 982-989 for a speech by Mr Francis Scott MP for Roxburghshire putting the squatters' point of view.

Waste Lands Occupation Act 1846. A subsequent Order in Council replaced annual licenses with long term leases and the squatters now had a preemptive right to buy. If the Crown ultimately wished to sell the squatters would have first refusal on their runs.

It was not until the 1860s that there was any further threat to the squatters. The government wanted to encourage arable farming and those wishing to take up the challenge were allowed to select plots freely for purchase. The squatters though were able to compete with the "free selectors" by purchasing only part of their runs. When a squatter had purchased the land on which his homestead stood together with the waterholes and riverbeds the rest was of little value to anyone else. The squatters remained an important, influential and wealthy section of the community for many years.

So far we have looked only at New South Wales which to start with was the entire eastern part of the continent known as New Holland. This continent began to be referred to as "Australia" about 1814 but it would be some years before the new term was generally adopted. Other colonies eventually emerged but British authority over the whole continent was not claimed until 1829.

The western border of New South Wales was originally set at 135° E but in 1825 was pushed further west to 129° E to include Melville Island on the north coast.[2] Here Fort Dundas had been established which it was hoped would secure the route between Sydney and Asia and perhaps develop as Singapore had done. Nothing came of this plan or of subsequent attempts on the Cobourg Peninsula but it was important that this region should be within the area of British administration. New South Wales also included unspecified "adjacent islands on the east". This included Norfolk Island from the beginning and would for a while include the islands that became New Zealand.

The initial spread of settlements beyond Sydney was basically the establishment of new penal settlements like those in Van Diemen's Land from 1803 and Newcastle in 1804. An attempt was also made to establish a penal settlement at Port Phillip in 1803 but this was abandoned and the convicts taken to Van Diemen's Land the next year. As free settlers arrived and settlements flourished it became difficult to maintain the strict discipline demanded by the home government and new penal settlements were established at Port Macquarie in 1821 and Moreton Bay in 1825.

It was perhaps natural that Van Diemen's Land, as an island, should eventually have a very large convict population. Lieutenant Governors were appointed from an early date but they were hampered in their administration by having no Supreme Court. Serious cases had to go to Sydney. The New South Wales Act of 1823 made good the deficiency and also made provision for the separation of Van Diemen's Land from New South Wales by Order in Council. The relevant Order came in 1825 and Van Diemen's Land became the first region to be detached from New South Wales as a separate colony.

The next colony to emerge from New South Wales was South Australia where an Act of 1834[3] provided for the setting up of a province or provinces under a scheme of emigration based on the ideas of Edward Gibbon Wakefield. The problems of land settlement and labour shortages that were troubling New South Wales could be avoided if land was priced high enough to discourage speculation but not so high that it would prohibit working class immigrants aspiring to land ownership altogether. The Act required that £35,000 would have to be raised from land purchase before settlement was allowed to go ahead. No convicts would

---
2 *Ralph Darling's Commission as Governor of New South Wales, 1825 instructed him to do this.*
3 *An Act to empower His Majesty to erect South Australia into a British Province or Provinces and to provide for the Colonisation and Government thereof (4 & 5 Will. IV. c. 95). (The South Australia Act 1834)*

be sent and the proceeds from land sales would assist suitable emigration from the United Kingdom. The price eventually fixed for land was a minimum of 12/- an acre compared with only 5/- in New South Wales at that time. The attraction to settlers was systematic colonization free of any convict stigma and the promise of their own constitution when a provincial population reached 50,000. By the end of 1835 sufficient land sales were guaranteed and an Order in Council of February 1836 allowed for the establishment of government in the Province of South Australia. The first settlers arrived later that year and the Colony was proclaimed by its first Governor on 28th December 1836. South Australia was carved out of the western part of New South Wales where thus far there had been no settlement. Its borders were the Southern Ocean, the longitudes of 132° E and 141° E and latitude 26° S. After an uncertain start the colony became viable in the 1840s, the initial area of settlement being the fertile region around Adelaide. The area north of 26° S remained part of New South Wales for the time being but plans to construct a trans Australia telegraph connecting ultimately with London led to changes. The route chosen ran from the north coast to Port Augusta in South Australia and, to facilitate construction, the whole area north of 26° S was annexed to South Australia in 1863. Palmerston (modern Darwin) was established on the north coast in 1869 and the cable was constructed 1870-1872.

The Port Phillip District of New South Wales became the separate colony of Victoria on 1st July 1851. This was allowed for in the Australian Constitutions Act 1850[4] to allow the settlers there a greater say in their own government. The northern part of New South Wales was divided off as Queensland in 1859 for much the same reason. This was accomplished by Letters Patent and Order in Council of 6th June 1859 which were published in Brisbane on 10th December.

While the division of New South Wales was just beginning a private initiative was planned to colonize the west coast of New Holland. Its leader, Captain James Stirling, pointed out that there was no British claim to the region and that the French might get there first. He suggested that a formal claim be made before his colony was established and HMS "Challenger" was dispatched from the Cape of Good Hope for that purpose. Her commander, Captain Fremantle, had instructions to take possession of "the western side of New Holland in His Majesty's name" at a place "as near as possible to the Swan River".[5] On 2nd May 1829 Fremantle stepped ashore at the mouth of the Swan River and formally took possession of all that part of New Holland which was not included in the territory of New South Wales. Britain now had claim to the whole of Australia.

It was fear of foreign intrusion which had led, at least in part, to the first settlement in Van Diemen's Land and to attempts to settle the north coast. In 1826 a small military detachment with a few convicts had been sent to King George Sound (modern Albany) for the same reason but had not prospered. The formal claim to the whole of the west was part of the same plan but it would still be some years before all fear of foreign intrusion in Australia had been laid to rest.

HMS "Challenger" remained until the first settlers were safely landed. James Stirling arrived with the first group at the end of May and on 18th June 1829 formally proclaimed the Swan River Settlement. In 1832 it received its official name of "Western Australia" although the old name continued in popular use for some years. Difficulty in attracting both capital and labour meant that development was slow and some settlers moved on to the eastern

---

4 An Act for the better Government of Her Majesty's Australian Colonies (13 &14 Vict. c. 59). (sometimes also referred to as the Australian Colonies Government Act 1850).
5 Instructions to the Admiralty to take formal possession of the western portion of the continent, 5th November 1828.

colonies. Eventually it was decided that if progress was to be made at all convicts would have to be used to meet the demand for labour. The first convicts arrived in Western Australia in 1850 just as transportation elsewhere was coming to an end but with labour now available for public works and infrastructure the colony at last began to prosper.

The colonial borders were adjusted from time to time but the separate colonies described above are those that would eventually join to form the Commonwealth of Australia on 1st January 1901. For clarity we can list them with their administrative capitals as:

New South Wales (Sydney)
Tasmania (Hobart)
South Australia (Adelaide)
Victoria (Melbourne)
Queensland (Brisbane)
Western Australia (Perth)

The configuration of South Australia, stretching from the south coast to the Timor Sea led to suggestions that it should more sensibly be named "Central Australia" but the northern part (north of 26° S) was separated from it in 1911 to form the Northern Territories.

Although the various colonies that emerged were separate from each other there were shared problems and common aspirations. The convict colonies, with the exception of Western Australia, were demanding an end to transportation and all of them wanted a greater share of government through representation. Both of these demands were initially resisted by the Home Government. Australia was where Britain sent her offenders and the idea of ex convicts, even their descendants, governing themselves appeared to some to be a recipe for anarchy. Nevertheless there were now large numbers of native born colonists who felt they had every right to representation in their government. These and the free settlers feared the moral effect of a continuing criminal influx and knew that while it continued and there were large numbers of expirees among them there would be little chance of attaining representative government.

Objections from the colonies to transportation therefore increased while in the United Kingdom there was a growing acceptance that convicts should be kept at home. Transportation to New South Wales was abolished in 1840 although "exiles" continued to be accepted at several of the settlements until 1850. "Exiles" had served part of their sentence and been pardoned on condition of transportation. The number of convicts sent to Van Diemen's Land naturally increased after 1840 but here too transportation was coming to an end and finally ceased in 1853. It was during this period of abolition that male convicts began to be sent to Western Australia. They continued to be shipped there until the final abolition of transportation in 1868.

Provision now had to be made for long term imprisonment in the United Kingdom and Pentonville (opened 1842) served as a model for many new prisons including Reading and a remodelled Dartmoor. Although these were state of the art prisons in their day they lacked the sunshine of Australia, hard labour and the cells were considered conducive to reform and there was little chance of a new life when sentences were completed. A colourful and somewhat effective experiment in penology had come to an end. The Australian colonies could breathe a sigh of relief and start a new chapter in their development.

With transportation ended the colonies could look forward not only to representative government but ultimately to responsible government (i.e. government responsible to an elected Assembly rather than to the Colonial Office). In 1842, just two years after the ending of transportation, the Legislative Council of New South Wales was increased to 36 members only one third of whom were appointed; two thirds elected and New South Wales had a representative government.⁶ Van Diemen's Land, still taking convicts, was not granted the same arrangement until 1850.

The next major step was the Australian Constitutions Act 1850.⁷ This was the Act that created Victoria but it also allowed all the Australian colonies, with some conditions, to seek Royal Assent for their own constitution acts which would give them a responsible government. For New South Wales the relevant Act received Assent on 16th July 1855 and the first meeting of the New South Wales Parliament took place on 22nd May 1856. Royal Assent for the Van Diemen's Land Constitution Act was granted on 1st May 1855. For some time the colony had been known popularly as Tasmania and a formal change of name took place on 1st January 1856. The Tasmanian Parliament met for the first time on 2nd December 1856. South Australia's Constitution Act received Royal Assent on 24th June 1856, her Parliament first meeting on 22nd April 1857.

Victoria had representative government as soon as it was separated from New South Wales and received Royal Assent for a new constitution on 16th July 1855. The 1850 Act allowed for further areas of New South Wales to be detached from it by Order in Council at any time in the future. Under this provision Queensland was created in 1859 and, as the parent colony already had responsible government, Queensland did not need Royal Assent for its constitution. It had representative government from the start and passed its own Constitution Act in 1867.

At the time of the 1850 Act Western Australia had just begun to import convict labour and its population was not large. The Act allowed for the setting up of a representative Legislative Council when certain conditions had been met. When that had been achieved the Act further allowed for Western Australia to apply for a constitution. Representative government was not in place until 1870 but further development was slow. Royal Assent for a constitution was not granted to Western Australia until August 1890.

By the 1890s all six colonies thus had their own constitution acts and all of them had moved smoothly to self government but there was another reason why the Australian colonies were quickly coming of age. Until 1850 wool had been the mainstay of the economy with farming in general beginning to achieve some importance but in 1851 discoveries of gold were announced in New South Wales and Victoria. These proved very rich and were followed by moderate finds in South Australia, Queensland and Tasmania. Significant finds were made in Western Australia in the 1890s. The various discoveries attracted immigrants in large numbers from all over the world and "diggers" soon took their place alongside squatters and free selectors in the story of Australia's development. The diggers came also from other parts of Australia at first leaving other industries undermanned and towns and farms deserted but, by the end of the 19th century, gold was just part of Australia's increasing industry. It had though put the Australian colonies on the world stage and contributed vastly to their development.

From an early date there had been suggestions that federation of the Australian colonies would be useful. At first the individual colonies saw little purpose in such a scheme. It would though remove trade barriers between them and the German annexation of part of New Guinea in 1884 highlighted the advantages there would be in matters of defence and foreign affairs. In 1885 a Federal Council for the Australasian Colonies was set up with power to legislate on matters of mutual and external interest. This was something that previously only the British Government had been able to do and was thus a first step towards the granting of

---

6 An Act for the Government of New South Wales and Van Diemen's Land (the Constitution Act 1842).
7 An Act for the better Government of Her Majesty's Australian Colonies (13 &14 Vict c. 59). (Also known as the Australian Colonies Government Act 1850).

federal powers to Australia. However, New South Wales and New Zealand (a separate colony since 1841) declined to be represented on it at all and South Australia only briefly so its effectiveness was limited. Nevertheless in 1889 the premier of New South Wales declared strongly in favour of federation in a speech which became known as the "Tenterfield Oration" and in the 1890s a series of conventions culminated in a draft Constitution which was to be put to a referendum in each of the Australian colonies. By 1899 all of them except Western Australia had agreed to accept it and the approved draft was taken to London to be passed into law. This was enacted as the main section of the Commonwealth of Australia Constitution Act 1900[8] which received Royal Assent on 9th July 1900. The Bill having been passed by the British Government, Western Australia held its own referendum in time to join the other colonies when the Act came into force on 1 January 1901. All six colonies thus became states of the Commonwealth of Australia. The Federal Parliament was to consist of the Queen, a Senate and a House of Representatives and a Governor General would be appointed by the Queen as her representative in the Commonwealth.

The seat of government was to be decided by the Commonwealth Parliament and would be in territory granted to or acquired by the Commonwealth in the State of New South Wales at least one hundred miles from Sydney. In 1909 New South Wales formally ceded the necessary territory which came under government control as the Federal Capital Territory on 1st January 1911. Here Canberra would be built but until its new home was ready the Commonwealth Parliament would meet at Melbourne.[9]

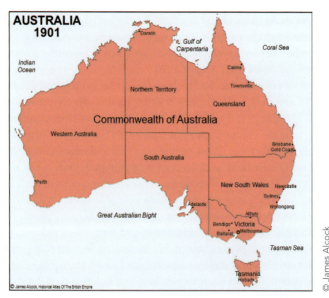

The six Australian colonies become states of the Commonwealth of Australia.

With self government came responsibility for defence and imperial troops were removed from the self governing colonies from about 1870. Colonial units were raised to replace them but as early as 1885 New South Wales was able to offer a contingent to support Imperial troops in the Sudan. Australian troops played a major part in the Second Boer War and we have already noted in Chapter six that the Australasian colonies agreed to subsidize the Royal

---

8 (63 and 64 Vict. c.12).
9 *The Commonwealth Parliament was shifted to Canberra from Melbourne in 1927. The territory officially became the "Australian Capital Territory" in 1938.*

Navy from 1887. The various colonial units began to be reorganized on federal lines in 1899 and were officially transferred to Commonwealth control in March 1901. When Britain declared war on Germany on 4th August 1914 Australia immediately took up arms. The ties with the "old country" were still too strong for any other course to be considered although there was also the small matter of a German presence in the Pacific.

We saw in Chapter six how an attempt was made in the 1820s to introduce the Spanish dollar as the legal currency of **New South Wales.** However, the United Kingdom Order in Council of 23rd March 1825 gave legal currency to British coins in the colonies generally in the hope that sterling silver would become the currency of the Empire. It laid down the concurrent rate of 4/4d for the Spanish dollar while sterling was being established.

The New South Wales Currency Act of 12th July 1826 therefore repealed previous legislation in favour of the dollar and promoted the circulation of sterling money of Great Britain in the colony. The Spanish dollar was to be the equivalent of 4/4d sterling and copper coins were to be legal tender as in Great Britain, no one being compelled to take more than twelve pence of them in any one payment. No bills were to be drawn for sums of less than twenty shillings. There was similar legislation for **Van Diemen's Land** which was now a separate colony although here the deficiency of British silver coin is specifically noted and circulating values given to subdivisions of the dollar down to the eighth (6½d). As the various other colonies were formed they too would take responsibility for their own currency regulations within the framework laid down by the British Government. Their isolation meant that the problems experienced in many other colonies with the erroneous rate fixed for the dollar and no fixed rate for foreign gold coins were of less importance in the Australian colonies. In fact the average rate for the dollar in NSW against bills over the previous few years had been about 4/4d as it had sunk in value from its official rate of 5/-. In Van Diemen's Land too the official rate for the dollar had been 5/- but her 1826 Act takes the trouble to explain that, although that had been the case, "*the sum of four shillings and four-pence Sterling is equal or more than equal to one Spanish Dollar*". [10]

The main problem in 1825 was that there was very little sterling coin in New South Wales or Van Diemen's Land, most of the circulating medium being dollars. During the next few years though, several shipments of British coins (silver and copper) arrived in New South Wales and in trade the dollar often changed hands at 4/2d (its intrinsic value) or less. In 1829 the Governor was able to order that, as a large sum of British coin was now in circulation, none of the Departments of Government would receive payments in foreign coin after 15th August. Exchange of "ring dollars" (i.e. holey dollars) and dumps for British silver would continue only until 30th September.[11] After their withdrawal from circulation the Colonial Treasury held about 28,600 holey dollars and 10,600 dumps.[12] These were sent to the Royal Mint in London where, to the obvious dismay of modern numismatists, these interesting relics of colonial Australia were melted.

Van Diemen's Land was generally less well provided with sterling coins during this period than was New South Wales and foreign coins continued in use for much longer. In 1835, there still being little British silver money, an Act was passed giving the sicca (Bengal) rupee legal tender status at 2/- but this Act was disallowed by the British Government. A further Act (of 28th November 1838) admitted dollars of the South American States and Mexico to legal tender at the same rate as the old Spanish dollars (4/4d) and this was amended in 1840 to clarify that this applied only to those of the full intrinsic value of the Spanish dollar. It was

---

10 *7 Geo IV No 3. 22nd September 1826, effective 8th October 1826.*
11 *General Order of 7th August 1829.*
12 *See Dr. W.J.D. Mira, "Coinage and Currency in New South Wales 1788-1829".*

only in 1842 though that Van Diemen's Land was able to follow the example of New South Wales and remove all foreign coin from legal tender.[13]

Although it had taken some time, British coinage was thus established in Australia more or less as the British Government had intended and the only coins legally current were sterling. Nevertheless, as was the case in other colonies, sterling silver coins had unlimited legal tender. An increasing population, particularly after the gold discoveries, required an increasing circulation and the unlimited use of "token" silver was not sound practice. The United Kingdom Order in Council and Proclamation of 16th October 1852 (noted in Chapter six) was therefore issued directing that the coins of the United Kingdom should pass current in the same manner as they did in the home country where silver had a legal tender limit of forty shillings only. This came into force separately in each of the colonies when published by Proclamation or Act and the currency of the Australian colonies was then on the same basis as that of the United Kingdom.

The huge discoveries of gold attracted many diggers to the goldfields but, because of the limited availability of specie, it was not always easy for them to exchange their finds for legal tender coin at anything like the correct price. Assay offices to test and guarantee quality would have been useful but the first of these was set up outside the gold producing colonies and primarily for a different reason. The diggers attracted to the finds in New South Wales and Victoria included many residents of **South Australia** who took much of their savings with them, mostly in the form of gold sovereigns. As the banks were required to back their paper issues with a certain amount of specie these large withdrawals created a dangerous situation in which issues of paper money may have to be restricted and the economy could face ruin. By 1852 the South Australian authorities felt forced to act with some urgency. The result was Act 1 of 1852[14], usually referred to as the Bullion Act, which passed through all its stages and was approved by the Lieutenant-Governor in one sitting of the Legislative Council. The Act authorized the setting up of an Assay Office in Adelaide to buy gold from the Victorian fields at the rate of £3-11s-0d an ounce. This was deliberately set higher than the price available in Victoria in order to attract the gold. The office would assay it deducting 1% in charges and strike it into ingots that would be held by the banks as a reserve against their paper issues. The paper money issued for the ingots would be legal tender in South Australia. The Act was a temporary measure and was to terminate in twelve calendar months. The speed with which the Bill passed through the legislative process and became an Act is indicative of how urgent the problem was seen to be. London had previously been informed of the developing situation but it was only on the day following the passing of the Act that a dispatch was sent explaining it and the reasons for it.

The Assay Office opened on 10th February immediately attracting deposits and the first ingots were issued on 4th March. The price offered for the gold was attractive but to ensure that as much as possible was sent home by South Australian diggers a police escort was arranged to carry it safely from Mount Alexander in Victoria to Adelaide. During the course of the Act more than £1 million worth of the gold processed by the Assay Office was brought in by the escort which continued to bring it for some months after the Office closed. In total it made eighteen round trips without loss.

The Act worked well in that credit and confidence were soon restored but there was immediate concern over some aspects of it. No limit was set on the amount of gold the banks were obliged to accept and pay for in legal tender notes. While the Act remained in force, but only while it remained in force, they could redeem their notes with ingots which could also be used to satisfy cheques, bills and other claims and demands made on them. Their notes

---

13 6 Vict No 7 of 14th September 1842 of Van Diemen's Land.
14 Of 28th January 1852.

though were payable in pounds sterling on demand and this obligation would put them in a difficult position when the Act expired or was perhaps disallowed by the Home Authorities. For the moment they still had very few sovereigns to hand and it would take time to attract them in exchange for bullion. The banks feared at least a temporary insolvency and sought amendment of the Act to deal with the problem. It was suggested that the cumbrous gold ingots of varied weight should be replaced by ingots of fixed value. If these were made legal tender in all business transactions they would not only relieve trade but provide an exchange for legal tender notes until sufficient sovereigns were available. For ease of use the new ingots should be of the size and character of a circulating medium (they should look like coins). Dies were prepared but by that time specie was beginning to arrive in useful quantities and the matter of the uniform ingots (or "tokens") may have been less urgent. In fact it was not until 11th November that the necessary Act was passed by the Legislative Council.[15] This repealed the part of the previous Act that required banks to issue legal tender notes for bullion and allowed for the striking of tokens of five pounds, two pounds, one pound and ten shillings at the rate of £3-11-0d per ounce. These could be issued directly as legal tender and used *"on all occasions on which a tender of money may legally be made"*. In the mean time a request had been made that a branch of the Royal Mint be set up in Adelaide to supply a proper coinage for the colony on a permanent basis.

Although dies had been produced for the five pounds and the one pound tokens, the only denomination struck when the new Act came into force was the one pound. The gold tokens were the same fineness as British gold coins (22 carats) but the Adelaide pound was based on the local gold price of £3-11-0d per ounce. As the price for an ounce of gold in London was £3-17-10½d the Adelaide pound was heavier and therefore worth more than the sovereign.[16] In fact a later assay at the Royal Mint gave it a sterling equivalent of £1-1-10·8d. By the time the first pound tokens were issued on 26th November large shipments of specie (silver as well as gold) were arriving in South Australia and it is perhaps because of this that the tokens were struck in fairly small numbers. The delay in producing them meant that by the time they were struck Australia's first gold "coins" were probably of limited use. It was obvious that they were worth more in London than if they remained in the colony. Also, banks would be unlikely to issue an Adelaide pound which the Act made legal tender at that rate in South Australia when a lighter sovereign was available to make the same payment. The Assay Office closed on 17th February 1853. All the gold tokens bear the date 1852.

The Adelaide pound 1852.

Such was the grinding slowness of communication before the advent of the telegraph that it was not until after all this had happened that there was any response at all from London concerning the Bullion Act and its amendment. Bills affecting the currency were a Royal Prerogative and local action could only be justified in cases of urgent necessity. It was therefore with some trepidation that the Lieutenant-Governor awaited replies to the various dispatches

---

15 Act 14 of 1852, sometimes referred to as "the Gold Token Act". It was given the assent of the Lieutenant-Governor on 23rd November.
16 The weight of the Adelaide pound, stated on the reverse, was **5 DWT: 15 GRS:** *(i.e. 135 grains) while the official weight of the sovereign was 123.274 grains.*

sent to his Secretary of State in London. These replies began to arrive on 4th May 1853. In general the responses from London applauded the original Act and its effects but the gold tokens could not be looked upon as anything other than a breach of the Royal Prerogative of Coining. At such a distance the authorities in London had no idea if the gold tokens had become an important part of the circulating medium so the amending Act was not disallowed. On general principles though, it was objectionable and should be repealed as soon as possible.[17] A branch of the Royal Mint at Adelaide would be quite unnecessary. Sydney had already been selected as the sight of a mint which it was hoped would service all Australia's coining needs.

In December 1851 **New South Wales** had already petitioned for a mint where unassayed Australian gold could be exchanged for current coin. During 1852 there was some correspondence concerning this and New South Wales was given two estimates. One was for a mint that could serve the whole of Australia, the other for a smaller mint to supply only the needs of New South Wales. As the senior colony it was generally assumed that the first option was the right one and plans were formed for a substantial mint at Sydney. However, large quantities of gold were soon coming from Victoria and in July 1852 they also requested a mint. A further request came from South Australia, also in 1852. The Lords of the Treasury examined the matter and published their findings in a Minute of 22nd March 1853. It recommended that Sydney should have a branch of the Royal Mint as promised. It should not though be on the scale originally envisaged as options should be kept open for the other gold producing colonies. Mints should only be established under the authority of an Order in Council. Although primarily established to coin Australian gold they should be available to strike any coinage her Majesty may direct.

An Order in Council of 19th August 1853 granted formal permission for a branch mint at Sydney and the mint opened on 14th May 1855. The coins struck were to be at the same standard as the British sovereign and would be legal tender throughout Australasia, not just in New South Wales. They would not, by law, be legal tender in the United Kingdom[18] and therefore had to be of distinctive design. Sovereigns with the reverse legend **SYDNEY MINT AUSTRALIA** were struck from 1855 to 1870, half sovereigns from 1855 to 1866.

Two different designs of gold coins, the Imperial and the Australian were now legal tender in Australasia while only one of them was legal tender in the United Kingdom. As they were both of the same weight and fineness this was clearly unsatisfactory and the colony began to press for full recognition of their coins. An Imperial Act of 1863[19] gave the Queen the power to declare the Sydney Mint gold coins legal tender in the United Kingdom although the relevant Proclamation was not made until February 1866. This though applied only to the United Kingdom and only to the Sydney Mint. It was clear that other branch mints could be established and a further Act was necessary to give the gold coins produced in all of them the same legal tender status as British gold coins. The Colonial Branch Mint Act of 1866[20] enabled the Queen to proclaim gold coins of any branch mint legal tender throughout the United Kingdom *and* throughout Her Majesty's Dominions. A resulting Proclamation of 10th November 1866 put Sydney gold on the same footing as that of the United Kingdom[21] and as other mints were established their gold too would be proclaimed legal tender throughout the Empire.

---

17 *In fact it was not repealed until 1934.*
18 *The 1816 Act to regulate the United Kingdom currency on a gold standard applied specifically to coins struck at "His Majesty's Mint in London". Coins struck at Sydney could therefore not be legal tender in the United Kingdom without a change in the law.*
19 *26 & 27 Vict. c. 74 (the Sydney Branch Mint Act, 1863).*
20 *29 & 30 Vict. c.65 (the Colonial Branch Mint Act, 1866).*
21 *In fact the legal tender of Sydney gold had been extended to Ceylon, Mauritius and Hong Kong in 1856. The 1866 Proclamation extended it to all other colonies except Canada and Newfoundland. A separate Proclamation of 14th May 1868 extended it to the North American colonies.*

When it became plain that a mint was to open in Melbourne it was plain also that another variant design would be confusing. The design of the Sydney gold coins was therefore altered to be exactly the same as the Royal Mint issues but for the addition of a small letter **S**. When Melbourne opened in 1872 these coins were also of imperial type but with mint letter **M**. After the finds of gold in Western Australia, Perth opened in 1899 using mint letter **P**. South Australia, where very little gold was found, was never granted the privilege of a branch mint.

Sydney Mint opened 1855

Sovereign 1866.

Half sovereign 1861.

Imperial style sovereigns and half sovereigns

Sydney sovereign 1876.

Melbourne sovereign 1881.

Sydney half sovereign (Jubilee head) 1891.

Perth half sovereign 1900.

(The George and dragon reverse was reintroduced for the sovereign in 1871 and for some years was issued concurrently with the shield reverse at all mints. The shield was thought more acceptable for use in India and the slaying of a dragon inappropriate for trade with China. The shield reverse continued to be used at London until 1874 and at the Australian mints until 1887. The half sovereign retained the shield reverse at all mints until the introduction of Victoria's veiled portrait in 1893).

Imperial style gold was struck at the Australian mints as follows:

Sydney	Sovereigns 1871-1926	Half sovereigns 1871-1916
Melbourne	Sovereigns 1872-1931	Half sovereigns 1873-1915
Perth	Sovereigns 1899-1931	Half sovereigns 1899-1918[22]

The primary purpose of these mints was to coin the gold found in Australia but it was proposed from the start that they should be available to strike other coins if required. In fact nothing but gold was produced at any of these colonial branches of the Royal Mint until some years after the Commonwealth of Australia introduced her own coinage in 1910. This we will look at in a moment but before doing so must take a brief look at the "small change" of the 19th century.

As population increased, particularly from about 1850, there were frequent shortages of small change and tradesmen requiring coins of small denomination often had to offer a premium to obtain them. As was the case elsewhere, this made the issue of tokens worthwhile and many of them give interesting insights into colonial life. The majority are of one penny denomination although some issuers also had halfpennies struck for them and there were a few silver tokens as well.[23] The first major issue was that of Annand, Smith and Company, family grocers, of Melbourne who imported a large number of pennies from Birmingham in 1849.

Imported tokens came from several of the major British manufacturers including Heaton and Sons and W. J. Taylor but there were local manufacturers as well. The first of these was probably J. C. Thornthwaite who struck tokens for Peek and Campbell in Sydney in the early 1850s. Lacking a screw press at the time Thornthwaite probably used a "drop-hammer" process giving these tokens their somewhat crude appearance. Another early manufacturer was Whitty and Brown of Sydney whose products are also somewhat crude. Thornthwaite went on to produce other tokens including silver threepences in his own name and some also for James Campbell of Morpeth. Hogarth and Erichson, jewellers of Sydney, are well known for their issues of silver threepences in their own name. In 1852 W. J. Taylor sent a coining press to Melbourne which produced several token issues with dies sent from London. In 1857 he sold this machinery and many of his dies to the local manufacturer, Thomas Stokes who went on to produce many Australian tokens. Some traders chose to countermark the tokens of others to avoid the trouble and expense of obtaining their own but, as names are clearly stated, redemption was presumably still guaranteed.

The penny and halfpenny tokens generally attempt the fabric of the heavy British copper coins of the time. Although Britain moved to a lighter bronze coinage in 1860 these did not arrive immediately in the colonies and Australian tokens continued to be struck in heavy copper for a number of years. From 1863 though, bronze tokens, more in line with the new British pennies and halfpennies, began to appear. However, the main period of issue was now over. The enormous numbers being produced were becoming an embarrassment and British bronze coins began to arrive in sufficient quantity to plan for a withdrawal of the tokens.

The first colony to attempt a ban was Victoria in 1863 after which many of her tokens found their way to other colonies. In New South Wales arrangements were in place by September 1868 to distribute the new British bronze coins. Their main function was to replace old regal copper coins but for a limited period they were also exchanged for tokens at the rate of 240 bronze pennies for 8 pounds by weight of the tokens. This was effectively full face value

---
22 The Perth Mint half sovereigns dated 1918 were in fact struck for export in 1919 and January 1920 (Howard Hodgson, COIN NEWS, January and February 2019).
23 An early silver shilling token of MacIntosh and Degraves in Tasmania dated 1823 probably did not circulate.

but to avoid possible fraud no tokens other than the heavy copper pieces were acceptable. Issuers who had recently imported bronze tokens were left with them on their hands at scrap value. In Tasmania it was not until an Act of 1875[24] that the bronze coins of the realm formally replaced the old copper coins and the same Act specifically disallowed the use of tokens.

Tokens exist from all six of the Australian colonies each of which was responsible for any legislation concerning them, their circulation and their withdrawal but the influx of the British bronze coins effectively brought their use to an end. The latest issues of the main series of Australian tokens are those of John Gidley Fleming of Hobart and John Henderson of Fremantle, both dated 1874, and an undated issue of Henderson attributed to 1878. An Order in Council and Proclamation of 1st August 1896 extended provisions of the United Kingdom Coinage Act 1870 to all the Australian colonies (and New Zealand). It is unlikely that any of the old tokens were circulating in Australia at that time but from the date of Proclamation in each colony only coins struck at the Royal Mint and gold from the branch mints could be made or issued *as a coin or a token for money*.

SOME AUSTRALIAN TOKENS
Early Australian struck tokens

Peek & Campbell penny by Thornthwaite.   Advance Australia penny by Whitty and Brown.

Countermarking

Annand Smith penny of Melbourne.

Another example countermarked for F. Cade.

---

24 39 Vict No 15 of 30th September 1875 (Tasmania). Proclaimed 11th October 1875.

Further tokens

Flavelle Brothers of Sydney and Brisbane struck by Taylor of London.

Copper penny of the Melbourne maker, Stokes 1862.

Penny and halfpenny of Lewis Abrahams of Tasmania 1855.

Hogarth Erichsen threepence 1860.

Later issues

Bronze penny of Ipswich, Queensland 1865.

Bronze penny of Fremantle, Western Australia c.1874.

Victorian Artillery canteen token (reminding us that the self governing colonies took responsibility for their own defence).

Most issuers of the Australian tokens can be traced in the extensive records of the period. Many of their stories have been told but I make no excuse for repeating one of them which brings the 19th century history of Australia vividly to life. Reuben Josephs was born in London in 1790 and became a tailor by trade. In October 1827 he was charged at the Old Bailey with two offences of feloniously receiving stolen silverware and was described as *"a general-dealer in the clothes line"*. His defence in both cases was that he had bought the items in good faith in the course of his trade. On the first charge the court agreed with him but on very similar evidence he was convicted of the second charge (for silverware totalling £2-12s-0d) and sentenced to transportation for fourteen years.[25] The life he had known came to an abrupt end and after a short spell in Newgate Prison he was received aboard the prison hulk "Ganymede" at Chatham on 19th November 1827. In March 1828, with about 190 other male convicts, he sailed from the Thames in the transport "William Miles" arriving in Hobart some four months later. Josephs appears not to have arrived empty handed and, unusually, his wife is recorded as having travelled on the same ship as a free settler. With Josephs assigned to her they set up business as general dealers and storekeepers at New Norfolk on the Derwent River. This rather cosy arrangement took him "off the store" and the records show that he was granted a ticket of leave in July 1833. In 1836 he was granted a conditional pardon and when his time expired in 1841 he received a certificate of freedom.[26] For a while their business seems to have prospered but in 1842 Josephs became insolvent and took up farming. Dinah, his wife, died in 1844 after which Josephs sold up and moved to Hobart. Here, in 1856, he would marry the widow Rachel Levein. After an unsuccessful tender for the New Town toll gate for 1851 he managed to secure the lease from 1852 to 1855 and again in 1857. It was here that he issued the penny and halfpenny tokens that would have allowed him to give exact change at the toll gate at a time when regal copper coins were scarce. It is interesting that at this late date Josephs, the ex convict, is the only Tasmanian issuer ever to use the name Van Diemen's Land rather than "Tasmania" on his tokens. The toll gate and the house where Josephs presumably lived appear on the obverse of his tokens. Under "Deaths" the Cornwall Chronicle (Launceston) of 29th November 1862 notes: *"On 21st inst at his residence, New Town, near Hobart Town, Mr. Reuben Josephs, an old respected colonist aged 72 years"*.

Arriving as a convict, he had worked on assignment, obtained his freedom, seen bad times and good and in maturity had achieved legitimacy and respect. And so it was with the land in which he lived which, by the time of his death, was making the first tentative moves towards federation.

Reuben Josephs' tokens (Van Diemen's Land) 1855

Penny. Halfpenny.

---

25 Both cases were heard consecutively on 25th October 1827 (numbers 2103 and 2104). In the court records his name is spelt "Joseph" without the "s".
26 For a brief summary see R. V. McNeice, "Coins and Tokens of Tasmania", 1969.

Prior to federation, legislation concerning the currency was a Royal Prerogative although each colony was responsible for bringing it into force and for the day to day regulation of coinage and currency. The Constitution Act of 1900 specified the legislative powers of the Commonwealth Parliament which included "*coinage, currency and legal tender*".[27] The Act also stated[28] that an individual State should "*not coin money, nor make anything but gold or silver coin a legal tender in payment of debts*". From 1st January 1901 responsibility for coinage and currency therefore rested firmly with the Commonwealth Parliament and with no one else.

By the later 19th century the Australian colonies were forming the opinion that they were entitled to a share in the profit made by the issues of sterling "token" silver coins for their own internal use. We have seen in earlier chapters that they were not alone in this but, unlike colonies elsewhere, there were fully functioning mints in Australia that could theoretically produce subsidiary coins as well as gold. In 1898 both New South Wales and Victoria negotiated the right to strike silver and bronze coins at their existing mints (Perth was not yet open) but, in the run up to federation and the years following it, nothing came of this. Gold sovereigns and half sovereigns continued to be struck at Sydney, Melbourne and Perth while imperial subsidiary coins in silver and bronze continued to come from the United Kingdom.

If Australia was to profit from the issue of subsidiary sterling coins then, as was the case elsewhere, she would need distinctive coins that would not be legal tender in the United Kingdom and for which she had full responsibility. The Coinage Act of 1909 and the Australian Notes Act of 1910 made the necessary provision for the first **Commonwealth of Australia** currency. The first coins to be issued were a florin (two shillings), shilling, sixpence and threepence in silver, all dated 1910 and bearing the portrait of Edward VII. The next year the portrait had to be changed to that of the new king, George V, and the first Commonwealth bronze coins (the penny and the halfpenny) made their appearance. There was no half-crown (2/6d) in the Australian series and no farthing. All the Australian coins were of the standard laid down for the United Kingdom coinage in the Coinage Act 1870. Although Australia was well provided with mints this new Commonwealth coinage was produced at the Royal Mint (occasionally sub contracted, like the imperial coinage, to Heaton's Birmingham mint) and this arrangement continued until the First World War. Supply problems then made it necessary to make alternative arrangements. Australian bronze coins were struck at Calcutta from 1916-1918 but it was the Melbourne branch of the Royal Mint that would now take over the main production of Australian coins. Here, silver was struck from 1916 and bronze from 1919. The Sydney branch mint struck some subsidiary coins from 1919 until its closure for economic reasons in 1926 and Perth struck the penny denomination in 1922.

The United Kingdom coins in circulation in Australia continued to be legal tender but arrangements were made after the 1909 Act for the withdrawal of £100,000 worth of British subsidiary coins each year. The Australian pound was of course exactly the same as the British pound and both were represented by the sovereign. In 1914 though Britain began to meddle with her gold specie standard (see Chapter fourteen) and by the time a gold standard was restored in 1925 the pound sterling was overvalued against the United States dollar. Britain's insistence on retaining the pre-war rate for gold caused grave problems and, as an emergency measure, Australia dropped the gold standard in December 1929. The United Kingdom was not forced to follow suit until September 1931 by which time the Australian pound had depreciated considerably. In December 1931 it was fixed at sixteen shillings (16/-) sterling and although it was pegged at that rate for many years the two currencies had parted company.

---

27 *Commonwealth of Australia Constitution Act, Chapter 1, Part V, Section 51 (xii).*
28 *Chapter 5, Section 115.*

In 1920 the price of silver momentarily rose to the level at which it was uneconomic to strike United Kingdom silver coins at their existing weight and fineness. The authorities acted very quickly and reduced the millesimal fineness of the British silver coins to 500. However, no change had been made to the Australian silver coins before the price of silver began to fall and they were able to retain their original sterling fineness of 925 until after the Second World War. Both coinages though were "token" in nature. British subsidiary coins continued to be legal tender in Australia but these divergences tended to remove the last of them from circulation. Sovereigns and half sovereigns left general circulation after the changes of 1914 and the issue of half sovereigns for internal Australian use ceased in 1915. Sovereigns continued to be struck at the Australian branch mints for reserve purposes and overseas payments until Britain abandoned the gold standard in 1931.

The Coinage Act was amended in 1936 to allow the issue of a Crown (5/-) denomination to commemorate the coronation of George VI. This denomination was not popular and was struck only in 1937 and 1938 at Melbourne. 1938 saw significant changes to the design of some of Australia's minor coins introducing the kangaroo to the copper coins and the ram's head to the shilling. This was not the first occasion when Australian fauna had been considered as a reverse design. In 1919 a coinage of pennies and halfpennies in cupro-nickel on square flans had been suggested and patterns were produced with a kookaburra as the reverse design. It did not though go into general circulation and the 1938 changes were perhaps inspired more by the recent introduction of the Irish coinage (Chapter fourteen).

The Second World War saw a further proliferation of mints. Perth again struck Australian coins from 1940 and would continue to do so, with Melbourne, for many years. Bombay struck bronze coins in 1942 and 1943 and two mints in the United States (Denver and San Francisco) struck large quantities of Australian silver coins in the period 1942-1944. The silver for the coins struck in the United States was provided under the wartime Lend-Lease scheme and had to be returned after the war. For this purpose the Coinage Act was again amended in 1947 to allow coins to be issued at a millesimal fineness of 500. The new debased issue allowed earlier coins to be withdrawn from circulation to recover the purer silver. It is interesting to note that cupro-nickel replaced silver completely in the United Kingdom coinage at the same time for similar reasons. The Australian silver coins continued at the 50% standard until decimalization in 1966.

Discussion on decimalization began in earnest in 1959 with the setting up of a Decimal Currency Committee. The Currency Acts of 1963 and 1965 made the necessary provisions and repealed the Acts of 1909, 1936 and 1947. The unit of currency chosen was the Australian dollar divided into one hundred cents and one pound of the previous currency was to be equivalent to two dollars. The Royal Australian Mint at Canberra (the first Australian mint that was not a branch of the Royal Mint) was opened in February 1965 specifically to produce the new coinage and decimalization took effect on 14th February 1966. The initial coins were produced in the United Kingdom, at Perth and at Melbourne as well as at Canberra and were dated 1966. The two remaining branches of the Royal Mint were dis-established in 1970, Melbourne having ceased production in 1968. The Perth Mint became a State institution producing collector coins and bullion.

COMMONWEALTH OF AUSTRALIA PRE-DECIMAL COINS.

Edward VII shilling 1910.

George V florin 1912. *George V shilling 1916, Melbourne mint*

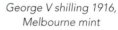

George V penny 1911.

George VI crown 1937. *George VI sixpence 1943, Denver mint.*

Elizabeth II florin 1960. *Elizabeth II Halfpenny 1961.*

The first Europeans known to have discovered **New Zealand** were the Dutch in the 1640s. They made no territorial claim but it derived its name, Nieuw Zeeland, from one of the seven United Provinces. It was Captain James Cook, on his initial great voyage of discovery, who would make the first formal claim to the islands. During his exploration of New Zealand Cook remained for some days at the place he named Mercury Bay on the east coast of North Island.[29] His journal entry for 15th November 1769 records that *"Before we left this Bay we cut out upon one of the trees near the watering place the Ships name, date etc, and after displaying the English Colours I took formal possession of the place in the name of His Majesty"*. A similar ceremony was conducted at the place he named Queen Charlotte's Sound on 31st January 1770 and claims had thus been made in both North and South Island. At Queen Charlotte Sound the local people were presented with items that were most likely to remain with them for some time and which would confirm the visit. These included spike nails impressed with the *"Kings broad Arrow"* and threepenny pieces of 1763 bearing the King's portrait. The ceremony completed, an empty wine bottle was also generously bestowed with which the recipient was recorded as being *"highly pleased"*.

Threepence of 1763.
Type recorded in Cook's journal as being given to the elders at Queen Charlotte Sound in 1770.

In the early 19th century the two main islands of New Zealand were referred to as the North (or Northern) Island and the Middle Island. This is because Stewart Island, much smaller than the two main islands, lies to the south. Middle Island is now named South Island and throughout this work, to avoid confusion, I use the names North Island and South Island as they would be used today.

By the end of the 18th century whaling and sealing vessels from Sydney and elsewhere were calling at New Zealand for supply and repair and the first permanent settlers came mainly from New South Wales. These included escaped convicts and deserters from ships and the main initial settlement was in the Bay of Islands on the east coast of North Island. Here they traded, mostly in firearms and rum, for local produce and generally lived a lawless and immoral existence free from any official control. Missionary societies were soon active, the first mission station being set up in the Bay of Islands by the Church Missionary Society in 1814. The various missionary societies (Anglican, Catholic and Methodist) would not only be active among the European settlers but would promote Christianity and European culture among the Maori (the indigenous Polynesian people of New Zealand). With their language skills and local knowledge missionaries often played an important part in early treaties and agreements.

In the 1820s the British Government had no intention of taking formal responsibility for New Zealand. Attempts at commercial colonization generally met with resistance and were not successful but in 1827, in the Marlborough Sounds, the first permanent whaling station was set up. Soon there would be more and it was plain that some sort of control should be exercised over British activity.

---

29 *Having observed the transit of Venus from Tahiti Cook observed the transit of Mercury from New Zealand on 9th November 1769.*

New Zealand lay within the compass of New South Wales so in theory the first settlers were subject to the jurisdiction of the Governor in Sydney. In practice, at such a distance, his authority was very slight. To improve this, a British Resident was appointed in 1832. James Busby's mandate was to protect legitimate British settlers and traders, to apprehend escaped convicts, to obtain the goodwill of the native chiefs and to prevent European violence towards the Maori. Without police or troops to support him, Busby could exercise little influence and his period of office coincided with increased French interest in the region. To deter this and to improve matters generally Busby encouraged the northern chiefs to declare themselves a nation under the title of The United Tribes of New Zealand. This they did in 1835 inviting the southern tribes to join them and seeking the protection of William IV for their new state.

The new state was recognized but their declaration of independence, foreign interest in the region and the continued lawlessness of British subjects were all causes for concern. Colonization seemed inevitable and British policy towards New Zealand began to change. When a New Zealand Association was formed in 1837 it was therefore planned that it should have a Royal Charter to take responsibility for the region on behalf of the British Government. Their aim was to establish a colony on the same lines as that recently set up in South Australia under the principles of Edward Gibbon Wakefield but there was soon some unease in government circles about the Association's attitudes towards the Maori and land purchase. In an atmosphere of reform these matters were important and the offer of a Charter was withdrawn. The Association was dissolved and reconstituted as the New Zealand Company in 1839. In the mean time the British Government had decided to negotiate with the Maori chiefs for a direct transfer of sovereignty to the Crown. Aware of this the Company, still without a Charter, was anxious to obtain as much land as possible before any restrictions were placed on its activities and a preliminary voyage under Wakefield's brother was hurried out from England in May 1839. Extensive tracts of land were purchased from the Maori and the main expedition arrived in January 1840 with settlers who had purchased land from the Company. They settled around what is now Wellington but this unseemly scramble and its after effects would sour relations between the Company, the authorities, the settlers and the Maori for many years.

In 1839 Captain William Hobson was appointed British Consul for New Zealand and left England with comprehensive instructions on how to turn it into a colony. The British Government was duty bound to recognize the independence of The United Tribes of New Zealand and there could be no change of sovereignty without full agreement. The chiefs though were to be left in no doubt that control could not be exercised over lawless British subjects and their lands would be at risk unless the Queen was recognized as sovereign. To start with New Zealand would have to be governed from New South Wales and to facilitate this letters patent of June 1839 had formally expanded the territory of New South Wales to include any territory that may be acquired in New Zealand. On the way out Hobson called at Sydney for detailed consultations with the Governor and took the oath of office for the additional title of Lieutenant Governor. Arriving in the Bay of Islands in January 1840, he immediately set about his task of obtaining British sovereignty.

Without delay a great meeting was held at Waitangi in the Bay of Islands between the British Authorities (Hobson and Busby) and the chiefs of the United Tribes of New Zealand. The Maori were informed that the British intended to settle and were offered the protection of the Queen. The Treaty of Waitangi was signed on 6th February 1840 by chiefs present at the meeting and in the following months by many other Maori chiefs all over New Zealand. It is unlikely that all of them had a full appreciation of what British sovereignty entailed and not all the Maori were represented by signatories to the Treaty. Nevertheless, it formed the basis of subsequent Anglo-Maori relations and was a genuine attempt to protect the Maori from land speculators and over-zealous settlers. Their lands were guaranteed and any they wished to sell could only be sold to the Crown. In return the Maori received the rights and privileges of British subjects.

On 21st May 1840, Hobson issued two proclamations. One proclaimed that the Northern Island had been ceded to Her Majesty absolutely from the date of the Treaty of Waitangi. The other proclaimed *"full Sovereignty of the Islands of New Zealand"* from 21st May and made it plain that it applied to the whole of New Zealand. The proclamations were published in the London Gazette of 2nd October 1840 and New Zealand, in its entirety, was subject to the Crown as part of New South Wales.

The proclamations had been made before all the signatures to the Treaty of Waitangi had been collected but Hobson was keen to forestall the New Zealand Company in its attempt to set up its own administration at Port Nicholson (now Wellington). Only after sovereignty had been fully settled did the Company finally receive its Charter on 12th February 1841. This allowed it to superintend the colonization of New Zealand but its relationship with government was never a happy one. The main problem for the Company and its settlers was the security of land grants. Initially, decisions on land usually favoured the Maori but very soon concessions had to be made to the settlers. As land tenure was also a major cause of Maori concern it was inevitable that problems would arise.

The first major incident occurred in 1843 in South Island when the Company tried to impose a disputed claim to the Wairau Valley without reference to the government's Land Commissioner. This led to the deaths of twenty two settlers and at least four Maori in what came to be known as the Wairau Affray. To the disgust of the settlers the Governor blamed the Company for the incident and the resultant fear of Maori insurrection almost brought immigration to a halt. In the economic climate of the day the Company did not properly recover from this and in 1850 surrendered its Charter to the Crown ending its involvement in the business of the colony.

The Maori Wars of the 19th century are usually referred to today as the New Zealand Wars and all took place in North Island, home to the majority of the Maori. Disputed claims, unauthorized sales, the increasing numbers of settlers seeking land and Maori fears for their future all contributed to a series of violent conflicts. The period from 1843 to 1848 saw major confrontations including the first New Zealand War of 1845-1846. At this time the settlers were heavily outnumbered by the Maori and the early governors had little military force to back their authority. The Maori though were not a unified force and many of them supported the colonial authorities allowing order to be restored.

Settlement continued apace and although many Maori were willing sellers others began to fear for the very existence of their tribes. In the late 1850s a Maori King was appointed which they hoped would give them some unity and enable them to resist further sales of land. The settlers though were far more numerous than they had been and the Governor could call on greater resources to back his authority. When trouble flared in 1860 over the obstruction of land surveys the colonial administration therefore had the confidence to confront the Maori and their "Kingite" movement and intermittent warfare continued throughout the 1860s. Imperial troops, Australian volunteers and locally raised forces grew in total to more than 14,000 and their successes were sealed with punitive confiscations of land (legalized by the New Zealand Settlements Act of 1863).[30]

---

[30] *27 Victoria 1863 No 8. This Act applied to North Island and allowed lands to be confiscated from those in rebellion and then sold to settlers. The proceeds would cover the costs of suppressing the insurrection and of local development. South Island had a much smaller Maori population and was not involved in the New Zealand wars.*

British policy at this time was for self governing colonies to take responsibility for their internal defence and despite this being a period of war the policy was applied also to New Zealand. Local forces were developed and would cope with the situation but when the last detachment of the 18th Regiment left New Zealand in February 1870 there were some among the settlers who felt they were being abandoned.

Although the fighting ended in 1872 there were continued problems. Tensions were eased in 1881 when the Maori King formally accepted peace but by the end of the century little land remained in Maori hands.

As soon as British sovereignty had been established arrangements began for New Zealand to become a Crown colony in its own right. Letters patent of 16th November 1840 announced and set forth the Charter for Erecting the Colony of New Zealand by detaching it from New South Wales. This was proclaimed by William Hobson in Auckland (where he had recently established his seat of government) on 3rd May 1841 on the same day on which he took the oath as Governor and Commander in Chief. His Proclamation noted the appointment of both Executive and Legislative Councils as required by the Charter and whose members were all *ex officio*.

The settlers were soon pressing for representation and in 1846 the Parliament of the United Kingdom passed a New Zealand Constitution Act.[31] From Auckland the Governor warned that some of the provisions of the Act would alienate loyal Maori at a very difficult time by interfering with the intentions and spirit of the Treaty of Waitangi. In 1848 the Act was accordingly suspended, it being recognized by Parliament that it was "*expedient that further and better provision should be made for the Government of New Zealand* ".[32] The New Zealand Constitution Act 1852[33] was drafted mainly by the Governor. It received Royal Assent on 30th June of that year and would remain in force until 1986. The purpose of the Act as finally passed in 1852 was to grant a representative constitution to the Colony. It created a General Assembly with an elected House of Representatives and established representative assemblies for the provinces. The first New Zealand Parliament opened on 24th May 1854 and full responsible government began with the second Parliament which opened on 15 April 1856.

A qualification to vote was the possession of freehold estate. As the Maori owned their land collectively they were automatically excluded from these constitutional developments and this was one of the factors that led to the founding of the Maori King movement and other political institutions. From 1867 though, four seats were reserved for Maori Representatives in the Lower House. Their electoral districts covered the whole of New Zealand and all adult male Maori were given the vote. There were Maori appointments to the Upper House from 1872.

The first settlers were self-sufficient farmers but wool exports were developed from the 1840s. Agriculture, particularly pastoral, became the mainstay of the economy and the advent of refrigerated ships in 1882 allowed the development of large scale meat exports. Gold began to be worked in the 1850s in various parts of New Zealand but it was not until 1861 that the gold rushes began in earnest in Otago stimulating large scale immigration. The finds were never as large as those in Australia but the discoveries increased the importance of South Island which had never been as populous as the North. In 1865 the capital of New Zealand was moved from Auckland to Wellington to ensure that the seat of government was not too remote from the growing communities of South Island.

New Zealand was represented at the conventions which led to the unification of the Australian colonies but was not strongly in favour of joining. The Commonwealth of Australia

---

31 *9 & 10 Vict. c. 103.*
32 *The Government of New Zealand Act 1848, 11 & 12 Vict. c. 5.*
33 *15 & 16 Vict. c. 72.*

Constitution Act 1900 defined the States of the Commonwealth as "*such of the colonies of New South Wales, New Zealand, Queensland, Tasmania, Victoria, Western Australia, and South Australia, including the northern territory of South Australia, as for the time being are parts of the Commonwealth*". New Zealand did not opt to join and remained a separate colony being granted her own Dominion status in 1907.[34] In August 1914, together with the other Dominions, New Zealand declared war on Germany in support of the United Kingdom.

The first Act passed by the Legislative Council of New Zealand was the New South Wales Laws Adopted Act 1841 which continued the use of the laws of New South Wales for the new colony "*in the like manner as all other the Laws of England*". The legislation was thus based on English law and the statutes of the Parliament of the United Kingdom with any adjustments that may have been made for the special circumstances of New South Wales. This meant that sterling was the only legal coinage of **New Zealand**. The first specific acknowledgement of this in New Zealand legislation appears in section 43 of the Paper Currency Act 1847[35] which defines cash as "*current gold and silver coin of the realm at the English mint price*". The first specific mention in United Kingdom legislation is the Order in Council and Proclamation of 16th October 1852 which brought New Zealand (as well as the Australian colonies and some others) into line with Britain's forty shillings legal tender limit on silver.

An Order in Council and Proclamation of 18th October 1854 noted that the Sydney Mint sovereigns and half sovereigns were intended to be "*current and lawful money*" in New Zealand as well as in the Australian colonies. The later Australian gold coins which were of the same design as United Kingdom gold coins were legal tender on the same basis as London Mint coins and were therefore legal tender in New Zealand.

Tokens made their appearance in New Zealand just a few years after they had come into general use in the Australian colonies. Those of New Zealand are very similar in appearance to the Australian tokens, often being produced by the same manufacturers, and they were introduced for the same reason – a great shortage of small change. The early story of New Zealand is one of confrontation between the Maori and the settler and between the ideals of a hardheaded company and an administration that considered itself to be humanitarian. In the middle of all this stood the settler, often arriving to find marsh and scrub where he had expected verdant pastures but determined nonetheless to carve out a future for himself and his family. In a very short space of time settlements grew into towns and cities and, as elsewhere, the tokens and their issuers help us to understand the story of this remarkable progress. They were issued by importers, builders, general stores, grocers, drapers and outfitters and others who collectively provided the vital needs of the growing settlements. Other needs (perhaps less vital) were met by such as wine and spirit merchants and even by a pawnbroker who issued a token in Auckland. The earliest New Zealand tokens are dated 1857 and the latest 1881. For much of that time they were a significant part of the small change in circulation but their usefulness was gradually phased out by increasing imports of the new bronze coin of the realm. In New Zealand the United Kingdom Order in Council and Proclamation of 1st August 1896, which applied to all the Australasian colonies, was published on 12th November. The Colonial Secretary had to remind the Governor that a local Proclamation was necessary to bring it into force and this was done in March 1897. Only coins struck at the Royal Mint and gold from the branch mints could now be made or issued *as a coin or a token for money*.

---

34 See Chapter fourteen for "Dominion status".
35 11 Vict. 1847. 16.

EXAMPLES OF NEW ZEALAND TOKENS

Auckland pennies, c. 1857.

Christchurch penny 1875.

Dunedin and Otago penny 1857.

New Plymouth penny.

In 1873 the Colonial Treasurer in Wellington wrote to New Zealand's Agent General in London asking him to find out if there would be any objections to the establishment of a mint in New Zealand. There was a growing need for silver coins for domestic use but also for use in the Pacific Islands who drew their requirements from the Australasian colonies. Also much of the copper coin in circulation was in the form of private tokens. A mint in New Zealand could solve both these problems by producing the silver and copper (or bronze) coins required. The Agent General was also asked to look into the costs of machinery and of coining to see if the enterprise was worth while. The response from the British Government was not favourable. There were already two branches of the Royal Mint in Australasia (at Sydney and Melbourne) and although the purpose of these was only to strike gold the Lords of the Treasury felt that for the time being there was no need for a third mint in the region. The matter was dropped and New Zealand continued to use United Kingdom coins for many years. It was only when the British and New Zealand pounds parted company in the turmoil of the 1930s that change finally came about. The circumstances of the day led to a great shortage of silver coin and it was at last decided that New Zealand would follow the example of Australia and others by taking full responsibility for her own coinage.

The Coinage Act 1933[36] allowed for the issue of silver coins of six denominations at the same weight and size as their British counterparts. They were to have a millesimal fineness of 500 in line with the current British coins rather than the sterling fineness still in use in Australia. The denominations listed in the schedule to the Act were the crown (5/-), half-crown (2/6d), florin (2/-), shilling, sixpence and threepence. British gold coins had unlimited legal tender under the Act but since 1914 these had been largely replaced with bank notes and in fact New Zealand had already come off the gold standard at the same time as the United Kingdom in September 1931.

The first silver coins in all denominations except the crown are dated 1933 and were struck at the Royal Mint. In 1935 a crown completed the silver series although this was struck in very small quantities and can not be considered a currency coin. It had a commemorative reverse celebrating the Treaty of Waitangi and was sold by the banks at 7/6d. The Act also allowed for British coins (other than gold coins) to lose their legal tender status by Proclamation and under this provision British silver coins were demonetized on 1st February 1935.

The Act further allowed for the subsequent issue of bronze or cupro-nickel coins by proclamation. It was uncertain which metal would best suit the coins of lowest denomination but, as supplies of imperial bronze coins continued to be adequate, there was no urgent need for them. In 1939 though it was decided to complete the whole range of denominations by introducing New Zealand pennies and halfpennies of distinctive design and these were to be struck in bronze at the same weight and size as the imperial coins. The first New Zealand bronze coins were dated 1940.

That same year was the centenary of the signing of the Treaty of Waitangi and a commemorative half-crown was issued to celebrate this. Unlike the "Waitangi crown" of 1935 this was struck in large quantities and went fully into circulation.

The British silver coinage was reduced to cupro-nickel in 1947 and New Zealand followed suit.[37] Nevertheless a small issue of crowns was made in 1949 at the old millesimal fineness of 500 to commemorate the proposed visit of George VI. A crown was again issued (in cupro-nickel) for the coronation of Elizabeth II in 1953.

As in Australia discussion on decimalization began in 1959 and New Zealand announced in 1963 that she would move to a decimal system of currency. The Decimal Currency Act 1964 made the necessary provisions, the unit of currency being the New Zealand dollar equivalent to ten shillings of the old money. Decimal coins first appeared in circulation on 10th July 1967.

---

36 *24 Geo V. 1933. 12.*
37 *Section 31 of the Finance Act 1947 amended the 1933 Coinage Act so that the new "cupro-nickel" coins, like the silver they replaced, were legal tender up to forty shillings.*

NEW ZEALAND COINS.

Half-crown 1933.

George VI penny 1942. George VI halfpenny 1942.

Cupro-nickel half-crown 1951.

Elizabeth II shilling 1965.

Penny 1964. Halfpenny 1964.

The first European contacts with **Fiji** were somewhat similar to those with New Zealand. Discovered and largely ignored by the Dutch the first European traders came mainly from New South Wales. They found they could buy bêche de mer and sandalwood that would sell in China and from the 1820s these traders, their agents and storekeepers began to settle. To avoid any problems with the East India Company's remaining monopoly of British trade United States citizens were often partners in these ventures and they too formed a presence in Fiji. By 1835 missionaries were also active. Tribal conflict was rife but in 1853 the Ratu Thakombau[38] united many of the tribes under his leadership and styled himself the King of all Fiji. The next year he was converted to Christianity.

The main European presence in Fiji in the mid 19th century was British but, as French claims began to be made in the South Pacific, it was obvious that the region was not automatically a British preserve. For their security the Australasian colonies would have liked Britain to have a stronger presence in the region. This was a period in which Britain was reluctant to assume any further colonial commitments but because of these concerns the annexation of Fiji began to be considered and a Consul was appointed in 1857. William Thomas Pritchard had been serving as Acting Consul in Samoa and arrived to take up his post at Levuka, Fiji's main port, in September 1858. In his own words he was given no instructions from the Foreign Office on how best to advance British interests other than their assumption that his experience in Samoa would stand him in good stead.[39] Shortly after his appointment an American warship arrived off Fiji to demand payment of debts admitted by the King of Fiji as due to United States citizens. The King agreed to make these payments by October 1859 but, aware that he would be unable to raise the $45,000 due, discussed the problem with Pritchard. The Consul suggested that Britain could settle the debt in return for grants of land and cession of the Fiji Islands to Queen Victoria all of which was agreed by Thakombau on 12th October 1858.

Pritchard immediately set off for London with the agreement in his pocket and the details of his trip are indicative of the problems of communication at that time. He travelled by mission schooner to Sydney from where he took the mail steamer to Suez via Ceylon and Aden. From Suez he travelled by rail to Alexandria and took a steamer to Malta. Another steamer took him to Marseilles from where he travelled by rail to Calais via Dijon and Paris. A ferry took him to Dover and a train to London Bridge station. After some months in London during which he was attached to the Foreign Office he was sent back to Fiji informed only that the cession was under consideration. Arriving back in November 1859 he found Thakombau in great difficulty maintaining his position. As the man on the spot Pritchard threw his considerable influence behind the King and in December 1859 had the cession ratified by the leading chiefs. In effect he assumed control, hoping that formal agreement of cession was on the way. He was concerned that the Americans would demand territorial concessions if their debt was not paid. After lengthy consideration though the British Government reached the conclusion that King Thakombau had not had the right to make the cession. It was decided to reject it and this was announced in Fiji in July 1862. For his pains Pritchard was removed from office in 1863 and British authority in Fiji was sorely dented. Nevertheless expectation of the cession had encouraged more settlers and during the 1860s cotton production began on a large scale. By 1870 Thakombau's American debt had been paid as part of a complex deal with a company based in Melbourne but as long as Fiji remained independent little control could be exercised over a European population that had increased to about 2,500.

---

38 Also spelt Cakobau. The title "Ratu" indicated Chiefly rank.
39 W.T.Pritchard, "Polynesian Reminiscences, or Life in the Pacific Islands", 1866.

Although Britain had rejected cession the Fiji islands were of increasing commercial significance and their position, between America and Australia, also gave them a strategic importance. European activity now included the unregulated import of labour to work the cotton plantations which was considered nothing short of slaving by the humanitarian movement at home. It was difficult to see how these concerns could be addressed by Britain without some sort of control over Fiji. Although the Colonial Office was still reluctant to take responsibility there were proposals in the early 1870s that Fiji should be annexed by one of the Australian colonies. While this was being considered a constitutional monarchy with a government dominated by European settlers was set up in Fiji under King Thakombau. By the end of 1871 the British Government had given this monarchy *de facto* recognition but this was not a permanent solution. Formal *de jure* recognition could only be considered if Fiji adopted effective labour laws to control imported labour and if its government was acceptable throughout the islands. By 1873 it was clear that Britain would have to decide between formal recognition of Thakombau's government and taking direct control. Annexation could only be justified by the full agreement of the people of Fiji.

Commodore Goodenough, on his way out to take command of the Australasian Squadron, and Edgar Layard, the new Consul for Fiji, were commissioned to inquire and report on what should be done. Goodenough arrived first and immediately formed the opinion that annexation was the only way forward. Layard arrived in January 1874 and agreed. It was clear that the settlers were in favour of annexation so Goodenough and Layard set about obtaining the agreement of the King and the Chiefs. At first they proved reluctant to agree but on 20th March 1874 Thakombau announced that he and the Chiefs were in favour. The offer of cession was accepted by Goodenough the next day and he at once made arrangements for an interim government. In accepting the cession Goodenough and Layard had acted well beyond their instructions but after examining and considering their report the situation was accepted by the British Government. The Governor of New South Wales was sent to Fiji to finalize arrangements and the Deed of Cession was signed on 30th September. Fiji was proclaimed a Crown colony on 10th October 1874.

Cotton growing in Fiji declined after prices slumped in 1870 but sugar soon took its place as the main product of the islands. The Colonial Sugar Refining Company, already well established in Australia, began operations in Fiji in 1880 bringing much needed experience and resources. Indentured labour began to be imported from India in 1879 to work the Fijian plantations and by the time the last group arrived on the S.S. "Sutlej" in November 1916 a total of more than 60,000 had gone to Fiji. Many indentured labourers opted to stay as settlers or traders after their time had expired and eventually persons of Indian extraction formed a major part of Fiji's population.

The British authorities soon decided that the administration should be shifted from Levuka to a more central site at Suva and this move was completed in 1882.

Fiji was governed indirectly through the provincial chiefs. From 1904 the Legislative Council became partly elective, providing some limited representation but Fiji remained a Crown colony until independence in 1970.

When Fiji became a Crown colony in 1874 the Laws, Acts and Statutes in force in New South Wales were adopted. The currency was therefore sterling with a legal tender limit of forty shillings for the silver coins. There was no indigenous coinage in Fiji at the time and a Proclamation of October 1875 gave sterling equivalents to the various coins that were presumably in most common use. The American dollar was rated at 3/6d, the Chilean thaler at 3/-, the French "thaler" (presumably the five francs) also at 3/-, the German thaler at 2/3d and the Bolivian half dollar at 1/3d. These coins would be accepted by the Colonial Government at the stated rates until 31st December 1875 after which no foreign coins of any denomination would be received. British silver soon became the main coinage in circulation. In 1881 the United Kingdom Coinage Act 1870 was formally applied to Fiji where it was proclaimed in March 1882.[40]

For many years British sterling coins provided the metallic currency of Fiji together with their Australian equivalents after that coinage was introduced in 1910. In 1933 the Fiji pound was devalued to bring it in line with the current rate for the New Zealand pound. It therefore lost parity with sterling and a separate Fiji coinage was introduced in 1934. The silver denominations (florin, shilling and sixpence) were struck at the Royal Mint at a millesimal fineness of 500 in line with that of the recently introduced New Zealand coins. They bore the portrait of George V changing to that of George VI for the 1937 coins. The penny and halfpenny denominations were struck in cupro-nickel and had central holes which precluded the use of the royal portrait. Some of the 1936 pennies are in the name of Edward VIII. The coins of 1942 and 1943 were struck in the San Francisco Mint, the silver coins at the enhanced millesimal fineness of 900 (which was the United States standard for silver coin) and the penny and halfpenny in brass. In 1947 a twelve sided threepence denomination in nickel-brass similar to those of the United Kingdom was introduced. After the Second World War the three larger denominations were not struck for some years. When they reappeared (the sixpence in 1953, the florin and the shilling in 1957) they were struck in cupro-nickel and bore the portrait of Elizabeth II. The halfpenny was last struck in 1954. A decimal coinage with 100 cents to the Fiji dollar was introduced in January 1969, the dollar being equivalent to ten old shillings.

FIJI

Florin 1934.

Cupro-nickel penny 1936 (Edward VIII)

George VI shilling 1943.

Nickel-brass threepence 1950.

Elizabeth II florin 1964.

---

40 R. Chalmers, "A History of Currency in the British Colonies", 1893.

The Treaty of London of 1824 (see Chapter twelve) defined British and Dutch interests in the East but **New Guinea** offered little in trade and was not in contention. It was though in the Dutch sphere of influence being at the eastern extremity of their activity in the East Indies. In 1828, for clarity, they made formal claim to the western part of the island up to 141° E. There was no claim from any quarter to the part of the island east of that meridian. New Guinea's proximity to Australia and the fact that in 1880 its eastern part was still unclaimed by any major Power was a constant concern for the British colonies that lay to the south. French and German activity was of particular concern but the British Government, having recently annexed Fiji, had little stomach for further responsibility in the region and was loathe to intervene. It was an Australian problem and it was Queensland that decided to address it.

In 1883 the Premier of Queensland instructed the resident magistrate of Thursday Island (which lies in the Torres Strait) to proceed to New Guinea and annex everything not previously claimed by the Dutch in the name of Queen Victoria. This he duly did, raising the Union Flag at Port Moresby and claiming everything between 141°E and 155°E including adjacent islands. When they were informed of this the Home Government disallowed the annexation but after some discussion it was agreed that New Guinea should become a Protectorate provided the Australian colonies would foot the bill. The Protectorate was formally declared on 6th November 1884 but just a few days earlier a German claim had been made on the north coast. This resulted in a New Guinea divided between three administrations. The Dutch held the west, the Germans the north east and the British the south eastern part of the island. A Special Commissioner was appointed to manage the British portion.

Full annexation as part of Her Majesty's Dominions took place in 1888 and the possession was named British New Guinea. An Administrator (later termed Lieutenant-Governor) replaced the Special Commissioner. Although appointed by the British Government he reported to the Governor of Queensland who in turn reported to London. In 1902 letters patent placed British New Guinea under the authority of the newly federated Commonwealth of Australia to take effect as soon as laws had been made for its government. This took some years to complete but the Papua Act 1905 (proclaimed on 1st September 1906) transferred full responsibility for British New Guinea to Australia and renamed it the Territory of Papua. Although under Australian administration Papua remained *de jure* a British possession.

In September 1914, shortly after the outbreak of the First World War, Australian forces took German New Guinea and for the rest of the war maintained a military administration. After the war it was granted to Australia under a League of Nations Mandate of December 1920 and civil administration began under that Mandate in May 1921.[41] The whole eastern part of the island was then administered by Australia as the dual "Territories of Papua and New Guinea" until the Japanese invasion of 1942. After the Second World War the Territory of Papua was still legally a possession of the Crown under Australian administration. The old mandated territory (ex German New Guinea) became the United Nations Trust Territory of New Guinea still also under Australian administration. The Papua and New Guinea Act 1949 arranged for both of these to be governed in an administrative union to be called the "Territory of Papua and New Guinea". Self government was gradually introduced and in 1973 the name of these combined territories became simply "Papua New Guinea". This name was retained at independence in 1975.

---

41 The New Guinea Act 1920 came into force 9th May 1921. For the system of League of Nations Mandates and the later United Nations Trusteeships see Chapter fourteen.

British coins formed the main circulation in British New Guinea (Papua) until the Currency Ordinance, 1911 declared that any coins that were legal tender in the Commonwealth of Australia would be legal tender also in the Territory of Papua. This allowed the new Australian coinage which had begun in 1910 to circulate alongside British coins as was the case in Australia. In Papua the Australian coins soon predominated.

The coins in use in German New Guinea were gradually replaced by Australian coins after the formal assumption of the mandate in May 1921. From 1929 to 1945 a distinct coinage was produced by the Australian authorities with the legend **TERRITORY OF NEW GUINEA**. The coinage began with cupro-nickel pennies and halfpennies dated 1929 and this was in fact the only date for the halfpenny. These cupro-nickel pieces were so similar in size to the Australian shilling and sixpence that, even though they had a central hole, they could be passed in rolls of those coins. Most of them were therefore melted and from 1936 the penny was struck in bronze. In 1935 a silver shilling was introduced and cupro-nickel sixpences and threepences followed. All these coins were struck at the Melbourne Mint and all have a central hole for ease of carriage by those without pockets. The three higher denominations have the unusual distinction of being the only coins of those values struck for any of the British overseas territories with a central hole. The silver content of the shilling matched the sterling fineness of 925 in use in Australia at this time although the coin is slightly lighter than the Australian shilling because of its central hole. While these coins were intended specifically for the Territory of New Guinea there is no reason to believe that they did not also circulate in the Territory of Papua.

After this brief but interesting coinage the normal currency of Australia was in use throughout Papua and New Guinea until independence.

NEW GUINEA

Shilling 1945.   Bronze penny 1936.

British subjects roving beyond New South Wales in the 19th century did not limit their activities to New Zealand, Fiji and the larger islands. Their trade and maritime ventures led them to almost every shore in the Pacific where, beyond the jurisdiction of the colonies, there was little control or restraint. In an attempt to improve this, the Foreign Office began to appoint Consuls to the larger islands such as Hawaii, Tahiti and Samoa from the 1820s and 1830s. They were recruited from the leading members of the local British community and their role was to promote friendly relations with the islanders and encourage British trade. They would also exercise what control they could over their countrymen but they had no resources to police them and perhaps little inclination to do so. Consuls were not appointed to the smaller islands where there was no established form of government with whom to confer. For most of the region the only effective British influence was therefore the occasional visit of a Royal Navy ship. By the 1830s there were regular cruises to the islands thought most in need of a visit but the commanders of these ships were given little detailed instruction by the Admiralty on how they should handle matters. They were told simply to impress the islanders with the power and friendly disposition of the British nation, to listen carefully to

British consuls and missionaries and to repress any tendency to usurp the rights of local chiefs. Operating beyond British jurisdiction any military action they took to protect British subjects would be an act of war. Unofficially the commanders of these ships took on the role of visiting magistrates and by and large settled disputes in an even handed manner, rarely using the force at their disposal when urged to do so by settlers, consuls and even missionaries. Acts of war were undertaken in retaliation for acts against British subjects rather than on request. Their reports often find fault with their countrymen and on occasion British subjects were placed under restraint and taken to Sydney. The Admiralty discouraged deportation as being of doubtful legality but in some cases there was no effective alternative.

By the mid 19th century the old problems of lawlessness and unethical trade caused by British subjects began to be overshadowed by the unregulated trade in native labour known as "blackbirding". Much of this trade was in British registered ships and supplied labour wherever it was required including the sugar plantations of Queensland and the cotton plantations of Fiji. It became obvious that some of the islanders transported in this way were less than willing and the British Government was obliged to act.

The Pacific Islanders Protection Act 1872[42] and subsequent legislation did not seek to end the traffic but placed it under strict regulation. Britain could of course lay down the rules for British colonies and British ships but otherwise, as had been the case in West Africa, she had no authority to do so. In most of the islands she had no control and ships could easily be transferred to other flags. The Act was therefore amended in 1875 in an attempt to improve its effectiveness. The new Act[43] allowed for the appointment of a High Commissioner for the region with a court of justice and extra territorial authority over British subjects allowing for punishment and deportation. The first appointment under the authority of this Act was made by Order in Council in 1877 when the Governor of Fiji became also High Commissioner (and Consul-General) for the Western Pacific. The post of High Commissioner was held *ex officio* by the Governors of Fiji until 1952 when it passed to the Governors of the Solomon Islands.

The authority of the High Commissioner extended to all the islands of the Western Pacific that were not in British hands or in the hands of any other civilized Power. The list of islands given in the Order in Council is a long one and, to ensure that nothing had been forgotten, finishes with the all embracing "other islands". It was not long though before the deliberations of the Berlin Conference of 1884-1885 curtailed this very broad approach. The purpose of the Conference was to bring some order to the division of Africa but it defined the rules under which the Powers could lay claim to territories. These were based on effective occupation and applied to the Pacific as much as to Africa. The claims of other nations already active in the region could not be questioned and these included France, the United States and, more recently, Germany. In April 1886 a Declaration between the governments of Britain and Germany defined their relevant spheres of interest. A demarcation line ran generally north eastwards from the Solomon Islands with the German sphere to the north and west, the British sphere to the south and east. Samoa, Tonga and Niue which all fell in the British sphere were to remain neutral as more than one Power was present. Nothing in the exclusive hands of any other civilized Power was to be claimed.

The High Commission had not been as effective as had been hoped in curbing labour trafficking and now international agreements were restricting British activity. Other nations were making claims and British concerns for the security of the region were added to those of the Australasian colonies. The solution to all of these problems was obvious. If law and order was to be maintained and if all the unclaimed islands were not to fall into the hands of others Britain would have to make formal claims to some of them.

---

42 *35 & 36 Vict. c. 19. Sometimes referred to as "The Kidnapping Act".*
43 *The Pacific Islanders Protection Act 1875, 38 & 39 Vict. c. 51.*

The **New Hebrides** (modern "Vanuatu") had been declared neutral by Britain and France in 1878. Britain would have been happy to leave these islands to France but pressure from the Australian colonies led instead to the setting up of an "Anglo-French Joint Naval Commission" in 1887. Naval Officers from both countries were appointed to protect the interests of British and French nationals in the islands. Civilian Residents were appointed by both Powers in 1902 and the New Hebrides Convention, ratified in London in 1906, created the Anglo-French Condominium that existed until independence in 1980.

Labour troubles in the **Gilbert and Ellice Islands** led to a protectorate being established over them in 1892 and the subsequent appointment of a Resident Commissioner. **Ocean Island,** to the west of the Gilberts, was unclaimed and of little interest to anyone until rich deposits of phosphate were discovered there by the Pacific Islands Company[44] in 1900. Knowing the enormous importance of the find, the Company immediately raised the Union Flag and pressed for official recognition. Ocean Island was formally included in the Gilbert and Ellis Islands Protectorate in September 1901.

Labour problems and fear of French annexation led to a protectorate being declared over the southern **Solomon Islands** in 1893. The Germans had already declared a protectorate over the northern Solomons but all of those south east of Bougainville joined the British Solomon Islands Protectorate as part of an 1899 agreement with Germany that recognized her claims in Western Samoa and elsewhere.

Tonga signed treaties of friendship with Germany in 1876 and with Britain in 1879. Germany gave up all claims in the Tonga group in 1899 (as part of the agreement on Western Samoa) and recognized Britain's position. Although it became a British protected state in 1900 Tonga was never annexed as a Crown colony and would retain her constitutional monarchy until and after independence in 1970.

Pitcairn Island lay far to the east of the main areas of concern and had been in the hands of British subjects for many years. The well known mutiny in which Captain Bligh was cast adrift from HMS "Bounty" occurred off Tahiti in 1789. Some of the mutineers returned to Tahiti and were later apprehended but nine of them, with Tahitian wives and a number of servants sailed the ship to Pitcairn arriving early in 1790. The island was uninhabited and here they remained undisturbed for nearly twenty five years. Two Royal Navy ships came across the settlement by chance in 1814, their commanders being astonished at finding an English speaking god-fearing "colony" of some forty six persons. The sole surviving mutineer was found to be a venerable old man exercising a paternal authority and it was wisely decided not to arrest him for his ancient crime. Once the settlement had been discovered ships began to call more frequently and in 1838 Captain Elliot of HMS "Fly" drew up a constitution for the island making the magistrate answerable to the Queen and giving them a Union Flag. His intention was simply to give this small community some protection from visiting ships but it is from that time that the islanders claim to have been a formal part of the British Empire. A loyal address in July 1853 accompanied by a gift of local craft work did not result in a requested document to confirm Pitcairn as a British colony. It did though draw thanks from Queen Victoria to *"her subjects on Pitcairn Island"* and subsequent events confirmed that Britain considered herself fully responsible for the settlement. There was no doubt that Pitcairn was a British colony under the British Settlements Act 1887.

Requests came from the **Cook Islands** and from **Niue** for British protection partly because of fears of French activity. Under pressure from New Zealand Britain finally agreed and declared a protectorate over the Cook Islands in 1888 and over Niue in 1900. New Zealand though was encouraged to take responsibility for these territories. A United Kingdom Order in Council of 13th May 1901 extended the limits of New Zealand to include the Cook Islands

---

44 *This was soon renamed the Pacific Phosphate Company and gained mining concessions in German Nauru in 1906.*

and Niue and a Proclamation by the Governor of New Zealand brought this into effect on 11th June.

Britain's main acquisitions in the Pacific had now been completed and the self governing colonies had taken responsibility for some of them (Papua, Cook Islands, etc). There was though other work to do. At the Colonial Conference of 1887 the construction of the last major link in the "All Red Line" (Chapter six) was agreed. This was the trans-Pacific section of the imperial cable system from Canada to Australia and if this was to be properly safeguarded various islands along its route would have to be secured.

The cable would run through a relay station on **Fanning Island**, south of Hawaii, and this was formally annexed in March 1888. Neighbouring **Washington Island** was annexed in 1889. These were part of the Line Islands, so named because they straddle the equator, and so important was the security of the cable that Britain formally annexed most of them together with the **Phoenix** and **Union Islands** to the south west. With these annexations complete Britain controlled a scatter of islands running from Fanning Island to Fiji from where the cable would extend to Australia and New Zealand. These annexations were completed by 1892 and the cable was fully operational late in 1902.

It only remained now for Britain to "tidy up" her administrative arrangements in the Pacific. The Gilbert and Ellice Islands became a Crown colony by Order in Council of November 1915 which came into force on 12th January 1916. Over the years several other islands would be added to this administration for the sake of convenience rather than proximity. Ocean Island, Fanning Island, Washington Island and the Union Islands (modern Tokelau) were added in 1916.[45] **Christmas Island** (one of the Line Islands) was added in 1919 and the Phoenix Islands in 1937.

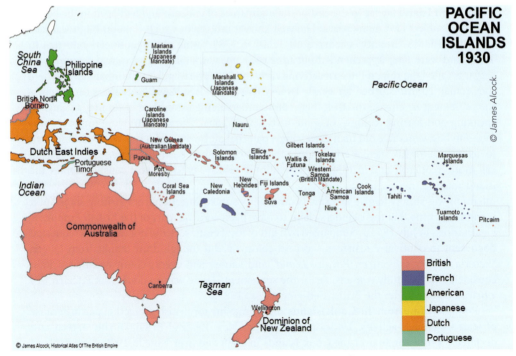

Islands and groups in the South Pacific

---

[45] *The Union Islands were transferred from the Gilbert and Ellice Islands Colony to New Zealand in 1926.*

Before European contacts the economies of the Pacific islands were uncomplicated and based on subsistence and barter. The currency of the first traders was mainly firearms and rum but as business became established coins of various currencies came into use. Although Pitcairn is not a typical Pacific Island its records clearly show that in the early years coins were not plentiful and that barter was still common. The laws of the island provided for fines in dollars for some offences but in shillings for losing the public anvil and sledgehammer. Schooling was to be paid for at the rate of one shilling a month but the schoolmaster was usually paid in food at specific equivalents or in labour at the rate of two shillings per day. Passing ships seeking supplies and fresh water found that clothing and tools, as well as money, were always acceptable in exchange.[46]

Many of the other islands had considerably more trade than Pitcairn and coin use steadily increased. Where British administrations were established sterling became the official currency and British coins came into use. Eventually these were supplemented by the Australian issues which began in 1910. This situation remained unchanged until the upsets of the 1930s altered the rates of the Australian, New Zealand and Fiji pounds against sterling and against each other. There was then some doubt as to which rate should apply in some of the smaller colonies and protectorates.

The territories under the direct jurisdiction of New Zealand were automatically on the New Zealand pound. These included the Cook Islands, Niue and the Union Islands but Western Samoa which had been taken over as a League of Nations mandate after the First World War would also use the New Zealand pound. In the same way the Australian pound was the rate in Papua and New Guinea. It may therefore have seemed obvious that the islands under British administration should have retained the sterling rate but, as much of their business was in the hands of Australian banks, it was decided that all of them except Pitcairn should use the Australian rate. Pitcairn was to have the New Zealand rate.

The result of all this was that Australian and New Zealand coins soon predominated and decimalization in the islands followed that of Australia (1966) and New Zealand (1967). None of these islands had coins of their own before that time but a small issue of tokens on the eastern limits of British activity deserves mention.

Long before the Pacific cable highlighted the importance of the Line Islands to Britain there had been British activity and development on both Fanning and Washington Islands. By 1864 the export of guano and coconut products was in the hands of a partnership formed by the Scotsman William Greig and the American George Bicknell. The necessary workforce was imported mainly from the Cook Islands. Both partners died in the 1890s leaving their estates to their children. Eventually their interests were sold on and the new owner formed Fanning Island, Limited in about 1907.

Aluminium tokens are known in four denominations (dollar, 50 cents, 25 cents and 12½ cents) with the legend WASHINGTON & FANNING ISLANDS CHECK. These were probably used to pay imported labour during their tour of duty and perhaps also for use in company stores. They are undated but it was not until the late 1880s that aluminium was produced cheaply enough for such a use. As they bear no reference to Fanning Island, Limited they probably pre-date the founding of that company.

---

46 *This information comes from Walter Brodie, "Pitcairn's Island and the Islanders in 1850".*

WASHINGTON AND FANNING ISLANDS

Aluminium dollar check.

We have now completed our geographical tour of the British world for the period from Waterloo to the First World War and looked at the coins region by region until independence or decimalization. We can now move to our concluding chapter which will look briefly at the 20th century and decolonization.

14

Climax and Decolonization

THE extent and form of the Empire changed little in the years before the First World War. As the light of the sun followed its daily course around the world it always shone on some part of Britain's far flung possessions and these were still protected by the most powerful navy in the world. The Empire though had reached its defensive climax and there were concerns in some quarters about its security and sustainability. Two World Wars in the space of just thirty one years would show that those concerns were valid. The Empire survived that period and increased in size but was afterwards set on a course that could hardly have been imagined in 1914.

By the end of the 19th century the self governing colonies were responsible for their own internal defence and were beginning to share the burden of increasing naval costs. There was now a very big difference between the Crown colonies (many of which had been obtained by conquest rather than settlement) and the self governing colonies which were becoming partners in Empire. This was reflected in the fact that only the self governing colonies participated in the Colonial Conferences which began in 1887. At the fifth Colonial Conference in 1907 it was agreed that the somewhat grander title of "Imperial Conference" was more appropriate and that the self governing colonies should be recognized as something more than just "colonies". They too should have a new title. The colonies that attended in 1907 were the Dominion of Canada, the Commonwealth of Australia, New Zealand, Newfoundland, Cape Colony and Natal. The two federated colonies (Canada and Australia) already had prestigious titles and shortly after the Conference New Zealand and Newfoundland were granted the title of "Dominion". In 1910 the newly formed Union of South Africa was also classed as a Dominion. Although there was now a new class of colony the new title did not immediately change their legal status (that would come after the First World War) but it did recognize their increasing role in Imperial affairs. When Canada, Australia, New Zealand and Newfoundland were recognized as Dominions in 1907 a Dominions Department was established within the Colonial Office but there would be no separate Dominions Office until 1925.

In 1914 Britain was considered to be the wealthiest and most powerful nation in the world and was a centre of world banking. With huge reserves of coal and her manufacturing industries she conducted a large proportion of global trade and nearly half the world's merchant shipping was British owned. She controlled an Empire covering perhaps a fifth of the world's land surface. Britain considered herself to be the centre of that Empire and the most important part of it. She had though neglected her agricultural industries in favour of manufacturing and free trade. The Empire certainly needed Britain for its finance, its supply and its defence but it was the Empire that fed Britain, bought much of her manufactures and provided investment opportunities. The First World War would clearly demonstrate the growing importance of the Empire to the mother country.

On 4th August 1914 Britain declared war on Germany (Chapter seven) and the whole of the Empire, including British India, was at war. Almost immediately large numbers of troops and the funding to support them were committed by the Dominions. India supported a huge number of British and Indian troops. British regiments in India could be sent elsewhere while the Indian Army not only covered for them but also sent units to serve overseas. The Government of British India was cautious in its imperial commitments fearing a backlash from political groups seeking more self determination. In the event the leaders of the Indian National Congress and other groups proved very supportive of the British war effort hoping, rightly, that this would further their cause. French Canadians and Afrikaners in South Africa had particular concerns but by and large the men, materials and money of the Empire were mobilized in support of the mother country without demur. France and Russia were already at war with Germany and further support came from Japan when she declared war on Germany on 23rd August in accordance with the Anglo-Japanese Alliance of 1902. The Triple Alliance of Germany, Austria-Hungary and Italy was seen by the Italians as defensive only. They therefore did not enter the war in August 1914 but in May 1915, convinced of the advantages of doing so, entered the war on the side of the Allies instead. Following secret agreements the Ottoman Empire (Turkey) entered the war on the side of the Central Powers and on November 5th 1914 Britain and France declared war on Turkey. Russia had already done so three days earlier. The United States was loathe to involve herself in Europe but the indiscriminate nature of the submarine war eventually persuaded her to join the Allies against Germany in April 1917. She did not though become involved in the war on Turkey.

Germany's colonial possessions in Africa and the Pacific were capable of supporting naval operations and were a threat to British commerce. Most of them were taken by allied forces in the early stages of the war and then administered by the occupying Power. Only in German East Africa did resistance continue until the general armistice of 1918. After the war the Treaty of Versailles granted all Germany's colonies to the victors.[1] In West Africa the administrations of both Togoland and Kamerun (Cameroon) had been divided between Britain and France whose forces had taken them and these divisions continued after the war. British Togoland was formally placed under British control as a League of Nations mandate in 1922 and was administered as part of the adjoining Gold Coast. The British Cameroons were similarly administered from Nigeria. South West Africa had been taken by South African forces in 1915 and was granted to the Union of South Africa after the war. Most of German East Africa went to Britain to become Tanganyika although some portions went to Belgium and Portugal. In the Pacific, German Samoa was granted to New Zealand whose forces had taken it at the beginning of the war. German New Guinea was granted to Australia. The Australian force that took it had also taken the German island of Nauru, an island rich in phosphates which had been exploited by a British company since 1906. Nauru would be administered by Australia after the war with the United Kingdom and New Zealand as co-trustees. The German islands north of the equator (the Marshall Islands, the Caroline Islands

---

1 *The armistice with Germany was signed on 11th November 1918 in a railway carriage near Compiègne in northern France. The Peace Conference opened in Paris on 18th January 1919 and after much negotiation a peace treaty with Germany was signed at Versailles on 28th June 1919. Separate treaties were signed later with Austria (at Saint-Germain), Bulgaria (at Neuilly), Hungary (at Trianon) and Turkey (at Sèvres).*

and the Mariana Islands) were all granted to Japan although Australia and New Zealand viewed this with some concern.

The First World War thus led to an increase in British colonial territory in Africa and the Pacific, some of it indirectly through the acquisitions made by Australia, New Zealand and the Union of South Africa. The world though was a changed place. For some years liberal thinking had been questioning the morality and purpose of imperialism and the United States, whose entry into the war had been a deciding factor in its outcome, had always opposed the very concept of colonialism. She was now unquestionably a powerful nation and ranked with Britain and France in the Peace negotiations in Paris. The position adopted by President Woodrow Wilson was that old fashioned imperialism would always be a threat to world peace. A League of Nations should be formed whose purpose was to remove the threat of future wars through open agreements, free trade, diplomacy and self determination. In the spirit of the day and in an atmosphere of great hope for the future the formation of such a League was the mainspring of Wilson's plan. The other Powers at the Peace Conference were deeply sceptical but were coerced into accepting it by the world's new economic giant. The League of Nations was set up as part of the Versailles Treaty. In line with Wilson's thinking Article XXII of the League's Covenant provided that the colonies reassigned at Versailles would be administered in trust by colonial Powers. They would steer them towards independence where possible and have specific responsibility for the wellbeing and progress of peoples not yet able to stand by themselves.

The grants made by the Treaty of Versailles were thus conditional. The ex German colonies were not to be absolute possessions but "mandates" under League of Nations supervision. Ironically France and the British Empire were founding members of the League of Nations but President Wilson was unable to persuade the United States Senate that it was in America's interest to join. In fact the Senate rejected the whole peace settlement because League membership implied a military commitment if things went wrong. The United States therefore had to make separate peace treaties with Germany, Austria and Hungary which excluded any provisions for League of Nations supervision and these were not completed until 1921.

The German Empire was not the only empire to be dismantled and redistributed as a result of the First World War. For many years the Ottoman Empire had been in decline but had been consistently supported by Britain because its existence prevented Russian expansion near the Mediterranean routes to India. The Anglo-Russian Convention of 1907 allayed those fears to some extent and when the Ottoman Empire took the side of the Central Powers the situation had changed completely. At war with Turkey, Britain had to think again about how the Suez Canal, the Persian Gulf and British India should be safeguarded. Cyprus, which had been under British administration for many years, was immediately annexed (Chapter seven) and Egypt became a British Protectorate (Chapter ten). It was also vital for the security of the whole region that the vast areas of the Middle East under Ottoman rule in 1914 should not fall into the wrong hands. Britain therefore set about securing the region through influence, intrigue and conquest.

By April 1914 the Ottoman Arabs were already planning armed revolt with the intention of establishing their independence in all the Ottoman provinces south of Turkey. This region was bordered by Persia and the Persian Gulf in the east, the Mediterranean and the Red Sea in the west and the Arabian Sea and Aden in the south. With the war under way it was in British interests to actively support such a revolt and foster friendly relations with any resulting independent Arab State. Correspondence concerning the revolt and the extent of British support took place between the British High Commissioner at Cairo (Sir Henry McMahon) and the Sharif of Mecca (Hussain bin Ali, the ruler of Hejaz) who would be the leader of the

Arab rebellion and intended nothing less than to become the Caliph of Islam in place of the existing Caliph at Istanbul. In this correspondence the High Commissioner expressed some reservations about the proposed limits of Arab independence but twenty thousand sovereigns were sent from Cairo to Mecca "*As an earnest of our intentions…*"[2] and both sides agreed that contentious matters could be re-examined after the war. When open revolt began in June 1916 there were thus one or two loose ends but the understanding was that Britain would support an independent Arab State. This allowed the Sharif (a member of the Hashemite dynasty) to declare the Hejaz independent of Ottoman rule with the expectation of greatly extending his dominion. British support for King Hussain (as he now was) and his revolt included the seconding of a young British Army officer to liaise with the Hashemite forces. His pre-war work as an archaeologist in parts of the Ottoman Empire and his understanding of the people and their language made T. E. Lawrence an ideal choice for the job. He was one of several advisors but his own exploits during the revolt, his leading role in it and his unwavering support for the promised independent Arab State would create the legend of "Lawrence of Arabia". Lawrence and King Hussain both assumed this independent State would be centred on Damascus and cover most of the region.

The British and French governments though had slightly different ideas on how the Ottoman Empire should be divided up and governed after the war. Arab independence was a major part of that plan but there were European interests in Syria and Mesopotamia (modern Iraq) that called for a more direct form of control. The Sykes-Picot Agreement of May 1916 (named after the chief negotiators) therefore decided in private that the northern Arab lands would contain areas of both British and French administration in what is today Iraq, Syria and Lebanon. Adjacent to these were large areas which would be under Arab rule but where either Britain or France would have priority of interest. It was envisaged that Palestine, with its holy places, would be under some form of international administration and neither Power would acquire territorial possessions in the Arabian Peninsula. Apart from the region of his homeland bordering the Red Sea this Anglo-French agreement therefore had little in common with the arrangement King Hussain thought he had made with Britain at about the same time.

Britain's political plans for the region were backed by military advances into Ottoman territory. From Egypt British forces fought their way into Palestine and Syria to protect the Suez Canal while forces mainly from British India fought their way into Mesopotamia to secure oil and other interests. These advances and Allied successes in Europe led to the armistice with the Ottoman Empire signed on 30th October 1918 leaving Britain in military control of much of Ottoman Arabia at the end of the war.[3] It was from this position of strength that Britain negotiated the re-allocation of the Arab provinces of the Ottoman Empire.

Discussion on the Ottoman Empire had not been completed when the Paris Peace Conference ended in January 1920. It continued in London and terms were finally agreed by the Allies at San Remo (Italy) in April. The resulting Treaty was signed by Ottoman and Allied representatives at Sèvres in August 1920.[4] As well as arranging for the reassignment of Ottoman provinces the Treaty also demanded the transfer of Turkish territory and this encouraged a nationalist movement to rise in protest. By November 1922 this movement had forced the Sultan from office before the Treaty of Sèvres had been ratified. The Allies were

---

2 *Letter from McMahon dated December 14th 1915.*
3 *The Ottoman armistice was signed on board HMS "Agamemnon" in Moudros Harbour on the Greek island of Lemnos and came into force the next day. It was not a surrender but left Britain in administrative control of the occupied Arab provinces.*
4 *The United States had not been at war with Turkey and did not take part in these later negotiations.*

compelled to renegotiate resulting in the Treaty of Lausanne in July 1923. This respected Turkey's borders and led to international recognition of the Republic of Turkey which was proclaimed on 29th October. The years of uncertainty immediately after the war together with French aspirations, British military occupation and Arab nationalism ensured that the distribution of the Ottoman Arab provinces was a rather muddled affair.

The Arab revolt had greatly assisted the British advance into the Levant. When Damascus was taken on 1st October 1918 it was arranged for Hashemite forces under the control of Prince Faisal (a son of King Hussain of the Hejaz) to raise the Arab flag before the main British force arrived. T. E. Lawrence was with the Hashemite forces and Faisal himself entered Damascus two days later. An Arab government under British protection was set up. Syria, like the Hejaz, had now been separated from the Ottoman Empire and the promised independent Arab State showed some signs of emerging. However, it was immediately made plain to Faisal that Syria was a French interest and it later became clear that there would be very little independence for the Arab State in that region. Feeling betrayed the Arab government at Damascus declared Syria to be a fully independent State in March 1920 with Faisal as its King. This led to military action by France and the expulsion of King Faisal after a reign of little more than four months. The French subsequently exercised strict control over Syria and Lebanon through a formal League of Nations mandate.

In return for a free hand in Syria the French dropped all claims in Mesopotamia which the Allies agreed would become a British mandate. When nationalist revolt made government difficult it was decided that the appointment of an Arab ruler who would work under British suzerainty would be a better option. Faisal, lately King of Syria, was therefore installed as "King of Iraq" in 1921 and Britain continued to control foreign and military policy. The nationalists reluctantly accepted this arrangement on the understanding that Britain would recommend independence at the earliest opportunity in line with Article XXII of the League of Nations Covenant. Britain retained control of Iraq until it became a fully sovereign kingdom on 3rd October 1932, still under Hashemite rule. An Anglo-Iraq treaty then allowed Britain to retain Royal Air Force bases and transit rights for her forces.

By the end of the war Britain was in military occupation of Palestine which was administered as occupied enemy territory. A High Commissioner for Palestine was appointed in July 1920 to establish civilian administration. There was little doubt that Palestine was part of the area pledged to the Arabs in the McMahon-Hussain correspondence of 1915-1916 but other considerations had arisen. For some years the Jews had been seeking a national home in Palestine and the British Government generally supported that aim. In November 1917 Lord Balfour, the Foreign Secretary, wrote to Lord Rothschild confirming British Government support for such a settlement. The letter was sent with the approval of the War Cabinet and was for the attention of the Zionist Federation. It became known as the "Balfour Declaration". British Government support was for a national home for the Jews within Palestine. A separate State was not envisaged and the Declaration made it plain that nothing should be done that would prejudice the civil and religious rights of existing non-Jewish communities. The Sykes-Picot Agreement had suggested some sort of international supervision for Palestine but as the war drew to a close Britain found herself in administrative control. It was felt that Jewish settlement could only improve the security of a sensitive area close to the Suez Canal and initially there was little Arab opposition to the plan as long as it did not interfere with their rights and freedoms. It was therefore accepted at the San Remo Conference in 1920 that the mandate for Palestine should be granted to Britain and that Britain would be obliged to manage Jewish settlement there under the terms of the Balfour Declaration. The settlement of Jews in Palestine while safeguarding the rights of the Palestinians would eventually present Britain with one of her most difficult imperial problems. In the end she was unable to solve it but in the inter-war years managed to maintain an uneasy control.

The geographical extent of Palestine was not fixed at the San Remo Conference. Some assumed that it would extend east as far as the British mandate for Mesopotamia but Britain had no intention of taking full responsibility for this vast region. She therefore decided that only the area west of the River Jordan would be under direct rule and contain the national home for the Jewish people. The area east of the Jordan would be granted to a Hashemite ruler and governed with a large measure of independence from Britain in a manner considered suitable for local conditions. In April 1921 the Emirate of Transjordan was established under Abdullah bin al-Hussain (another son of the King of Hejaz) and the Transjordan Memorandum detailing these arrangements was subsequently written into the mandate agreement. In May 1923 Britain recognized Transjordan as a State preparing for independence as set out in the League of Nations Covenant. Britain would retain overall responsibility but none of this part of the mandate would be available for Jewish settlement.

All of this had occurred before the mandate formally came into effect in September 1923 following ratification of the Treaty of Lausanne.

With sons installed in Iraq and Transjordan, King Hussain of the Hejaz felt justified in claiming to be King of all the Arabs. When the office of Caliph at Istanbul was abolished by the new Republic of Turkey in March 1924 he claimed this long coveted title as well. Hussain's claims though and problems of access to the holy places of Islam angered his neighbours in Nejd. The ruler of Nejd was Abdulaziz Ibn Saud with whom Britain had a general understanding. His claims in the Arabian Peninsula were recognized in exchange for which he respected British interests in the Persian Gulf and Iraq. In 1924 Ibn Saud's forces captured Mecca from King Hussain and moved on to capture the whole of the Hejaz. Britain would not take sides in what she considered a religious war but at the end of it recognized Ibn Saud as the legitimate ruler of Hejaz as well as Nejd. In 1932 Ibn Saud united his dominions into the Kingdom of Saudi Arabia. The holiest places of Islam thus came into the care of the Saudis and the office of Caliph lapsed. King Hussain went into exile.

Although there were present and potential problems Britain was generally content with her lot in the Middle East after the First World War. Palestine and Transjordan were British mandates and she had effective treaty arrangements with Iraq. The rise of Ibn Saud made the Hashemite rulers of Iraq and Transjordan more dependent on their British connection and Saudi Arabia had no quarrel with Britain. Although Egypt achieved independence in 1922 a substantial British military presence continued and Aden remained in British hands. The United States had not been at war with Turkey and had little to do with the Middle Eastern arrangements after the war. In the inter-war years Britain continued to be the pre-eminent western Power in the region and effectively controlled the Suez Canal, the routes to India and the oil of the Persian Gulf.

Although mandated territories were not colonies in an absolute sense Britain's responsibilities in them included a responsibility for coinage. We have seen what happened in the ex-German colonies in previous chapters. The ex-Ottoman territories already had a functioning currency and Iraq did not need a new coinage supply during the brief period of direct British administration. For **Palestine** though a new coinage was soon required. During the period of military administration the Egyptian pound and the coins described in Chapter ten came into use with the troops who came from Egypt but this was a temporary measure. In 1926 a Currency Board for Palestine was appointed to arrange the introduction and management of a new currency. It was decided that this would be based on a Palestine gold pound equivalent to the British sovereign and divided into one thousand mils. An Order in Council of February 1927 allowed for the introduction of the pound coin and for silver coins of one hundred mils and fifty mils. The Order also allowed for lower denominations as may be approved. The gold pound was never struck but the two silver denominations at a millesimal fineness of 720 were introduced in 1927 and continued to be struck until 1942. Lower denominations also came into issue in 1927. The twenty, ten and five mils were struck on holed flans in cupro-nickel with a two mils and one mil struck in bronze. From 1942-1944 the cupro-nickel denominations were struck in bronze as a wartime measure and 1944 was the last striking of the twenty mils. Cupro-nickel was re-introduced in 1946 for the ten mils and five mils but coins of that year were the last to be issued as currency before the British mandate expired. All the coins were struck at the Royal Mint to a simple design that it was hoped would offend no section of the community. Legends were in English, Arabic and Hebrew.

Because of its functional appearance this brief Palestinian coinage has often been dismissed as inartistic, unremarkable and therefore uninteresting. In fact it is a product of its time and place. Everything about it from the names of the denominations to the design features and the positioning of elements of the legend is a compromise to make it acceptable to the people who used it and the authorities who issued it. As such it is a very interesting coinage fully illustrating a difficult period of British imperial history.

PALESTINE

One hundred mils 1927.

Cupro-nickel five mils 1939.

Bronze two mills 1927.

The Peace treaties arranged after the First World War effectively redrew the political map of the world with gains to Britain in Africa, the Pacific and the Middle East. With the mandated territories the British Empire can now be said to have reached its greatest extent.

Wartime losses at sea had highlighted Britain's dependence on supplies of colonial food and materials. This and the support received during the war led to a reappraisal of how Britain viewed her colonial possessions. The Empire and the investment in it would materially aid financial recovery after the war was over and it was becoming plain that Britain needed her Empire at least as much as the Empire needed Britain.

The contribution that the Empire was making to the war effort was formally recognized in 1917 when the Dominion Prime Ministers and representatives from India were invited to join special sessions of the War Cabinet. The War Cabinet was a permanent body but these special sessions were held in conjunction with the Imperial Conference of that year. These enlarged sessions were known as "The Imperial War Cabinet" and the Imperial Conferences of 1917 and 1918 are usually referred to as "Imperial War Conferences". Their purpose was to involve the Empire (or at least the Dominions and India) in discussions on urgent questions affecting the war and the possible conditions for peace. Until this time the Dominions (like other colonies) had no say in their foreign affairs but at the 1917 Conference it was resolved that future constitutional arrangements should be *"based on a full recognition of the Dominions as autonomous nations of an Imperial Commonwealth, and of India as an important portion of the same"*. The Dominions and India should have *"the right... to an adequate voice in foreign policy and in foreign relations"*. It was also resolved that *"The time has arrived when all possible encouragement should be given to the development of Imperial resources, and especially to making the Empire independent of other countries in respect of food supplies, raw materials, and essential industries."*[5]

The term "Commonwealth" to refer to the Empire had been used before but what was being suggested here was literally a system of "common wealth" to protect the essential needs of the Empire. This was almost reminiscent of the good old days of tobacco, sugar and rum but in 1917 any form of trade protection conflicted sharply with Britain's well-established views on free trade. Circumstances though would soon combine to alter those views.

When war had begun in Europe in 1914 international trade and finance had momentarily ceased to function. The Government was deeply concerned about this aspect of the war because Britain's power depended on her dominance of trade and her financial resources as much as on her military and naval strengths. Her gold reserves had to be protected but to abandon the free market in gold would seriously damage the credibility of the "City". Steps therefore had to be taken to protect the financial system while retaining the gold standard. Even before Britain declared war the bank rate was raised to discourage withdrawals of gold and attract new deposits. Where possible overseas debts were called in and the Bank of England made useful guarantees to banks with liquidity problems. Perhaps of more interest to the numismatist was the Currency and Banknotes Act 1914 which received Royal assent just one day after the declaration of war.[6] The main provision of the Act was for the immediate issue of currency notes of £1 and 10/- (ten shillings) by the Treasury, both denominations to have unlimited legal tender. A particular function of the Treasury notes was to allow the sovereign and half sovereign to be withdrawn from circulation and added to the reserves sorely needed to uphold British credibility. Also, as there was no effective restriction on the amount of Treasury notes that could be issued, the Government was able to print whatever notes it required to cover its obligations.[7] Although issued by the Treasury (and therefore on the credit of the nation rather than the Bank of England) the new notes were redeemable under the Act in gold coin at the Bank of England. This was not stated on the notes themselves but by June 1915 much of the gold coin in circulation had been withdrawn. The willingness of the British people to accept Treasury notes instead of gold is a measure of their confidence in a financial system that in fact needed some assistance to survive the shocks of war. By 1918

---

5 *These quotes are from "The War Cabinet Report for the Year 1917".*
6 *4 & 5 Geo V. c. 14 of 6th August 1914.*
7 *The Bank of England was required by the Bank Charter Act 1844 to cover its note issues with securities and gold. Section three of the 1914 Act allowed for a relaxation of these provisions if temporarily authorized by the Treasury. This had been done before in times of financial crisis but on this occasion the issue of Treasury notes proved sufficient.*

there were virtually no gold coins in circulation in the United Kingdom and internally Britain had effectively suspended the gold specie standard.

As well as an enormous loss of life the First World War had cost Britain a huge amount of money. The national debt rose from about £700 million in 1914 to nearly £7,500 million after the war. An increasing imbalance of trade with the United States had strained Britain's gold reserves and she ended the war as a debtor nation.

For most of the war the pound sterling had been pegged against the US dollar at a little below its pre-war par of $4·8665. This disguised the fact that the pound was increasingly overvalued but in March 1919 the peg was removed and the pound fell swiftly to $3·38. To protect reserves unlicensed gold and bullion exports were prohibited by Order in Council of 28th March 1919. This wartime measure (the Treaty of Versailles had not yet been signed) was replaced by the Gold and Silver (Export Control) Act 1920 which placed a legal embargo on similar exports of bullion and coin. In spite of internal arrangements Britain had officially remained on the gold standard throughout the war and had paid her overseas debts in gold when wartime conditions allowed. The measures of 1919 and 1920 formally took Britain off the gold standard with the stated aim of returning to it as soon as conditions were right.

The pre-war international gold standard was a voluntary arrangement whereby the major currencies were pegged against gold at fixed rates and paper money was convertible into gold on demand. Adherence to it effectively limited growth and money supply to the rate at which gold could be accumulated but it had been a period of great stability. It was assumed that a return to it would bring stability to the post-war economy. Under the system the pound sterling was the equivalent of 113 grains of pure gold and the US dollar was 23·22 grains. This gave the pound sterling its par exchange rate of US$ 4·8665 and it was a point of honour for Britain to return to the gold standard at that rate. It was some time before conditions were deemed suitable for this during which Britain pursued a deflationary policy and the pound improved against the dollar. The move was made in 1925 but it was not a return to the old gold specie standard. Bank of England notes and the Treasury notes issued since 1914 were no longer convertible into gold coins on demand. They could only be exchanged for gold bars "*containing approximately four hundred ounces troy of fine gold*" and Britain was now on a gold bullion standard.[8]

Britain was not alone in returning to the gold standard but her adherence to the pre-war rate overvalued the pound and put some stress on her balance of payments. This made it difficult to maintain gold reserves and in 1931 the failure of Austria's largest commercial bank triggered turmoil in the world's money markets. This included a run on gold in London that could only be contained by a suspension of payments in gold. The Gold Standard (Amendment) Act 1931 was rushed through Parliament on 21st September and took Britain permanently off the gold standard. Now floating, the pound dropped quickly by about 25% to $3·69. Most subsequent commentators conclude that the return to the restrictions of the gold standard in 1925 had been a mistake and that it contributed to Britain's economic problems of the inter war years. Certainly those countries that came off it first (like Britain) can be shown to have recovered soonest and by 1934 the pound had more than regained its losses. In 1936 the last of the major currencies left the gold standard.

Throughout this period the **sovereign** continued to be a legal tender coin. The Royal Mint ceased striking half sovereigns in 1915 and sovereigns in 1917. A new issue of sovereigns was

---

8 *The Gold Standard Act 1925 (15 & 16 Geo V. c. 29) introduced the gold bullion standard and at the same time ended the gold specie standard. Gold coins could no longer be obtained for Bank of England or Treasury notes. The Currency and Banknotes Act 1928 finally transferred responsibility for the Treasury notes (issued since 1914) and their associated gold reserves to the Bank of England. For the first time the Bank of England was authorized to issue notes of less than five pounds and all the denominations were legal tender to any amount.*

struck in 1925 as Britain returned to the gold standard but these were mainly for reserve purposes and were the last Royal Mint issues before Britain came off the gold standard in 1931. The Currency and Banknotes Act 1914 applied only to the United Kingdom and the Isle of Man. All other British possessions were specifically exempted from its provisions and we have seen in previous chapters that the sovereign continued to be struck at some branches of the Royal Mint until the gold standard was finally abandoned. The production of sovereigns and half sovereigns at the Royal Mint branches in the Dominions and India for the whole period of their operations is summarized in Table 2. Although Australia came off the gold standard in 1929 the Royal Mint branches there continued to strike sovereigns for reserve purposes and overseas trade until Britain came off the standard in 1931. South Africa did not come off the gold standard until 1932.

TABLE 2 Gold Production at the Royal Mint Branches		
Mint (and mint mark)	Sovereigns	Half Sovereigns
Sydney (Australia style)	1855 - 1870	1855 - 1866
Sydney (S)	1871 - 1926	1871 - 1916
Melbourne (M)	1872 - 1931	1873 - 1915
Perth (P)	1899 - 1931	1899 - 1918[9]
Ottawa (C)	1908 - 1919	-
Bombay (I)	1918	-
Pretoria (SA)	1923 - 1932	1923 - 1926

After the abandonment of the gold standard the sovereign became *de facto* a bullion coin. In 1937 a proof issue of sovereigns and half sovereigns was struck in the name of George VI and in 1957 their issue was resumed on a regular basis as currency coins[10]. New issues of the sovereign ensured that wherever it was in use the coin did not fall into disrepute. Occasionally

---
9 Although the last half sovereign dies used at Perth are dated 1918 the coins were actually struck in December 1919 and January 1920.
10 A few proof sovereigns were struck in 1936 in the name of Edward VIII as part of a proof set of gold coins. They are dated 1937, the proposed year of his coronation, but his abdication in December 1936 meant that they were never issued and very few exist.

they also facilitated overseas payments by the Foreign Office. The sovereign is still struck at the standard laid down in the Coinage Act 1816 and contains almost exactly 113 grains of pure gold. Its bullion value is now many times its face value but holders of the sovereign in 2020 can rest assured that it is still legal tender in the United Kingdom for one pound sterling and to any amount at that rate.

THE GOLD SOVEREIGN

Edward VII 1904.

George V 1932 SA.

Elizabeth II 1957.

The period between the wars was one of great economic uncertainty. There were phases of optimism but it is remembered mainly as a period of stagnation and deflationary policies leading to wage cuts, high unemployment and depression. A period that included German hyperinflation, the General Strike of 1926, the Wall Street Crash of 1929, the Great Depression that followed it in the 1930s and the abandonment of the international gold standard. It was in this atmosphere that the Imperial Conference of 1932 met in Ottawa to discuss what could be done to protect the economic wellbeing of the Empire.

The status of the Dominions whose representatives met at Ottawa had now changed. After taking part in the Imperial War Conferences of 1917 and 1918 the Dominions were given independent voices at the Paris Peace Conference in 1919. They also became founder members of the League of Nations which appeared to give them the same status as sovereign states. The Dominions felt that they were ready for exactly this sort of status but their legal position as colonies within the Empire had not changed. The post-war Imperial Conferences addressed this matter.

At the 1923 Conference the need for a more devolved, autonomous relationship between Britain and the Dominions was recognized. The proceedings of the 1926 Conference adopted a report by Lord Balfour[11] which described Great Britain and the Dominions as "*autonomous Communities within the British Empire, equal in status, in no way subordinate one to another in any aspect of their domestic or external affairs, though united by a common allegiance to the Crown, and freely associated as members of the British Commonwealth of Nations.*" The conclusions reached in 1926 were restated at the 1930 Conference and led directly to the passage through Parliament of the Statute of Westminster 1931 granting the Dominions the exclusive right to legislate for themselves and to manage their own foreign affairs.

---

11 *Balfour was Lord President of the Council. He attended the Conference as part of the British delegation and his report was written as Chairman of the Inter-Imperial Relations Committee.*

The changing status of the self governing colonies is reflected in the coinage. The Royal Titles Act 1901[12] gave Edward VII the additional title of king of "*the British Dominions beyond the Seas.*" The legend on British coins was changed accordingly from the **BRITT· REG·** (Queen of the United Kingdom) used by Victoria to **BRITT: OMN: REX** (King of all the Britains) for the new coinage of Edward VII. The change was made in consultation with the self governing colonies and was designed primarily to recognize the support they were providing during the Boer War. When Australia introduced her own version of sterling subsidiary coins in 1910 they used the same formula. So too did the silver coins of the West African Currency Board introduced in 1913. Other territories though did not use this additional title.

Use of BRITT· REG· and BRITT: OMN: REX

British halfcrowns of Victoria and Edward VII

Australia shilling 1910

British West Africa Shilling 1914

By 1931 the Dominions were enjoying equal status with the United Kingdom and most of them were issuing their own coins. For many years the United Kingdom coinage had used a civic (bare headed) portrait of the monarch while colonial coins, to indicate their subordinate status, had shown a crowned portrait[13]. The Statute of Westminster notwithstanding, George V was reluctant to vary this practice but after the change of reign in 1936 the coins of Canada, Australia, New Zealand and South Africa began to use the same portrait as United Kingdom coins to reflect their equal status. Coins of the colonies, where the Crown retained supremacy, continued to use a crowned portrait.

---

12 1 Edw. VII. c. 15.
13 *This did not apply to the sovereigns and half sovereigns struck at the Royal Mint branches which, after the initial "Australia" type from Sydney, had always been an integral part of the Imperial coinage.*

14 Climax and Decolonization

UNCROWNED AND CROWNED PORTRAITS

United Kingdom

British florin 1937.   British florin 1967.

Dominions   *Colonies*

Australia florin 1938.   British West Africa two shillings 1938

Canada fifty cents 1960.   Hong Kong dollar 1960.

The newly autonomous Dominions, equal in status to each other and to Great Britain, met at Ottawa in 1932 and it was these Dominions that for some time had been the strongest advocates of protection for the Empire's trade and resources. The worldwide effects of the Great Depression, the abandonment of the gold standard and protectionism elsewhere now persuaded Britain also that it was time to move on from the 19th century ideal of free trade.

While it was generally agreed at Ottawa that something should be done, it proved difficult to find a solution that was acceptable to all. The various Dominions had differing needs and in fact the Empire was not self sufficient in all aspects of supply and demand. Nevertheless, in anticipation of agreement being reached at the Conference the Import Duties Act 1932[14] was passed which imposed a general 10% tariff on imports but gave temporary exemptions to the Dominions, India and Southern Rhodesia[15]. The subsequent Ottawa Agreements Act 1932 extended exemptions to the Empire as a whole and made them permanent. In return for these preferences the colonies and India were obliged to make reciprocal arrangements and the Dominions were expected to do the same. The various tariffs and quotas agreed at Ottawa amounted to a comprehensive scheme of Imperial preferences. Although subject to considerable modification Imperial Preference continued in use until the 1960s.

---

14 *(22 & 23 Geo. V. c. 8).*
15 *Southern Rhodesia was not a Dominion but had been self governing since 1923.*

The Dominions recognized as autonomous communities within the British Empire in 1926 and 1931 now included the Irish Free State as noted in Chapter seven. Acceptance of Dominion status within the Commonwealth implied Irish allegiance to the Crown and the acceptance of the partition of Ireland both of which were difficult concepts for a republican free state. This led to bitter faction fighting in Ireland between those who accepted the Anglo-Irish Treaty of 1921 and those who did not before matters were settled in favour of the Treaty early in 1923. For many though Dominion status was not a permanent solution while on the other side of the Irish Sea the fragmentation of the United Kingdom had been difficult to accept. The forced marriage of 1801 had become separation and the relationship between the two countries was an uneasy one. Inevitably it would end in divorce.

In the mean time, with her new status, the Irish Free State attended the Imperial Conferences from 1923 to 1930 that laid the groundwork for the Statute of Westminster. In 1932 Fianna Fáil (the republican successor to Sinn Féin) was able to form a minority government replacing the moderates who had supported Dominion status. The legislative independence guaranteed by the Statute of Westminster now allowed Fianna Fáil to remove any of the provisions of the 1921 Treaty that it found objectionable. The role of the Crown in the internal affairs of the State was therefore attacked and the oath of allegiance was discontinued. By 1937 the Irish Free State had written herself a new Constitution as "*a sovereign, independent, democratic state*" the name of which would be "*Éire, or, in the English language, Ireland*".

The Irish Free State decided not to attend the Imperial Conference of 1937 and her continued membership of the Commonwealth came into question. Her External Relations Act however still recognized the King in his capacity as the constitutional head of the Commonwealth and the final rupture did not come until 1949. The Republic of Ireland Act 1948[16] which came into effect in April of the following year removed the remaining constitutional duties of the King. Ireland became fully independent as the Republic of Ireland and left the Commonwealth.

In 1922 the new State continued to use sterling but, like other Dominions, soon made arrangements to issue her own version of sterling subsidiary coins. The Coinage Act 1926 provided for the issue of silver, nickel and bronze coins and the currency was to be managed by a Currency Commission. This Commission was created by the Currency Act 1927 but would be dissolved under the Central Bank Act 1942 when its powers and duties were transferred to the Central Bank of Ireland. While the 1926 Act allowed for Ireland's own subsidiary sterling coins the main purpose of the 1927 Act was to create a separate Saorstát (Free State) pound as a standard of value which would be pegged exactly to sterling. The Act allowed for the receipt of gold bullion and the issue of gold coins of the same standard as the sovereign "*at a place for the time being appointed*". In the event a Saorstát gold pound was never issued but this should not surprise. The United Kingdom had recently adopted the gold bullion standard and sovereigns were no longer being struck at the Royal Mint. In practice the Saorstát pound was represented in circulation by Currency Commission notes with unlimited legal tender.

The silver, nickel and bronze coinage though went ahead. These were to be of the same denominations as the British coins which were already in circulation and which continued to be legal tender. The new Free State coins came into issue in 1928. The half-crown, florin and shilling were the same size and weight as their sterling counterparts but had the higher millesimal fineness of 750. British silver coins had been somewhat hurriedly reduced to a fineness of 500 in 1920 when the price of silver looked likely to continue rising. In 1926

---

16 *This was an Act of the Irish Parliament.*

though the higher fineness was affordable and was designed to give credibility to this new and innovative coinage. The bronze coins (penny, halfpenny and farthing) were to the same specification as their British equivalents. The intermediate denominations (sixpence and threepence) were struck in nickel and were both larger than the British denominations of the same value. Both the nickel denominations would be changed to cupro-nickel in 1942. The Irish coins were all struck at the Royal Mint.

The designs adopted for the coins fully reflect the independent and republican feelings of the time. While the other Dominions automatically accepted the King's portrait as their obverse design the Free State coins use a harp and the simple legend **saorstát éireann**. Their reverses show examples of Irish fauna. The new Constitution in 1937 led to a change of obverse legend to **éire** but there was no further change when Ireland left the Commonwealth in 1949. Although these coins are startlingly "foreign" in appearance all those of the Irish Free State and those of Ireland until 1949 are Commonwealth coins and are part of our story. While the coins are highly distinctive the Saortstát pound itself (officially the "Irish pound" after the new Constitution) retained exact parity with the pound sterling throughout the difficult interwar years and would do so until 1979. Ireland had joined the European Monetary System in 1978 and adherence to its Exchange Rate Mechanism made the break with sterling unavoidable the following year.

SAORSTÁT ÉIREANN

Half-crown 1928. Penny 1937. Cupro-nickel sixpence 1935.

EIRE

Florin 1939. Shilling 1939. Halfpenny 1942.

There was a feeling in British Government circles that the Home Rule issue in Ireland could have been better managed. If handled differently the end result would probably have been the same except that Ireland may have remained within the Commonwealth. After the First World War a similar but rather more complex situation was developing in India where there were also demands for home rule. In dealing with this the British Government determined to avoid confrontation as much as possible.

Before the First World War demands were already beginning to surface for the sort of self government enjoyed by the Dominions. The support received from India during the war led to her attendance, with the Dominions, at the Imperial War Conference of 1917 and to an announcement by the Secretary of State for India on future British policy. This amounted to a pledge to move stage by stage towards responsible government for India within the British Empire. The Secretary of State (Edwin Samuel Montagu) then went to India to discuss this with the Viceroy (Lord Chelmsford). The resulting Montagu-Chelmsford Report formed the basis of the Government of India Act 1919. This gave increased powers to Provincial Councils and required a review after ten years to assess what progress had been made and to recommend further stages on the road to self government. The provisions of the Act though did not move things as far or as fast as the nationalists, represented by the National Congress Party, would have liked. Congress was a Hindu organization which from 1921 was effectively led by the charismatic Mahatma Gandhi. Its political aims at this time did not conflict with those of the Muslim League so Congress could claim to represent an all-India nationalist movement. They recommended a policy of non cooperation to accelerate the process of change.

In 1928 the Commission required by the 1919 Act arrived in India under the chairmanship of Sir John Simon. By this time Congress was demanding immediate Dominion status. Failing that they threatened a further campaign of non cooperation with the goal of complete independence. It was mainly for this reason that the Simon Commission had arrived earlier than required but its final report looked no further than the original plan of staged progress towards internal self government. London strongly resisted the idea of full independence but there were also practical objections to immediate Dominion status. If India was to succeed as an autonomous state and preferably remain within the British sphere of influence, the sub continent had to be properly federated and the Native States would have to be included. This was problematic as their political ethos would seriously limit the effectiveness of Congress. As frustration mounted at the lack of progress all the parties concerned were invited to London for a series of Round Table Conferences which took place in 1930, 1931 and 1932. Congress was only represented at the second of these and by one delegate, Mahatma Gandhi. The Native States though were well represented. The Conference findings were examined by Parliament and led eventually to the Government of India Act 1935. Among other things the Act allowed for the creation of the "Federation of India" when certain conditions had been met and there was a growing acceptance that full responsible government and Dominion status would follow. Burma and Aden had been part of British India for many years but did not sensibly fit into the proposed Federation. The 1935 Act therefore allowed for their separation.

The main concern of the Congress Party was the future of the provinces of British India but federation would have to take place in a way that was also acceptable to the Native States. By this time too the Muslim League were beginning to have concerns about religious freedoms. Apart from the separation of Burma (which became a distinct unit within the British Commonwealth in 1937) and Aden (which became a Crown colony in the same year) nothing had been settled before the Second World War began. Constitutional change was put on hold for the duration of hostilities.

On 3rd September 1939 Britain declared war on Germany because of a guarantee that had been given to Poland in the event of invasion. The colonies were automatically at war too but the Dominions (who had not been consulted over the Polish guarantee) now managed their own foreign affairs. Should they too go to war?

Events in Ireland and India and concerns about Palestine may give the impression that the Empire was beginning to crumble but the troubled world of the 1930s had tended to draw much of it closer together. Britain was still a great power and was still the world's banker. She invested heavily in the Dominions and was a market for their produce. For Australia and New Zealand the Imperial connection was seen as essential and as the best guarantee of their safety. For Canada and South Africa the connection was still very useful and even Ireland was reluctant to make the final break[17]. There was therefore little doubt that the Dominions would assist the "Mother Country". Assurances of support in the event of war had already been received and within a few days all the overseas Dominions had declared war on Germany. Only Ireland remained neutral, and would do so throughout the war, although many thousands of her people enlisted in British units and served in British merchant ships.

From India's summer capital at Simla the Viceroy unilaterally declared India to be at war without consulting any of the political parties or provincial governments. As the representative of the Emperor of India this was within his constitutional rights but it so angered the Congress Party that they withdrew from government and eventually developed the Quit India movement. British authority in India was strong enough to deal firmly with this wartime challenge and many Congress leaders were imprisoned for the rest of the war. The Indian Army, the Civil Service and other organizations remained loyal and India played a major part in this war as she had done in the last.

The Second World War would bring irreversible change but when it got under way the Empire was probably more united in purpose than it had ever been before.

In 1939 the defence of the Empire was still based on the strength of the Royal Navy which was the most powerful navy in the world and was supported by ships of Australia, New Zealand and Canada. About one third of Britain's peacetime army was stationed in India where there was also a large Indian army including Gurkha regiments recruited in Nepal. In the Middle East there were garrisons in Egypt, Sudan and Palestine and in the Far East in Singapore, Hong Kong and the concessions in China at Shanghai and Tientsin. British troops were also stationed permanently in Gibraltar, Malta and Jamaica and there were smaller units in some other colonies. The Dominions had their own forces and many of the colonies had locally raised units which could be reinforced by British troops if required. The Royal Air Force had squadrons in Malta, Egypt, Sudan, Palestine, Aden, Iraq, India and the Far East (mainly Singapore) and the overseas Dominions had their own air forces. In total this was an impressive military resource but it was designed to defend the British Empire and maintain order within it. It was not designed to wage a world war on all fronts.

Britain's prime concern was the defence of the homeland and for this, her navy was concentrated more in home waters and the Mediterranean. To start with Britain and France were ranged against Germany but it was not long before the British Expeditionary Force, outflanked by a German advance, had to be evacuated from Dunkirk in a hurry with heavy losses in men and equipment. In June 1940 France fell and Italy entered the war on the German side. The French ports were now available for German use and thus began the dark days of the war. The shipping lanes of the Atlantic and the Mediterranean were at threat from

---

17 *The provisions of the Statute of Westminster of 1931 were mainly at the insistance of Canada, South Africa and Ireland. Australia did not formally adopt the Statute until 1942 and New Zealand until 1947.*

German and Italian submarines and Britain herself was vulnerable to invasion. In September 1940 Italian troops crossed from Libya into Egypt threatening the Suez Canal and initiating a long desert campaign that soon also involved German troops. At this time the British Empire stood alone against the Axis Powers of Germany and Italy and the forces of Vichy France.

On the other side of the world Australia and New Zealand were concerned not only for Britain's safety but for their own. The Anglo-Japanese Alliance of 1902 which had given Britain useful support in the Pacific in the First World War had lapsed in 1921. It had not been renewed, mainly because the United States opposed it. Without Japanese support in the Pacific Britain needed to pay more attention to the defence of the region and the building of the Singapore naval base began. Even with this completed (in 1939) Britain was unable to keep pace with the build up of Japanese military power.

Already the Japanese had invaded parts of China. In doing so they had not attacked foreign troops in the mainland concessions but it was clear that British units in Shanghai and Tientsin (Tianjin) were a potential flash point. It seemed unlikely that Britain's Asian Empire could be adequately defended if war did erupt with Japan and to reduce the risk of that the last British troops were withdrawn from Shanghai and Tientsin in August 1940.

In an effort to curb Japan's imperial aspirations in China the United States had imposed sanctions on certain Japanese imports. These sanctions were tightened when Japanese activity extended to Vichy held Indo China and in July 1941 Japanese assets in the United States and Britain were frozen. Japan needed the resources of South East Asia to service her industry and decided she would have to take them. The most important of these were the rubber, tin and oil of British held Malaya and Burma and the oil of the Dutch East Indies. Assuming that an attack on British and Dutch colonies would provoke an American response, a preemptive strike on the United States Pacific Fleet was part of Japan's plan. The attack came on 7th December 1941 at Pearl Harbour (8th December in Japan which was on the other side of the date line). Hong Kong, Malaya and Thailand were attacked almost simultaneously a few hours later. The war was now truly a world war with which the British Empire was not equipped to deal. As feared, the Japanese war machine could not be resisted. Hong Kong surrendered on Christmas Day and the British North Borneo territories, Malaya, Singapore and Burma were all lost in rapid succession by May 1942. By April the whole of the Dutch East Indies and the Philippines were in Japanese hands and landings had been made in New Guinea, uncomfortably close to Australia.

The Japanese had achieved nearly all their objectives in just four months. Singapore had been the biggest British surrender in history and with Burma taken Japan was poised on the borders of British India. The loss of Britain's Far Eastern colonies was an enormous blow to her economy and to her reputation. Hard pressed in Europe and with Suez under threat it was obvious that Britain's Australasian Dominions had to look elsewhere for their ultimate safety. Still they supplied ships and men to the European theatre and the desert campaign but they now sought greater contact with the United States.

In September 1940 Japan had joined the Rome-Berlin Axis in a Tripartite Pact pledging mutual assistance. A few days after Pearl Harbour Germany and Italy therefore declared war on the United States in Japan's support. America was now at war in the Atlantic as well as the Pacific and Britain at last had the full and complete support she needed. Slowly the fortunes of war were turned, in the Atlantic, in North Africa, in Europe itself and finally in the Pacific and the Far East. VE-Day (Victory in Europe) was celebrated on 8th May 1945 and VJ-Day (Victory over Japan) on 15th August.

The Empire had emerged from the war victorious and intact but, once again, at enormous human and financial cost. During it Britain had liquidated overseas investments, used most of her foreign currency reserves and hugely increased her foreign debt. After it she was economically and financially exhausted and relied heavily on further substantial loans from the United States and Canada. Britain was not a spent force but her economic recovery now depended heavily on the American loans and on further assistance from the United States.[18] For her future wellbeing Britain pinned her hopes on increased exports, on the protectionist arrangements she had with the Empire and on the safeguards of the Sterling Area. The "Sterling Area" comprised those countries that used sterling or pegged their currencies to it. In 1939 many of these had agreed to protect the pound sterling by forming a single exchange control area which was more or less coterminous with the British Empire. Within the area there was no exchange control of sterling payments but transfers outside it were strictly controlled from London. The agreement was a wartime measure but when convertibility was restored Britain again found it necessary to impose similar exchange controls.[19] Member countries maintained large balances in London, an important resource that could back sterling when required. The Sterling Area was a major currency bloc until the 1950s and continued in existence for another twenty years after that.

The Empire on which Britain pinned much of her hopes for the future was adapting rapidly to the upheavals of the Second World War. The Dominions, already independent within the Commonwealth, had been forced to rethink their complete dependence on the old Imperial system and diversify their economic as well as their strategic links. By the end of the war Australia, New Zealand and Canada had all been drawn closer to the United States and, as we have seen, Ireland was on course to leave the Commonwealth completely.

Before the war, Government expenditure in the colonies was generally limited to the revenues that could be raised in them. Wartime demands on colonial supplies though brought an acceptance that development would have to be funded and if the Colonial Empire was to be a source of future prosperity even more would have to be invested in it. These were straightened times but the Colonial Development and Welfare Acts of 1940 and 1945 attempted to address these matters. The war had brought many colonial subjects into closer contact with the wider world through service overseas, through military personnel based in the colonies and now also by the greater attention to their development and welfare. All of this led to a greater awareness of democracy, freedom and national identity – the very ideals for which the war had been fought. While most of the colonies had not suffered invasion or occupation, those in the Far East had become acutely aware of Britain's inability to defend them in 1941-1942. Although all of them had been regained as the war drew to a close, this had not been achieved without United States involvement and British prestige had been damaged.

In the Middle East Palestine was causing serious concern. Zionists always assumed that a Jewish majority would one day be achieved and that a Jewish State would result. Even before the war it proved difficult to control Jewish immigration and this contributed to a serious Arab revolt against British rule. In her role as mandate trustee it was Britain's duty to move Palestine towards independence. All options were considered but in the end Britain maintained the principle that Palestine should provide only a homeland for the Jews and there should be

---

18 The United States' Marshall Plan of 1948 was designed to enable the economic reconstruction of Europe and her subsequent Mutual Security Act of 1951 provided funds for the defence spending of her allies. Both of these initiatives were intended to deter the spread of communism and in both cases Britain was a major recipient.
19 The Exchange Control Act, 1947 (10 & 11 Geo. VI. c. 14). The first schedule of the Act defines the countries of the Sterling Area, listing them as "Scheduled Territories".

no separate State. After the war there was little chance of stemming the flow of arrivals and Britain's continued attempt to establish a binational independent Palestine now stirred the Jews into armed rebellion. Already (in 1946) Britain had moved neighbouring Transjordan successfully to independence but for Palestine there seemed no way forward. The British Government therefore announced in 1947 that it wished to terminate its trusteeship and place the question of Palestine's future in the hands of the United Nations. The UN recommended partition into separate Arab and Jewish States whose independence would terminate the mandate. Britain effectively walked away from the problem, giving up the mandate on 14th May 1948. The State of Israel was declared on the same day.

The League of Nations which had granted the various mandates after the First World War did not survive the effects of the Second World War. It held its final meeting in April 1946 but its successor, the United Nations, had already been chartered in the previous year. A Trusteeship Council was set up to oversee moves to independence of the old mandates. These would become United Nations Trust Territories.

By far the biggest change at this time was the independence of India. In all her long history India had never been one nation. Under British rule it had almost become so although the Native States were still nominally independent. Nevertheless the diverse nature of India had not prevented the rise of nationalist demands from an early date and by the Second World War it was understood that self government as a Dominion would be achieved when hostilities ceased. During the war, in order to obtain full cooperation in India, more specific promises were made but these did not satisfy the Indian National Congress Party. Their subsequent demands that Britain should quit India (at a time when the Japanese were already in Burma) divided nationalist opinion and allowed the Muslim League to become more influential. India now had little chance of moving to independence without partition.

After the war Britain strove to hand over India in an orderly fashion. She agreed that independence should take place in 1948 and that there should be partition between regions that were predominantly Hindu or Muslim. Violence though was erupting, particularly in the proposed border areas and Britain was anxious to reach a dignified conclusion. Independence was therefore brought forward by some ten months. The Indian Independence Act, 1947[20] provided for the setting up in India of two independent Dominions to be known as India and Pakistan and for suzerainty of His Majesty over the Indian (Native) States to lapse. Pakistan was created as two predominantly Muslim regions, separate from India and from each other, on 14th August 1947 (East Pakistan would later become Bangladesh). India became an independent Dominion the next day. The Indian States were urged to join one or other of the new Dominions and had little choice but to do so. This was not an ideal solution but it allowed an orderly British hand over and withdrawal and both countries remained within the Commonwealth. The last British troops had left by March 1948 and the crucial role India had played in Imperial defence came to an end.

The Indian Independence Act gave the assent of Parliament for the omission by Royal Proclamation of the words "Indiae Imperator" and "Emperor of India" from the Royal Style and Titles. The necessary Proclamation though did not come from Buckingham Palace until nearly a year later on 22nd June 1948[21] and only then could the title **IND IMP** or **EMPEROR** be legally dropped. Although India was independent the coins of the United Kingdom (and Australia) thus continued with legal correctness to use the **IND IMP** title for coins dated 1948 only coming into line with the rest of the Empire for those dated 1949.

---

20 *10 & 11 Geo. VI. c. 30.*
21 *The London Gazette, number 38330 22nd June 1948.*

14 Climax and Decolonization

COINS WITH AND WITHOUT TITLE OF EMPEROR

British penny 1948. *British penny 1949.*

Seychelles ten cents 1943. *Seychelles ten cents 1951.*

New Zealand sixpence 1947. *New Zealand sixpence 1948.*

Burma, which had been part of British India until 1937, was firmly nationalist after recovery from the Japanese, became independent in January 1948 and opted not to join the Commonwealth. Ceylon (modern Sri Lanka) was not part of British India but had reached a similar level of development. Nationalist politics had surfaced in the early 20th century but not of the vigorous Indian style. Ceylon moved very smoothly to independence and Dominion status in February 1948, the first actual colony to do so.

By 1949 the Indian sub continent and Ceylon had gained independence and Burma and Ireland had left the Commonwealth. Canada, Australia and New Zealand were forging links with the United States. Britain had left Palestine and many of the colonies were developing their own sense of identity. The pre war assumption that the system of imperial defence could offer an independent strategic umbrella to the Dominions, the colonies and India had been proved unworkable. The traditional economic links had been damaged and the cost of maintaining a military presence around the world was unsustainable. The inevitable consequence of the war was therefore the end of the existing Imperial system. Britain's financial resources could no longer support the worldwide commitments of a Great Power and the twenty years that followed the Second World War would be a period of adjustment.

In spite of the immediate post war changes there was still an assumption that Britain's decline was temporary and that the Empire and Commonwealth would provide for her economic recovery. World opinion was now strongly anti-imperial but at least until 1960 the United States viewed Britain's colonial Empire as a bulwark against the spread of Soviet influence. In spite of her anti-colonial traditions she therefore found it in her interests to support Britain as a colonial Power. Nevertheless both the United States and the United Nations saw independence as the ultimate goal for all colonies and Britain herself was coming to the same view. If the Colonial Empire could no longer be maintained by force or adequately protected it could perhaps be joined with the Dominions to form a multi racial Commonwealth of independent countries maintaining economic ties for mutual benefit.

The principle of self determination for the colonies was thus conceded but it was assumed that the pace of change would be gradual. It would take place over many years with the ultimate goal of Commonwealth membership for each colony. Ceylon had been the first part of the Colonial Empire to achieve independence after the Second World War and the way in which it had successfully become a Dominion within the Commonwealth was held up as an example for future decolonization.

The term "Commonwealth" has been used freely in this chapter and we should now attempt to define it. It is to Lord Rosebery[22], in a speech delivered in Adelaide in 1884, that the first mention of "a commonwealth of nations" in this context is attributed. He was describing the growing independence of the more advanced colonies (particularly Australia's bid for nationhood) and it is perhaps because of his speech that the federation of Australian States formed in 1901 adopted the title Commonwealth rather than Dominion. The War Cabinet Report for 1917 describes the Dominions collectively as an "Imperial Commonwealth" but the first official use of the term "British Commonwealth of Nations" appears in the Anglo Irish Treaty of 1921. It now officially describes the self governing colonies that had achieved Dominion status and which would be represented by the Dominions Office from 1925. After the Second World War India, Pakistan, Ceylon and then smaller colonies began to achieve independence and join the Commonwealth. Many of them would become republics and would recognize the monarch only as head of the Commonwealth, not as their own head of state. The nature of this exclusive club therefore had to change and this was discussed at the Commonwealth Prime Ministers' Conferences of 1948 and 1949. It was decided that member states would no longer need to have Dominion status and that all of them, old and new, would be independent "members of the Commonwealth". The word "British" was dropped from the title and it became the "Commonwealth of Nations". A major change occurred in 1965 when a Commonwealth Secretariat was established giving the organization its own autonomy. Today the "Commonwealth of Nations" is often referred to simply as the "Commonwealth".

The changing form of the Commonwealth led to an adjustment of coin legends. The Royal Titles Act 1953[23] altered the Queen's titles to reflect more clearly the new constitutional relations of the members of the Commonwealth. The term *Britanniarum Omnium* was no longer appropriate for the all embracing organization that the Commonwealth had become and **BRITT: OMN:** was dropped from the coinage of those countries that used it (the United Kingdom, Australia and British West Africa).

COINS WITH AND WITHOUT BRITT: OMN:

British shilling 1953.   *British shilling 1954.*

---
22 *Lord Rosebery was a Liberal statesman and future Prime Minister.*
23 *1 & 2 Eliz. II. c. 9.*

Under Elizabeth II the specific use of crowned/uncrowned portraits for territories of different status also comes to an end with the introduction of Arnold Machin's "tiara" portrait in the 1960s. This was made available to any territory wishing to use it and was used in the United Kingdom when decimal denominations began to come into issue.

THE ARNOLD MACHIN PORTRAIT

United Kingdom ten new pence 1968.

Jersey (Crown dependency) ten new pence 1968.

Rhodesia (colony) two shillings 1964.

Canada (Commonwealth realm) fifty cents 1965.

The post war changes to the Imperial system meant that central control in London also had to change. In 1947 the Dominions Office took responsibility for any remaining business of the old India Office and was renamed "Commonwealth Relations Office". As Britain's colonial interests declined this was combined with the Colonial Office in 1966 to form the "Commonwealth Office" and a further merger in 1968 formed the "Foreign and Commonwealth Office" to deal with all of Britain's overseas interests.

As decolonization began in earnest it was important to the British Government that it should be managed in an orderly manner. As far as possible, colonies should be properly prepared for independence with democratic governments in sympathy with British aims and the handover should be to moderates who favoured Commonwealth membership. Decolonization should be seen as the completion of planned policy, not as a measure forced on Britain through economic conditions, world opinion, nationalist pressures, or communist subversion. In practice, in order to pre-empt the rise of extreme nationalism, this could not always be done. The pace of decolonization was sometimes faster than the Colonial Office would have liked.

The next colony to achieve independence was the Gold Coast which became an independent member of the Commonwealth, as Ghana, in March 1957. This was followed by the Federation of Malaya in August of the same year. It is well beyond the scope of this book to examine the details of independence for each of the colonies but a brief explanation of how matters progressed must be attempted. As smaller colonies began to join the Commonwealth there was concern among the existing members that this fundamental change to its character would be detrimental. There were some attempts to federate smaller territories before independence (for example those in the Malay Peninsula) to avoid having too many such members in the Commonwealth but this was not always successful. The proposed federation of the West Indies for example was never achieved. When Cyprus became a member in 1961 the precedent was set for all colonies, however small, to join the Commonwealth which soon had a majority of smaller members, many of them republics.

These changes were difficult for some of the old Dominions to accept and this was particularly the case in Southern Africa. The policies of South Africa were completely out of step with the new Commonwealth's aims of equality and this led to her leaving the Commonwealth in 1961. Self governing Southern Rhodesia had a similar segregated government run exclusively by white settlers. Here there was deep concern at Britain's insistence on African power sharing as the colony was moved towards independence and this led to a unilateral declaration of independence by the white settlers in 1965. The Rhodesian problem was not sorted out until 1980 when Britain granted her independence as Zimbabwe. South Africa would not be welcomed back into the Commonwealth until 1994.

The segregated governments of Southern Africa and the settler colonies obviously did not prepare the indigenous majority for self determination but neither did the colonies of tropical Africa. Britain had ruled many of these indirectly through existing or appointed local rulers. This had perpetuated the old traditional systems of autocratic rule and prevented the development of the democratic systems deemed desirable for independence in the 20th century. Perhaps a bigger problem was the way in which many of the colonial borders had been delineated by latitude and longitude during the great "Scramble for Africa".[24] Inevitably this had cobbled together different ethnic groups in box shaped colonies that are still in evidence on a political map of Africa today. This had worked reasonably well under the umbrella of colonial rule and was largely ignored in what became a rush towards independence. It would though cause grave problems in post colonial Africa.

As a Dominion South Africa's affairs were her own business and she had chosen the strictly segregationist policy termed "apartheid". Britain was therefore concerned for the future of the High Commission territories of Basutoland (now Lesotho), Bechuanaland (now Botswana) and Swaziland (now eSwatini). The original intention was that these would one day become part of South Africa but apartheid and South Africa's exit from the Commonwealth meant this was no longer possible. They thus became independent members of the Commonwealth between 1966 and 1968.

Elsewhere in the world problems did arise with decolonization but not to the same extent as in Africa. Although independence was often granted earlier than planned, the arrangements put in place under imperial rule generally allowed Britain to withdraw in good order. There were exceptions to this (like Palestine and Aden) but most of the colonies became independent members of the Commonwealth.

The nature of the Commonwealth as it finally emerged was somewhat different to that

---

24 See Chapter nine.

which had been planned. The original intention was that it should be a strong economic alliance which, with defence agreements, would restore and maintain Britain's position as a world power. In the end it became more a forum to advance freedom, equality and cultural links. In fact the changing pattern of the world's economy after the Second World War tended to make any sort of formal empire irrelevant.

By the early 1960s Britain's economy had revived. The old Dominions were diversifying their trading links and the cost of keeping what remained of the colonial empire tended to make it a burden rather than an asset. Britain was looking more to Europe for economic security and, as the main threat to Europe was from Soviet Russia, her defence arrangements had to concentrate on the nuclear threat. Even so Britain was reluctant to give up her role as a world power and independence arrangements with the colonies often included the continued use of military bases. Events though had already begun to unfold that would show conclusively where Britain now stood in the league of world powers.

In 1951 Iran nationalized the assets of the Anglo-Iranian Oil Company. This was the British company that had developed Iran's oil industry and had a monopoly of production and export. The British Government was the Company's main shareholder and the Abadan refinery was probably Britain's largest overseas asset. Iran wanted a bigger share of the profits and a greater role for her nationals in the running of the Company but negotiations had stalled and nationalization was her reaction. Rather than a direct military response Britain opted to mount a legal and economic challenge but the matter was not settled until 1954. For Iran this was a period of great economic distress culminating in the overthrow of her elected government. Nevertheless, when a new concession was agreed with the Shah Britain had lost control of Abadan and the Company (renamed British Petroleum) had lost its monopolies in Iran.

Elsewhere in the Middle East Britain's handling of the Iranian issue was seen as weak and indecisive. When Egypt had ceased to be a Protectorate in the 1920s British troops remained at Suez to protect the Canal and in 1936 there was agreement that they should remain there for another twenty years. The Second World War had proved their worth and the subsequent loss of India and Palestine had left Suez as Britain's main base in the region. With a garrison of some 80,000 its function had now changed to include Imperial defence. Its continued existence at that level was viewed by Egypt as inappropriate and completely out of step with what had been agreed in 1936. Late in 1951 she therefore announced the end of that agreement and demanded the immediate withdrawal of the garrison. This Britain refused to do but it was clear that when the time came there would be no extension of the 1936 agreement and a phased withdrawal had to be negotiated for 1956. Safeguards were agreed in the event of an external attack on Egypt and it was also agreed that control of the Suez Canal Company would pass to Egypt in 1968. The last British troops left Suez in July 1956 but within weeks of the withdrawal President Gamal Abdel Nasser (Egypt had become a republic in 1953) had nationalized the Suez Canal.

On this occasion Britain took immediate action mounting a massive invasion with French assistance and Israeli support. The intention was to regain the Canal and depose President Nasser. The military operation began well but the United States and others immediately entered the political fray. Economic pressure and world opinion left Britain and France little alternative but to withdraw. Nasser had not been deposed and the Suez Canal remained in Egyptian hands. The final withdrawal from Egypt at the behest of the United States was a humiliation that turned Suez into a disaster. It shattered Britain's reputation as a world power and was pivotal in defining her future role in world affairs.

After Suez that role was increasingly a shared one through NATO[25] and, eventually, the EEC[26]. Membership of these organizations focused on the defence of Britain and on economic and political ties with Europe. In many ways Britain found it difficult to adjust to membership of the European Community. She had so recently been a world power and the head of a great Commonwealth and Empire all of which made her reluctant to surrender any of the sovereignty of the British Parliament[27]. She was reluctant too to give up the old Imperial ties even though the Commonwealth was economically less important and the old Empire had become irrelevant. For some years it was hoped that its essential elements could be maintained by the retention of military bases in remaining and former colonies such as Gibraltar, Malta, Cyprus, Aden and Singapore but in the end Britain's commitments still had to be adjusted to her resources. The nuclear deterrent designed to keep the Soviet Union at bay was expensive and Britain's historic world role had to suffer. In 1968 a decision was made to withdraw all forces east of Suez and this clearly signalled the end of Britain's role as a worldwide imperial power. By the end of 1971 this withdrawal was effectively complete and when Britain joined the European Community in 1973 the economic significance of the Commonwealth also came to an end.

With forces withdrawn east of Suez and decolonization more or less complete it would be reasonable to assume that our story had come to an end but inevitably one or two loose ends remained. We will look first at a major exception to the general move towards independence.

Hong Kong, situated on the coast of mainland China, was a special case. The treaties creating the colony had granted Hong Kong and Kowloon to Britain in perpetuity while the New Territories (adjoining the colony) were on lease from China until 1997. A separate existence for Hong Kong, independent or otherwise, without the New Territories was hardly practicable. China had long held the view that the treaties creating the colony had been forced upon her and that Hong Kong was hers by right. She would not tolerate a grant of independence and was powerful enough to prevent it if the need arose. Independence was therefore out of the question but so too was an indefinite British administration. It would have to be returned to China. It was though in the interests of China, Britain and most of the people of Hong Kong for this thriving capitalist emporium to remain undisturbed as far as possible by the restrictions of Communist China. Arrangements were therefore made to return the whole of the territory to China when the New Territories lease expired in 1997. It was to become a Special Administrative Region of the People's Republic of China for a guaranteed period of fifty years to safeguard its way of life and capitalist system. Hong Kong thus remained in British hands far longer than most of the old colonies and was handed over with due pomp and ceremony on 1st July 1997.

Our main chapter on the East took the story of Hong Kong's colonial coinage to 1952 and we must now take it to its conclusion. The period from the accession of Elizabeth II in 1952 to the hand over to China in 1997 was generally one of increasing prosperity for Hong Kong and this is reflected in the variety of coins issued in Elizabeth's name. There were variations in metal content, changes in flan size, new flan shapes and new denominations. In 1952 the only

---

25 *The North Atlantic Treaty Organization is a military alliance recognizing the importance of trans Atlantic cooperation for the security of Europe. It is based on an original treaty of 1949.*

26 *The European Economic Community was created by the 1957 Treaty of Rome as was the European Atomic Energy Community. The European Coal and Steel Community was already in existence. Britain first applied for membership in 1961 and joined all three Communities in 1973. In 1993 (Maastricht Treaty) the three Communities became one of the "pillars" of the European Union. The Treaty of Lisbon merged the pillars of the European Union into a single legal entity in 2009.*

27 *This attitude lingered on and a British referendum of 23rd June 2016 resulted in a vote to leave the European Union.*

coins in issue were the fifty cents in cupro-nickel and the ten cents and five cents in nickel-brass. In 1960 a cupro-nickel dollar was added to the series. The twenty cents was reintroduced in 1975 after an absence of 70 years and a new denomination, the two dollars, was introduced in the same year. Both of these were struck on flans with scalloped edges, the twenty cents in nickel-brass; the two dollars in cupro-nickel. The next year the cupro-nickel five dollars denomination made its debut on a ten-sided flan. In 1978 the dollar was reduced in size and 1979 saw the last currency issue of the five cents (the lowest post war denomination). The five dollars denomination was struck on a smaller round flan from 1980. As the time for hand over approached the Queen's name and portrait were removed from the coins and replaced with the new symbol of Hong Kong, the flower of the bauhinia blakeana.[28] The latest coins of Britain's last major colony to bear the royal portrait are dated 1992.

HONG KONG UNDER ELIZABETH II

Cupro-nickel dollar 1960.

Two dollars 1975.   Five dollars 1978.

Dollar 1992 (reduced weight).

Five dollars (now round) 1987.   Five dollars 1993 (bauhinia type).

---

28 *A hybrid orchid originally cultivated in Hong Kong and generally known as the Hong Kong orchid.*

Hong Kong was not the only overseas territory for which Britain retained responsibility in the 1990s. There were those who did not seek or need independence, some that were too small to achieve it satisfactorily and some, like the British Antarctic Territory, with no permanent population at all. Until 1983 most of these were Crown colonies. The British Nationality Act 1981 which came into force on 1st January 1983 defined and restricted the Right of Abode in the United Kingdom and renamed the Crown colonies "British Dependent Territories". The British Overseas Territories Act 2002 relaxed many of the restrictions which had applied to citizens of the Dependent Territories and renamed them "British Overseas Territories". At the time of writing there are fourteen such territories although four of these have no permanent population. The ten which are permanently inhabited are shown in Table 3, the others in Table 4.

TABLE 3
BRITISH OVERSEAS TERRITORIES
(INHABITED)

Name	Location	Flag	Population (approximate)	Currency
Anguilla	Caribbean		15,500	East Caribbean Dollar
Bermuda	North Atlantic		64,800	Bermuda Dollar
British Virgin Islands	Caribbean		27,800	US Dollar
Cayman Islands	Caribbean		57,000	Cayman Islands Dollar
Falkland Islands	South Atlantic		2,950	Falkland Pound
Gibraltar	Europe		30,000	Gibraltar Pound
Montserrat	Caribbean		5,100	East Caribbean Dollar
Pitcairn Islands	Pacific		56	New Zealand Dollar
St Helena, Ascension and Tristan da Cunha	South Atlantic		5,530	St Helena Pound
Turks and Caicos Islands	Caribbean		31,500	US Dollar

TABLE 4
BRITISH OVERSEAS TERRITORIES
(NO PERMANENT INHABITANTS)

Name	Location	Flag	Population
Akrotiri and Dhekelia	Cyprus (Sovereign Base Area)		Military personnel and staff
British Antarctic Territory	Antarctica		Scientific staff only
British Indian Ocean Territory (Chagos Islands)	Indian Ocean		Military personnel and staff (mainly United States)
South Georgia and the South Sandwich Islands	South Atlantic		Scientific staff and administrators

Table 3 shows that just three of the permanently inhabited Overseas Territories still use the pound as their currency and this in fact is the last vestige of the old sterling area. The Falkland Islands, Gibraltar and St Helena all have currency boards which back their currencies with sterling securities and peg their pounds to sterling. They issue coins and notes of the same denominations as the United Kingdom but of distinct designs. This revives the practice begun in the early 20th century when several of the Dominions and colonies issued their own versions of sterling denominations in order to secure the profits of coinage.

Decimal day in the United Kingdom was 15th February 1971 after which there were 100 "new pence" to the pound. This replaced the old system where there had been twelve pennies to the shilling and twenty shillings to the pound. It was some years (1983) before a one pound coin was introduced for practical purposes to replace the quick wearing pound note. This was the first time that the United Kingdom had had a one pound denomination in base metal but nevertheless, like the pound note it replaced, this nickel-brass coin was given unlimited legal tender. It was only after decimalization that the Falkland Islands, Gibraltar and St Helena introduced their own sterling equivalent coins.

Closer to home, Jersey, Guernsey and the Isle of Man continue to be Crown dependencies separate from the United Kingdom. They all use sterling coins but since decimalization have also issued their own versions which are legal tender only within each dependency. The currencies of the Crown dependencies are guaranteed by their governments and, like those of the Overseas Territories, are kept at par with the United Kingdom pound.

UNITED KINGDOM POST-DECIMAL POUND 1983

POUND COINS OF OVERSEAS TERRITORIES

Falkland Islands 1987. *St Helena 1984.*

Gibraltar 1988.

POUND COINS OF THE CROWN DEPENDENCIES

Jersey 1992. *Isle of Man 1983.*

Guernsey 1986

14 Climax and Decolonization

We noted in the Introduction that the ending of our story is necessarily a rather ragged affair. We have ended it as independence occurred or approached and for some of the Commonwealth realms at some other convenient point. Independence did not specifically bring change to the currency in use although a change of issuing authority obviously required a change of coin design. In fact even before independence the general trend in coin design is away from the purely heraldic devices common in the early 20th century and towards the use of national symbols. These are often based on local flora and fauna, a trend perhaps initiated by the Ceylon coins as early as 1870 but taken a step further by the Irish coinage of 1928. We have seen that by the mid 19th century it was clear that sterling would not become the standard uniform coinage of the Empire and that some colonial coins had to be struck in other currencies. We have also seen that, as silver prices fell, a desire on the part of the colonies and dominions to profit from the token nature of the British silver coinage led some of them to introduce their own versions of sterling coins. The divergence of the Australian, New Zealand and Fiji pounds from sterling as the gold standard was abandoned led to further versions of sterling coins, some of the silver now at different standards to that in use in the United Kingdom. As our story draws to a close the 19th century ideal of uniformity was but a dim memory and the coinage of the dominions and colonies was probably more diverse than it had ever been. Commonwealth coinages of course continue but each now pursues its own individual course with its own separate story and it is beyond the scope of this book to examine these.

The British Empire was a product of its time. With the benefit of hindsight it would be easy to find fault with colonial adventure and all that it entailed. It would also be easy to take pride in the achievement and in the humanitarian and liberal advances of the day. History though is not about opinion or about what should have been or what might have been. It is about what actually happened and to judge those of yesteryear other than by the standards of the times in which they lived would be wrong.

This book has sought neither to glorify nor condemn the Imperial achievement. Almost every motive and every agency combined to create it. The adventurer, the merchant, the humanitarian, the soldier, the sailor, the missionary, the explorer, the colonist, the colonized, the politician, the administrator, the convict, the slave and even the quarrelsome Sierra Leone brides with their black eyes all, for better or for worse, played their part in creating the complex dominion that became the British Empire. This has simply been their story and the story of the money that they used.

Gazetteer

Place	Location	Approximate Latitude and Longitude
Abadan	Iran	30-22 N 048-20 E
Aboh	Nigeria	05-34 N 006-31E
Acapulco	Mexico	16-51 N 099-56W
Adelaide	South Australia	34-52 S 138-30 E
Aden	Yemen	12-48 N 045-02 E
Aix la Chapelle (Aachen)	North Rhine	50-47 N 006-04 E
Akrotiri	Cyprus	34-35 N 032-59E
Albany	Western Australia	35-01 S 117-53 E
Alberta	Canada	55-00 N 115-00 W
Alderney	Channel Islands	49-42 N 002-12 W
Alexandria	Egypt	31-10 N 029-53 E
Alma (Battle of)	Crimea	44-50 N 033-41 E
Amalfi	Italy	40-39 N 014-35 E
Amiens	France	49-54 N 002-16 E
Amirante Islands	Seychelles Group	06-00 S 053-00 E
Amoy	China	24-25 N 118-04 E
Amsterdam	Netherlands	52-23 N 004-54 E
Andaman Islands	Bay of Bengal	12-30 N 092-50 E
Anguilla	Leeward Islands	18-12 N 063-05 W
Antigua	Leeward Islands	17-05 N 061-47 W
Arakan	Burma	19-00 N 094-15 E
Archangel	Russia	64-32 N 040-35 E
Arcot (Arkat)	India	12-53 N 079-20 E
Ascension Island	Atlantic Ocean	08-00 S 014-15W
Assam	India	25-45 N 92-30 E
Auckland	New Zealand	36-51 S 174-44 E
Ava	Burma (Myanmar)	21-51 N 096-00 E
Awadh (Oude)	India	26-50 N 081-00E
Azores	North Atlantic	38-44 N 029-00 W
Baffin Island	Canada	68-00 N 071-00 W

Bagamoyo	German East Africa	06-27 S	038-54 E
Baghdad	Iraq	33-20 N	044-28 E
Bahamas	Western Atlantic	25-00 N	078-00 W
Bahrain	Persian Gulf	26-00 N	050-30 E
Balaklava	Crimea	44-30 N	033-36 E
Bandar Abbas	Persia	27-12 N	056-15 E
Bangladesh	Asia	23-00 N	090-00 E
Bandjarmasin	South Borneo	03-20 S	114-35 E
Bantam	Java	06-08 S	106-10 E
Barbados	West Indies	13-05 N	059-35 W
Barbuda	Leeward Islands	17-35 N	061-50 W
Basra	Iraq	30-30 N	047-50 E
Bassein	Burma (Mandalay)	16-50 N	094-44 E
Basutoland (Lesotho)	Southern Africa	30-00 S	028-00 E
Batavia (Jakarta)	Java	06-09 S	106-49 E
Bay of Islands	New Zealand	35-15 S	174-06 E
Bechuanaland (Botswana)	Southern Africa	22-00 S	024-00 E
Beijing	China	39-55 N	116-25 E
Bencoolen	Sumatra	03-48 S	102-12 E
Bengal	India	23-00 N	088-00 E
Benin	West Africa	10-00 N	002-00 E
Berbice	British Guiana	05-50 N	057-40 W
Berlin	Germany	52-31 N	013-24 E
Bermuda	Atlantic	32-17 N	064-47 W
Bihar	India	25-00 N	086-00 E
Birmingham	England	52-29 N	001-55 W
Blantyre	Nyasaland (Malawi)	15-47 S	035-00 E
Bloemfontein	Orange Free State	29-06 S	026-13 E
Blood River	Natal	28-06 S	030-32 E
Blue Mountains	New South Wales	33-40 S	150-00 E
Bermudas	Atlantic	32-45 N	065-00 W
Bombay (Mumbai)	India	18-55 N	072-50 E
The Bogue	Pearl River, China	22-46 N	113-37 E
Boston	Massachusetts	42-21 N	71-04 W
Botany Bay	Australia	34-00 S	151-14 E
Botswana	Southern Africa	22-00 S	024-00 E
Bougainville	Pacific	06-00 S	155-00 E
Île de Bourbon (Réunion)	Indian Ocean	21-00 S	055-30 E
Brisbane	Queensland	27-26 S	153-02 E
Bristol	England	51-27 N	002-35 W
British Columbia	Canada	50-00 N	123-00 W
British Guiana	South America	06-00 N	059-00 W
British Honduras	Central America	17-00 N	088-30 W
Brunei	Borneo	04-50 N	115-00 E
Brussels	Belgium	50-51 N	004-21 E
Buenos Aires	Argentina	34-36 S	058-23 W

Bulawayo	S. Rhodesia (Zimbabwe)	20-09 S	028-35 E
Bultfontein	Orange Free State	28-17 S	026-09 E
Burma (Myanmar)	Asia	20-00 N	096-00 E
Bushire	Persia	28-55 N	050-50 E
Cachar	Assam	25-05 N	092-55 E
Cairo	Egypt	30-03 N	031-14 E
Calais	France	50-57 N	001-51 E
Calcutta	Bengal	22-34 N	088-22 E
California	United States of America	38-00 N	122-00 W
Callao	South America	12-02 S	077-08 W
Cameroon	West Africa	04-00 N	012-30 E
Canberra	Australia	35-18 S	149-07 E
Cannanore	South India	11-52 N	075-21 E
Canton (Guangzhou)	China	23-08 N	113-15 E
Cape Blanco (Ras Nouadhibou)	West Africa	20-46 N	017-03 W
Cape Breton Island	Nova Scotia	46-00 N	060-00 W
Cape Coast Castle	Gold Coast (Ghana)	05-06 N	001-15 W
Cape Cod	New England	42-02 N	070-14 W
Cape of Good Hope	South Africa	34-21 S	018-28 E
Cape Verde Islands	North Atlantic	16-40 N	024-30 W
Caroline Islands	Pacific	08-00 N	150-00 E
Castile	Spanish Kingdom	40-00 N	004-30 W
Cayman Islands	Caribbean	19-15 N	080-30 W
Cephalonia	Ionian Islands	38-14 N	020-30 E
Cerigo (Kythira)	Ionian Islands	36-14 N	023-00 E
Ceylon	Bay of Bengal	07-00 N	081-00 E
Chagos Islands	Indian Ocean	06-00 S	072-00 E
Channel Islands	English Channel	49-30 N	002-30 W
Charlottetown	Prince Edward Island	46-15 N	063-08 W
Christmas Island	Indian Ocean	10-30 S	105-35 E
Christmas Island	Pacific	01-53N	157-24W
Chuenpee	China	22-46 N	113-39 E
Cobourg Peninsula	Australia	11-20 S	132 15 E
Cocos (Keeling) Islands	Indian Ocean	12-05 S	096-50 E
Colombo	Ceylon (Sri Lanka)	06-56 N	079-50 E
Comfortless Cove	Ascension Island	08-00 S	014-15W
Compiègne	France	49-25N	002-49E
Congo	Central Africa	03-00 S	023-00E
Connecticut	New England	41-40 N	072-40 W
Constantinople (Istanbul)	Turkey	41-01 N	028-58 E
Cook Islands	Pacific	20-00 S	160-00 W
Corfu	Ionian Islands	39-38 N	019-50 E
Cormantine (Kormantin)	West Africa	05-12 N	001-06 W
Crimea	Black Sea	45-00 N	034-00 E
Cuba	Caribbean	22-00 N	079-00 W
Cumberland House	Saskatchewan	53-57 N	102-19 W

Curaçao	Caribbean	12-11 N 069-00 W
Cyprus	Mediterranean	35-00 N 033-00 E
Dahomey	West Africa	07-00 N 002-30 E
Damascus	Syria	33-31 N 36-18 E
Danube (River)	Central and Eastern Europe	Germany to Black Sea
Dar es Salaam	East Africa	06-50 S 039-18 E
Darien	Central America	08-50 N 077-40 W
Darwin	Australia	12-27 S 130-50 E
Davis Strait	Canada	65-00 N 058-00 W
Delhi	India	28-40 N 077-14 W
Demerara	British Guiana	06-48 N 058-10 W
Derwent River	Tasmania	42-50 S 147-20 E
Dhekelia	Cyprus	34-59 N 033-45 E
Dijon	France	47-17 N 005-03 E
Dindings	Malay Peninsula	04-15 N 100-35 E
Dodowa	Gold Coast (Ghana)	05-53 N 000-06 E
Dominica	Caribbean	15-25 N 061-20 W
Douglas	Isle of Man	54-09 N 004-29 W
Dover	England	51-08 N 001-19 E
Dublin	Ireland	53-21 N 006-15 W
Dunedin	New Zealand	45-52 S 170-30 E
Dunkirk (Dunkerque)	France	51-02 N 002-22 E
Durban	Natal	29-53 S 031-02 E
Dutoitspan	Northern Cape Province	28-44 S 024-47 E
Elba	Italy	42-45 N 010-14 E
Elmina	Gold Coast (Ghana)	05-05 N 001-21 W
Equatoria	Southern Sudan	05-00 N 031-00 E
Essequibo	British Guiana	06-48 N 058-25 W
Falkland Islands	South Atlantic	52-00 S 059-30 W
Fanning Island	Pacific	03-51 N 159-22 W
Farrukhabad	Bengal	27-22 N 079-38 E
Fashoda	Sudan	09-53 N 032-07 E
Fiji	Pacific	17-30 S 179-00 E
Florida	North America	28-00 N 082-00 W
Foochow (Fuzhou)	China	26-05 N 119-18 E
Fort Cornwallis	Penang	05-25 N 100-21 E
Fort Dundas	Melville Island, Australia	11-24 S 130-12 E
Fort St George (Madras)	India	13-06 N 080-17 E
Foxe Channel	Canada	66-00 N 080-00 W
Freetown	Sierra Leone	08-29 N 013-14 W
Frobisher Bay	Canada	63-00 N 067-00 W
Gambia	West Africa	13-30 N 016-00 W
Gandamak	Afghanistan	34-17 N 070-02 E
Geneva	Switzerland	46-12 N 006-09 E
Genoa	Italy	44-25 N 008-56 E
George Town	Penang	05-23 N 100-15 E

Georgia	North America	32-00 N	082-00 W
Ghana	West Africa	06-00 N	001-00 W
Ghent	Belgium	51-03 N	003-44 E
Gibraltar	Europe	36-08 N	005-21 W
Gilbert and Ellice Islands	Pacific	02-00 S	175-30 E
Gold Coast (Ghana)	West Africa	06-00 N	001-00 W
Gombroon (Bandar Abbas)	Persian Gulf	27-12 N	056-15 E
Good Hope (Cape of)	South Africa	34-21 S	018-28 E
Granada	Spain	37-11 N	003-36 W
Graham's Land (Graham Land)	Antarctica	70-00 S	062-00 W
Grain Coast	West Africa	06-00 N	010-00 W
Grand Banks	Western Atlantic	45-00 N	050-00 W
Gravelines	France	51-00 N	002-08 E
Great Fish River	South Africa	33-00 S	027-00 E
Grenada	Windward Islands	12-07 N	061-40 W
Grenadines	Windward Islands	12-40 N	061-20 W
Griqua Town (Griekwastad)	Northern Cape Province	28-51 S	023-15 E
Guadeloupe	Caribbean	16-15 N	061-35 W
Guangzhou	China	23-08 N	113-16 E
Guernsey	Channel Islands	49-27 N	002-33 W
Guinea	West Africa	10-30 N	011-00 W
Gunzburg	Bavaria	48-27 N	010-16 E
Haiti	Caribbean	19-00 N	072-00 W
Halifax	Nova Scotia	44-40 N	63-37 W
Hanover	Europe	52-22 N	009-43 E
Havana	Cuba	23-08 N	082-23 W
Hawaii	Pacific	19-30 N	155-30 W
Hejaz	Arabia	22-00 N	040-00 E
Heligoland	North Sea	54-11 N	007-52 E
Herat	Afghanistan	34-20 N	062-12 E
Herm	Channel Islands	49-29 N	002-28 W
Hobart	Tasmania	42-53 S	147-19 E
Honduras	Central America	15-00 N	086-30 W
Hong Kong	China	22-17 N	114-10 E
Hudson Bay	Canada	58-00 N	085-00 W
Inkerman	Crimea	44-36 N	033-37 E
Ionian Islands	Mediterranean	38-00 N	020-00 E
Iraq	Middle East	32-00 N	044-00 E
Isle of Man	British Isles	54-10 N	004-40 W
Istanbul	Turkey	41-01 N	028-58 E
Ithaca	Ionian Islands	38-22 N	020-43 E
Ivory Coast	West Africa	07-30 N	005-00 W
Jalalabad	Afghanistan	34-26 N	070-27 E
Jamaica	Caribbean	18-00 N	077-00 W
Jamestown	Virginia	37-13 N	076-47 W
Jask	Persia	25-39 N	057-46 E

Java	East Indies	07-30 S	108-00 E
Jersey	Channel Islands	49-12 N	002-07 W
Johore (modern Johor)	Malay Peninsula	02-00 N	103-30 E
Jordan	Middle East	31-00 N	036-00 E
Kabul	Afghanistan	34-32 N	069-10 E
Kandahar	Afghanistan	31-37 N	065-42 E
Kandy	Ceylon	07-18 N	080-38 E
Kedah	Malay Peninsula	06-00 N	100-30 E
Kelantan	Malay Peninsula	05-30 N	102-00 E
Kew	England	51-29 N	000-17 W
Khartoum	Sudan	15-33 N	032-32 E
Kimberley	Northern Cape Province	28-44 S	024-46 E
King George Sound	Western Australia	35-02 S	117-56 E
Kingston	Jamaica	17-59 N	076-48 W
Kingston	Ontario	44-14 N	076-30 W
Klaarwater (Griqua Town)	Northern Cape Province	28-51 S	023-15 E
Kormantin (Cormantine)	West Africa	05-12 N	001-06 W
Kowloon	Hong Kong	22-19 N	114-11 E
Kuala Lumpur	Malay Peninsula	03-08 N	101-41 E
Kuching	Borneo	01-34 N	110-21 E
Kumasi	Ghana	06-40 N	001-37 W
Kuria Muria Islands	Arabian Sea	17-30 N	056-00 E
Kuwait	Persian Gulf	29-20 N	048-00 E
Labrador	Canada	53-00 N	060-00 W
Labuan	Borneo	05-19 N	115-13 W
Laccadive Islands	Indian Ocean	10-30 N	072-30 E
Lagos	West Africa (Nigeria)	06-27 N	003-24 E
Laird's Port (Onitsha)	Nigeria	06-09 N	006-47 E
Laird's Town (Lokaja)	Nigeria	07-48 N	006-45 E
Lake Victoria	East Africa	01-00 S	033-00 E
Larut	Perak	04-57 N	100-50 E
Lausanne	Switzerland	46-31 N	006-38 E
Lebanon	Middle East	34-00 N	036-00 E
Leeward Islands	Caribbean	17-30 N	63-00 W
Leith	Scotland	55-59 N	003-10 W
Lemnos	Greece	39-55 N	025-15 E
Lesotho	Southern Africa	30-00 S	028-00 E
Levuka	Fiji	17-41 S	178-50 E
Libya	North Africa	29-00 N	17-30 E
Limpopo River	Southern Africa	20-57 S	030-00 E
Lintin Island	China	22-25 N	113-48 E
Lisbon	Portugal	38-43 N	009-08 W
Lokoja	Nigeria	07-48 N	006-45 E.
Lombok	East Indies	08-30 S	116-30 E
London	England	51-30 N	000-08 W
Macao	China	22-12 N	113-33 E

Madras (Chennai)	India	13-06 N	080-17 E
Magellan (Strait of)	South America	52-30 S	069-00 W
Malacca (Melaka)	Malay Peninsula	02-15 N	102-15 E
Malacca Strait	Asia	03-00 N	101-00 E
Malawi	Central Africa	12-30 S	034-00 E
Maldive Islands	Indian Ocean	04-00 N	073-00 E
Malta	Mediterranean	35-53 N	014-30 E
Maluka (Maloeka)	South Borneo	03-30 S	114-40 E
Mandalay	Burma (Myanmar)	21-58 N	096-05 E
Manila	Philippines	14-36 N	120-59 E
Manipur	India	24-30 N	094-00 E
Manitoba	Canada	55-00 N	097-00 W
Mariana Islands	Pacific	17-00 N	145-00 E
Marlborough Sounds	New Zealand	41-09 S	174-05 E
Marseilles	France	43-18 N	005-23 E
Marshall Islands	Pacific	10-00 N	168-00 E
Martaban	Burma (Myanmar)	16-32 N	097-37 E
Martinique	Caribbean	14-40 N	061-00 W
Maryland	North America	39-00 N	077-00 W
Massachusetts	New England	42-25 N	072-00 W
Masulipatam (Machlipatam)	India	16-10 N	081-09 E
Mauritius	Indian Ocean	20-20 S	057-30 E
Mecca	Arabia	21-26 N	039-50 E
Meerut	India	28-59 N	077-42 E
Melbourne	Victoria	37-45 S	144-58 E
Melville Island	Australia	11-30 S	131-00 E
Mercury Bay	New Zealand	36-47 S	175-48 E
Mesopotamia (Iraq)	Middle East	32-00 N	046-00 E
Mexico	Central America	20-00 N	100-00 W
Minorca	Balearic Islands	40-00 N	004-00 E
Moldavia	Eastern Europe	47-00 N	027-00 E
Molopo River	Southern Africa	25-40 S	24-30 E
Mombasa	East Africa	04-03 S	039-40 E
Montreal	Canada	45-30 N	073-35 W
Montserrat	Leeward Islands	16-45 N	062-12 W
Morant Bay	Jamaica	17-53 N	076-24 W
Moreton Bay	Australia	27-15 S	153-15 E
Mosquito Coast	Central America	14-00 N	084-00 W
Moudros	Greece	39-52 N	025-16 E
Mount Alexander	Victoria	37-00 S	144-18 E
Murshidabad	Bengal	24-11 N	088-16 E
Muscat	Arabian Sea	23-37 N	058 33 E
Mysore	India	12-18 N	076-39 E
Nanking (Nanjing)	China	32-05 N	118-46 E
Natal	South Africa	29-00 S	030-00 E
Nauru	Pacific	00-32 S	166-55 E

Negri Sembilan	Malay Peninsula	02-40 N	102-10 E
Nejd	Arabia	26-00 N	042-00 E
Neuilly	France	48-53 N	002-16 E
Nevis	Leeward Islands	17-06 N	062 36 W
New Amsterdam *(see New York)*			
New Brunswick	North America	46-30 N	066-00 W
New Guinea	Pacific	05-00 S	145-00 E
New Hampshire	New England	43-00 N	072-00 W
New Haven	New England	41-18 N	072-56 W
New Hebrides (now Vanuatu)	Pacific	16-00 S	168-00 E
New Jersey	North America	40-00 N	074-30 W
New Netherlands *(see New York)*			
New Norfolk	Tasmania	42-47 S	147-03 E
New South Wales	Australia	34-00 S	150-00 E
New York	North America	40-43 N	074-00 W
New Rush (Kimberley)	Northern Cape Province	28-46 S	024-46 E
Newcastle	New South Wales	32-56 S	151-47 E
Newfoundland	North America	48-00 N	055-00 W
Nicobar Islands	Bay of Bengal	08-00 N	093-30 E
Ningpo (Ningbo)	China	29-52 N	121-33 E
Niue	Pacific	19-03 S	169-55 W
Norfolk Island	South West Pacific	29-02 S	167 58 E
Normandy	France	49-00 N	000 30 W
North Cape	Norway	71-11 N	025-47 E
North Western Territory	Canada	62-00 N	115-00 W
Northern Rhodesia (Zambia)	Central Africa	15-00 S	025-00 E
Northwest Territory *(see North Western Territory)*			
Nova Scotia	North America	45-00 N	064-00 W
Nyasaland (Malawi)	Central Africa	12-30 S	034-00 E
Ocean Island (Banaba)	Pacific	00-52 S	169-32 E
Oil Rivers	Nigeria	04-30 N	006-00 E
Omdurman	Sudan	15-39 N	032-29 E
Onitsha	Nigeria	06-09 N	006-47 E
Ontario	Canada	46-00 N	080-00 E
Orange River	Southern Africa	30-40 S	026-00 E
Orissa	India	21-00 N	085-00 E
Oro, Rio de	West Africa	23-43 N	015-56 W
Osaka	Japan	34-42 N	135-29 E
Otago	New Zealand	45-30 S	170-30 E
Ottawa	Canada	45-25 N	075-42 W
Oude (Awadh)	India	26-50 N	081-00 E
Pahang	Malay Peninsula	03-30 N	102-30 E
Palestine	Middle East	32-00 N	034-50 E
Palmerston (modern Darwin)	Australia	12-27 S	130-50 E
Panama	Central America	08-56 N	079-31 W
Pangkor	Malay Peninsula	04-13 N	100-33 E

Papua	New Guinea	07-30 S	145-00 E
Paris	France	48-52 N	002-20 E
Paxos	Ionian Islands	39-12 N	020-10 E
Pearl Harbour	Hawaiian Islands	21-22 N	157-59 W
Pei-ho River (Hai River)	China	38-57 N	117-43 E
Peking (Beijing)	China	39-55 N	116-25 E
Penang	Malay Peninsula	05-23 N	100-15 E
Pennsylvania	North America	40-00 N	076-00 W
Perak	Malay Peninsula	04-40 N	100-50 E
Perim	Gulf of Aden	12-40 N	043-25 E
Perlis	Malay Peninsula	06-25 N	100-15 E
Perth	Western Australia	31-56 S	115-52 E
Phoenix Islands	Pacific	03-30 S	172-00 W
Piedmont	Southern Europe	45-00 N	007-30 W
Pietermaritzburg	Natal	29-37 S	030-23 E
Pitcairn Island	Pacific	25-04 S	130-06 W
Plassey (Palasi)	India	23-48 N	088-15 E
River Plate	South America	35-00 S	057-00 W
Plymouth	England	50-22 N	004-09 W
Plymouth	New England	41-57 N	070-40 W
Poitiers	France	46-35 N	000-20 E
Port Augusta	South Australia	32-30 S	137-46 E
Port Blair	Andaman Islands	11-40 N	092-42 E
Port Jackson	New South Wales	33-51 S	151-14 E
Port Louis	Mauritius	20-10 S	057-30 E
Port Macquarie	New South Wales	31-26 S	152-54 E
Port Mahon	Minorca	39-52 N	004-18 E
Port Moresby	Papua	09-27 S	147-12 E
Port Natal (Durban)	Natal	29-53 S	031-02 E
Port Nicholson (Wellington)	New Zealand	41-17 S	174-50 E
Port Phillip	Australia	38-00 S	144-50 E
Port Stanley	Falkland Islands	51-42 S	057-52 W
Pretoria	Transvaal	25-45 S	028-11 E
Prince Edward Island	North America	46-15 N	063-00 W
Prince of Wales Island (Penang)	Malay Peninsula	05-23 N	100-15 E
Providence	North America	41-49 N	71-25 W
Province Wellesley	Penang	06-20 N	100-25 E
Pulo Run	Spice Islands	04-33 S	129-40 E
Punjab	India	32-00 N	073-00 E
Qatar	Persian Gulf	25-30 N	051-15 E
Qishn (Sultanate)	Aden Protectorate	15-20 N	051-40 E
Queen Adelaide Province	Southern Africa	32-50 S	027-25 E
Queen Charlotte Sound	New Zealand	41-10 S	174-15 E
Queensland	Australia	26-00 S	150-00 E
Quebec	Canada	46-49 N	071-13 W
Ramsey	Isle of Man	54-19 N	004-23 W

Rangoon (Yangon)	Burma (Myanmar)	16-48 N	096-09 E
Ras-al-Khaima	Trucial Coast	25-47N	055-57 E
Redonda	Leeward Islands	16-56 N	062-21 W
Réunion (Île de Bourbon)	Indian Ocean	21-00 S	055-30 E
Rhode Island	New England	41-30 N	071-30 W
Rhodesia (see Southern Rhodesia, Northern Rhodesia)			
Rio de Oro	West Africa	23-43 N	015-56 W
Roanoke	Modern North Carolina	35-56 N	075-42 W
Rodrigues Island	Indian Ocean	19-45 S	063-25 E
Rome	Italy	41-54 N	012-29 E
Run (Pulo Run)	Spice Islands	04-33 S	129-40 E
Rupert's Land	Canada	52-00 N	085-00 W
Ryswick (modern Rijswijk)	Netherlands	52-02 N	004-20 E
Saint-Germain	France	48-54 N	002-06 E
Saint Lô	France	49-07 N	001-05 W
Saintes	Caribbean	15-50 N	061-37 W
St Christopher (St Kitts)	Leeward Islands	17-18 N	062-44 W
St Helena	South Atlantic	15-57 S	005-42 W
St John's Island (Prince Edward Island q.v.)			
St Kitts (St Christopher)	Leeward Islands	17-18 N	062-44 W
St Lawrence (Gulf of)	Canada	48-00 N	063-00 W
St Lawrence River	Canada	47-00 N	070-50 W
St Lucia	Windward Islands	14-00 N	061-00 W
St Thomé	India	13-05 N	080-17 E
St Vincent	Windward Islands	13-10 N	061-10 W
Samoa	Pacific	13-54 S	171-50 W
San Remo	Italy	43-49 N	007-47 E
Sand River	Orange Free State	28-05 S	027-08 E
Sandakan	North Borneo	05-50 N	118-07 E
Sandwich Islands (now Hawaii)	Pacific	19-30 N	155-30 W
Santa Maura (Levkas)	Ionian Islands	38-43 N	020-39 E
Santo Domingo	Caribbean	19-00 N	070-00 W
Sarawak	North Borneo	03-00 N	114-00 E
Sardinia	Mediterranean	40-00 N	009-00 E
Sark	Channel Islands	49-26 N	002-22 W
Saskatchewan	Canada	55-00 N	115-00 W
Savoy	Southern Europe	46-00 N	006-20 E
Sevastopol	Crimea	44-35 N	033-31 E
Selangor	Malay Peninsula	03-15 N	101-40 E
Senegal	West Africa	14-40 N	016-40 W
Senegambia	West Africa	13-50 N	016-40 W
Seringapatam	India	12-25 N	076-42 E
Sèvres	France	48-49 N	002-13 E
Seychelles	Indian Ocean	04-50 S	055-40 E
Shangani River	Matabeleland	18-48 S	027-45 E
Shanghai	China	31-13 N	121-27 E

Sharjah	Trucial Coast	25-22 N	055-23 E
Sicily	Mediterranean	37-30 N	014-30 E
Sierra Leone	West Africa	08-30 N	012-30 W
Simla	India	31-06 N	077-10 E
Sind	British India (later Pakistan)	26-00 N	069-00 E
Singapore	Malay Peninsula	01-18 N	103-51 E
Sinop	Turkey (Black Sea)	42-02 N	035-10 E
Slave Coast	West Africa	06-30 N	003-00 E
Socotra.	Indian Ocean	12-30 N	053-40 E
Solomon Islands	Pacific	08-00 S	158-00 E
Somers Islands (Bermudas)	Atlantic	32-17 N	064-47 W
Sourabaya (Surabaja)	Java	07-16 S	112-45 E
South Australia	Australia	32-00 S	138-00 E
South Georgia	South Atlantic	54-30 S	037-30 W
South Orkney Islands	South Atlantic	60- 40 S	045-30 W
South Sandwich Islands	South Atlantic	59-00 S	025-00 W
South Shetland Islands	South Atlantic	62-00 S	058-00 W
Southern Rhodesia (Zimbabwe)	Southern Africa	20-00 S	030-00 E
Strait of Magellan	South America	52-30 S	069-00 W
Straits Settlements (Penang, Malacca, Singapore and the Dindings q.v.)			
Sudan	North East Africa	15-00 N	030-00 E
Suez	Egypt	29-58 N	032-33 E
Sulu	Eastern Archipelago	06-00 N	121-00 E
Sumatra	East Indies	01-00 S	102-00 E
Sunda Strait	Eastern Archipelago	06-20 S	105-30 E
Sungei Ujong (Seremban)	Malay Peninsula	02-45 N	101-55 E
Surat	India	21-10 N	072-50 E
Suva	Fiji	18-08 S	178-26 E
Swan River	Western Australia	32-03 S	115-50 E
Swaziland	Southern Africa	26-30 S	031-30 E
Sydney	New South Wales	33.52 S	151- 13E
Syria	Middle East	35-00 N	038-00 E
Syriam (Thanlyin)	Burma (Myanmar)	16-44 N	096-15 E
Tahiti	Pacific	17-40 N	149-25 W
Tanganyika (Tanzania)	East Africa	05-00 S	035-00 E
Tangier	Morocco	35-46 N	005-48 W
Tasmania (Van Diemen's Land)	Australia	42-00 S	147-00 E
Teheran (Tehran)	Iran	35-42 N	051-25 E
Tel el Kebir	Egypt	30-30 N	031-55 E
Tenasserim	Burma (Myanmar)	13-00 N	098-45 E
Tenterfield	New South Wales	29-03 S	152-01 E
Ternate	Spice Islands	00-49 N	127-22 E
Texas	North America	31-00 N	098-00 W
Thursday Island	Australia	10-33 S	142-12 E
Tientsin (Tianjin)	China	39-08 N	117-11 E
Tobago	Caribbean	11-16 N	060-36 W

Togoland	West Africa	60-30 N	001-20 E
Tokelau (Union) Islands	Pacific	09-10 S	171-50 W
Tonga	Pacific	21-00 S	175-00 W
Toronto	Canada	43-42 N	79-25 W
Torres Strait	Australia	10-20 S	143-00 E
Tortola	Virgin Islands	18-23 N	64-42 W
Toulon	France	43-07 N	005-56 E
Tournai	France (now in Belgium)	50-36 N	003-23 E
Transjordan (modern Jordan)	Middle East	31-00 N	036-00 E
Trengganu	Malay Peninsula	05-00 N	103-00 E
Trianon	France	48-49 N	002-06 E
Trincomalee	Ceylon (Sri Lanka)	08-33 N	081-14 E
Trinidad	Caribbean	10-30 N	061-10 W
Tristan da Cunha	South Atlantic	37-07 S	012-17 W
Turks and Caicos	Western Atlantic	21-35 N	071-25 W
Union Islands (now Tokelau)	Pacific	09-10 S	171-50 W
Utrecht	Netherlands	52-05 N	005-07 E
Vaal River	Southern Africa	27-00 S	026-30 E
Valparaiso	South America	33-02 S	071-38 W
Van Diemen's Land (Tasmania)	Australia	42-00 S	147-00 E
Vancouver	Canada	49-15 N	123-07 W
Vanuatu (New Hebrides)	Pacific	16-00 S	168-00 E
Venice	Italy	45-26 N	012-21 E
Versailles	France	48-48 N	002-07 E
Vichy	France	46-07 N	003-25 E
Victoria	Australia	37-00 S	145-00 E
Victoria (Lake)	East Africa	01-00 S	033-00 E
Vienna	Austria	48-12 N	016-22 E
Virgin Islands	Leeward Islands	18-20 N	064-40 W
Virginia	North America	37-00 N	076-30 W
Wadelai	Uganda	02-48 N	031-35 E
Wairau Valley	New Zealand	41-40 S	173-30 E
Waitangi	New Zealand	35-16 S	174-05 E
Wallachia	Eastern Europe	44-30 N	026-00 E
Washington Island	Pacific	04-41 N	160-23 W
Waterloo	Belgium	50-43 N	004-24 E
Weihaiwei	China	37-31 N	122.07 E
Wellington	New Zealand	41-17 S	174-47 E
Wesselton	Northern Cape Province	28-44 S	024-46 E
Western Australia	Australia	30-00 S	117-00 E
Whampoa	China	23-06 N	113-23 E
White Highlands	Kenya	00-30 S	037-00 E
Windward Islands	Caribbean	13-00 N	061-00 W
Witu	East Africa	02-23 S	040-25 E
Winnipeg	Manitoba	49-53 N	097-08 W
Yandabo	Burma (Myanmar)	21-38 N	095-22 E

Yangon (Rangoon)	Burma (Myanmar)	16-48 N	096-09 E
Yucatan Peninsula	Central America	20-00 N	088-00 W
Zambia (Northern Rhodesia)	Central Africa	15-00 S	025-00 E
Zambesi River	Central Africa	17-35 S	025-00 E
Zante	Ionian Islands	37-48 N	020-45 E
Zanzibar	East Africa	06-10 S	039-20 E
Zimbabwe (Southern Rhodesia)	Southern Africa	20-00 S	030-00 E
Zululand	Southern Africa	28-00 S	031-00 E

Glossary

Afrikaner	An ethnic group in Southern Africa descended predominantly from the early Dutch settlers.
All Red Line	A communication system of cables (mainly submarine) connecting the main countries of the Empire. Completed in 1902 with the lengthy trans-Pacific section.
Amir	A nobleman, commander or chief.
Anna	The sixteenth part of a rupee.
Asiento	Permission to supply slaves to the Spanish Empire. Due to the Papal division of the world the Spanish could not generally trade directly for slaves on the West African coast which was a Portuguese sphere of interest. The asiento was granted to Britain in 1713 after the War of the Spanish Succession and managed by the South Sea Company until the privilege was lost to Britain in 1750.
Baganda	The people of Buganda (q.v.).
Bêche de mer	The sea cucumber, found mainly in the South West Pacific.
Blackbirding	Labour trafficking in the Pacific.
Boer	Dutch and Afrikaans for "farmer". Not all Afrikaners were Boers the Boers were all Afrikaners.
Buganda	The land of the Baganda people. Buganda eventually formed the nucleus of the British protectorate of Uganda.
Calicoes	Light cotton cloths. A generic term for many types of cotton goods exported from India.
Caliph	The leader of Islam. Considered to be a religious successor to the Prophet Muhammad.
Candareen	One hundredth of a tael of silver.
Cash	Small copper or base metal coin.
Cent	The hundredth part of a higher denomination, usually the dollar.
Challie	In Ceylon, one fourth of a stiver.

Co-Hong	The select group of Chinese merchants who dealt with the European traders at Canton. Until the opening of Chinese trade in the 19th century this was the only group authorized to handle foreign trade in the whole of China.
Commissariat	Originally a civilian service under direct Treasury control. It was responsible for the supply of the essentials of life to the army (food, fodder and non-military stores). It also acted as banker to the army being the agent of the Treasury for the supply of money to the military. It played a vital role in the early years of colonies such as New South Wales and Sierra Leone being responsible to the Treasury for the safekeeping of specie and the issue of Bills of Exchange. In the Crimean War the system of supply under strict Treasury control was found wanting and changes began to be made. In December 1854 the Commissariat became the responsibility of the War Department. It continued to operate as a civilian (though uniformed) service under Treasury regulation until 1869 when it came under full army management as part of the newly formed Control Department. After several administrative changes "Commissariat and Transport" was reorganized into the Army Service Corps in 1888.
Commonwealth	The British Commonwealth of Nations originally comprised the self governing colonies which had achieved Dominion status. In the era of decolonization it became more inclusive and aimed to attract all the colonies as they achieved independence. The word "British" was dropped from the title in 1949.
Commonwealth realm	An independent Commonwealth country which retains the British monarch as its constitutional head of state.
Condominium	A territory over which more than one power agree to share equal dominion and exercise their rights without dividing it into separate zones. Examples are the Anglo-Egyptian Sudan and the Anglo-French arrangement for the New Hebrides.
Corn Laws	British trade laws designed primarily to protect the price of home grown cereals.
"Country" trade	The private trade carried on by East India Company servants and others in the East. This could include anything other than the direct trade to Europe.
Cowry	A shell used for many years as currency in parts of Asia and Africa. The variety used was the shell of the *Cypraea moneta*, a type of cowry found mainly in the Indian Ocean.
Crown	Five Shillings (one quarter of a pound sterling).
Crown colony	A colony with a Governor appointed directly by the Crown and governed mainly through appointed councils. Originally termed "royal colonies" they began to replace proprietary colonies in the 17th century. In later years Crown colonies achieving full representative government, self government and then responsible government could move on to become dominions. In 1983

	the remaining Crown colonies became "British Dependent Territories" which in 2002 were reclassified as "British Overseas Territories".
De facto	Latin "concerning fact". It refers to what has become normal practice without specific legal sanction.
De jure	Latin "concerning the law". It refers to what the law actually says rather than what happens in practice.
Diwan	Receiver general of a province and Chief Justice in civil cases in India.
Doit (Dutch "duit")	A small Dutch copper coin.
Dollar	The large silver coin which became known as the "Jaochimsthaler", named after the rich silver mines at Jaochimsthal in central Europe. The term was soon shortened to "thaler" and then corrupted into English as "dollar". When the Spanish American eight reales became the established international trade coin it too would be referred to as a dollar.
Dominion	A self governing colony granted special status. The Dominions were the basis of the British Commonwealth of Nations and were granted the right of independence within the Commonwealth in 1931.
Doubloon	Spanish coin, originally the doblón (double escudo). By the mid 18th century the term "doubloon" was in general use for the coin of eight escudos. The eight escudo doubloon was the same weight as the silver piece of eight reales and passed for sixteen dollars.
Entente Cordiale	A series of agreements between Britain and France signed in 1904. These were aimed at settling various colonial and international matters of mutual concern but marked the beginning of what would be an alliance against Germany.
Ex officio	Latin "from the office". This describes a position held by an official by virtue of holding a specific office elsewhere. The Governor of Fiji, for example, was ex officio the High Commissioner for the Western Pacific. The post of High Commissioner was held by the Governor of Fiji irrespective of who that individual may have been. In Crown colonies colonial officials were often ex officio members of Executive and Legislative Councils.
Fanam	Small gold coin of southern India. From 1689 the East India Company struck the fanam in silver.
Fante	The predominant coastal people of the Gold Coast (Ghana).
Farthing	One quarter of a penny. Originally a "fourthling".
Firman	An order, mandate or imperial decree.
Florin	A medieval gold coin but in 19th century Britain a silver coin of two shillings (one tenth of a pound sterling). Introduced in 1849 as a first tentative step towards decimalization (a process not completed until 1971).
Franc	Unit of French currency.

Free Selector	A prospective arable farmer allowed by the New South Wales government to freely select plots of Crown land for purchase before survey. Much of this land was already in use by squatters (q.v.) for sheep farming.
Garda Costas	Coast Guard vessels charged with policing the Spanish monopoly.
Gold Standard	The international gold standard in use before the First World War provided a mechanism for price and exchange rate stability. The major currencies were pegged against each other in terms of gold (see "par exchange rate" below). Any deviation in the rate above or below certain points caused by imbalances of trade or changes in bank rates made it profitable to import or export gold. When gold approached its export point the Central Bank would raise its interest rate to attract gold. When it approached its import point the "rules of the game" were that the Bank rate would be lowered. Under this system Bank notes were fully convertible into gold coin which was in general circulation. The First World War led to a suspension of this system but when attempts to restore it were made in the 1920s most nations were unwilling or unable to abide by the rules. Gold coins did not come back into general circulation and banknotes could only be exchanged for gold bullion. It was therefore referred to as the "gold bullion standard" rather than the previous "gold specie standard". All the major currencies left the gold standard in the 1930s.
Guilder	Dutch unit of currency. In medieval Europe it had been a "golden" coin but was struck in silver by the Dutch from the 17th century.
Halifax currency	The rate for the Spanish dollar in Nova Scotia (5/-) which became generally accepted throughout British North America by the early 19th century.
Imam	An Islamic community and religious leader.
Impi	An armed body of Zulu men usually used to describe a Zulu regiment.
Indentured labour	Labour contracted for a specific period. This system was used to provide European labour for many of the colonies until it was largely superseded by slavery. When slavery was abolished large numbers of indentured labourers were again recruited, mainly from the Indian sub continent, to work the plantations of the Caribbean, Mauritius, Fiji and elsewhere.
Industrial Revolution	The move to increased industrial output in Britain from the later 18th century. It was enabled by mechanical methods of production, the increasing use of steam power and a willingness to invest in new ventures. It led to a population shift away from the countryside, to a huge increase in urban development and to fundamental social change. It occurred in Britain some years before it occurred elsewhere.

Jingoism	A belligerent and patriotic stance on foreign affairs.
Johannes	Portuguese series of gold coins so named because they superseded the moidore coinage in the 1720s during the reign of Johannes V. The first examples thus bore his name. The largest coin of the series was the 12,800 reis denomination known as the "dobra" in Portugal and the 6,400 reis (the "peça") was correctly the half johannes. In the colonies though it was the peça that was in common use and it was this denomination that was generally referred to as the johannes.
Kabaka	The title of the King of Buganda.
Kanganie	Often spelt "Kangany". An overseer of imported workers, particularly Tamils recruited for the plantations and mills of Ceylon and Malaya. His responsibilities included recruitment, advances of pay and administration.
Keping	Small copper coin used in the Eastern Archipelago.
Khedive	Title claimed by the Ottoman Wali (governor) of Egypt from the early 19th century. The title was not acknowledged by the Ottoman Sultan until 1867. When Egypt became a British protectorate at the start of the First World War the last Khedive was deposed and a Sultanate of Egypt proclaimed.
Larin	Unit of currency in the Maldive Islands.
League	An obsolete measure based on the distance a man could walk in one hour. It varied considerably but was usually about 3½ statute miles (roughly equivalent to 3 nautical miles). At sea the distance of the horizon varies with the height of eye but is about 3 nautical miles (one league) at a height of 7 feet.
Lepton	A fractional unit of currency in the Greek speaking world from ancient times. In the Ionian Islands in the 19th century it was a fraction of the obol.
Letters Patent	Latin "litterae patentes ". Litterae (plural) in the sense of something written, patentes from the Latin verb pateo (to be open). A letters patent is a written order by a head of state giving effect to a specific decision. Traditionally the seal was attached to the document but did not have to be broken for the document to be read. It was an open letter, its contents intended to be public knowledge.
Mace	One tenth of a tael of silver.
Mahdist	Follower of the Mahdi (the prophesied redeemer of Islam).
Mandate	Territory granted to a colonial power by the League of Nations after the First World War. The Power administering the mandate was obligated to the League of Nations to respect minority interests and, where possible, prepare the mandate for independence. Armies were not to be raised in them nor naval bases established. There were three classes of mandate. Class A were ex Ottoman territories considered almost ready for self

	determination (e.g. Palestine and Mesopotamia). Class B were ex German colonies in Africa (e.g. Tanganyika, Cameroon and Togo) which required a greater level of control. Class C mandates were ex German territories that were considered best administered as part of the Mandatory power (e.g. South West Africa administered by South Africa, Western Samoa administered by New Zealand and New Guinea administered by Australia).
Maori	The indigenous Polynesian people of New Zealand.
Marathas	A loosely confederated Hindu people of northern India.
Maritime Provinces	The eastern provinces of Canada (Nova Scotia, New Brunswick and Prince Edward Island).
Maundy	Maundy money is coin distributed as Royal Bounty to the poor at a ceremony on Maundy Thursday. Originally current coin it is now given in the form of four denominations of specially struck silver coins (fourpence, threepence, twopence and penny).
Mil	A unit of currency, generally one thousandth. In Hong Kong the mil was one thousandth part of the dollar. In Palestine (and later in Cyprus) it was one thousandth of the pound.
Millieme	The Egyptian equivalent of the mil. One thousandth of the Egyptian pound.
Moghul (or "Mughal")	The Moghuls were the Mongol invaders of India in the 16th Century. They became the paramount rulers of India, the Moghul Emperor having his seat at Delhi. The last Emperor was expelled by the British in 1858 after the Mutiny.
Mohur	A gold coin generally used as bullion and usually equivalent to about fifteen rupees. Also spelt "muhr" and sometimes termed "ashrafi".
Moidore	A Portuguese gild coin eventually of 4,800 reis. It was superseded by the johannes in the 1720s.
Navigation Acts	The Acts of Parliament designed to protect the trade of the English, later British, world.
Nawab	Under Moghul government, the governor of a province. Also used as a courtesy title for persons of high rank or station.
New World	The Americas, not known by the European nations to contain continental land masses until the discoveries of the early 16th century.
Obol	A unit of currency in the Greek world from ancient times. In the Ionian Islands under British rule it was a copper coin.
Obverse	The front or "heads" side of a coin
Order in Council	An Order made by and with the advice of the Privy Council in the name of the monarch. An Order can be made in accordance with existing primary legislation (an Act of Parliament) or it can be an exercise of the Royal Prerogative in which case the Order itself becomes primary legislation. The Order in Council of 1825 giving legal currency to sterling coins in the colonies and the

	subsequent amending Orders are examples of the exercise of the royal prerogative.
Par exchange rate	Under the international gold standard units of currency were equivalent to declared weights of pure gold. The pound sterling was 113 grains, the US dollar was 23.22 grains with other currencies at their various declared rates. There was thus an exact or "par" exchange rate between the various currencies. The pound sterling was equivalent to 4·8665 United States dollars (113 ÷ 23·22 = 4·8665).
Pasha	An honorary title in the Ottoman Empire granted to persons of high military or political rank. Granted also to foreigners in the service of the Empire (e.g. Emin Pasha, the Khedive's governor in Equatoria).
Peça	Portuguese gold coin of 6,400 reis (see "Johannes").
Penny	One twelfth of a shilling.
Piastre	A standard unit of currency in several countries, mainly in the Mediterranean region.
Pice	In British India, one sixty fourth of a rupee and thus a quarter anna.
Pistareen	Name given to the Spanish silver coin of two reales.
Plantation	The plantation colonies were those producing cash crops like tobacco and sugar for the European market. In the early days the colonies in general were often referred to as "the plantations".
Porte	Sometimes "Sublime Porte" or "High Porte". These were terms used to describe the central government of the Ottoman Empire and were derived from the gate in Istanbul where foreign diplomats were received and which gave access to the main government buildings. During the final years of the Ottoman Empire the term "Porte" referred specifically to the Foreign Ministry.
Presidency	An administrative unit under the East India Company.
Preventative Squadron	The West Africa Squadron (q.v.)
Proprietary colony	A colony with a proprietor governing under a Royal Charter. Most of the early settlements were proprietary colonies.
Protectorate	A British "protectorate" was a territory that had not been formally annexed but over which Britain exercised power by treaty or other lawful agreement. A "protected state" was a territory under an independent ruler whose foreign (but not internal) affairs were controlled by Britain.
Pulau	Island (as in "Pulau Penang").
Rajah	A Hindu title originally inferring "king" but later applied to lesser princes, nobles, etc. Broadly similar in meaning to the Mohammedan term "Nawab".
Rajah Mudah	The heir to a Rajah.

Ratu	The title "Ratu" indicated Chiefly rank in Fiji.
Real	Basic unit of Spanish silver currency.
Reis	Portuguese plural of real, the basic unit of Portuguese currency. The Portuguese real last existed (as a small copper coin) in the mid 16th century. Eventually it was a very small unit there being 4,800 reis to the moidore.
Responsible government	Government of a colony by an executive responsible to an elected assembly in the colony rather than to the Colonial Office in London. This gave self governing colonies responsibility for and control of revenue and internal affairs but did not give them any control of foreign affairs.
Reverse	The opposite side of the coin from the obverse. The "tails" side.
Rix dollar	A European silver coin given a maximum circulating value in Queen Anne's Proclamation of 1704 of 4/6d throughout the colonies. When sterling was introduced to the colonies in 1825 it was still a unit of currency in some of the ex-Dutch colonies but, apart from a small issue under the British administration in Ceylon, was no longer a coin. By that time it was equivalent to 1/6d sterling.
Rupee	The standard silver coin of India.
Shroff	A money changer or banker in Asia.
Scramble for Africa	The period from the 1880s when the European Powers competed against each other to obtain colonial interests in Africa and divided the continent between them.
Sepoy	A native Indian foot soldier in the employ of a European army.
Shah	King. Title used by the ruler of the Persian Empire, latterly Iran. His full title was Shahanshah (king of kings).
Sharif	Title of the protector of the holy cities of Mecca and Medina.
Sheikh	Arabic leader or governor.
Shilling	One twentieth of a pound sterling.
Sicca	In India, term applied to coins of the current year's minting indicated by the regnal year. Only newly struck coins passed at the full rate, older coins at a discount. In colonies outside India which used the rupee the term "sicca rupee" refers specifically to the Bengal Murshidabad rupee which was struck by the East India Company with the fixed regnal year 19 from 1777 to 1835 to avoid discounting.
Sirdar	A military commander.
Sixpence	British silver coin (half a shilling).
Sou	A French coin of low denomination. A popular name for the five centimes but in Canada the equivalent of a halfpenny.
Sovereign	The gold coin that for many years represented the pound sterling.
Specie	Coined money.

Squatter	In Australia sheep farmers who initially had little or no right to the Crown lands on which they grazed their sheep were termed "squatters". During the 19th century they gradually became a wealthy and influential sector of Australian society associated with large scale land ownership and often referred to as "the squattocracy".
Sterling	The official currency of the United Kingdom. See separate Note on Sterling Denominations which follows the Glossary.
Stiver	A Dutch unit of currency. One twentieth of a guilder.
Suku	Malay term for a quarter dollar.
Sultan	A sovereign ruler.
Sycee	A medium of exchange in China for many years. An ingot of fine silver, the quality and weight of each one guaranteed by the individual issuer, not by the State.
Tael	A weight of fine silver in China, there being several different standards.
Thaler	Dollar (q.v.).
Token	1. A token coin is one that does not contain its full face value in precious metal. The British silver coinage from 1816 for example was a token coinage – twenty silver shillings passed for one pound in circulation but were not intrinsically worth a gold sovereign. Token coins were legal tender but usually to a limited extent. 2. Private tokens (usually in copper or base metal) carried a written or implied promise that they would be exchanged for a particular service or for legal tender coin but they were not in themselves a legal tender.
Treaty ports	Chinese ports opened to foreign trade by treaty following the opium wars.
Viceroy	An official who administers a territory as the appointed representative of the monarch.
Vichy	The government of occupied France during the Second World War which collaborated with Germany. It was named after the town of Vichy in which it was set up.
West Africa Squadron	Royal Naval squadron set up to enforce Britain's ban on the slave trade. Ships were first sent to West Africa to police the ban in 1808 and worked actively until 1860.

Note on Sterling Denominations

Pounds, shillings and pence

The pound sterling today consists of 100 pence (this term being the plural of penny). The decimal system was introduced in 1971 to replace what many considered to be an outmoded and complicated system of 20 shillings to the pound and 12 pence to the shilling. There were thus 240 pence to the pound with two halfpence to the penny and two farthings (originally "fourthlings") to the halfpenny. This was the system in use for most of the period covered in this book and it may be useful to look briefly at what it was and at how sums in sterling were recorded in contemporary documents.

The sterling system of pounds, shillings and pence was usually abbreviated £.s.d. or l.s.d. where "l" stood for *librae* (pounds), "s" for *solidi* (shillings) and "d" for *denarii* (pence). The pound symbol (£) was in general use before and after decimalization.

A figure in the old pounds, shillings and pence system could be shown in several ways. One hundred pounds could be written as £100, as £100-0s-0d, as £100-0-0d, as £100-0-0 or even as £100/0/0. Five shillings could be 5/- or 5s. Six pence would be written as 6d. Five shillings and sixpence would be 5/6d. The fractions of a penny would be shown as they were: a halfpenny as ½d and a farthing as ¼d. Three farthings would be written as ¾d.

Just as items for sale today can be priced at, say, £1.99 to make them more attractive than at £2 the farthing was often used in the same way. An item of clothing priced at 1/11¾d (usually rolled off the tongue as "one and eleven three") seemed more attainable than if it had been priced at two shillings (2/-).

The actual denominations were the sovereign (£1) and half sovereign (10/-) in gold until these were replaced with paper money from 1914. The larger silver denominations were the crown of five shillings (5/-) and the half-crown (2/6d). From 1849 a two shilling piece, the "florin," also circulated. At one tenth of a pound the florin (2/-) was a first step on the long road to decimalization and a double florin (4/-) was struck briefly from 1887 to 1890. The smaller silver denominations were the shilling (1/-), sixpence (6d) and threepence (3d) although the 3d was struck as a twelve sided nickel-brass coin from 1937. The copper denominations were the penny (1d), halfpenny (½d) and farthing (¼d) all of which were struck in bronze from 1860.

Popular slang terms for some of these denominations can sometimes be encountered in journals, court records and contemporary fiction the commonest perhaps being "quid" for the pound, "half a dollar" for the half-crown (2/6d), "bob" for the shilling (1/-) and "tanner" for the sixpence (6d).

Before the adoption of the gold standard in 1816 and the introduction of a twenty shilling sovereign the following year the standard gold coin had been a little heavier and had not had a fixed relationship to the silver coins. It was termed a "guinea" and in 1817 it stood at 21/-. Many of these older gold coins continued in circulation at that price for a number of years and such is sentiment that long after their withdrawal the term "guinea" continued in popular use to mean 21/-. Racehorses and works of art particularly continued to be priced in guineas into the 1950s and beyond.

Although the pre decimal system may seem complicated to those who have never used it, it was in many ways a very simple one. The twenty shillings of the pound were readily divisible by ten, five, four or two and there were eight half-crowns to the pound. It was of course a simpler age when prices, wages, etc. tended to be rated in line with these divisions. 17/6d was not the arbitrary figure it may seem but was seven eighths of a pound. As most grocery items were sold by the dozen, twelve pence to a shilling was also very useful. If eggs were 2d each they were 2/- a dozen. If they were 1/6d a dozen they were 1½d each.

When reading the prices on old coin tickets it is useful to know that numismatic tradition was to price everything under £5 in shillings and pence. A coin selling at £4-15-0d would usually be priced on the ticket at 95/-. 62/6d was £3-2-6d and £5/15/- on a coin ticket was exactly what it said. 21/- was a popular price tag in some series and was of course a guinea.

Select Bibliography and References

There is an enormous amount of information on British colonial and British Indian history. It is in many forms including official and private documents of all sorts, correspondence, reports and returns, company records and of course in very many published works. Together they cover every aspect of the subject but those that interest us most deal with exploration and settlement, political, civil and military history, commerce and economic history, social history and of course numismatics.

In this select bibliography I attempt only to note those items that seem most useful in understanding the subject matter of this book. Many of the publications noted below have their own bibliographies which should be consulted for a fuller awareness of relevant works. Perhaps the largest collection of records is that of The National Archives at Kew but manuscript sources and records exist in many other locations in the United Kingdom and around the world. These are too numerous to record here but the most important will also be noted in the bibliographies of some of the cited works.

The list of works is given by region, an arrangement that requires some titles to be listed more than once.

CATALOGUES

GENERAL CATALOGUES IN ORDER OF APPEARANCE

ATKINS, James, *The Coins and Tokens of the Possessions and Colonies of the British Empire,* 1889. This was the first attempt at a comprehensive listing of British colonial coins and tokens. In his preface Atkins points out the difficulties of compiling a pioneering work and disclaims *"any pretension to finality or completeness".*

WRIGHT, L. V. W., *Colonial and Commonwealth Coins,* 1959. Excludes gold coins and most of the tokens but otherwise extends Atkins' coverage to the 1950s.

FRIEDBERG, Robert, *Coins of the British World Complete from 500 AD to the Present,* 1962. As well as colonial and Commonwealth coins this includes coins of the British Isles from the early Saxon period and the Anglo-Gallic series.

Select Bibliography and References

PRIDMORE, F., *The Coins of the British Commonwealth of Nations to the end of the reign of George VI 1952*. Published, by Spink, in four parts from 1960 to 1980.

Part 1 European Territories, 1960.
Part 2 Asian Territories, 1965.
Part 3 Bermuda, British Guiana, British Honduras and the British West Indies, 1965.
Part 4 India
   Volume 1, *East India Company Presidency Series c1642-1835,* 1975.
   Volume 2, *Uniform Coinage East India Company 1835-58. Imperial period 1858-1947,* 1980.

Pridmore's standard works were intended as a complete revision of Atkins extending the record to 1952. Sadly Fred Pridmore died prematurely in 1980 leaving North America, Africa and Australasia undone. His work has been amended, updated and supplemented in various journals and publications in subsequent years by Pridmore himself (until 1980) and by others.

REMICK, Jerome and JAMES, Somer, *The Guidebook and Catalogue of British Commonwealth Coins,* 1967. A general catalogue covering much of the series in one volume. The third edition, 1971, co-authored also by Anthony Dowle and Patrick Finn is much more comprehensive and includes a useful section on the Native States of India by Ken Wiggins.

De CLERMONT, Andre P. and WHEELER, John, *Spink's Catalogue of British Colonial and Commonwealth Coins,* 1986. This is the latest general catalogue of the whole series bringing the story to the 1980s.

KRAUSE PUBLICATIONS, *Standard Catalogue of World Coins* is published in several volumes covering the periods 1601-1700, 1701-1800, 1801-1900, 1901-2000 and 2000-date. Although these cover the whole world they include most colonial and Commonwealth coins. The volumes covering the 20th and 21st centuries are particularly useful as they cover the period after the publication of de Clermont and Wheeler and are frequently updated.

AREA SPECIFIC CATALOGUES

British Isles and Europe

LYALL, Bob, *The Tokens and Checks of Malta,* 1999.

LYALL, Bob, *The Tokens and Checks of Gibraltar,* 2010.

McCAMMON, A. L. T., *Currencies of the Anglo Norman Isles,* 1984 with Supplement 1993 updating the catalogue section.

PRIDMORE, F., *The Coins of the British Commonwealth of Nations to the end of the reign of George VI 1952, Part 1 European Territories,* 1960.

SPINK, *Coins of England and the United Kingdom.* Previously *Seaby's Standard Catalogue of British Coins.* Updated yearly.

North America

BRETON, P. N., *Illustrated History of the Coins and Tokens Relating to Canada,* 1894.

CHARLTON PRESS, *The Charlton Standard Catalogue of Canadian Colonial Tokens,* 2012.

North America *continued*

CHARLTON PRESS, *The Charlton Standard Catalogue of Canadian Coins*. Updated annually and now in two volumes.

CROSBY, Sylvester S., *The Early Coins of America and the Laws Governing Their Issue*, 1875.

West Indies

LYALL, Bob, *The Tokens, Checks, Metallic Tickets, Passes, and Tallies of the British Caribbean & Bermuda*, 1988.

PRIDMORE, F., *The Coins of the British Commonwealth of Nations to the end of the reign of George VI 1952. Part 3 Bermuda, British Guiana, British Honduras and the British West Indies*, 1965.

Africa and the Atlantic

HERN, Brian and JACOBS, Allyn, *Hern's Handbook on Southern African Tokens*, 2009.

KAPLAN, Alec, *Catalogue of the Coins of South Africa*. Several editions, now by Alec Kaplan and Sons.

MAYNARD, E. J., *Tokens of Southern Africa. A Catalogue Based on the Collection of the Africana Museum*, Johannesburg, 1966.

PARSONS, H. Alexander, *The Colonial Coinages of British Africa with the Adjacent Islands*, 1950. Covers the whole of Africa (except for South Africa) together with St Helena, Mauritius and the Seychelles.

VICE, David, *The Coinage of British West Africa and St.Helena 1684-1958*, 1983.

India, the East India Company and the Indian Ocean

PRIDMORE, F., *Part 4 India*, volumes 1 and 2 have been the standard work on British Indian coins since publication but are in process of being updated, mainly by Dr. Paul Stevens.

STEVENS, Dr. Paul, *The Coins of the Bengal Presidency,* 2012. A detailed description and catalogue of the East India Company coins of Bengal.

STEVENS, Dr. Paul, *The Coins of the English India Company. Presidency Series*, 2017. A detailed catalogue of the coinage of all three presidencies.

STEVENS, Dr. Paul and WEIR, Randy, *The Uniform Coinage of India 1835-1947,* 2012.

KRAUSE PUBLICATIONS, *South Asian Coins and Paper Money*, Indian edition 2013. A general catalogue edited by George S. Cuhaj and Rajender Maru which replaces the 1982 edition. The sections on the coins of the East India Company and British India are covered in more detail by Pridmore and/or Stevens but it has a useful section, with map, on the coins of the Native States.

Asia

PRIDMORE, F., *The Coins of the British Commonwealth of Nations to the end of the reign of George VI 1952. Part 2 Asian Territories*, 1965.

Select Bibliography and References

Asia *continued*

PRIDMORE, F., *Coins and Coinages of the Straits Settlements and British Malaya 1786 to 1951* published by Spink in 1968. This covers the coinages of that region in more detail than his *Asian Territories*, particularly the Singapore merchants' tokens.

MA, Tak Wo, *Illustrated Catalogue of Hong Kong Currency*, 2013.

TAN, Steven, *Standard catalogue Malaysia – Singapore – Brunei Coin and Paper Money*, 2012.

Australasia and Oceania

ANDREWS, Arthur, *Australasian Tokens and Coins*, 1921.

CLARKE, Robert L., *The Coins and Tokens of British Oceania*, 1971.

GRANT, Anthony W., *New Zealand Coin and Banknote Catalogue*, 2014.

RENNIKS (Editor Michael T. Pitt), *Australian Coin & Banknote Values*, 2017 (28 editions since 1964).

RENNIKS (Editor Michael T. Pitt), *Australian & New Zealand Token Values*, 2012.

OTHER WORKS ON THE COINS AND CURRENCY

General

CHALMERS, Robert, *A History of Currency in the British Colonies*, 1893. Updates and expands Pennington (*q.v.* below). Brings together much original material and is still the basic reference on the currency history of the colonies. Chalmers was a Treasury official and the work was originally published by Her Majesty's Stationery Office.

HOWORTH, D. F., *Colonial Coins and Tokens*, 1890 (fourth edition 1906).

LINECAR, Howard W. A., *British Commonwealth Coinage*, 1959.

(PENNINGTON, James), *The Currency of the British Colonies*, 1848. Originally published anonymously by Her Majesty's Stationery Office. Pennington was the Treasury official responsible for the remedial legislation of 1838.

PLANT, Richard, *Arabic Coins and How to Read Them*, 1980.

British Isles and Europe

NELSON, Philip, *The Coinage of William Wood 1722-1733*, 1959.

RUDING, The Rev. Rogers, *Annals of the Coinage of Great Britain and its Dependencies*, 1840 (third edition).

SEABY, Peter, *The Story of the British Coinage*, 1990.

North America

CROSBY, Sylvester F., *The Early Coins of America and the Laws Governing Their Issue*, 1875.

DURST, Sanford J., *Comprehensive Guide to American Colonial Coinage it's Origins, History and Value*, 1976.

FAULKNER, Christopher, *The Holey Dollars and Dumps of Prince Edward Island*, 2012.

North America *continued*

FAULKNER, Christopher, *Coins are Like Songs. The Upper Canada Coppers, 1815–1841*, 2016.

FAULKNER, Christopher, *Imperial Designs. Canada's Ships, Colonies & Commerce Tokens*, 2019.

KLEEBURG, John M. (Editor), *Canadas's Money,* 1994. A collection of essays by several authors.

McCULLOUGH, A. B., *Money and Exchange in Canada to 1900,* 1984.

NELSON, Philip, *The Coinage of William Wood 1722-1733,* 1959.

NETTELS, Curtis Putnam, *The money supply of the American Colonies Before 1720,* 1934.

NEWMAN, Eric P., *Coinage for Colonial Virginia,* 1956.

NEWMAN, Eric P., *The Early Paper Money of America,* 1967 with later editions. Gives many illustrations of Bills of Credit.

NOE, Sydney P., *The Silver Coinage of Massachusetts,* 1973.

West Indies

GORDON, Ralph C., *West Indies Countermarked Gold Coins,* 1987.

LYALL, R. (Bob), *West Indian Coinage – Some New Discoveries,* c.1998. Publishes new source records. Appends a useful list of papers on British West Indian coinage appearing in SNC since the publication of Pridmore's West Indian volume.

Africa and the Atlantic

SHAW, E. M., *A History of Currency in South Africa,* 1956.

THERON, Dr. G. P., *Tokens of Southern Africa and their Story,* 1978.

VICE, David, *The Coinage of British West Africa and St.Helena 1684-1958,* 1983.

India, the East India Company and the Indian Ocean

FERNANDO, B. W., *Ceylon Currency. British Period 1796-1936,* 1939.

MALHOTRA, D. K., *History and Problems of Indian Currency 1835-1939,* 1939.

STEVENS, Dr Paul, *The Coinage of the Bombay Presidency. A Study of the Records of the EIC,* 2019. A detailed study of the Bombay records referring to coins and currency.

THOMPSON, Peter R., *The East India Company and its Coins,* 2010.

Asia

BUCKNIL, John, *The Coins of the Dutch East Indies,* 1931. Useful for the Dutch coins circulating in the East and for its section on *The Netherlands Indies under British Administration.*

PRIDMORE, F., *Coins and Coinages of the Straits Settlements and British Malaya 1786 to 1951* published by Spink in 1968. This covers the coinages of that region in more detail than his *Asian Territories*, particularly the Singapore merchants' tokens. Although basically a catalogue this work is extremely useful for the detailed numismatic story including transcripts of relevant Orders in Council, Proclamations, etc.

THOMPSON, Peter R., *The East India Company and its Coins,* 2010.

Australasia and Oceania

CRELLIN, Andrew, *The Coinage of Colonial Australia*, 2004.

DEACON, J. Hunt, *The "Ingots" and "Assay Office Pieces" of South Australia*, 1954.

HYMAN, Coleman P., *An Account of the Coins, Coinages, and Currency of Australasia*, 1893.

MIRA, Dr.W.J.D., *Coinage and Currency in New South Wales 1788-1829*, 1981.

McNEICE, Roger V., *Coins and Tokens of Tasmania 1803-1910*, 1969.

PEPPING, Robert, *New Zealand History Coined. Coins of New Zealand (1933–1965)*, 2017.

SUTHERLAND, Allan, *The Numismatic History of New Zealand*, 1941.

THOMAS, E.R. and DALE, L.J. (Editors), *They Made Their Own Money. The Story of Early Canterbury Traders & their Tokens*, 1950.

HISTORY

General

BEER, George Louis, *The Origins of the British Colonial System*, 1959.

BEER, George Louis, *The Old Colonial System 1660-1754*, 1958, two volumes.

CARTER, Marina, *Voices from Indenture*, 1996. Examines the system of indentured labour.

HUSSEY, W. D., *Discovery Expansion and Empire*, 1954.

KEITH, A. Berriedale, *The Governments of the British Empire*, 1936.

THE OXFORD HISTORY OF ENGLAND. Published in 16 volumes from 1934 to 1985 with reprints until 1988. A consolidated Index was published in 1991. The series covers the whole period from Roman Britain to 1945, those from volume 8 (*The Reign of Elizabeth 1558-1603*) being relevant to this work.

THE NEW OXFORD HISTORY OF ENGLAND began publication in 1989 and will eventually replace *The Oxford History of England*. Well over half the planned volumes have been published (2014) taking the history of the nation to 1990. In both series the term "England" does not restrict the geographical cover.

THE OXFORD HISTORY OF THE BRITISH EMPIRE. Published in 5 volumes in 1998 and 1999, volume 5 being the *Historiography* only.

LUCAS, C. P., *Historical Geography of the British Colonies*. A work in seven volumes plus an introductory volume covering the colonies and British India. The series was published in the late 19th and early 20th centuries and although always referred to as "Lucas" two volumes (Newfoundland and Australasia) were written by J.D.Rogers and both parts of the volume on India were written by P.E.Roberts.

POPE, Rex, *Atlas of British Social and Economic History since c.1700*, 1989.

PORTER, A. N. (Editor), *Atlas of British Overseas Expansion*, 1991.

ROYAL COMMISSION, *Her Majesty's Colonies*, 1886. Produced for the Colonial and Indian Exhibition of 1886. A general description of each colony at that time. Has an introduction by J.R.Seeley (*q.v.* below) who was Regius Professor of Modern History at Cambridge University.

SAMHABER, Ernst, *Merchants Make History*, 1960, English translation 1963.

HISTORY, General *continued*

SEELY, J. R., *The Expansion of England* 1883. This was the publication of an influential series of lectures justifying the Empire as an extension of the British State. It was reprinted several times.

SMITH, Adam, *An Enquiry into the Nature and Causes of the Wealth of Nations,* 1776.

SOMERVELL, D. C. and HARVEY, Heather, *The British Empire and Commonwealth,* 1954 (revised 1959). This work supersedes Somervell's *The British Empire,* 1930.

STARKEY, David J., Van HESLINGA, E.S.van Eyck and De MOOR, J.A. (Editors), *Pirates and Privateers,* 1997.

WILLAN, T. S., *Studies in Elizabethan Foreign Trade,* 1959.

YOUNG, D. M., *The Colonial Office in the Early Nineteenth Century,* 1961.

British Isles and Europe

DROWER, George, *Heligoland,* 2002.
FIELING Keith, *A History of England 1950.*
HARVEY, Maurice, *Gibraltar. A History,* 1996.
PREBBLE, John, *The Darien Disaster* 1968.
SPIERS, Edward M., *The Late Victorian Army 1868-1902,* 1992.

North America

BARNES, Viola Florence, *The Dominion of New England,* 1923.

BEER, George Louis, *The Commercial Policy of England toward the American Colonies,* 1948.

COLDHAM, Peter Wilson, *Emigrants in Chains,* 1992.

GOVERNOR AND COMMITTEE of the Hudson's Bay Company, *Hudson's Bay Company. A Brief History,* 1934.

MASON, Frances Norton, *John Norton and Sons Merchants of London and Virginia,* 1968.

NEWMAN, Peter C., *Empire of the Bay* 1989. An illustrated history of the Hudson's Bay Company.

West Indies

CARTER, Marina, *Voices from Indenture,* 1996. Examines the system of indentured labour.

CRATON, Michael, *Empire Enslavement and Freedom in the Caribbean,* 1997.

GREEN, William A., *British Slave Emancipation,* 1976. The sugar colonies 1830-1865.

HIGHAM, C. S., *The Development of the Leeward Islands* under *the Restoration 1660-1688,* 1921.

LUBBOCK, Basil, *The Coolie Ships and Oil Traders,* 1955. Examines the carriage of indentured labour.

PITMAN, Frank Wesley, *The Development of the British West Indies, 1700-1763,* 1917.

PREBBLE, John, *The Darien Disaster* 1968.

THOMAS, Hugh, *The Slave Trade,* 1997.

WEST INDIA ROYAL COMMISSION, 1938-1939, Report, 1943.

Africa and the Atlantic

BAKER, Geoffrey L., *Trade Winds on the Niger,* 1996.

COLEMAN, Deirdre (Editor), *Maiden Voyages and Infant Colonies,* 1999.

De GRAMONT, Sanche, *The Strong Brown God,* 1975. The story of the Niger.

De KIEWIET, C. W., *A History of South Africa Social and Economic,* 1941.

DUFF, H. L., *Nyasaland Under the Foreign Office,* 1903.

FYFE, Christopher, *A History of Sierra Leone,* 1962.

GALE, W. D., *One Man's Vision. The Story of Rhodesia,* 1935.

GOSSE, Philip, *St Helena 1502-1938,* 1938.

HOCKLY, Harold Edward, *The Story of the British Settlers of 1820 in South Africa,* 1948.

JOHNSTON, Sir Harry H., *British Central Africa,* 1898.

MARTIN, Eveline C., *The British West Africa Settlements 1750-1821,* 1927.

SHERIFF, Abdul, *Slaves, Spices & Ivory in Zanzibar,* 1987.

St CLAIR, William, *The Grand Slave Emporium,* 2006. The story of Cape Coast Castle and the slave trade.

THOMAS, Hugh, *The Slave Trade,* 1997.

VERE-HODGE, E. R., *Imperial British East Africa Company,* 1960.

WARD, W. E. F., *A History of the Gold Coast,* 1948.

WILSON, Ellen Gibson, *The Loyal Blacks,* 1976. The story of those slaves emancipated after the American war of independence who were subsequently transported to Sierra Leone.

India, the East India Company and the Indian Ocean

BRUCE, George, *The Burma Wars 1824-1886,* 1973.

CARTER, Marina, *Voices from Indenture,* 1996. Examines the system of indentured labour.

CHESNEY, General Sir George, *Indian Polity,* 1894. Describes the system of administration in British India as it was in the later 19th Century but with a useful historical summary.

COTTON, Sir Evan, *East Indiamen,* 1949. A study of the East India Company's maritime service edited by Sir Charles Fawcett.

GARDNER, Brian, *The East India Company,* 1971.

KEAY, John, *The Honourable Company. A History of the English East India Company,* 1991.

LUBBOCK, Basil, *The Coolie Ships and Oil Traders,* 1955. Examines the carriage of indentured labour from India.

MALLESON, Colonel G. B., *An Historical Sketch of the Native States of India in Subsidiary Alliance with the British Government,* 1875.

MISRA, B. B., *The Central Administration of the East India Company 1773-1834,* 1959.

MISRA, B. B., *The Administrative History of India 1834-1947,* 1970.

POWELL, Geoffrey, *The Kandyan Wars,* 1973. Ceylon 1803-1818.

ROBERTS, P. E., *History of British India Under the Company and the Crown,* 1958.

SUTTON, Jean, *Lords of the East,* 2000. The ships of the East India Company.

Asia

BEECHING, Jack, *The Chinese Opium Wars,* 1975.

COLLIS, Morris, *Foreign Mud,* 1946. The events leading to the founding of the colony of Hong Kong.

LUBBOCK, Basil, *The Opium Clippers,* 1933.

MILLS, L.A., *British Malaya 1824-67,* 1960.

MORGAN, Susan (Editor), *A Decade in Borneo,* 2001. With additions to the original by Ada Pryer, first published in 1893.

WOODCOCK, George, *The British in the Far East,* 1969.

Australasia and Oceania

BATESON, Charles, *The Convict Ships 1787-1868,* 1959.

BROOKE, Alan and BRANDON, David, *Bound for Botany Bay,* 2005.

BURNS, Sir Alan, *Fiji,* 1963.

COLEMAN, Deirdre (Editor), *Maiden Voyages and Infant Colonies,* 1999.

MURRAY, Thomas Boyles, *Pitcairn: the Island, the People and the Pastor,* 1860 (twelfth edition).

SCARR, Deryck, *Fragments of Empire. A History of the Western Pacific High Commission 1877-1914,* 1967.

SHAW, A.G.L., *The Story of Australia,* fifth edition (revised) 1983.

SHAW, A.G.L., *Convicts and the Colonies,* 1966.

SINCLAIR, Keith, *A History of New Zealand,* 2000.

SINCLAIR, Keith, *The Oxford Illustrated History of New Zealand,* 2nd edition 1996.

Twentieth Century

Relevant volumes of *The Oxford History of England, The New Oxford History of England* and *The Oxford History of the British Empire* cover this period.

JOURNALS

BNJ	British Numismatic Journal (the journal of the British Numismatic Society).
JNSI	Journal of the Numismatic Society of India.
JONS	Journal of the Oriental Numismatic Society.
ONS	Oriental Numismatic Society Newsletter. After issue 185 (Autumn 2005) this becomes JONS.
JRAS	Journal of the Royal Asiatic Society.
SCMB	Seaby's Coin and Medal Bulletin.
SNC	Spink's Numismatic Circular.

Index

Abolition	69, 77-78	Antigua	9, 61-62
Adelaide Assay Office	276-277	Arab State	307-308, 309
Ingots	276-277	Arcot rupee	20
Adelaide pound	277	Army (British)	94, 306, 321
Aden	174-175, 310, 320, 328	Assam	206, 211
		Tea garden tokens	206
Currency	175-176	Ascension Island	78, 151, 332
Administration		Ashanti	152, 153
Board of Trade	31	Asiento	46
Central administration	29, 31-32, 113, 174-175, 305, 327	Australia	79-80, 270-275
		Australia sovereign	278-280
Chartered Company	29, 249-250	*Currency*	275-286
Colonial Assembly	30, 31	*Tokens*	280-283
Colonial Council	30	See also New South Wales	
Crown colonies	30, 31	Commonwealth of Australia	
Self governing colonies	113, 120, 137-138, 165, 272-273	Australian pound (1931)	284
		Austrian Succession (war)	46
Proprietory colonies	15, 29		
Under Parliament	29		
Protectorates	113, 154	Bahamas	2, 62
Malta	107	*Penny 1806*	56
Ionian Islands	108-9	*19th/20th century currency*	147-148
West Indies	137-139	Bahrain	90-191
See also: Colonial Office		Banda Islands	23
India Office		Bandjarmasin	244-245
Dominions Office		Barbados	9, 61-62, 137-139
Commonwealth Office			
Responsible Government		*Coins and tokens*	54-55, 64
Afghanistan	193-194, 209-211	*Later currency*	143
		Barbary Coast	5
African Company	42-43, 70-71, 151	Barbary ducat	50-51
		Basutoland (Lesotho)	162, 165, 328
Coins (Gold Coast)	71-73	Bechuanaland	163-164, 165, 328
Agents (colonial)	31		
Aix la Chapelle (treaty)	46	*Currency*	167
Alberta	121	Belgian Congo	153, 178
Alwar	204-205	Belize	
American War of Independence	48, 61	See British Honduras	
		Bencoolen	21, 230
American War of 1812	118	See also Fort Marlborough	
Amirante Islands	223	Bengal (early trade)	20
Anchor money	82-83, 154	Berbice	62
Andaman Islands	206	*Currency*	139
Andaman rupee	206	Berlin Conference	154
Anglo Gallic coins	13-14	Bermuda	8-9, 332
Anglo Irish coins	13-14	*Coins and currency*	56, 148
Anguilla	139, 332	See also Somers Islands	

369

Bikanir	204-205	British West Indies	61-62, 136-139
Bills of Exchange	33-34	*Currency*	34, 36, 62-68, 139, 142-145
Board of Trade	31		
Boer	158-164	BRITT: OMN: legend	316, 326
Boer Republics	162-165	Brooke, James	245-246
Boer War, *First*	163	Brunei	246, 248
Second	165	Bullion	
Bojador, Cape	2	*Spanish treasure*	2, 5
Bombay (Mumbai)	22, 23, 196-197, 201	*For East India Company*	11-12, 15
		Burma	211-212, 320, 322, 325
Borneo	244-246		
Boston Mint	17-18	*Currency*	212
Botany Bay	73		
Botswana	328		
See also Bechuanaland		Cabot, John	3, 7
Boulton's Soho Mint	56, 71, 83, 213, 230	Calais (as an English mint)	13-14
		Calcutta Mint	91, 197
Breda (treaty)	30	Cameroon	306
British Antarctic Territory	332, 333	Canada	4, 61, 74
British Central Africa		*Development*	118-121
See Nyasaland		*Early currency*	84, 122
British Columbia	120-121	*Currency, coins and tokens of*	
Proposed gold coinage	132	*Lower and Upper Canada*	122-123
Decimal Currency Act	133	*Province of Canada coins and tokens*	123-126
British Dependent Territories	332		
British Guiana	62, 136-138	*Dominion coinage*	126-128
Currency and coins	88, 139-140	Canary Islands	2
British Honduras	62, 138-139	Canberra Mint	285
Currency and coins	141-142	Cape Breton Island	118
British India	98, 191-195, 208-211, 320-321, 324	Cape Colony	158-163
		19th century currency	160-161, 167
Nationalism	320-321, 324	Cape Verde Islands	2
Independence	324	Caribbean	61-62, 136-139
Currency, coins and tokens	196-208	Carolina	
British Indian Ocean		*"God Preserve" tokens*	53
Territory	223, 333	Caroline Islands	306-307
British Isles	59-60	Cartier, Jacques	3
British Malaya	234-236, 322-323	Cayman Islands	139, 332
		Currency	142
Coins and currency	243-244	Ceylon	212
British North America	117-121	*Early colonial coins*	83
Currency	122-134	*Currency and coins*	213-217
British North Borneo	249-251, 322	*Tokens*	217-218
Coins and currency	250-252	*Independence*	325-326
Tokens	253-254	Chagos Islands	223, 333
British North Borneo Co.	249-250	*See also* British Indian Ocean Territory	
British Overseas Territories	332	Channel Islands	101
British South Africa Co.	163-164	China	255-258
British (trade) dollar	239, 261-262	Christianity	1-2, 7
British Virgin Islands	332	Christmas Island (Indian Ocean)	224
See also Virgin Islands			
British West Africa	151-154	Christmas Island (Pacific)	302
Currency Board coins	157	Clunies-Ross family	223-224

Cocos (Keeling) Islands	223	Cyprus	111, 307, 328, 333
Tokens	223		
Coin supply to colonies		*Coinage and currency*	111-112
Early years	15-17, 32-34		
18th Century	52-56, 62-64	Darien Company	44-45
Small change	52-56	De Beers	162
Early 19th century	82-84	*Tokens*	170-171
Colonial branch mints		Decimalization	
Act of 1866	278	*Australia*	285
Sydney (1855)	278	*New Zealand*	293
Melbourne(1872)	279	*Fiji*	297
Perth (1899)	279	*UK*	333
Ottawa (1908)	127	Decolonization	325-326, 327-328
Bombay (1918)	201		
Pretoria (1923)	168	Defence	94-95, 97
Colonial Conferences	94, 305	Dewas (Senior and Junior)	204-205
See also Imperial Conferences		Dhar	204-205
Colonial Office	113, 175, 305, 327	Dindings	235
		Dollar	
Columbus, Christopher	2	*Origin*	15
Commerce	93-94	*Spanish American eight reales*	15, 32, 35-37, 39-40, 49, 64
Commodity money	32-33, 34		
Commonwealth	312, 315, 318, 323, 325, 326, 327-329	*Sterling rate (19th century)*	86-88
		See also: British (trade) dollar	
Commonwealth of Australia	272, 273-274	Hong Kong dollar	
Currency and coins	284-286	Lion dollar	
Commonwealth Office	327	Maria Theresia dollar	
Commonwealth Relations Office	327	Dollar using colonies	89, 122, 238, 258-259
Connecticut	9	Dominica	62
Higley coppers	54	*Cut coins*	63, 64
Consignment merchants	18	*Currency 19th century*	143
Convicts	1, 41, 267-269, 271-272	Dominion of Canada	120-121
		See also Canada	
Cook, Captain James	73, 79, 287	Dominion of New England	29-30
Cook Islands	301	Dominions	305, 312, 315-317, 321, 323
Corn Laws	92-93		
Repeal of	93	Dominions Office	305, 326, 327
Council of Trade	31	Drake, Francis	6, 7, 8
Crimean War	113-114	Dutch East India Company	7
Cromwell, Oliver	9, 23, 29	Dutch wars	44
Crown colony	30, 305, 332		
See also: Administration British Dependent Territories British Overseas Territories		East Africa	174, 177-181, 183
		Currency	181, 183-187
Curaçao	137	East Africa Protectorate	178, 181
Currency Boards		*Coins*	183-184
British Caribbean	145	East African Currency Board	185-186
West African	157	East African shilling	185-186
Kenya, Uganda	184	*In Aden*	176
East African	185-186	*In Somaliland*	176
Cut & Countermarked coins	63-68	*In Zanzibar*	182, 186
Cut coins	62-66		

East India Company	7, 11-12, 18-22, 48, 79, 91, 191-192, 193-195	Foreign coins in use	15, 34-39, 49-52, 62
Civil administration	193, 194, 208-209	Foreign Office	113, 174, 175
Paramount power	92, 192-193	Foreign policy	97-98
United Company	19	Fort Marlborough	21
In Burma	211	Free Trade	48, 77, 93-94, 256, 265, 312, 317
In Ceylon	212	French wars	45-48
In Indian Ocean	174-175	Fur trade	4, 117-118
In Java	18, 21, 228-229		
In Malay Peninsula	225-228, 233-234		
In Persian Gulf	189-191	Gambia	42, 60, 151-153
In Sumatra	230-232	*19th century currency*	155
Coins	19-23, 91-92, 196	Gandhi, Mahatma	320
East India Company (Dutch)	7	Germany	114-115, 154, 179
East India Company (French)	45	Ghana	328
Egypt	173-174, 307, 310, 322, 329	See also Gold Coast	
Currency and coins	176-177	Gibraltar	46, 105-106, 330, 332
Eight reales	15, 32, 35-37, 39, 49, 64	*Cut coins*	63
Empire		*Currency*	106-107, 333-334
18th century expansion	57, 74	Gilbert and Ellice islands	301, 302
19th century	114	Gilbert, Sir Humphrey	7
20th century	305-306, 311-312, 315, 317, 321, 323, 325-326, 329, 330, 335	Glorious Revolution	30, 105
		God Preserve London tokens	53
Entente Cordiale	115, 173	Gold Coast	1, 151-153
Essequibo and Demerara	62	*Coins (African Company)*	71-73
Cut and countermarked coins	83-84	*19th century currency*	155
Colonial coins	83, 139-140	*Independence (as Ghana)*	328
Europe		Gold discoveries	
Balance of power	98-99, 113-115, 119, 232	*Canada and California*	122
European Union	330	*Transvaal*	163
		Australia	273, 276
		New Zealand	290
Factory	18	Gold standard	313
Falkland Islands	149-150, 332	*UK*	82, 313
Currency	150, 333	*West Indies*	36
Fanning Island	303-304	*Straits Settlements*	239
Fashoda incident	180	*South Africa*	314
Federated Malay States	235	Good Hope, Cape of	1-2
Fiji	295-296, 300	*Dutch in possession*	23
Currency and coins	296-297	*British rule*	98
Fiji pound	297	See also Cape Colony	
Firman	24	Gordon. Major-General	174
First World War	306-307, 308, 311-312	Great Game	193
		Grenada	61, 62
Origins	114-115	*Currency 19th century*	143
Effects	306-310	Griqua Town	159
Foreign and Commonwealth Office	327	*Coins*	161
		Griquas	159, 162
		Guadaloupe	61

Guernsey	59, 101, 333	Ireland	6, 104, 318, 321
Coins and currency	103, 333	*Coins and tokens*	104-105
Guinea (coin)	43, 359	*Free State coins*	318-319
Guinea Coast	5, 42-3	Irish pound	318
Guinea Company	42	Islam	1, 190, 307-308, 310
Gulf of Mexico	3	Isle of Man	59, 99, 333
		Coins and tokens	99-100, 333
Half-crown	358	Israel	324, 329
Halifax currency	84, 122, 131	*See also* Palestine	
Hanover	97, 99, 105		
Hare, Alexander	223, 244-245		
Hawkins, William and John	5	Jamaica	9, 61-62, 137-138
Heaton's Birmingham Mint	127, 134, 176, 182, 196, 220, 238, 247, 251, 284	*Early currency*	32
		Countermarked coins	63
Hejaz	307-310	*18th century tokens*	54-55
Heligoland	110, 179	*Later currency and coins*	142-143
Hibernia coins (William Wood)	53-54	Jameson Raid	164-165
High Commissioner for Southern Africa	162	Japan	306-307, 322
		Jardine and Matheson	256
High Commissioner for Western Pacific	300	Java	18, 21, 228-229
		Coins (19th century)	229
Higley coppers (Connecticut)	54	Jenkins's Ear (war of)	46
Home Office	113, 267	Jersey	59, 101, 333
Hong Kong	257-258, 262, 322, 330	*Currency, coins and tokens*	101-103, 333-334
Currency and coins	258-262, 330-331	Jingoism	114, 174
Hong Kong dollar	238, 259-260	Johannes	51
Hong Kong Mint	238, 259-260	*Clipped, false and plugged*	52, 67
Hudson, Henry	3	Johor	235
Hudson Bay	4	Joint Stock Companies	4, 70
Hudson's Bay Company	4, 46, 117-118, 121		
Made Beaver tokens	132	Kandahar	209-210
		Copper falus	210
		Kenya	178, 181
Imperial British East Africa Company	179-180	*Currency*	182-185
		Khartoum	173-174
Coins	182-183	King's Norton Metal Co. Ltd.	157, 176
Imperial Conferences	305, 312, 315	Kookaburra patterns	285
See also Colonial Conferences		Kormantin	5, 42
Imperial preference	317	Kuching	245, 246
Indentured labour		Kuwait	190
Early period	41-42		
19th/20th centuries	137, 296		
India Office	113, 174-175, 327	Labuan	246, 249
Indian Mutiny	194-195	*Currency*	249
Ionian Islands	108-109	Laccadive Islands	222
Coins and currency	109-110	Lagos	152-154
Iran (Persia)	4, 189-191, 194, 210-211, 329	*19th century currency*	155-156
		Land grants	11, 29
Iraq	308-310	Lawrence of Arabia	308-309

League of Nations	307, 324	Mariana Islands	306-307
Mandate	307, 310	Marshall Islands	306-307
Lebanon	308, 309	Martinique	61
Leeward Islands	61-62, 136, 138-139	*Plugged gold coins*	67
		Maryland	9
Currency	143	*Coins*	17-18
Legal tender limits		Mashonaland	163-164
United Kingdom	82, 89	Massachusetts	9
British colonies after 1825	86, 88-89	*Coins*	17-18
Australia	275, 276	Matabele	158-160, 163-164
British India	199		
Canada	122, 125	Mauritius	218-219
Ceylon	215	*Coins and currency*	82, 84, 219-221
Hong Kong	259-260	"Mayflower"	9
Jamaica	142	Mediterranean	98, 105-111
Mauritius	220	Melbourne Mint	279, 284
New Zealand	291, 293	Mesopotamia	308-309
St Helena	151	*See also* Iraq	
Southern Africa	167	Middle East	307-310, 323-324, 329
Straits Settlements	236-238		
West Indies	139	Minorca	46, 107
Z.A.R. coins	168	Moghul rule in India	92, 192-195
Legislation		Mohur	196-200
General	31-32, 60, 61	Moidore	51-52
Currency	35-39, 86-88	Mombasa	177-179
Paper money	56-57	*Coins*	182-183
British sterling coins (1825)	86-88	Montserrat	9, 62, 332
Lesotho	328	*Currency 19th century*	143
See also Basutoland		Morocco	5
Lion Dollar	49-50	Mosquito Coast	61
Lower Canada	61, 118, 119	Muscovy Company (Russia Company)	4
Currency, coins and tokens	122-123		
Macau	255, 257	Napoleon	98, 151
Macgregor Laird	152, 156	Napoleonic War	48, 98-99
Madras	19	Natal	159-160
Mint	19, 20, 197	*Currency*	161, 167
Magellan, Ferdinand	2	Native States of India	194, 203-204
Malacca	228, 232-233, 234	*Coins*	203-206
Malay Peninsula	225-228, 232-236	Nauru	306
Malay States	234-236	Navigation Acts	27-28, 92
Currency	239, 243	*Repeal of*	93-94
Maldive Islands	222-223	Nejd	310
Malta	107	Netherlands	6-7
Currency	107-108	Nevis	9, 61-62
Third farthing	89-90, 108	New Brunswick	61, 118, 120
Maluka	244-245	*Currency, coins and tokens*	130
Coins	245	New England	9, 28, 29,
Manitoba	121	*Coins*	17-18
Maori	287-290	*Dominion of*	29-30
Maria Theresia dollar	175-176, 181, 182, 191	*"God Preserve" tokens*	53
		New France	3

New Guinea	298, 306, 322	Opium wars	94, 257-258
Currency and coins	299	Orange Free State	162
New Hampshire	9	Orange River Colony	165
New Haven	9	Orange River Sovereignty	162
New Hebrides	301	Ottawa Mint	127
New Jersey	30	Ottoman Empire	1, 98, 111, 173-174 190-191, 306, 307-309
St Patrick Coins	53-54		
New Netherlands	3, 23-24, 30	Overland route to India	1, 98, 174, 189-190, 307
New South Wales	73, 79-80, 267-273		
Early currency	74, 80-81		
Holey dollars and dumps	80-81, 275	Pacific Islands currency	303
Currency after 1825	275	Pacific Ocean	2, 299-302
Tokens	280-282	Pakistan	324
New York		Palestine	308, 309-310, 323-324
Transfer from Dutch	23-24, 30		
Coins	50, 52	*Currency and coins*	310-311
New Zealand	270, 274, 287-291, 301-302	Pangkor Engagement	235
		Paper money	33-34, 49, 56-57
Currency and coins	291-293	*18th century depreciation (North America)*	56-57
Tokens	291-292	*Berbice*	139
New Zealand Company	288-289	*British West Indies*	144-145
New Zealand pound	293, 303	*Canada*	132
Newfoundland	3, 7, 118, 120, 133	*Cape Colony*	160-161
		Ex Dutch colonies	83
British claim recognized	46	*East Africa*	184, 185
Currency, coins and tokens	133-135	*Falkland Islands*	150
Nicobar Islands	222	*Hong Kong*	261-262
Nigeria	152, 154	*Ireland*	318
Coins and currency	156, 157	*Jamaica*	142
Nine Years' War	45	*Newfoundland*	134
Niue	300, 301-302	*New South Wales*	80-81
Norfolk Island	79, 268	*North Borneo*	250-251
North Borneo	249-250	*Seychelles*	221
See also British North Borneo		*South Australia*	276
North East Passage	4	*Straits Settlements*	243
North West Company	117-118	*United Kingdom*	82, 312-313
North West Passage	3, 4	Papua and New Guinea	298-299
Northern Rhodesia	165	See also New Guinea	
Northern Territories	272	Pax Britannica	77
Nova Albion	6	Pearl Harbour	322
Nova Scotia	46, 61, 118	Penal settlements	73, 267-268, 270, 271
Currency, tokens and coins	128-129		
Nyasaland (British Central Africa)	165-167	Penang	225-226
		Work tallies	225
Currency and tokens	167, 170-171	*Currency and coins*	226-227
		Penny	358
Ocean Island	301, 302	Persia (Iran)	4, 189-191, 194, 210-211, 329
Old Colonial System	27-28, 46-48		
End of	59, 93	Persian Gulf	189-191, 307, 310
Oman	177, 190		
Opium	255-258	Perth Mint	279, 284, 285

Phoenix Islands	302	Roanoke	7-8
Piece of Eight		Rosa Americana coins	53-54
See Eight reales		Royal Air Force	309, 321
Pilgrim Fathers	9	Royal Africa Company	43
Piracy	2, 4/5, 78, 189-190	Royal Mint branches *See* Colonial branch mints	
Pistareen	36, 39, 49, 62, 64	Royal Navy	78, 94-95, 97-98, 189, 246, 265, 299-300, 321
Pistole			
Scots	45	Royal Niger Company	154
Spanish two escudos	49, 51	Royal portrait	92, 316-317, 327
In Ireland	104	Royal title	
Pitcairn Island	301, 332	*Britt: Omn:*	316, 326
Currency	303	*Emperor/Empress of India*	191, 195, 200
Plantation token (tin)	53-54	Rupee	
Pope	2, 6	*Uniform East India Company rupee 1835*	91, 196
Portcullis coins	11-13		
Portrait (crowned/uncrowned)	316-317, 327	*Bengal sicca rupee*	84, 91, 215, 219, 226
Portugal	1-3, 7		
Portuguese gold coins	51-52	*British India*	196-197
Pretoria Mint	168	*In East Africa*	181, 182-183
Prince Edward Island	118, 120	*In Persian Gulf*	191
Cut and countermarked coins	68-69	*Mauritius rupee*	220-222
Currency, coins and tokens	131	*Seychelles rupee*	221-222
Privateering	4-5	*Zanzibar rupee*	182
Privy Council	30-31	Russia (Muscovy) Company	4
Proclamation rates 1704	35	Ryswick (treaty)	'45
Proprietory colony	15		
Protectorates	97, 113, 154		
Pulo Run (Banda Islands)	23, 30	St Helena	23, 150-151, 332
		Currency	150-151, 333-334
		St Kitts (St Christopher)	9, 61-62
		St Lawrence, Gulf, River	3
Qatar	190	St Lucia	61-62
Quebec Act 1774	61	*Currency 19th century*	143
Queensland	271, 273, 298	St Patrick coins	53-54
		St Vincent	61-62
		Sailana	204-205
Raffles, Thomas Stamford	226, 228-233	Samoa	299, 300
Ralegh, Walter	7-8	*See also* Western Samoa	
Real	64	Sarawak	245-246
Regal imitations (of British halfpennies)	54-55	*Coins*	246-247
		Saskatchewan	117, 121
Responsible Government	113, 119	Saudi Arabia	310
Restoration	29, 30	Scramble for Africa	153-154, 162, 174, 175, 178, 181
Revenues (Quit rents)	31		
See also Taxation		Second World War	321-322
Revolutionary War (France)	48	Security	94-95, 97
Rhode Island	9	Senegal and Senegambia	60
Rhodes, Cecil	162, 163-165	Settlers and Settlement	1, 7-8, 41, 79-80, 158-159, 269-270, 289-291
Rhodesia	164-165		
See also: Southern Rhodesia Northern Rhodesia		Seven Years' War	46
		Seychelles	221-222
Rix dollar	36, 86, 213	Shilling	358

Sierra Leone	69-70, 78, 151	Sterling coins: system of supply from Royal Mint	144, 156
Coins (Sierra Leone Co)	71-72		
Currency (19th century)	154-155	Sterling denominations (UK)	358-359
Silver		Sterling denominations struck specifically for colonial use	89-90
Mint price	82, 86-88		
19th century price decline	139, 141, 142, 143, 144, 151, 155, 156, 200	Straits Settlements	234-235
		Currency and coins	236-243, 252
20th century price fluctuations	157, 168, 185, 201-202, 239-240, 262, 285	Sudan	173-174, 178, 180
		Suez	329
Singapore	232, 322	Suez Canal	98, 173, 307, 308, 309, 310, 322
Currency	233		
Merchants' tokens	233-234	Sugar	9, 137, 296
Slave trades	5, 42-43, 69, 177	Sumatra	21, 230
Slavery	42, 60, 69	Coins	21, 230, 233
Small change	39, 52-56, 62, 68	Supply of sterling coins to the colonies	156-157
Socotra	175		
Soho Mint		Swan River Settlement	271
See Boulton's Soho Mint		Swaziland	165, 328
Solomon Islands	300, 301	Sydney Mint	278, 284
Somaliland Protectorate	175	Sycee	258
Somers Islands (Bermudas)	8-9	Syria	308, 309
Coinage	16-17		
South Africa	162-163, 165-167, 305, 306, 328	Tael	258-260
		Tahiti	299, 301
Currency, coins and tokens	167-171	Tanganyika	178, 183
South Australia	270-271, 272, 273	Currency	185-186
		Tariffs	92-93, 317
Currency	276-277	Tasmania (Van Diemen' Land)	79, 268, 270, 273
Gold ingots	276-278	Currency	275-276
South Georgia	150, 333	Tokens	170, 281, 283
South Orkney Islands	150	Taxation	47-48
South Sandwich Islands	150, 333	See also Revenues	
South Shetlands	150	Tea garden tokens	206-207
South West Africa	163, 306	Telegraph	95, 271, 302
Southern Rhodesia	167, 317, 328	Ternate	6
Coins and currency	169	Thomason, Edward	72
Sovereign	82, 134, 167, 278, 312, 313-315, 358	Tobacco	8, 9, 33, 250
		Tobago	61-62, 136, 138
In Australia	277, 278-280, 284	Currency 19th century	144
In British North America	125-129, 133-134	Togoland	306
In Cyprus	111	Tonga	300, 301
In East Africa	184	Tortola	62
In India	199-200	Coins and currency	64-65, 143
In Southern Africa	167-168	Tournai	13
Spain	2-3, 6-7	Trade	1, 43-45, 48
Spanish Armada	6-7	See also Free Trade	
Spanish gold coins	51	Transjordan	310, 324
Spanish Succession (War)	46, 105, 107	Transportation	1, 41, 267-268, 272
Spice Islands	2, 3		
Stamp Act 1765	47-48	Ending of transportation	272
Sterling Area	323	Transvaal	162-163
Sterling coins made current in the colonies	86-90	See also Zuid-Afrikaanche Republic (Z.A.R.)	

Transvaal Colony	165	Virginia	7-8
Treaty ports	258, 265	*And Bermuda*	8-9
Trinidad	62, 136, 138	*Commodity money*	33
Currency	144	*Copper halfpennies 1773*	56
Triple Alliance	115	Voce Populi tokens	54-55
Triple Entente	115		
Tristan da Cunha	151, 332		
Turks and Caicos	139, 332	Waitangi Treaty	288-289
Turkey	306, 308-309	Wakefield, Edward Gibbon	270-271, 288
		Wales	59-60
		Washington and Fanning	
Uganda	178, 179-180	Islands	302, 303
Currency	183-184	*Tokens*	303-304
Union (United Kingdom)	44, 59-60. 104	Watt, James & Co	196, 238
Union Islands	302, 303	West Africa	5, 42-43
Union flag	60	*See also* British West Africa	
United Nations	324	West Africa Settlements	153
Trust Territories	324	West Indies	61-62
United States	48, 98, 118-119, 306, 307, 322, 323, 325-326, 329	Western Australia	271-272, 273, 274
United States dollar	122	Western Samoa	301, 303
Upper Canada	61, 118, 119	*See also* Samoa	
Currency, coins and tokens	122-123	Westminster, Statute of 1931	315
Utrecht (Peace of)	46, 107	Windward Islands	62, 138-139
		Currency	143
		Wood's Hibernia coinage	53-54
Van Diemen's Land			
See Tasmania			
Vancouver	120	Zanzibar	177-178, 179, 180
Currency	133		
Versailles	306, 307	*Currency and coins*	182
Vespuchi, Amerigo	2	Zimbabwe	328
Victoria (Australia)	271, 273	*See also* Southern Rhodesia	
Tokens	280	Zuid-Afrikaanche Republiek	
Vienna Congress	98-99	(Z.A.R.)	162-163
Virgin Islands	61-62, 332	*Coins and currency*	167-168
Currency 19th century	143	Zululand (and the Zulu)	159, 163

Index

The Story of the Coins and Tokens of the British World